OCT 1 - 1991

DATE DUE

OCT 17 1991	JUN 12 1992	
NOV 01 1991		
NOV 05 1991	JUN 25, 1992	
NOV 30 1991		
JAN 17 1992	JUN 31 92 JUL 16 1992	
DEC 26 199	AUG 25 1992	
APR 04 1992		
MAY 21 1992		

THE CAMBRIDGE SPIES

THE CAMBRIDGE SPIES

The Untold Story of Maclean, Philby, and Burgess in America

VERNE W. NEWTON

Madison Books
Lanham • New York

Published by Madison Books
4720 Boston Way
Lanham, Maryland 20706

Published in the U.K. by The Macdonald Group,
Orbit House, 1 New Fetter Lane, London EC4A 1 AR
under the title The Butcher's Embrace

Distributed by National Book Network

The paper used in this publication meets the minimum
requirements of American National Standard for
Information Sciences—Permanence of Paper for
Printed Library Materials, ANSI Z39.48–1984. ∞™
Manufactured in the United States of America.

Library of Congress Cataloging-in-Publication Data

Newton, Verne W.
The Cambridge spies : the untold story of Maclean, Philby, and
Burgess in America / Verne W. Newton.
p.   cm.
Includes bibliographical references and index.
1. Espionage, Soviet—Great Britain.
2. Secret service—Great Britain.   3. Philby, Kim, 1912-
4. Burgess, Guy Francis de Moncy, 1911-1963.
5. Maclean, Donald Duart, 1915-   .   I. Title
UB271.R9N47   1991
327.1'247'041—dc20   91–7889 CIP

ISBN 0–8191–8059–9 (alk. paper)

"Stalin's actions were inconsistent with the norms of civilization."

August 1990 decree by
Mikhail Gorbachev

For
MOM AND DAD
who taught us to value freedom

ACKNOWLEDGMENTS

In any project of this length and complexity there are invariably times when it seems like it will not get done. In those periods of discouragement and despair, I was fortunate enough to have friends and colleagues who would not allow me to abandon it.

First among them was John Costello. Researchers become alarmed when they discover another who is dusting off the same yellowed and brittle files. Eventually John and I bridged that chasm of suspicion and collaborated as two sleuths pursuing the same clues to solve different mysteries.

No less enthusiastic was Andrew Lownie. He not only became my agent, but his skills as a Cambridge-trained historian and writer reignited this project.

And even while he was helping me on another project, Arthur Schlesinger, Jr. admonished me to see this book through to its completion.

I benefited too from many other kindnesses. Robert T. Crowley, a retired CIA officer and an expert on Soviet intelligence, was exceedingly generous with both his time and his files. Hayden B. Peake, another writer on intelligence matters, unselfishly shared his extensive resources.

Colonel Russell J. Bowen, a noted intelligence bibliophile, allowed me special privileges in using his vast collection, which is housed and expertly administered at Georgetown University.

I had long talks with many prominent American diplomats who knew and worked with Donald Maclean. Sadly, Loy Henderson, Theodore Achilles, and John D. Hickerson died before this book was completed. Among Maclean's British colleagues, Valentine Lawford, Wilfrid Mann, Sir Isaiah Berlin, Sir Robert Mackenzie and Robert Cecil were extremely kind and helpful.

From the American intelligence community Richard Helms, Robert Lamphere, Tom McCoy and the late James J. Angleton and Robert Amory, though always properly circumspect, helped shed light on intelligence matters.

The staffs at the National Archives in Washington, D.C. were ever helpful, especially Sally Marks in the diplomatic section, and the redoubtable John Taylor in the military section. Likewise the staff of the Public Record Office provided a warm and congenial refuge during one of England's bitterest winters. Helen Neer's professionalism and openness made the FBI Library a richly rewarding place to do research. Sharon Kotok at the State Department went beyond the call of duty to retrieve from its chaotic files what the system often claimed was not there. Ellen M. Macdonald did invaluable research at the New York Public Library.

Nancy and Miles Rubin, Carol and Tom Wheeler, Sue and Don Kaul, and Pam, David and (my godson) Davey Brunnel provided reprieves from days of isolation with wonderful meals and conversation. In New York, old friends Ken Auletta and Amanda Urban offered early and critically important encouragement, while Bill Samuels and Meredith and Richard Cohen could always be counted on for hospitality.

The support of so many generous people does not carry with it any liability for the book's deficiencies.

CONTENTS

INTRODUCTION

"Why has the American side of this story never been told?" a frustrated Senate investigator demanded to know about the Maclean and Burgess case in 1957. By then six years had passed since the two British diplomats had fled England for Russia and touched off the largest manhunt in history.

Both had once served in Washington, where Maclean was by far the more senior. Entrusted with secrets denied the Congress, the Parliament, and often the cabinets of both governments, he was well known to American officials (he met with four serving or future secretaries of state) as he rose to become the youngest counsellor in Britain's diplomatic service.

Maclean vanished in May 1951, just as British security authorities, convinced that he was a Soviet agent, were about to confront him. Within a year, books began to appear detailing his rise within the Foreign Office and his dramatic escape with Burgess. None gave more than a passing glance to their period in America (Maclean served in Washington from May 1944 to September 1948; Burgess from August 1950 through April 1951).

The Senate investigator, Dr. Edna Fluegel, who was also chairman of the Political Science Department at Washington's Trinity College, tried to explore the innumerable American angles: Maclean and his sister both married Americans, and two of his children were born in the States; Burgess vanished with Maclean just three weeks after his disastrous posting to Washington ended, and one of the last persons to see him before he disappeared was an American who briefly became a key figure in the story.

More important, Maclean's longest overseas assignment was in the United States at a time when it was American secrets that the Soviets were after. It did not seem farfetched to assume that Washington represented not only the pinnacle of his diplomatic career, but his zenith as an espionage agent.

Fluegel's efforts to follow these threads set off alarms throughout Washington. An FBI analysis of several articles that she wrote for *The American Mercury* was nearly as long as the articles themselves. When it was released under the Freedom of Information Act twenty-five years later, that analysis was still heavily excised.[1]

Director J. Edgar Hoover must have been ruffled at how close Fluegel had come to several targets. Although she had no proof, she was sure that Donald Maclean and Alger Hiss knew each other. The FBI had the proof—wiretaps of phone conversations between Hiss and Maclean. Although at the time Hoover was still engaged in efforts to discredit Hiss, for some reason he did not want this story to come out; perhaps because it was one of several instances when the Bureau had had Maclean in its sight and let him pass as harmless.

Fluegel was equally certain that Maclean must have passed information during the Korean War that could have cost American lives. Again she was correct, and to a degree that even she could not have fathomed. She did not suspect the ultimate American connection, however. It was American investigators who found the evidence that eventually condemned Maclean.

In 1963 Kim Philby, who had served in Washington as a senior British intelligence officer from October 1949 to June 1951, claimed that he was the Third Man who had dispatched Burgess from Washington to warn Maclean that he must flee. Then Philby bolted for Moscow. This, in addition to the exposure of Anthony Blunt as the Fourth Man in 1979, and Michael Straight's public acknowledgment that he, too, had been recruited to the Soviet cause while a student at Cambridge, inspired a steady stream of books between 1968 and the early 1980s. These shared some common attributes with the earlier works. All were by British writers, and all largely ignored the American side of the story. (Straight is an American, but his book, partly autobiographical, partly *apologia pro vita sua,* contained almost nothing about either Philby or Maclean.)[2]

The Cambridge Spies is the first book on the Maclean-Philby-Burgess story by an American, and the first to detail their years in the United States. It was inspired, however, by a desire to answer the question: Did these spies truly make a difference?

This required a different approach from the preoccupation about British spies who were spying on Soviet spies who were spying on them. Rather than attempting to flush out unknown spies—Fifth or Sixth Men—or chasing imagined Soviet moles hither and yon through the bowels of British and American intelligence (grist for the fiction mill rather than the stuff of serious history), the greater challenge was to gauge the impact by known enemy agents on policies and events.

Over the years readers have had to be satisfied with such bromides as, "they betrayed every secret they knew," or "they passed to Moscow every secret that crossed their desk." No doubt. But what did they know, and what did cross their desks?

This book represents years of digging through British and American archives to answer those questions. Several conclusions can be drawn.

First, it is clear that from Stalin's point of view, Maclean was far more valuable than either Burgess or Philby. The Soviet dictator wanted to know what the President and Prime Minister and their closest advisers were saying in moments when they thought that only their most trusted colleagues were listening. Maclean alone could tell him. Maclean also proved to be a devastatingly effective saboteur, able to work undetected behind enemy lines to foul the machinery of Western foreign policy.

This made him, former CIA Director Richard Helms believes, the most valuable known Soviet agent ever to operate in the West. Still, he obviously did not tip the Cold War scales in the Soviet Union's favor, but that may have had less to do with his effectiveness as an enemy agent than with Stalin's failures to comprehend the complexities and nuances of the postwar world. Indeed, when Stalin's advantages are realized, his string of failures between 1945 and 1951 is all the more astonishing.[3]

Maclean provided the Soviet ruler with a direct pipeline to high-level Western strategy sessions. It was not a two-way hookup. At the same time that he was furnishing Moscow with direct exchanges between president and prime minister, H.D. "Doc" Matthews, a senior adviser to Secretary of State James F. Byrnes, complained to Michael Wright at the British embassy, that "the State Department has little information from Moscow which might shed any light on

Stalin's intentions."[4] For these reasons, and because he spent almost twice as much time in America as Philby and Burgess combined, this book is much more about Maclean than the other two.

In addition to their efficacy, a second question nags. Why did they do it? The long-accepted answer is that they were communists. But at best this is a non sequitur and may be completely wrong. It is possible, in fact, that they were recruited by the Soviets precisely because they were unencumbered by Marxist dogma. But even if they had been ideologues, this explains nothing.

After conceding that Maclean and Burgess may have been communists, a British journalist asked the essential question in 1955:

> But so were thousands of other liberal-minded young men who turned to Communism in the dark days of the mid-thirties . . . *Why should Russian agents have selected just these two from all the other university Communists* who have since become irreproachable citizens—and patriots?[5]

This question applies equally to Philby, Blunt, and, to the extent that he was recruited, Straight. As undergraduates none were more offended by poverty, outraged by injustice, or horrified by fascism than their contemporaries. Three made the popular undergraduate pilgrimage to the Soviet Union, but the two who served it most blindly never set foot on Russian soil until as fugitives they went there to die.

These men did not become Soviet agents because they were committed to Karl Marx's vision of a workers' paradise. What impelled them was an addiction to the drug of deceit. Their greatest enemies were not Nazis—not one ever fired a shot at a fascist—but defectors from Stalin's atavistic horrors such as General Walter Krivitsky and Whittaker Chambers.

Once in Moscow, Philby and Soviet propagandists peddled the message that only the best of the 1930s generation spied for Stalin; everyone else was morally defective. Philby hawked this line to his death. His implicit message to the 1980s generation was that they would have made the same choice.

PROLOGUE

THE PACT

The meeting was not spontaneous. How could it be? The two deserters from Joseph Stalin's army of secret agents were being stalked by his assassins. And, imbued with the paranoia of Soviet underground life, neither Walter Krivitsky nor Whittaker Chambers would have agreed to anything unless every detail had been planned. "It had all been set in advance," said the wife of Isaac Don Levine, the man who initiated the meeting. "You didn't play games with this sort of thing. Everything was prearranged."[1]

It took place in late May 1939, not long after Germany and Italy signed their grandiose "Pact of Steel." After fifteen intense hours of nonstop conversation, Krivitsky and Chambers made their own pact. It hardly rivaled in importance the Axis alliance. But its consequences would reverberate through history long after Hitler and Mussolini were dead, outliving even the two men who made it.

Chambers was the first to arrive at the five-story townhouse at 38 East 64th Street, tucked away between Park and Madison avenues. At thirty-eight, short, pudgy, in a rumpled, ill-fitting suit, he looked more like a plumber's assistant than someone whose life had been and would continue to be the stuff of baffling contradictions. Reared in an intellectually gifted but emotionally turbulent Philadelphia family, by the age of seventeen he was adrift, living in New Orleans with pimps and prostitutes. Eventually, he gravitated back north, enrolling and dropping out of both Williams College and Columbia University. Then, at the age of twenty-four, he discovered communism.[2]

"It offered me what nothing else in the dying world had power to offer at the same intensity—faith and a vision, something for which to live and something for which to die." He started as an editor of the *Daily Worker,* but Moscow soon changed his assignment from propagandist to secret agent, and for six years he shuttled between New York and Washington collecting secrets from Americans who belonged to an underground Soviet-controlled network that had burrowed its way into almost every major government agency.[3]

By 1937, however, as the dimensions of Stalin's vast and bloody purges began to take hold in the West, Chambers was seized with wrenching doubts. Finally, in April 1938, he and his wife made their break. They spent the next year hiding in remote houses along the Eastern seaboard; at night Chambers maintained an armed lookout while his family slept. Penniless and desperately in need of a job, Chambers's life was restored to a minimum level of normalcy after friends arranged for him to get a job with *Time* magazine. It was at that same time, April 1939, that *The Saturday Evening Post* began publishing Krivitsky's stories exposing the nightmarish world Stalin had inflicted upon Russia.[4]

Their effect was to convince Chambers he should tell his story of life in the communist underground. But first, a meeting between the two outlaws, Chambers and Krivitsky, was arranged. It was clear, as Chambers took his seat in one of the two chairs arranged before the fireplace, that he was still a man on the run. Awkward, self-contained, lacking in friendliness and warmth, his darting, furtive eyes conveyed immense distrust. But on this night they also betrayed the powerful effect that meeting one of Stalin's most reviled enemies was having on him.

Approximately fifteen minutes later Krivitsky walked into the large bookcase-lined living room at the front of the apartment. As always, his expression was intense and brooding. Chambers offered his hand. The Russian did not pause nor look down, and any contact seemed to be accidental. He took the chair opposite Chambers.

Short, wiry, with piano-thin legs that barely touched the floor, he did not look the part of a man who had once been close to Stalin. But his high cheekbones, crooked lips, menacing blue eyes, and thick red hair combined to suggest an explosive inner strength that had made Krivitsky one of Europe's most ruthless and feared revolutionaries.

As a teen-ager "I joined the Bolshevik Party with my whole soul," wrote Krivitsky. "I seized the Marxist and Leninist Faith as a weapon with which to assault all the wrongs against which I had instinctively rebelled."[5]

By his mid-twenties he was sowing the seeds of revolution in Germany, Italy, Spain, Holland, and Austria, dashing frenetically from city to city, matching his multiple languages with forged passports and aliases. Thrown in prison and narrowly escaping death, he conspired with the flotsam of underground life—murderers, thieves, reactionaries, and thugs—until he became the head of Soviet intelligence for Western Europe.

But as Stalin liquidated Krivitsky's Bolshevik and Red Army colleagues in the purges, he, too, decided to break with Moscow, becoming, as *The Times* (London) noted, "the first military dignitary to refuse obedience to the Kremlin while abroad." Instead of joining other Russian political exiles, he accepted an offer of protection from the French government. But after two attempts on his life, he came to the United States. "Krivitsky has joined the petty bourgeoisie," Leon Trotsky sneered from his Mexican fortress. "He has become a democrat."[6]

The two men stared into the fireplace. Each shared the same unspoken fear: When Stalin's assassin appeared, would he be cloaked as a rabid anti-Stalinist? Finally, Krivitsky broke the silence.

"*Ist die Sowjetregierung eine faschistische Regierung?*" he asked in German, his only common language with Chambers. Is the Soviet government a fascist government? At first Chambers said nothing. Then, in a very deliberate voice tinged with sadness, he replied, "*Ja, die Sowjetregierung ist eine faschistische Regierung.*" Yes, the Soviet Government is a fascist government.

Soon after that exchange, and with some prodding from Don Levine, they overcame their fears and were deep in conversation. "By comparing dates and places, descriptions and plots, they discovered they knew a number of the same agents, though often by different names." Chambers would mention a colleague who had been murdered; Krivitsky would tell him who did it and the reason why. For the first time Chambers learned which branch of the Russian intelligence service had employed him (Fourth Section, Military Intelligence) and his boss's real name (Boris Bykov).[7]

They talked through the night. "We were like two survivors from another age of the earth, like two dated dinosaurs, the last relics of the revolutionary world that had vanished in the Purge," Chambers later wrote. Finally, exhausted, they parted, but not before they made their pact.

To Krivitsky, Stalin was a totalitarian despot who differed from Hitler only in the socialist phrases to which he hypocritically clung. To have worked for him was to have abetted his crimes. Now they had to atone. "In our time," he told Chambers, "informing is a duty." They had incurred an obligation to help the very Western governments they had once sworn to destroy by identifying those still implementing Stalin's criminal policies. They must inform not only on Russian-born agents operating illegally abroad, but also on Westerners who were secretly working for the Soviets.

Chambers "knew at that moment if the opportunity offered, I would inform."[8]

CHAPTER ONE

Every crime was possible to Stalin, for there
was not one he had not committed. . . . Let us
hope for all time to come—to him will fall
the glory of being the greatest
criminal in history.

Milovan Djilas[1]

A FATEFUL DUTY

Events in Europe and the United States had conspired to make
inconvenient Walter Krivitsky's November 1938 arrival in
America. At the Munich Conference in late September, England and
France humiliated themselves before a blustering Hitler. On Tuesday,
November 8, the Republican Party delivered a jarring blow to
President Franklin Roosevelt's efforts to break the isolationist's stran-
glehold on American foreign policy by scoring their biggest congressional gains in ten years. And the very next night—*Kristall-
nacht*—thousands of young Nazis swept through Germany on an
anti-Semitic rampage shooting Jews, burning synagogues, and
smashing the windows of Jewish stores.

The following day, Thursday, the French liner *Normandie* pulled
into New York harbor with Krivitsky aboard. He was not naive
about the complexities of American politics. But, as Flora Lewis
wrote years later in *The Washington Post*, "things were different in
the United States, much more than Krivitsky at first realized. In this
country too, it was a strange time." His determination to spread the
story of Stalin's atavistic horrors unwittingly put him on a collision

1

course with progressives, who were struggling to convince an American public still fighting its way out of the Depression of the threat posed by a Hitlerized Europe.

"If Hitler were bad, Stalin, whom he attacked, must be good," reasoned the progressives. But, they feared, if people thought otherwise it would be impossible to arouse them against Hitler. This unwritten axiom—that only Hitler could be portrayed as evil—"led not only to a tolerance of Communist sympathies in the government and intellectual society, but to an irritated intolerance of those who denigrated Communism."[2]

Thus, many political and literary circles fostered, sometimes with accusatory anger and a preening impudence, a benign attitude toward Stalin's dictatorship. It did not take Krivitsky long to discover that, as the highest-ranking Soviet official ever to defect to the West, his mere presence in America was considered by some to be threatening.

The moment he, his wife Antonia—a striking blonde from Leningrad whom he had met in the revolutionary underground—and their son Alex stepped from the *Normandie*'s gangway onto American soil, immigration officials abruptly informed them that their "application to enter the United States had been turned down by the Department of Labor." They were led away and placed in detention while Labor officials (who then had authority for the Immigration Service) in Washington debated over whether Krivitsky could be deported as a Soviet agent.[3]

Before Labor could act, however, William C. Bullitt, U.S. ambassador to France, intervened. In Paris, Bullitt was instrumental in securing the French and American travel papers Krivitsky had needed to leave Europe. Now, back in Washington to discuss the European crisis with Roosevelt, Bullitt was annoyed to discover that his own government was toying with Krivitsky's fate. Long an FDR favorite, the rich, aristocratic, and sometimes mystical Bullitt—who had been America's first ambassador to the Soviet Union—used his considerable influence to get Krivitsky a 120-day visitor's pass.[4]

Labor issued it grudgingly, and only after they had held Krivitsky for twelve days. But the matter was not settled. During the next two years, almost to the day of his bloody and violent death, Krivitsky would continue to be hounded by Immigration authorities in what his supporters considered a vendetta.[5]

Bullitt's empathy for Krivitsky reflected a fissure in the attitude toward Moscow between American diplomats who had served in the Soviet Union and other senior government officials who had no direct experience. The former almost without exception eschewed the latter's indulgent attitude toward the Kremlin. The leader of the hardliners was Loy Henderson, one of the State Department's most respected career men. He was the architect of the powerful Division of East European Affairs, long renowned for its youthful, Ivy League educated, Russian-speaking Foreign Service officers, and its extensive collection of Russian books and materials. From 1934 to 1938, he practically ran the Moscow embassy under Bullitt, profoundly influencing the coming generation of American diplomats including George Kennan, Charles "Chip" Bohlen, and Edward Page.

All had front-row seats in Moscow for the Great Terror's grizzly opening act in June 1936. That was when Stalin announced—to shocked Russians and Westerners alike—that the patriarchs of the Bolshevik Revolution had become German and Japanese spies. Men who had endured czarist persecution with Lenin, and had seized power and served with him, were picked up in waves of arrests. For the next eighteen months, Henderson and the others were aghast as Kamenev and Zinoviev, along with Rykov, the former premier of Russia, and finally the immensely popular Bukharin, were charged with treason, espionage, and terrorism. These men were not just the intimates of the deity Lenin. All had helped to boost Stalin up the ladder from his obscure Georgian origins to the Kremlin's inner sanctum, and had plotted with him to oust Trotsky.

Stalin, General Secretary of the Communist Party since 1922 and the Revolution's improbable trustee, targeted his one-time allies as he vowed "a merciless uprooting and destruction of wreckers, diversionists, spies and murderers."[6]

Bohlen was in the courtroom for the most chilling spectacle of all—the confessions. One after another the Bolshevik Old Guard admitted they were guilty of these "crimes," and one after another they were taken out and shot. Soon every member of Lenin's Politburo except for Trotsky (whom Stalin had forced into exile in 1929) and Stalin were on trial. More than 1,100 of the 1,961 delegates to the Seventeenth Party Congress were rounded up and arrested. One after another they confessed "to having entered into secret agreements with the Nazis by which they were to dismember the Soviet Union and cede vast slices of Soviet territory to Germany and Japan." Such inventions assured that all the accused were well beyond the reach of martyrdom. To dull the appetite for revenge, wives, children, relatives, and friends were denounced and arrested.[7]

This was only the beginning. According to an article in *The New York Times* of July 24, 1937, Stalin commanded all citizens "to act as informers against suspicious neighbors, and to help the government smoke out all fascist agents and destroy them as mad dogs."

"Little people anxious to curry favor and win plaudits are being paid off," Harold Denny, *The New York Times*'s Moscow correspondent, reported. Stalin decreed that only the person who betrayed a friend could be trusted; to not inform was considered a criminal act. "Lying, hypocrisy, humiliating obeisances, violence towards one's deepest convictions, and disloyalty to friends were a small price to pay for being kept out of prison. No one knows who to trust." Schoolchildren, taught that only Stalin was above suspicion, were instructed to watch parents, siblings, neighbors, and teachers for symptoms of espionage and sabotage. "Death to the fascist reptiles," students hissed at pictures of Bolsheviks long enshrined as heroes. "Let the enemies tremble," one student leader warned, "They will be utterly destroyed."[8]

At least 350,000 were liquidated in the first stages of the purge. Teachers, professors, scientists, doctors—it was a massacre of Soviet talent. As Denny told his readers, "the writer does not know intimately what the position of the Communist Party members is in Italy, Germany and other rabidly anti-communist countries. But it is difficult to believe they face any greater hazards than here. For here they have been shooting them."[9]

Once the political leadership of Russia was exterminated, Stalin turned on the elite Red Army officer corps. Every senior air force officer, all but one admiral, three out of five marshals, thirteen out of fifteen army commanders, 90 percent of all generals—a total of thirty-five thousand in all—were executed. "The reptile of Fascist espionage has many heads," *Pravda* boasted, "but we will cut off every head, paralyze and sever every tentacle, and extract the snake's venom."[10]

For Henderson, Page, Kennan, and Bohlen, the trials and executions were "unavoidably a sort of liberal education in the horrors of Stalinism" and brought to an end the honeymoon in Soviet-American relations. But witnessing it first hand also left them at odds "with official thinking in Washington for at least a decade thereafter." Because back in the United States, as Joe Alsop complained to his readers in *The New York Times,* "liberals were made to feel that a blood purge was a small thing between friends."[11]

Indeed, the Roosevelt administration was so worried that the antipathy of Henderson and the other Soviet experts might endanger efforts to cultivate an anti-Hitler Kremlin that, in the midst of the purges, it abolished the Division of East European Affairs. The end came, ironically, with a decree signed by Undersecretary Sumner Welles on June 15, 1937. This was only three days after Marshal M.N. Tukhachevsky—Chief of Staff of the Red Army, Russia's most able, successful, and revered soldier, who was also highly regarded in the West—was executed with a bullet to the back of the head.[12]

When Henderson returned to Washington from Moscow in October 1938, the bureaucratic carnage of the once mighty division was complete. Its officers had been reassigned to the European Division, of which it was now a subsection, or transferred to other regions. Even the precious library, with articles in Russian that were unobtainable even in Russia, had been dismantled. Two desks were moved into Room 385—one for Poland and the Baltic states, and the other for Russia. They were occupied by Edward Page and Loy Henderson, who did not even have a secretary.[13]

But Henderson, who ran America's "listening post to Russia" from Riga, Latvia, preceding the recognition of the USSR, was determined to stay current with the Soviet Union. So, shortly after Krivitsky arrived in the United States, Henderson phoned Isaac Don Levine, "a Russian-speaking writer fluent in the special skills of popular journalism, highly knowledgeable in Communist affairs, warm, voluble," and a friend of twenty years, who was helping Krivitsky market a series of articles. He told Levine he wanted to meet with Krivitsky.[14]

The Ukrainian-born Levine had come to America with his family in 1911 at the age of nineteen, and later had returned to Russia as a journalist to cover the Bolshevik revolution. He had become friendly with Lenin and Trotsky and had reported favorably on the changes sweeping the country. But, as the Revolution soured, he had begun using his typewriter to wage a holy war against Stalinism. It was Levine who would, several months hence, arrange the meeting between Krivitsky and Chambers.

"There is no use telling the government anything in confidence," a skeptical Krivitsky told his lawyer Louis Waldman after being informed of Henderson's request. Washington "is so sloppy about security, and so honeycombed with agents" that everything would get back to Moscow within forty-eight hours. The only result, he explained, would be increased danger to him and his family.[15]

But Levine and Waldman countered with other considerations. There was no reason to believe that the Labor Department would extend his visa when it expired in March. Perhaps cooperation with the State Department might lead to a more sympathetic treatment for his citizenship application. So on January 10, 1939, just two months after his arrival in America, Krivitsky was sitting in the cramped offices of Room 385 on the State Department's eastern corridor. As he stood at the window, he could look down on the White House and its gardens.[16]

The two Americans listened spellbound as Krivitsky answered their questions about the purges, plots, counterplots, and subplots that even foreigners in Moscow could not have known. How many had died? At least 500,000, Krivitsky thought, perhaps more, perhaps many more. What about Stalin's campaign to destroy the independent peasantry? Krivitsky answered with this vignette: After the director of the Soviet census bureau documented matter-of-factly for the Politburo that twenty million Russians had perished during the 1933–34 famine, an irritated Stalin ordered the director and his entire staff put to death.[17]

Why had Stalin decapitated Russia's political, military, and intellectual leadership at the very moment his archenemy Hitler was raising Germany to the level of a top military power? The State Department's experts had deduced the obvious. By accusing the nation's political leadership of betraying Russia to foreign enemies, Stalin was able to eliminate his rivals—real and imagined—absolve himself of blame for the government's abysmal economic failures, and increase traditional Russian fears of foreigners.[18]

But Henderson and Page had never even remotely anticipated what

Krivitsky told them next: What animated Stalin was his determination to forge a pact with Hitler. Not only that, but it was *Hitler* who had consistently rebuffed *Stalin*. Krivitsky had found out that Stalin, in late 1934, had sent a trusted schoolboy chum—David N. Kandelacki—to Berlin as a Soviet commercial attaché. His real mission, however, was to probe Nazi willingness to enter into a political alliance with the Soviet Union.

That was the reason that Stalin had to turn against the old Bolsheviks and the Red Army officers. They were inflexibly and unalterably opposed to any alliance with Hitler. So, in the name of antifascism, Stalin exterminated the antifascists. And, though the Nazis had so far resisted Stalin's persistent efforts, Krivitsky predicted that the two dictators would yet come to terms. Even to staunch anti-Stalinists like Henderson and Page this must have seemed beyond comprehension.[19]

After lunch, Krivitsky met with Ruth B. Shipley, head of the State Department's Passport Division, who was anxious to interrogate him about Soviet illegals—agents who had entered the country using forged or stolen passports—operating in the United States. They were astounded by his retentive mind. As he sat looking through large photo albums, Krivitsky started reeling off names, backgrounds, code names, and often the type of forged passports. For instance, this is how he described Nicholas Dozenberg:

> The Chief of the Soviet Military intelligence in the United States traveled on the *Normandie,* first class, from New York on May 8, 1937, using a Greek passport . . .

Impressed by his encyclopedic memory, Shipley insisted that Krivitsky return to the Department the following day for a second session. After two days, Krivitsky had provided enough information to keep the passport officials busy for months. Although he was trained to be distrustful, Krivitsky managed to establish a rapport with Henderson, who, at forty-nine, with a large bald head, warm intense eyes, and a broad mustache, radiated a nineteenth century elegance and charm that gave him the serene looks of an Old World philosopher.[20]

Yet, Krivitsky's apprehension that the visit would cause him trouble also seemed to be borne out. Several weeks later, the Labor Department turned down his application to extend his visa. Then he received what he assumed was a warning from Stalin.

On Tuesday evening, March 7, shortly after he and a friend were seated in a Times Square cafeteria, four men entered and took the table next to Krivitsky's. He immediately recognized one of the men as Serge Bassoff, a skilled Soviet assassin. Krivitsky rose from the table and walked to the middle of the room where Bassoff, a husky, redheaded former sailor from the Crimea in his early forties, joined him.

"Have you come to shoot me?" Krivitsky demanded.

"No," Bassoff insisted, "this is unofficial. I have just come for a chat. You have nothing to fear," he exhorted Krivitsky, "if you return to Russia. You still have friends in high circles, and would get no more than two years in prison."

But Krivitsky would have none of it. He asked Bassoff if he was not afraid to approach him so publicly. No, Bassoff responded, pointing out that he, not Krivitsky, had American citizenship.

"What has become of my family and Antonia's?" Krivitsky asked.

"They have all been shot," Bassoff replied, "Antonia's brothers suffered greatly."

"Leave at once!" Krivitsky boomed, "and do not speak to me again."

Later, after things had calmed down, he turned to his friend and said quietly, "They will not stop until they kill me. They have ways of bringing about my death in such a manner as to make it appear to be accidental."[21]

That night the Krivitskys, Ruth and Don Levine, and several others gathered at Alexander Kerensky's Manhattan apartment. Kerensky had been living in exile since his government, which had succeeded the czarists, had been overthrown by the Bolsheviks. As the couples sat in the living room discussing the day's events, Lydia Kerensky, an alluring Australian and amateur palmist, reached over and took Krivitsky's hand. As she studied it, Krivitsky's normally reproachful features broke into a sardonic smile. But after only seconds Lydia suddenly released his hand, fumbling for the banal comment that "you have lived such an interesting life." Later she confessed darkly to Ruth Levine, "I saw only death."[22]

In mid-April *The Saturday Evening Post* hit the newsstands with the first of five articles by Krivitsky and Levine. The contents tore away Stalin's revolutionary mask, sending shockwaves through Western circles. The first article detailed Stalin's betrayal of the Spanish Civil War. Subsequent installments revealed his pursuit of Hitler and predicted a German-Soviet pact that would lead to world war. Although large numbers of readers—including Whittaker Chambers—were enthralled at this exposé of Soviet rule, official Washington and London reacted with hostility.

"Twaddle," "rigmarole," and "nonsense," hooted the Foreign Office's Soviet specialists. "On the whole we do not consider that these would-be hair-raising revelations of Stalin's alleged desire for rapprochement with Germany are worth taking seriously."[23]

In Washington, FBI Director J. Edgar Hoover was infuriated. Krivitsky was already on his enemies list for providing information to the State Department—the FBI's bitterest rival in the field of foreign intelligence. It was the sort of crime Hoover was completely incapable of forgiving. But Krivitsky's articles were both a personal affront and an unforgivable assault on the bureau itself.[24]

For years Hoover had boasted that foreign spies posed no threat to America, because none could possibly penetrate the Bureau's steel nets. But Krivitsky described Soviet agents effortlessly entering the United States on forged passports, spending large rolls of counterfeit money, and using assassinations to keep American communists in line. The idea that Moscow-dispatched assassins could gun down Americans in their homes—even if they were communists—was a public relations debacle for the FBI.[25]

The Labor Department was soon back on the warpath. On June 28, midway through the articles, Krivitsky provided Mrs. Shipley with so much information in a three-hour session that it filled nineteen typewritten pages. The very next day, the Labor Department had a warrant out for his arrest. An enraged Levine, already worried that the Russians were about to kill or kidnap Krivitsky, called Shipley and practically accused her of conspiring with his pursuers.[26]

In fact, the opposite was true. The State Department was scheming for ways to delay the Labor Department's deportation of Krivitsky, at least until it could "get as much information as possible."

They were also aware that time could be short because, as Shipley concluded, Krivitsky "has but a slight chance to survive."

The strong-willed Shipley, whom Roosevelt once publicly called an "ogre," was not easily intimidated. Yet, shaken by Levine's menacing call, she immediately phoned Byron H. Uhl, the district director of Immigration and Naturalization at Ellis Island. Aware of rumors throughout Washington that Krivitsky was refusing to co-operate, and naively believing this might be the source of the Labor Department's displeasure, Shipley told Uhl that Krivitsky had "ren-dered great service to the Department."[27]

Levine also complained directly to Uhl's boss in Washington, James L. Houghteling, about harassment of Krivitsky by "political activists inside the Department of Labor." He singled out a Stanley White. But Houghteling responded by denying any anti-Krivitsky sentiment and insisting the department had no Stanley White on its rolls. This did not assuage Krivitsky's backers who believed, as did Assistant Secretary of State Adolf A. Berle, that the Labor Depart-ment's campaign "looks suspiciously like Communist maneuvering to get Krivitsky out of the country."[28]

Perhaps their protests did some good, because a July 1 writ ordering Krivitsky to leave the country was rescinded after Krivitsky and Waldman appeared before Uhl on July 6. His visa was extended to December 31.[29]

Krivitsky's scathing portrait of Stalin made him the *bête noire* of the fashionable literary set. They undertook a relentless effort, questioning everything about his background from his name to his rank in the Red Army. "Oh God," Ruth Levine recalled years later, "the attacks were terrible, just never ending." Lewis adds that "in the public print, [Krivitsky] lost reality as a man and became a windy controversy. Somehow, he couldn't make his facts weigh, only the fury that surrounded them. It was an ironic contradiction of the sharp-edged, hard-minded man he was."[30]

But the earth was about to open on Krivitsky's critics. On Monday, August 21, Dashiell Hammett, Max Lerner, Clifford Odets, Vincent Sheehan, James Thurber, and three hundred and ninety-five other poets, writers, artists, journalists, and playwrights placed an ad in publications around the country savagely attacking the Krivitsky-inspired suggestion that "the fascist states and the

Soviet Union equally menace American institutions and the democratic way of life.''[31]

Before the sun set on that same day, paralyzing news came
screaming out of Berlin: the two titans, Stalin and Hitler, history's
most implacable ideological foes, had become—as Krivitsky had
predicted—allies. No one doubted what forces the pact unleashed.
Stalin had just given Germany permission to invade Poland; war was
now unavoidable. The world's capitals were in convulsions. In London, the deadliest high explosives could not have caused more
damage; in Rome, Mussolini was taken completely unawares; in
Paris, there was near hysteria—France was suddenly without a
continental ally. In Tokyo, the entire cabinet, humiliated by its
failure to prevent or even predict the pact, resigned. In Moscow,
bewildered Russians watched in stunned silence as Soviet officials
passed out Nazi flags, while Warsaw rushed troops to its border with
Germany.[32]

In the early dawn of Friday, September 1, over a million German
troops invaded Poland. The next morning, as Panzer tank units were
rolling over the dry Polish plains and the world waited to see if
Britain and France would make good on their pledge to aid Poland,
Levine burst into Chambers's *Time* magazine office. Aware of the
pact between Krivitsky and Chambers, the journalistic crusader
sought to capitalize on it.

"I've arranged for us to meet with Adolph Berle, the assistant
secretary in charge of security. Tonight. Will you be there?" Chambers nodded in grim silence.[33]

Berle, forty-three, one of FDR's original Brain Trusters, was dark,
compact, still boyishly handsome, and known for his abrasive brilliance. He ran the State Department's informal intelligence network
and was liaison to the FBI. The son of a liberal Boston minister, he
had a lightning start in life, graduating with honors from Harvard at
eighteen. Three years later he also had a Harvard M.A. and Law
School degree, and, at twenty-three, was an adviser on Russian
affairs to President Woodrow Wilson at the Versailles Conference.

Berle lived at Woodley Oaks in Northwest Washington, which he
rented from Henry Stimson, a prominent Republican lawyer. It was
the perfect setting for Chambers to make good on his pledge to
inform. Not because of Woodley's tranquil view across Rock Creek

Park toward the center of the Capital, but because ten years earlier, as Hoover's secretary of state, Stimson had abolished the "Black Chamber," a secret cryptographic bureau that intercepted coded transmissions of other governments. He later defended the controversial decision with the admonition that "gentlemen do not read each other's mail."

Now, on this warm, humid night, Whittaker Chambers would reveal just how Moscow had been reading other gentlemen's mail—including Stimson's—for years.[34]

After dinner in the old Southern colonial house that dominated the estate, Berle, Chambers, and Levine adjourned to sit underneath the moonlit shadows of a magnificent old elm. Breathing in the sweet scent of honeysuckle, Chambers described in an even, unemotional, almost subdued voice how two underground Soviet spy rings, each containing officials in shockingly high positions, operated throughout official Washington. Berle was amazed as Chambers, who had never stepped foot inside the State Department, described with calm exactitude its chain of command and division of responsibilities. He knew the men who occupied the desks, too, and reeled off the names of six State Department officials, including Alger Hiss, who were part of the communist underground. Berle wrote furiously, protesting, "But I know him, I know him."[35]

It was nearly 1:00 A.M. when Chambers left Woodley Oaks. He returned to New York that morning and collapsed into bed. Twenty-four hours later, thousands of miles away in London, British Foreign Secretary Halifax handed a note to the German chargé d'affaires: "I have the honor to inform you that a state of war exists between our two countries as from 11:00 A.M. today, September 3."[36]

Levine, meanwhile, remained in Washington to attend to some unfinished business. During their collaboration on the *Post* articles, Krivitsky had once told him about several Soviet spies inside the British Foreign Office. At the time Krivitsky, "who was torn between the satisfaction of revealing Stalin's monstrous conspiracies and lies and the desire still to protect old comrades, old ideals, old devotions," refused to include the information in the articles.[37]

But for Levine, "the thought of Soviet spies in the highest offices of the British government sharing information with their Nazi allies became unbearable," so he sought an appointment—through Hen-

derson—with the British ambassador, Lord Lothian (known as Philip Kerr until he inherited his father's title).

"There is a Soviet agent working in the Foreign Office code room as a cipher clerk," Levine began almost as soon as he was seated in the large, elegantly furnished study at the ambassador's residence. "For some time he has been providing the Russians with cables." The staggering implication was that Great Britain had gone to war depending on a worldwide communications system that its enemy could read. But rather than alarm, a smile of incredulity spread across Lothian's angular face. Like many diplomats of the day, he found spying a distasteful concept, unseemly, and surely—because it was quite obviously something only the low-born would do—of trivial importance. With amused condescension Lothian finally asked, "And what is his name?"

"King," Levine answered with a trace of annoyance. "That's his last name and that's all I know." Ignoring the less than receptive atmosphere, Levine described a second agent whose name he did not know, saying he was of good family and assigned to an office within the British Cabinet.[38]

Loy Henderson was in his office when a discouraged Levine arrived from his session at the embassy. The ambassador had made him feel like a crank. Lothian had not even bothered to ask him where he could be reached. Things soon changed, according to Henderson:

Some time later the secretary through whom I had arranged for the interview telephoned me in what seemed to be an air of excitement, and asked me how to get in immediate touch with Mr. Levine.

It turned out that Lothian had dutifully cabled Levine's information to the Foreign Office, and John Herbert King, a fifty-five-year-old cipher clerk in the Communications Office, was put under surveillance. This led to questioning, and eventually King broke down and confessed to being a paid Soviet agent. He was sentenced to ten years in prison.[39]

Urged to come back to Washington immediately, Levine arrived at the embassy on Massachusetts Avenue to discover that solicitation had replaced condescension. Victor Mallet, the embassy's towering six-foot six-inch Counsellor, confessed that "the British government

wants Krivitsky's cooperation in ferreting out the Soviet espionage agents who, in view of the Stalin-Hitler Pact, could be regarded as Nazi collaborators."[40]

Apparently, the State Department had already shared with the British embassy a warning it had received from its embassy in Moscow:

> Soviet agents now in the United States or who may hereafter be sent there to operate either as individuals or through Amtorg [the New York-based Soviet trading company] will endeavor to acquire in the United States such material supply as the German government may desire.

And from Brussels came

> positive proof that the German and Soviet governments are working together in matters of espionage and sabotage. Soviet agents are being used for most important jobs as they are more likely not to be suspected.[41]

Krivitsky soon explained the setup to a House Committee:

> Stalin's pact with Hitler is really an alliance of the two armies, operating in specific zones. I have no doubt that such exchanges of military secrets and information are indispensable to both Hitler and Stalin.[42]

Within weeks officials from three nations were working to get Krivitsky to England. It was not easy. To begin with, Krivitsky could not "believe a government whose communications office has been compromised, could keep secret from Stalin such a threatening mission." So Waldman began making elaborate security arrangements with personal friends in the British Labour Party (Krivitsky feared Conservative Prime Minister Neville Chamberlain's government might turn him over to Stalin or Hitler).

Then Washington got into the act. Apparently agreeing that Moscow would inevitably find out about it, and fearing Stalin would think Krivitsky's trip was a U.S.-inspired anti-Soviet vendetta, the

government insisted that Krivitsky could not leave for England from American soil.[43]

This approached overkill. The Labor Department had finally succeeded in denying Krivitsky any further extensions on his visa. And though he had testified on Capitol Hill to placate critics on the right and left, any hope of friendly congressional intervention evaporated after Wisconsin Representative Edward Schafer stood on the floor of the House and bellowed to his colleagues, "Let's get Krivitsky out of America *tout de suite*." The Republican congressman complained that he was tired of Krivitsky "posing as a patriot." Facing an expiration date of December 31, Krivitsky had no choice but to leave the country for six months and then reenter, register as an alien, and start over on his citizenship campaign.[44]

To satisfy all the American conditions, the British made arrangements for the Krivitskys to establish temporary residence in Canada. But only two days before his scheduled departure, which was so secret that not even his closest New York friends knew about it, Krivitsky spotted two men keeping his apartment under surveillance. Knowing that Moscow would stop at nothing to keep him from getting to England, he called Loy Henderson at his home on Christmas Eve.

As a result, two nights later the Radical Squad, a special heavily armed unit of the New York police, escorted Krivitsky and his family to the Canadian border, where they were turned over to the protection of the Royal Canadian Mounted Police. In early January, with his family in hiding at a secret location outside Montreal, Krivitsky boarded a Royal Navy submarine for the trip to England. Having decided to move to Virginia once he became an American citizen, Krivitsky passed the twelve-day crossing reading *Gone With the Wind*.[45]

He arrived in England on January 19, and the first spy he may have flushed out was not British, but an American. Tyler Kent, a twenty-nine-year-old Virginia blueblood, was a cipher clerk in Ambassador Joseph Kennedy's London embassy. After attending Princeton and the Sorbonne, he studied Russian in Paris. Then, although he had backing from Virginia's powerful Byrd family, he was admitted to the Foreign Service and served in the first American diplomatic mission to Moscow. Malcolm Muggeridge, the British journalist, described him as "one of those intensely gentlemanly Americans who wear well-cut tailor-made suits, with waistcoats and watch-chain, drink wine instead of highballs, and easily become furiously indignant."[46]

Shortly after he arrived in London on October 5, 1939, he was using a set of unauthorized keys to remove cables, "true readings" (meaning in enemy hands they could be used to crack American codes), from the cipher room where he worked as a clerk. He shared what he filched with German and Italian intelligence agents, which may have further proved the close cooperation of the Soviet and Nazi underground.[47]

For President Roosevelt, Kent's arrest may have preserved a victory in his controversial quest for a third term. Kent had copies of the highly secret exchanges Roosevelt had initiated with Churchill (then First Lord of the Admiralty), a correspondence few in either government even knew about. Roosevelt was always guarded in his response to Churchill's blandishments to bring America into the war. Even so, had their exchanges become public during the antiwar heat of the 1940 American election, "they could have proved disastrous" for FDR "and destroyed his hopes for a third term."[48]

During three weeks of "skilled and systematic debriefing" by British intelligence, Krivitsky identified "ninety-three agents working around the world," sixty-one of whom were operating in Great Britain: Soviet illegals with fake passports, spies working under Soviet diplomatic cover, and two Western journalists.[49]

It was the British who would next have a rude awakening. According to Krivitsky, the Soviets had successfully recruited privileged British youth who were among those destined to run the Empire. For some reason, however, the higher up the suspect, the more vague Krivitsky's clues, or so the Foreign Office has always maintained. This is strange in that it might be expected that the more important the spy the more someone of Krivitsky's senior rank would know about him.

Yet, Gladwyn Jebb, who interrogated Krivitsky, maintains he had little information, only that

there was a man "of good family" in the Foreign Office who was giving away information to the Russians, but as he could go no further in describing this person—who as it turned out later was clearly Donald Maclean—we were unable to pursue our investigation very far.[50]

This seems more like a combination of a memory dimmed by years of many other great crises—Jebb's distinguished career extended into the 1960s—and devotion to the largely discredited official Foreign Office line: Whitehall could not possibly have known, based on Krivitsky's vague clues, that Maclean was a Soviet agent.

Yet, if he told the British only what he had already told Levine, it should have been enough for them to identify Maclean. According to Levine, Krivitsky knew a good deal more than Jebb remembers, including that the Soviets had recruited "a young Scotsman who had been imbued with communism in the early thirties, and who subsequently was induced to enter the service of the British diplomacy." Krivitsky did not know the man's name, but he was of good family and had been educated at Eton and Oxford and as "an idealist [was] working without payment." He was an artistic type, sometimes wore a cape, and had a prominent father.[51]

Maclean's father, Sir Donald, had been a Member of Parliament, a Cabinet officer, leader of the Liberal Party, and one of the most respected men in British public life. The younger Maclean had gone to Gresham's School and Trinity Hall at Cambridge (a minor discrepancy because most foreigners, especially Soviets, believe that all well-bred Englishman go to Eton and Oxford). Alienated during the turbulent 1930s, he became a self-described communist and vowed to move to Russia following graduation. But these plans were redirected once he had been recruited by Soviet intelligence, who instructed him to enter the Foreign Office.[52]

In September 1935 Maclean passed the rigid Civil Service written and oral exams on his first try, something of a rarity. He began his service as a Third Secretary in the Diplomatic Service that October. In 1938 he was assigned to Paris—at about the time Krivitsky was beginning to make his break—and frequented the Left Bank haunts of the artistic set, which is where he met his future wife, Melinda Marling.

If Krivitsky had told the British this much, it should have been enough. Krivitsky said the spy had been recruited in the early 1930s and had joined the Foreign Office subsequent to that recruitment. An Oxbridge graduate would have entered the Foreign Office only through the annual competitive examination. Between 1932 and 1936 only six to eight passed the necessary exams (seven were accepted in Maclean's class of 1935). This means that at its largest (assuming no deaths, resignations, dismissals, and so forth), the pool of suspects in 1940 could not have numbered more than thirty to forty.

Even if the number could only have been halved by concentrating on Scots (Donald's grandmother was a Scottish matriarch who spoke Gaelic to her dying day) and those with prominent fathers ("for a quarter of a century he has been a distinguished and respected figure in the political life of this country," King George V wrote after Sir Donald's sudden death), it would have left a pool of no more than twenty. And of those it is a near certainty that only one—Donald Maclean—would have been so brazen as to virtually advertise his split loyalties. For surely none of the others told his Foreign Office examiners that while at Cambridge, "I did have some [strong communist] views—" and "I haven't entirely shaken them off." But not for the last time Maclean would be the beneficiary of a combination of upper-class arrogance and ineptitude among Western intelligence services.[53]

Krivitsky also told of five other well-placed British government officials who were Soviet agents. Although he did not know any by name, he did have clues—even more vague—to the identity of one other. He was a "young English journalist sent to Spain during the [Spanish Civil] War." Admittedly, this would not have led to Kim Philby. He was merely one of many young men such as Claude Cockburn, George Orwell, Arthur Koestler, and Jim Lardner who rushed to cover the civil war. Many were freelance propagandists or on Moscow's payroll. But as journalists they did not pose a threat to Britain's national security, and British intelligence can be forgiven for not starting an investigation.

What they cannot be forgiven for, however, is their decision to permanently ignore Krivitsky's de facto warning: should any British journalist who covered the Spanish Civil War subsequently try to join the British government, beware that he might be a Soviet agent. Instead, when Kim Philby, a Cambridge graduate who covered the Spanish Civil War for *The Times* (London), later—under specific instructions from Moscow—penetrated British intelligence, they embraced him as one of their own.

The problem with what Krivitsky was saying was not with his clues, vague or otherwise; rather it was with the incapacity of the British Foreign Office (under whose authority MI6, or Secret Intelligence Service, operated) to grasp what Krivitsky was telling them: proper British gentlemen can betray country and crown. When Krivitsky's clues led to the arrests of an ill-bred loser like King, a lower-class Briton who was an army washout, and Kent, a foreigner after all, that was splendid. But once he implicated the British upper classes, his vagueness, we are to believe, left his interrogators helpless.

★ ★ ★

None of Krivitsky's leads would have pointed directly to twenty-nine-year-old Guy Burgess, who had been close to both Maclean and Philby at Cambridge, and was, like them, a Soviet agent. During the summer of 1940 he seemed about to move into a league of his own by breaking into the senior ranks of British intelligence.

His opportunity came in June 1940, shortly after Sir Stafford Cripps, a self-styled Marxist, was appointed ambassador to Moscow. At the time Burgess was thriving in Section D, a special wartime intelligence unit whose mission was to sabotage the Germans behind enemy lines. However, either he or the Soviets decided that rather than fight the Soviet Union's ally, Burgess could be more valuable inside the British embassy in Moscow serving as a pipeline to the Kremlin. Accordingly, Burgess got himself assigned to the embassy as a British intelligence officer working under diplomatic cover.

He left London in early July with Isaiah Berlin, an Oxford philosopher who had been convinced by the Foreign Office to assume the dubious position of press attaché at the British embassy in Moscow. (Berlin had protested to Harold Nicolson that "the possibility of influencing the Russian press was smaller than it can ever have been before, and that the job did not seem to me very real.") Berlin was even less certain about Burgess's job.[54]

Before Berlin left London, Gladwyn Jebb briefed him on what he could expect in Moscow. As Berlin got up to leave, Jebb added, "By the way, Guy Burgess is to go with you—he has his own work to do about which you need know nothing; but for convenience sake he may have to be attached as your assistant—have you any objection?"[55]

"I knew nothing about GB's work, had no suspicion then, or, indeed, until he absconded of his being a Communist, let alone a Soviet agent, so I said I had no possible objection," Berlin recalled decades later.[56]

Because the path through Europe was cut off, Burgess and Berlin were to proceed via Washington to Japan, eventually taking the Trans-Siberian Railway to Moscow. But two days after they arrived in Washington, their mission was canceled. Cripps, as it turned out, objected to the Foreign Office staffing his embassy.[57]

Burgess used his brief stay to look up Michael Whitney Straight, another Cambridge classmate. Straight had been one of the most glamorous undergraduates of his day. A handsome, smart, popular and exceedingly rich American, he was also very left-wing and belonged to one of the many communist cells that flourished on the campus by the mid-1930s (Straight went up to Cambridge in 1935). In 1937, however, he received what he understood to be orders directly from Moscow to drop out of Cambridge and return to America to further the Soviet cause. He did so that summer.

His first job interview was at the White House over tea with President and Mrs. Roosevelt. This was the kind of access that came from being scion to one of the greatest fortunes in America, derived from intermarriage among the Whitneys, the Vanderbilts, and the Paynes of Standard Oil. Straight's mother was a liberal activist and social reformer who had started and privately financed the influential *New Republic* magazine, and Mrs. Roosevelt considered her a friend.

The President seemed nonplussed by the young Straight, and suggested he get some experience in the private sector before seeking government employment. Mrs. Roosevelt, however, sent him to the State Department where, in January 1938, he began a low-level job in the economics division. He was quickly contacted by Michael Green, assigned by the Soviets to be his control officer.[58]

In March 1939 Straight left the Department because he claimed, "[I was not] willing to be a Soviet agent in the Department of State." Leaving had been "a welcome escape. It was an escape from the trap that had held me captive." Once out of the State Department, Straight felt he had achieved "my first, small foothold on the possibility of leading an honest and an honorable life." Next he joined a presidential speechwriting team lead by the one-time New Deal "whiz kids" Tommy Corcoran and Ben Cohen. But it was disbanded in the summer of 1940, and Straight was at loose ends. Then Burgess arrived.[59]

During their talks, Straight claims to have realized for the first time that it was Burgess who had been behind the scheme to have him abandon his promising Cambridge career to return to America. After a final dinner with Burgess at his house, Straight confessed to his wife that he and Burgess were both involved with Soviet intelligence and that he, Straight, had been holding clandestine meetings with Green. She insisted he begin to break off contact with Michael Green.[60]

Later that same summer, Straight was back in the State Department. When asked why he would return to "the trap" he had so recently and eagerly fled, Straight maintains his thinking at the time was rather simple: "a fear of being unemployed." Having been without a job for several months, he felt out of place in a city running on the high octane of a world in crisis.

According to Straight, this came about when Assistant Secretary of State James C. Dunn called and offered him a "vacant desk" in the European Division. Dunn was certainly an improbable benefactor for Straight. The only thing the two had in common was immense unearned wealth. Son of a Newark bricklayer and a high school dropout, Dunn escaped the tedium of minor State Department administrative posts when he married the heiress to the Armour meat-packing fortune. But where Dunn was an arch-conservative, Straight was ultra-liberal, and where Dunn became the son Secretary of State Cordell Hull never had, Straight's ties were to the White House, which treated Hull as if he were a leper.[61]

"Poppycock," Jack Hickerson, the assistant chief of the European Division, later replied when told of Straight's assertion that Dunn had offered him a job. According to Hickerson, there was no vacant desk at the time, and if there were, he would not have considered the twenty-four-year-old Straight qualified to fill it. "We tried our damndest to keep Straight out," he recalled over forty years later in a voice still trembling with rage. "We didn't want him. He wasn't our choice. He was not a professional. He had political pull and he used it." In fact, Straight had the best political pull in town—a letter from the president of the United States.[62]

Straight had continued access to the White House as part of the Corcoran-Cohen speechwriting team. He also managed to see Mrs. Roosevelt fairly frequently, and was an occasional White House dinner guest. As recently as February 1940, he and his wife dined alone with the Roosevelts. But Straight, labeling Hickerson's account as "nonsense," claims he was unaware of the letter until years later, and that the president wrote them for all members of the speech team.

Any opposition quickly buckled. The Department, especially after the Tyler Kent affair, was already in enough trouble with FDR. Following routine clearances, Straight began work on August 27 as a Grade 4 full professional at $3,800 a year in the European Division.[63]

The event is important, because it put Straight in proximity to Walter Krivitsky's State Department lifeline. For the past eight months, Krivitsky had been hiding out in Canada, but he was due back in the United States soon to resume his campaign to become a citizen. It is possible that given, as we shall see, the degree of Soviet penetration of the Canadian government, Moscow knew of Krivitsky's whereabouts. If not, Straight maintains he could not have helped them because he was not reporting to Green, and he had never even heard of Krivitsky.

Krivitsky quietly reentered the United States in late October. His apprehension, if anything, had increased, for on August 20 an assassin dispatched by Moscow had succeeded in driving an ice pick through Trotsky's skull. Only weeks earlier Trotsky, the man who built the Red Army and was once Foreign Commissar, had told an American visitor, "General Krivitsky is right. We are the two men Stalin is determined to kill." Now only Krivitsky was left.[64]

Krivitsky registered as an alien applying for American citizenship. He felt increasingly isolated and despondent. The world was now engaged in a life and death struggle and, after twenty years of preparing for this moment, he was on the sidelines. He was convinced England would do nothing with what he had told them.

Perhaps the totalitarian view of democracy as inherently weak and vacillating was true.

For months, before her husband broke with him, Ruth Levine saw Krivitsky often:

> He couldn't adjust to freedom. He was a tormented, unhappy man, pursued by the furies. After all he had done, after all the sacrifices and deaths in the Soviet Union, the Revolution had ended with a Stalin dictatorship. Russia was worse off than anything it had known in its history. He just could never accept that. It haunted him.[65]

His petulant and demanding nature also caused his one-time protege, Paul Wohl, to break with him. Yet, after Krivitsky's death, Wohl wrote, "no other Bolshevik ever left the Soviet world to become so lonely and desperate." He would often lapse into silence, looking "as if his heart were breaking." Once when he and Wohl were out on a walk in the misty early morning light, Krivitsky suddenly "sank on a bench and on his ashen face was an expression of unspeakable pain," caused by life without the Party, the legend of the Revolution, and his homeland. Some days he would go to the docks and spend hours watching the loading of ships bound for Russia.[66]

Krivitsky spent more and more time with Chambers "tramping the streets, taking circuitous routes and watching, as in the old underground days, to see if we were followed." By now they knew that Chambers's meeting with Berle had been perfunctorily dismissed (for reasons that would later be hotly disputed). All the Soviet agents Chambers identified were still at work. In fact only weeks after Chambers was there, the Berles had as their dinner guests at Woodley Oaks Priscilla and Alger Hiss.[67]

Seeking to fill the void in his life, Krivitsky asked Chambers "if I could arrange for his instructions so that he could be baptized and confirmed in the Episcopal Church." Chambers agreed. Several days later, on Thursday, February 6, Krivitsky was at the State Department with Loy Henderson. The two had maintained close contact. Henderson had always been willing to lend a sympathetic ear, or arrange an appointment, or try to alleviate his immigration problems. Now, as they talked, Krivitsky told him he was going to spend the weekend in Virginia, return to Washington on Sunday, and then take a train to New York. While he was in Virginia, he added, he intended to buy a gun. A Soviet assassin who had made two attempts on Krivitsky's life in France had recently been spotted in New York.[68]

Although Henderson knew that if Krivitsky were caught carrying a gun he could be immediately deported, he apparently did not try to dissuade him. These were dangerous times, especially with Trotsky's assassination. Neither man knew, of course, that Michael Straight, sitting near Henderson's office, was in America primarily because Moscow had ordered him there.[69]

That same afternoon, Krivitsky left Washington for Eitel and Marguerite Dobert's ninety-acre chicken farm in rural Virginia, a trip that would contribute greatly to the suspicious circumstances surrounding his death.

The Doberts lived in a 150-year-old two-room log cabin near the village of Barboursville, fifteen miles northeast of Charlottesville. She was a thin, attractive brunette, half Turkish and half Greek. He had been a Nazi stormtrooper until the early 1930s, when a stay in Switzerland made him "a convert to freedom." After he renounced his German citizenship, they moved to America where he wrote and lectured against the Nazis and began to associate with, if he did not actually join, the communists.[70]

They had met Krivitsky at a writers' colony in upstate New York several months earlier and described to him the splendors of rural isolation in Virginia. The Russian decided it would be a secure place to move his family. Although Krivitsky had obviously planned the trip in advance, the Doberts, who did not have a phone, would later claim not to have known he was coming. And, in that case, he could not have been sure they would even be there. How he even got to the farm is a mystery.

"There was a knock on the door, I opened it and there was Walter," Mrs. Dobert said later. "I never thought to ask him how he got there. Perhaps a taxi." But the farm was so remote that even a taxi from Charlottesville would have been unlikely unless the driver knew its exact location. There were later reports that an American, never identified, gave Krivitsky a ride down from Washington.

On Saturday Mrs. Dobert drove Krivitsky to the Charlottesville Hardware Company where he bought a .38-caliber automatic pistol for fifteen dollars. He also bought two boxes of mushroom bullets. Krivitsky was in a good mood, and told manager Charles Henshaw he would soon be moving to the area. Most of the rest of the day was spent target practicing. That night, according to Mrs. Dobert, Krivitsky had trouble sleeping. He knocked on the door to the bedroom and asked for some aspirin. Later, he interrupted them again, and asked for some paper so that he could write letters. She gave him several sheets of inexpensive drugstore stationery.

She too had planned to go to Washington on Sunday, so at 1:00 P.M. the two of them headed north in her 1936 Buick. He was in excellent spirits, and so absorbed in wondering whether he could afford to buy any of the small farms they passed in the dense woods of the Blue Ridge foothills, that he hardly noticed that Mrs. Dobert—constantly checking the rearview mirror to be sure they weren't followed—missed a turn and got lost. They approached Union Station as the last light was being drained from the pewter sky. "Do you want me to mail your letters?" she asked as Krivitsky was getting out of the car.

"No," he replied, "they're nothing for you to bother with."

"Do you have your artillery?" He nodded as he patted his canvas bag. Then he gave his usual, if somewhat morbid, farewell: "If anything should happen to me, look after Tonya and Alex."[71]

Krivitsky never boarded the train to New York. Instead, he went almost directly to the small, quiet Bellevue Hotel only a few blocks from the station, checking in at 5:47 P.M. This was odd. He had a room permanently reserved in a large downtown hotel, where he always stayed when he was in Washington, because he considered it safer.

At 9:30 A.M. the following morning Thelma Jackson, a twenty-one-year-old maid, knocked several times on the door of Room 532. When there was no answer, she used her passkey to enter, pausing at the door when she saw Krivitsky lying on the bed. He was fully dressed but his head was toward the foot of the bed. She asked if she should come back later. There was no answer. She walked over to the bed. It was only then she saw the blood. A .130 grain mushroom bullet had been fired into his head above the right temple and exploded out below the left ear, leaving a gaping wound the size of a man's fist.

Because he had registered under an alias, the police were not sure who the dead man was. But eventually J.B. Matthews, a congressional aide who had worked with Krivitsky, arrived on the scene. "It's Krivitsky all right. And it's murder, I have no doubt about it," he later told reporters. At their last meeting Krivitsky had told him, "They'll get me sure as hell. But when I'm dead, don't ever believe it was suicide." Over the next several days, at least six others reported Krivitsky had pleaded with them never to believe he would commit suicide, no matter how convincing the evidence. For Soviet intelligence, staging a murder to look like a suicide, he cautioned, was child's play.

But, "the Metropolitan police who know little or nothing of the devious methods attributed to Red undercover agents," according to *The New York Times,* "stood on the bare physical facts they encountered when they entered Krivitsky's hotel room." To them it was an obvious case of suicide. Their report, probably written only after the second-guessing started, left little room for any other conclusion. The door and windows were locked from the inside; three suicide notes were found written on cheap stationery bearing the script, "Charlottesville, Virginia": one to his wife (in Russian); one to his lawyer Louis Waldman (in English); and one to his friend Suzanne LaFollette (in German; she was an anticommunist intellectual and a cousin of Wisconsin Senator Bob LaFollette). According to one of the notes, "on the farm of Dobertov I wrote this yesterday [Saturday]."[72]

By 11:30 A.M., just two hours after the body had been discovered, Coroner A. Magruder MacDonald issued a certificate of suicide. By 1:00 P.M. the room had been scrubbed clean. By 2:00 P.M. it was back on the hotel's inventory of available rooms.

Then Waldman arrived on the scene. Forty-nine and (like Levine and Krivitsky) born in the Ukraine, he had been twice elected to the New York State Assembly while in law school. He later ran three times for governor of New York on the Socialist ticket, and was virulently anticommunist. He dismissed the police investigation as a joke and demanded that the FBI take on the case.[73]

Krivitsky's death had not softened Hoover's attitude toward him. He refused either to comment publicly on the case or to allow anyone to receive Waldman. "We are not in this case and we are not going to be baited into it . . ." he instructed his staff. Hoover was so determined to blacken Krivitsky's name that he lied to the Attorney General by insisting that to his knowledge "Krivitsky never furnished any information of value to other Federal agencies." This even though he had copies of Henderson's, Page's, and Shipley's memoranda which attested that Krivitsky had provided information of unsurpassed importance.[74]

Although Hoover was unmoved, a number of reporters started digging. Within hours, the police's airtight case collapsed. First, the window had not been locked from the inside; in fact, the police had found it open. Nor was the door locked in such a way that it could only have been opened from the inside. The maid used a passkey hanging from a nearby unlocked broom closet, an arrangement, as regulars at the Bellevue knew, that could be found on every floor; Krivitsky's door may not have even been locked to begin with. The bullet that shattered Krivitsky's brain was never found. Therefore, it was never established that it was fired from his gun, nor that his gun was even fired, although an empty shell was found on the floor.[75]

The trajectory of the bullet was such that if Krivitsky had fired it, his right arm would have to have been fully extended away from his body. And the recoil would have also been to the right. Yet Krivitsky's gun—which was never checked for fingerprints—was found on his left side. Finally, although the Bellevue's guests habitually complained because every snort and cough passed undimmed through the hotel's thin walls, no one reported hearing a gunshot that night. Yet, the rooms on both sides of Krivitsky's were occupied, and his gun had no silencer. The police never interviewed any of the hotel guests.[76]

By Tuesday "the police were smarting under the charge of inexcusably sloppy work," and Dr. MacDonald retracted his verdict of suicide. By then journalists had converged on the Dobert farm. Eitel Dobert, isolated though he was, was completely familiar with the story. He alone among Krivitsky's friends was certain that the Russian had committed suicide. And he provided what, for the police, became the clinching piece of evidence: Krivitsky, he maintained, had written the suicide notes at the farm on Saturday night.

As her husband was describing Krivitsky's final days, Mrs. Dobert arrived from Washington with the following story. She had spent

Sunday night there checking into the Capitol Park Hotel adjacent to the Bellevue, unaware that just two minutes before Krivitsky had registered at the latter. She left the next morning Monday, just as the coroner was announcing his verdict. That night, still unaware of what had happened, she remained in Washington, this time at the home of a friend. It was not until she picked up *The Washington Post* the next morning that she discovered her weekend houseguest had been found dead. She then drove straight back to Virginia without contacting the police.

Uneasy at finding herself in the middle of a press conference, Mrs. Dobert at first hesitated to agree with her husband that Krivitsky wrote the letters on Saturday night. After a few minutes, however, she said that she too was certain that Krivitsky had written the notes at the farm before leaving for Washington. That was enough for the police. Coroner MacDonald again issued a certificate of suicide to the District Health Department.[77]

During the ensuing years, attention remained focused on the suicide notes. None of the three recipients ever saw the originals, though for years all tried to get them. Instead, the police gave them translations. Mrs. Krivitsky, Waldman, and LaFollette all said that the words and the syntax did not *sound* like Walter.

On February 15 Waldman issued a public statement pointing out glaring errors in the police translation of the suicide notes. In the one to his wife and son, Krivitsky was to have intoned "Good people will help you but no enemies." The correct translation included two Russian words previously omitted, so that the note actually read, "Good people will help you but no enemies of the Soviet people."

"This fact now available puts an entirely different complexion on this letter," Waldman insisted. He and others familiar with Soviet intelligence claimed that the words sounded like those dictated by Soviet agents to give the impression that for Krivitsky suicide was an act of contrition. Scores of thousands of Russians, it was pointed out, had been executed during the purges after being branded as "enemies of the Soviet people."

Similarly, the line "I want to live very badly, but it is impossible" had been translated to make it appear that Krivitsky had come to the end of his rope and could not bear to go on. But the correct translation reads "I want very badly to live, but I must not live any longer," which suggests his death was mandated by someone else.[78]

Each note also carried a sentence beneath his signature, although "he had never been a man to write postscripts, a man to have afterthoughts." And each postscript mentioned a third party, in one case a man (Dobert) Krivitsky hardly knew. It was unlike him to drag the name of strangers into what he knew would be a scandal.[79]

Even more troubling, the postscripts sounded labored, which suggests they may have been dictated by someone who was trying to close loopholes to make an execution appear like a suicide: why he went to Virginia (to buy the gun); why he committed suicide in Washington (he hadn't had the strength in New York); and why he wrote the notes on the farm (he planned his death). All the postscripts were clumsy and irrelevant.[80]

Only one thing is certain. The notes he was alleged to have written were on "Charlottesville, Virginia" stationery. But there is no way anyone, including the Doberts, can be sure that he wrote them on Saturday night, or that he wrote them at all. Perhaps, however, Krivitsky did commit suicide. Perhaps an assassin forced him to write the notes, promising to spare his family if he cooperated in his own suicide. Perhaps someone set him up, lured him to the hotel—and brought with them blank stationery and the cartridge the police found in the room—and then executed him.[81]

Mrs. Krivitsky and Alex were left destitute. She was barely able to scrape together the $108 needed to bury her husband. The day after the funeral, they went into hiding with Whittaker Chambers's family in Florida. Months later Tonya and Alex returned north. She got a job in an apron factory to pay rent on a fifty-five dollar per month apartment in the Bronx, where she still lives nearly half a century later. She is alone now; her son died of a brain tumor before he reached the age of forty. Her English is still broken, and she has never spoken of her husband's death even to such friends as Ruth Levine and Marguerite Dobert.[82]

Not long after Krivitsky was found dead, Michael Straight decided to leave the State Department. He denies he was providing information to the Soviets, or even reporting to his control during his final State Department tour. There is no evidence to contradict him. Still, it must be noted that the Soviets' indifference to his activities is almost without precedent. Soviet intelligence officers, for instance, met weekly with Philby, Maclean, and Burgess even when they had nothing to report, or were unemployed altogether. Yet, even though he dined at the White House and worked in the State Department, Straight maintains the Soviets left him in peace.[83]

Even though Straight may not have known anything about Krivitsky, it is almost certain the Soviets did have some way of tracking the Russian. In fact, several years later, a witness told the Senate Subcommittee on Security that Jack Parilla, who was the head of a Soviet liquidation squad in the United States, came to Washington on Friday, February 7, the day after Krivitsky was at the State Department discussing his plans. Parilla, who because of a deformity was known as "The Hunchback," remained in Washington through the weekend. Several days later, he was back in New York and was drinking with merchant seamen at the National Maritime Union headquarters.

"He loafed around for quite a while. He got on a drunk, became very vicious, and dropped a hint of the murder to several of the trusted seamen, who were comrades at the time," according to the witness.[84]

Straight was unsettled by Krivitsky's death. A few nights after his body was found, Straight heard a commotion in his home. For a fearful moment, "I thought: They've come for me." He should have been scared. He walked away from the State Department, a top priority for Soviet penetration, and never held another government job until the Nixon administration.[85]

"Stalin does not permit agents to leave his service," said Krivitsky, who knew. To Stalin there was "no wavering. There could be no such thing as resignation from a task assigned because it caused a crisis of conscience. He who did not obey perfectly, accept everything, was a traitor." And for traitors there was only liquidation. National borders meant nothing.[86]

Yet, Straight claims he was not a spy because he chose not to be one, and the Soviets had no say in the matter. He, not Stalin, decided what he would do. And he, unlike the countless others were killed for disobedience to Moscow, was allowed to walk away from the whole business to write for his family magazine.

He must have been jolted by the *New Republic* editorial that greeted him in the first issue after Krivitsky's death:

> We are beginning to learn that anybody who enters the secret service of a totalitarian ruler has already in a sense committed suicide. He is a dead man from the moment he takes the oath.[87]

CHAPTER TWO

The keeping of secrets acts like a psychic
poison, alienating their possessor from the
community.

Carl Jung, 1935[1]

THE ETHIC OF CONSPIRACY

During the 1920s and 1930s the Soviet Union, relying upon a highly sophisticated psychological screening process mastered during the Bolsheviks' prolonged underground struggle against the czarists, launched a campaign to recruit Western citizens as spies. The primary targets were those imbued with what a Royal Canadian Commission investigating this campaign's techniques described as "the Ethic of Conspiracy."[2]

The campaign had its greatest successes at Cambridge University among young Britons whose birth and breeding ensured their membership in the British Empire's governing elite. Using "ingenious psychological development," Soviet recruiters were able to persuade a handful of carefully selected individuals "to engage in illegal activities directed against the safety and interests of their own society." Among those who became entangled in the Soviet net either while at Cambridge or shortly thereafter were Donald Maclean, Kim Philby, Guy Burgess, Anthony Blunt, Alan Nunn May, and the American Michael Straight.[3]

Maclean and Philby went on to penetrate the British—and eventually the American—sanctum sanctorum. Little is known about the precise place and time when they or the others received, as Philby

33

characterized it, "the proposition." But it is certain that their recruit-ment was part of a prolonged and subtle operation.

The gradualism was not owing to reluctance on the part of the targeted recruits. If, after five years of mining Cambridge, the Soviets came away with twenty spies, they could have had 200 or perhaps twice that number. The Soviets, however, were not inter-ested in quantity, but in quality. Moscow maintained complete control of the process and an eagerness to betray was hardly sufficient to gain admission into what Philby proudly called its "elite force."[4]

They chose well; so well and with such precision that no one turned them down and then reported the proposition to the British authorities. In fact, from the time the Soviet campaign began until 1946, there was not a single known instance in the English-speaking world where an individual had been approached to engage in espio-nage, refused, and reported the criminal request to the proper authorities. This does not mean that no one refused them. But the targeting of the individual and the subsequent approach were so expertly conceived that even if the individual did refuse, he either did not realize that he was being invited to commit treason (perhaps he had only declined to attend regular study group sessions), or did not feel compelled to report it to the authorities.[5]

How did they do it? The technique varied in each country. In the United States, Soviet intelligence worked through the American Communist Party until 1943 when, at Moscow's uncompromising insistence, full control of the Party's espionage cells was transferred to Soviet intelligence.[6]

In England the Communist Party of Great Britain played a more marginal role. At Cambridge, for instance, the Party neither re-cruited nor directed spies. Overt student communists who belonged to the Party might be used to invite other students—those, for instance, who had expressed an admiration for communism and the Soviet Union, or who had a marked antipathy to their own coun-try—to attend study groups. The study groups' ostensible purpose was to discuss Marx and Lenin, as well as current affairs. But

these study groups were in fact "cells" and were the recruiting centers for agents, and the medium of development of the necessary frame of mind, which was a preliminary condition to eventual service of the Soviet Union in a more practical way.[7]

Moscow opened a file on each invitee to be updated as he progressed through the study group. Those judged to have promise were often encouraged to refrain from openly joining the Party, and often to conceal their radical beliefs. Those who showed potential as agents were quietly separated from the larger group and placed in even smaller and more select cells.[8]

How many were thought to have the stuff of duplicity? Not many. In 1935 Cambridge's student population was five thousand. Perhaps 500 to 600 were active in socialist or communist organizations. At most, 150 were meeting in secret cells. Of those, perhaps three or four each year were finally invited to secretly join the Soviet underground as spies to be run individually and directly by Soviet intelligence.[9]

What was Moscow looking for? The most valued attribute a potential spy could possess was a love of conspiracy, or what the Canadian Commission described as a predisposition for conspiratorial relationships. This trait is common enough among adolescents who form secret clubs that ostentatiously exclude other playmates. Even for such youthful and innocuous conspirators "secrecy presupposes a separation between those that have the secret and those that are excluded from it," Brandeis's Sissela Bok has written. "This separation between insider and outsider is essential" to the thrill of belonging to secret organizations.[10]

By their teens, most young men have passed through this phase. But Cambridge had a history of being dominated by sanctimonious and introverted coteries that perpetuated the adolescent cult of secrecy. Clusters of students and faculty constituted themselves self-appointed elites by forming clubs whose oaths, membership, and activities were cloaked in ritualistic secrecy. Nonmembers, the great mass of students, were scorned as rabble. Burgess, Blunt, and Straight all belonged to the Apostles, Cambridge's ultimate secret organization that the historian Hugh Trevor-Roper has described as "an egregious secret society of self-perpetuating, self-admiring narcissi." Oxford, Trevor-Roper contends, was "gayer, more sophisticated, more cosmopolitan" and would have laughed Cambridge's plethora of secret societies off the campus.[11]

Cambridge's elitist pretensions made it fertile territory for Soviet recruiters. Their invitation to attend a study group was calculated to gauge a targeted student's conspiratorial bent. The recruit would have been approached by a fellow student, likely one he did not know, along these lines:

> *I saw your letter-to-the-editor last week about the need to work for peace and justice. There are others on campus who agree with you. Some of us are meeting to share our views at John's house on Thursday night at eight o'clock. The address is 50 Lorcum Lane. But you mustn't write any of that down. Nor can you bring anyone with you or tell anyone you're coming. Our host's real name is not John, but that is what you will call him that night. And your name will be Andrew.*

Some might have been put off by such ludicrous secrecy surrounding something that was perfectly legal. Others might have mocked the absurdity of extending an adolescent's fascination with secret clubs and passwords into the adult world of politics.

Such people were of no interest to the Soviets. Moscow wanted the ones who would attend, and then keep coming back, not to exchange ideas between like-minded colleagues, or to better understand Marx, but because of their eagerness to engage in conspiratorial activity even when neither the circumstances nor an identifiable enemy required it. Once they were "hooked," the drug of deceit was administered in ever larger doses. Secret meetings, secret acquaintances, and secret objectives were invented and zealously guarded by the initiates. Even the most routine and legal activities were made to appear as though they were dangerously illegal (ironically, in the Soviet Union, they would have been).

> The prolonged habitual emphasis on a conspiratorial atmosphere is to isolate the individual from the great mass of people, who in the beginning he was going to save.[12]

The masses, however, could not be trusted because they were being manipulated by the government authorities. These were the same authorities, it was repeatedly stressed, whose hostility to the study groups' discussions of Marxism, peace, and justice necessitated such life and death secrecy among the guileless "conspirators."

With Britain's educated elite, as with the Bolsheviks, the sharing of secrets in a highly charged atmosphere of conspiracy offered a "form of human contact and exhilaration [they] cannot find elsewhere." According to Trotsky, "nobody did any revolutionary work during endless tea-table discussions" that were the staple of his underground days. The important point was "the secret highly conspiratorial methods" that framed their sessions. It was the excitement, the feeling of daring and the intimacy to conspire, not any actual revolutionary activity, that produced "a reverence" for their meetings that "was almost mystic."[13]

"For comfortable public school types already drawn into a homosexual subculture, and infused with at least a modicum of Marxist self-guilt," Stanley Weintraub, a history professor at Penn State University later observed, "there was the thrill inherent in the excitement and danger of a covert double patriotism—not to one's own country and to communism, but to the subterranean worlds of male bonding and class betrayal . . . few were doctrinaire communists."[14]

There was no discussion initially about espionage or serving the Soviet Union in the British cells. "A spy doesn't become an espionage agent overnight," concluded a New York Times study published in 1948. "He has perhaps since the early Thirties been experiencing a sense of outrage with social injustices, a feeling of frustration with what he feels is ineptitude with the liberal parties." Cell meetings talked not about the virtues of spying, but about the imperfections of Western society.[15]

A new allegiance to international ideals—peace and justice—was cultivated. These values transcended artificial and retrograde loyalties to such bourgeois concepts as the British nation. Eventually, as the West's appalling deficiencies were hammered home, it became evident that only the Soviet Union—where there was no unemployment, no poverty, no inequality, and where peace was revered—shared the recruit's ideals and merited his loyalty. But this was not yet the final stopping point.

The greatest loyalty, it was finally revealed, must be to the Party—

not the party of Marx and utopian idealism, but the underground party of Soviet intelligence. As Whittaker Chambers told the FBI, once recruited, a "person is segregated from the Party proper" and becomes a member of the Soviet intelligence network. The Canadian Commission found the same thing: "Loyalty to the [underground] Party in due course takes the place in the member's mind of the earlier loyalty to certain principles professed by the party propaganda." The underground party is a rigid, semimilitary, hierarchical organization in which these new recruits were mercilessly at the bottom. They "were now to become not open propagandists of the communist cause, but secret agents of Stalin's machine."[16]

The Party's authority eclipsed the individual's obligation not only to country and ideals, but to family and friends. Its authority could never be questioned. If the Soviets chose and developed the recruit adequately, he would not object when "the quest for justice becomes indistinguishable from loyalty to a profoundly unjust system of totalitarian domination."[17]

It is only at this point that the recruit is introduced to the necessity of espionage. Western governments, it is explained, use secrecy to oppress people. The Soviet Union, conversely, welcomes discussions about peace and justice, and believes all information should be freely shared. "Supplying information to Soviet intelligence was, in the beginning, an incidental activity." The spy who considers himself an ideologue

> . . . does not like espionage. He would rather be on the picket lines or writing propaganda to further his cause. But "psychologically developed" to the point where he believes he is helping to build a better world, he sees the "practical" application of his ideals—the act of espionage—simply as routine.[18]

Donald Maclean carried that attitude to his grave. Once in Moscow he inelegantly characterized his fifteen-year career as a Soviet spy in this way: "It's like cleaning toilets; it's a stinking job but someone has to do it."[19]

Why? Why were the Soviets consumed with the need to have spies throughout Western governments? "Never in history has there been a government which has placed greater faith in, and greater emphasis on, political *razvedka* [reconnaissance]," David Dallin, a Russian-born expert on Soviet intelligence, has written. "And never has there existed such an insatiable and formidable quest for information from other countries" as in the the the Soviet Union.[20]

Stalin was so obsessed with intelligence operations he often functioned as a case officer, monitoring every detail of important missions abroad. According to Alexander Orlov, a high ranking Soviet intelligence officer who later defected to the West, Stalin had no interest in public speeches, newspaper reports, cocktail gossip, or official diplomatic notes. All were Western tricks created to mislead the Kremlin. "Stalin warned his intelligence chiefs time and again to keep away from hypotheses and equations with many unknowns." He would contemptuously toss aside reports that had unsubstantiated assumptions and personal views, demanding of his lieutenants, "Don't tell me what you think, give me the facts and the source!"

His demands all boiled down to this: What were Western policymakers thinking and planning? In conversations where it was assumed all who were listening could be trusted, what Soviet move did they most fear, and what Western opportunity were they plotting? Stalin wanted his intelligence apparatus to "get at the facts and figures hidden in the secret vaults of foreign governments." So from 1932 on the NKVD sent Stalin "only summaries of important documents stolen from other governments and reports from exceptionally valuable secret informers."[21]

Maclean and Philby started their careers too late to help Stalin as he emerged on the world stage and cast about for the alliances that would enable the Soviet Union to survive the perilous and uncertain 1930s. But both were excellently positioned to help the Kremlin in its fight to dominate postwar Europe and Asia.

Few if any Soviet agents were more valuable in the first crisis-driven years of the Cold War than Maclean. Former CIA Director Richard Helms believes that during the four tension-filled years when Maclean was stationed at the British embassy in Washington, Stalin would have repeatedly demanded of his intelligence chief Lavrenti Beria or Foreign Commissar Molotov, "What does Maclean know?" or "What has our man inside the British embassy sent us on this?"

Western investigators like Helms were astonished years later when they discovered Moscow's usual contempt for its spies did not apply

to Maclean. This unusual, almost unprecedented relationship between spy and master reflected both Maclean's analytical skills and
his ability to be at the center of many of the most pressing crises,
from the extinction of political freedom in Poland to the consideration of the use of the atomic bomb in Korea. In all these instances
and many more he pulled from Western vaults the secrets that Stalin
craved.[22]

The Soviet ruler was not alone. Prime Minister Winston Churchill
"had a greater faith in, and fascination for, secret intelligence than
any of his predecessors." He understood the advantage of reading
what U.S. Secretary of State Henry Stimson once called "other
gentlemen's mail." Intercepting what a government regards as secret
and secure conversations between senior officials, Churchill maintained, is

> a means of forming a truer judgment of public policy in these spheres
> than any other sources of knowledge at the disposal of the state . . .
> [they are] the most valuable source of secret information respecting
> their policy and actions.

One of Britain's most respected diplomats, Sir Horace Rumbold,
who also happened to be the father of Maclean's closest Foreign
Office friend, believed the world leader who knows other men's
most intimate thoughts is "in the position of a man who plays bridge
and knows the cards in his adversary's hands."[23]

By joining organizations whose function was to collect and guard
secrets—the Foreign Office and the Secret Intelligence Service—
Maclean and Philby gained the special knowledge shared by only a
few others. Their sense of superiority came from the realization that
even among these few, none knew the most important secret of all—
that they were Soviet spies. As Robert Conquest, an expert on Soviet
history observes, "People are totalitarian revolutionaries because, for
one reason or another, they reserve the right to impose their dogmas
by any means up to and including killing anyone who hampers their
plans. When they act or speak otherwise, it is merely tactics."[24]

CHAPTER THREE

> "System, System, System"—that is what
> British Intellectuals run crying as soon as they
> lose faith in Nanny Imperialism.
>
> Dmitri Mirsky[1]

PHILBY: THE DRUG OF DECEIT

Kim Philby was raised in the shadow of his legendary father, St. John Philby. Desert explorer, writer, convert to Islam, friend of "Lawrence of Arabia," adviser to kings, and bane of the Foreign Office, the elder Philby was so overbearing that his cowering son had acquired a lifelong stutter by the age of four. The dutiful Kim attended his father's schools, graduating from London's Westminster at the top of his class. But any precociousness or spontaneity had been knocked out of him long before; he was subdued, hesitant to call attention to himself, and reluctant to share his views, if, indeed, he had any. "He made no impact to speak of . . . he was not a leader."[2]

Philby arrived at Cambridge in the autumn of 1929 within days of Wall Street's Great Crash. The first shockwaves struck Britain only a glancing blow, and, as a scholarship student, Philby was not threatened. But it did ring the death knell for the trendy intellectuals of the "Bloomsbury set" whom the Russian writer Mirsky characterized as "extremely intrigued by their own minutest inner experiences." In the words of their leader John Maynard Keynes, "nothing mattered except states of mind . . . timeless, passionate states of contemplation and communion."[3]

But with Western financial institutions collapsing, industrial unemployment soaring, and fascism on the march in Europe, the
escutcheoned and battlemented Gothic buildings that sheltered Oxbridge's lush green courtyards could no longer provide a cozy
sanctuary from the world's brutal realities. Politics soon replaced
poetry as the reigning passion.

Not that Philby, with his dark, angular good looks and soft,
melancholy eyes which lit up when he flashed his contagious smile,
was in the forefront of the political movement. He did join the
Cambridge University Socialist Society, and, in his third year, as
student communists were taking it over, Philby became its treasurer.
By then communism was sweeping Cambridge like some medieval
plague. The Great Depression had made England a sea of misery for
the working class, and Karl Marx's prophecy that its own internal
contradictions would cause capitalism to perish was ringing with
seductive clarity across Britain's elite campuses. For impatient and
impressionable young men searching for absolutes, Marxism became
"the new orthodoxy that fastened itself upon the minds of the
undergraduates."[4]

Engels had declared that the mere discovery of socialism would
conquer the world because of the undeniable power of its wisdom.
As the only nation bold enough to embrace Marxism's self-evident
truths—thus sparing its citizens the degrading experience of unemployment and poverty—the Soviet Union was an object of adoration.
And where the British establishment feared its youth, "Russia is
young. Men and women in position of authority are young. Young
in years," gushed Hewlett Johnson, the "Red Dean" of Canterbury,
"but also young in spirit, and possessed of all the mental and moral
qualities of youth."[5]

Philby never has been able to explain the reason that he became a
spy. Instead he described at great length the reason that he became a
communist, as if there were a self-evident connection between the
two. Of course, thousands of his contemporaries—many with cre-
dentials vastly superior to Philby's—were communists, but only a
handful became spies. So, clearly, being a communist had little if
anything to do with becoming a Soviet agent.

When Eleanor Philby, his third wife, discovered that her husband,
with whom she thought she shared everything, was a spy, she felt

"the victim of a prolonged and monstrous confidence trick." Yet she followed Kim to Moscow. "Daily I half expected him to take me aside, throw an arm around my shoulder and say: 'My dear, it's like this. I did so-and-so all these years, because I believed in such-and-such . . . These beliefs are my philosophy, my reasons for living . . .' but he said no such thing."[6]

Although he supposedly told a friend in 1932 that he considered himself a communist, Philby later wrote the revelation did not come until his final term at Cambridge. "It was a slow and brain-racking process," he insists. Two years were spent just converting from "a socialist viewpoint to a communist one." Philby's "convictions" it is to be understood, were not the result of faddishness or youthful passion; they were arrived at with a scientist's respect for the truth. This also explains the reason that his "convictions" did not waver, and why he "stayed the course," while so many of his more frivolous contemporaries fell by the wayside just because Stalin aligned himself with Hitler.

Philby's four-year search for the truth would also explain how in a time of such passions, when his fellow students were marching and shouting their convictions, he departed having joined no clubs, played no sports, developed no network of friends, written no articles, given no speeches, nor created any memorable impression.

"The early life of Kim Philby is doubly important: all Kim's life was early," John Le Carré, the master espionage writer, has argued. It was doubly important because emotionally and intellectually Philby never developed beyond adolescence. In addition, because so much of the manufactured-in-Moscow Philby mythology has its roots in the years between his graduation in 1933 and his hire into British intelligence in 1940, it is necessary to sort out fact from the abundance of fiction.[7]

Following graduation, Philby headed toward Austria, in part to study German, but also to witness a country on the brink of civil war. The British came in such numbers to Vienna that the fascists derisively referred to them as "English do-gooders." Among them were Hugh Gaitskell, a future leader of the Labour Party; Elwyn-Jones, later attorney general under Prime Minister Harold Wilson; Teddy Kollek, as of this writing still mayor of Jerusalem; the British writer Naomi Mitchison; Emma Cadbury, a British heiress, as well as an American heiress named Muriel Gardner; and a multitude of Oxbridge students, including such Philby contemporaries as Christopher Isherwood, Stephen Spender, and John Lehmann.

As fighting raged through the city, nearly all joined various underground cells, took code names, ran safe houses to hide injured or hunted freedom fighters, made secret drops of money and literature, and set up clandestine communication channels.[8]

With so many "do-gooders" there ahead of him, Philby's presence was little noticed. One Austrian writer thought of him as "a shaggy bumbling Englishman overwhelmed by the passions swirling around him. To what extent he shared them I don't know. Certainly he talked. But more often he listened."

In fact Philby seemed oddly detached from the city's apocalyptic action. Shortly after renting a room in a private home, his passions were directed to his landlord's dark, attractive, and energetic daughter, Litzi. She was two years older than he, and had already been married and divorced. Romance blossomed and she—or so Philby's friends believe—relieved him of his virginity. Eventually, they moved into their own apartment. It was Litzi's association with a student communist group that allowed Philby what adventures he had while in the city. In February, in the aftermath of the worst of the fighting, he and Litzi were married. "Why, that silly young man has gone and done it!" Gaitskell guffawed when he heard the news. It was worse than silly, it was a blunder that would nearly derail Philby's British intelligence career before it began.[9]

Was Philby already working for the Soviets before he left for Europe? One who knew him in Vienna argues that he was "directed [by the Soviets] to go there to gain his first revolutionary experience," while many others assume that he was not actually recruited until after he arrived. In the KGB-authorized version of his life, Philby claimed somewhat churlishly that "how, where and when I became a member of the Soviet intelligence service is a matter for myself and my comrades." Yet, he was reported to have told his children when they visited him in Moscow that "I was recruited in 1933," before he left for Vienna.[10]

But in January 1988, less than a year before he died in Moscow, Philby decided to again rewrite his history in the form of interviews with British journalist Philip Knightley. Indeed, most of Philby's intelligence career—twenty-five years of propaganda work in Moscow compared with only eleven years in British intelligence—was spent inventing stories about himself. "The process of Philby's beatification as a spy-hero," as British writer Andrew Boyle puts it, "has gone on almost without interruption from 1963 until the present." The resulting legend is "out of all proportion to the slender merits, mixed motives and debatable exploits of the man himself."[11]

Initially Philby had been modest about his year in Vienna, claiming only that he engaged in "illegal activities" (under Chancellor Dollfuss, almost all activities were illegal). But twenty years later he told Knightley that

> My work in Vienna must have caught the attention of the people who are now my colleagues in Moscow because almost immediately on my return to Britain I was approached by a man who asked me if I would like to join the Russian intelligence service.

Like most of Philby's fabrications, this one—that he was recruited based on his daring revolutionary behavior in Vienna—serves a multiplicity of purposes. First, it implies that his life was as bold as the fictionalized accounts have it. Second, the notion of a Soviet intelligence officer strolling up and asking him if he would care to work for the Soviet Union, suggests that brave communists revolutionaries were precisely what Moscow was looking for.[12]

John Le Carré warned that this would happen. Moscow, he wrote, would reinvent Philby, they would "call him a vanguard man; they will give him medals, publish his arid, post-office prose, extol his ideological virtue." Soviet intelligence received immense help in this enterprise. Western writers seemed determined to create an even more dangerous, charming, and romantic rogue than Ian Fleming's mythical James Bond. Even before Philby's own rationalizations appeared, a mountainous masterspy was being sculptured out of an inconsequential amount of clay.[13]

In 1968 a group of British journalists, of whom Knightley was one, explained, for instance, that Philby's distance from the action in Vienna was simply "displaying the discretion about his own part in events that was later to become an integral part of his professional facade." Still, they suggested, after his "first taste of intrigue, his

first experience of the Great Game," it was understandable if Philby
(and the reading public) was reminded of Rudyard Kipling's *Kim*,
about whom the chronicler of British imperialism wrote:

> From time to time God causes men to be born who have a lust to go
> abroad at the risk of their lives and discover news . . . these souls are
> very few and of these not more than ten are of the best. [14]

By 1988 Knightley had decided that Philby's Vienna role was even
more glamorous. In a chapter darkly titled "A Bloody Initiation" he
imagines that "they were heady days for the young Englishman,
barely twenty-two—days of police charges, broken heads and sabre
wounds; nights of conspiracy and fierce debates." [15]

One of the ten best? Broken heads and sabre wounds? Certainly
none of this remotely applied to Philby. Hundreds of do-gooders
flocked to Vienna and almost all seemed to have been more involved
in the city's cataclysmic events than he. There is no evidence, for
instance, that the risks Philby took matched those of Gardner and
Cadbury, the British and American heiresses or even, for that matter,
exceeded those taken by Lehmann, Spender, and Isherwood. Those
truly in the thick of the action saw Philby as silly, bumbling, naive,
or, at best, duplicitous. [16]

"Philby was there of course," one militant underground leader
later recalled, "but only as one might glimpse a person out of the
corner of his eye." No one saw Philby sustain any wounds or charge
any police barricades. [17]

His preoccupation was with Litzi. "It was his first sexual experience and his emotional involvement was, as a consequence, much
deeper" than hers, most of his friends thought. For her the marriage
served a very practical purpose. There was a possibility she might be
arrested and "one way I could avoid arrest was to marry Kim, get a
British passport and leave the country. This is what I did. I wouldn't
exactly call it a marriage of convenience. I suppose it was partly that
and partly love." [18]

Marriage as the product of juvenile eroticism and calculated convenience did not conform to the image of a swashbuckling Philby
being created by the British press. So the marriage was recast (in the
borrowed words of T.S. Eliot) as another act of heroism, "the awful

daring of a moment's surrender" when Philby used his British passport to snatch his beloved co-conspirator from the executioner's blade: martyrdom through marriage. But Litzi had been in no real danger. As another pair of British journalists concluded, she and Kim were doing little more than playing an "exhilarating game of hide and seek" with the authorities.[19]

Litzi herself confirmed this. "Apart from marrying me, a communist, Kim took no part in communist underground activities while he was in Vienna." When presented with this statement long after the need for cover stories had vanished, Philby, ever the misty-eyed romantic, maintained "this is exactly what we agreed she would say [a half-century before] and I'm moved that she kept our bargain." Communism with a human face.[20]

Up to his dotage and death Philby furiously peddled the idea that he became a spy to fight for the underdog. Le Carré rejected the hoax from the start. "I do not much believe in the political motive of Kim Philby," he wrote. "Such political opinions as sustained him are the opinions of his childhood . . . from there on, [he] simply ceased to develop. He was left with a handful of clichés whose application had ceased in 1931." Others have come to agree.[21]

"If anything is certain, it is that Philby's motivations were not ideological," says Edward Sheehan, an American diplomat who knew him in Beirut. "He may have been a Soviet spy, but he was not a communist." Rupert Allason, who writes on intelligence under the nom de plume of Nigel West, wrote of Philby, "to this day I am convinced that he was not an ideologue. Spying was just his way of being above lesser mortals." *The Guardian* agreed: "It is hard to believe he was a communist for very long, if at all. Even if it all began with youthful idealism he was hardly a champion of the proletariat or a devoted internationalist."[22]

In his most penetrating if unwitting insight into his own motives Philby wrote, "to betray you must first belong; I never belonged." Born in India, raised in Arabia, "Philby has no home, no women, no faith," Le Carré observed. "Behind the inbred upper-class arrogance, the taste for adventure, lies the self-hate of a vain misfit for whom nothing will ever be worthy of his loyalty. In the last instance, Philby is driven by the incurable drug of deceit itself."[23]

When Philby's American wife confronted him in Moscow and

angrily demanded to know which was more important, she and the children, or the Party, he instantly responded, "the Party of course." This has been taken as an almost shocking answer of a devout apostle of the communist faith. ("He [Philby] believed in Stalin as some men believed in God," Boyle has written.) But Philby was talking about his blind obedience to the semimilitary underground party whose orders he obeyed without reference to any system of beliefs, morals, or ideology. When Philby made his pledge, he abandoned Marxism (if indeed he ever embraced it) as surely as he abandoned any loyalties to country, family, or friends.[24]

Philby's spirit was anything but revolutionary. With traditional institutions collapsing and the world torn by competing dogmas, he, like many of his contemporaries, found the chaos and flux unbearable. He developed a craving for authority to instill order. It was a craving he never lost. In Moscow, around senior intelligence officers, he was like a puppy starved for attention and affection. The spectacle upset his adoring wife, Eleanor. "He sometimes seemed pathetically pleased by the approbation of the Russians," she wrote. "Every pat on the back was like a medal or a bouquet of flowers. The Russians understood his psychological need for reassurance," she believes. But, "he went down in my estimation."[25]

Once he turned himself over to the Soviet underground's supreme authority, the youthful Philby relinquished any further responsibility for his own decisions; all his thinking would be done by someone else. Henceforth his beliefs would never be challenged or exposed, all criticism of his "ideas" would be shut out. What feedback he received would be calculated to increase his dependency on the central authority. As he grew older his reaction to every great crisis was to drink himself into unconsciousness, sometimes for weeks at a time.

This is what led Jung to describe secret organizations as "crutches for the lame, shields for the timid . . . nurseries for the irresponsible . . . [and] a land of promise for disillusioned vagrants and weary pilgrims." Having abandoned all responsibility for his own life, the servile Philby could never accept any responsibility for others—especially for his various wives and children.[26]

If any of Philby's accounts can be believed, he was enrolled as a "probationary agent" in Soviet intelligence by no later than mid-

1934, by which time he and Litzi were living in London. This also allowed him to claim that it was the Soviets who ordered him to join the Anglo-German Fellowship, a large, aristocratic organization established to foster ties between the two countries, and contemptuously referred to as part of "the Heil Hitler Brigade" by Churchill.[27]

Philby's explanation is that he became a fascist sympathizer because "overt and covert links between Britain and Germany at that time were of serious concern to the Soviet government." This last part is certainly true. Stalin, as Krivitsky warned and captured German documents later confirmed, was pursuing Hitler overtly and covertly. At the Seventeenth Party Congress in February 1934 Stalin pleaded that "the existence of a fascist regime in Germany was no more of an obstacle to good relations between the U.S.S.R. and Germany," than Mussolini's accession to power had been. And, he noted with pride, Moscow enjoyed "the most excellent relations" with Italy. Meantime David Kandelacki was in Berlin with secret instructions from Stalin to seek an alliance with the Germans.[28]

For Bukharin and the older Bolsheviks, "the idea of an alliance with a power as openly predatory and barbarous as national socialist Germany was much more abhorrent than a policy of alliance with the more orthodox 'imperialists.' " Stalin remedied this problem by having Bukharin and thousands of other like-minded ideologues shot.[29]

Because he did not suffer from Bukharin's ideological discomfort, Philby fitted in well with the cryptofascists. He even flew several times to Berlin to meet, he claims, with Foreign Minister Joachim von Ribbentrop and various Third Reich propaganda officials. His Western admirers insist that Philby must have found all this distasteful, but Philby makes no similar claims, and there is no reason to believe that he did.[30]

"Authoritarian governments appeal to a certain sort of person," Malcolm Muggeridge, whose friendship Philby long coveted, has written. "And as has been shown again and again, those with a taste for it, like it in any version." Muggeridge thought Philby the classic type to find Hitlerism as appealing as Stalinism: "ambitious, romantic, weak and violent." It was not "Marxist theory or utopian aims, but rather [the USSR's] inexorably brutal practices" that appealed to Philby's baleful fascination with ruthless dictatorships. "He admired

Goebbels and once told me he easily could have worked with him,"
claims Muggeridge, who thought Philby "protests too much in
claiming that he already had settled convictions and was bluffing the
Germans at the Russians' behest. I still think he was bluffing himself." Le Carré agrees and suggests that Philby acquired from his
father the neofascist instincts of a slightly berserk Englishman.[31]

St. John Philby "spent a lifetime renouncing his native land, railing
against her perfidy, deceit and moral decline." As a candidate for
Parliament in 1939, he hailed Hitler as a peacemaker while castigating
Churchill as a warmonger. With a characteristic penchant for being
wrong on the major issues of his day, he insisted "Mr. Hitler does
not want war and anyone who tells you that he does is a liar." He
won all of 576 votes.[32]

Perhaps this, more than the elections of 1931, was the calamity
that caused his adoring son to doubt "the validity of the assumptions
underlying parliamentary democracy." To Kim's querulous mind,
democracy had failed *him,* had let *him* down. Obviously it could not
be trusted to do the right thing. Whatever prompted his disillusion-
ment, by his own account Philby's first political conviction was a
distrust for the masses. After that, he sought to align himself with
authoritarian regimes in his war—*My Silent War,* he called it—against
democracy.[33]

The Canadian Royal Commission later found, among the spies
whose background and beliefs it investigated, a "fascination by what
may appear to them to be the efficiency of the unusual and essentially
totalitarian system of Party organization." And for those like Philby
"there is apparently an emotional appeal and glamour, as it were a
sense of adventure, inherent in the conspiratorial methods." Philby
had little interest in whom he was conspiring for or against.[34]

In his memoirs Philby cautioned writers to stick to explanations
that were simple and true. But many Western writers, uncomfortable
with Philby's extensive Nazi ties, devised—independent of Philby—
the explanation that he consorted with fascists as part of a grand
Soviet plot to throw Western intelligence off Kim's well-traveled
communist past.[35]

But such a precaution seems unnecessary for a person whose
"communist past" consisted of joining an organization whose members by 1938 included 20 per cent of the entire Cambridge under-

graduate student body, and a stay in Vienna at a time when it appeared that a healthy chunk of the British literary establishment was there. Philby may have told several people at Cambridge and Vienna that he considered himself a communist. But that would place him in the most nonselect group of the decade. In Vienna, his only "initiation," bloody or otherwise, seems to have been with sex. Certainly he was less visible than others like Gaitskell and Kollek whose ambitions to enter government service were not thwarted by having been in Vienna.[36]

He did come away from Vienna with one appalling liability— Litzi. It was not because she was a communist, although that might have become a problem. It was more that it made Philby's habitually untidy personal life downright messy. She and Philby were soon living apart and he not only took up with other women, but eventually moved in with one and fathered a child, although he had not yet filed for divorce from Litzi. Perhaps this too was all part of the Soviet master plan. More likely, however, it is further proof of Philby's inability to take responsibility for his personal life. Captives of the secret world, as Professor Sissela Bok explains, eventually develop "an incapacity to plan, or choose."[37]

Whatever his status in Vienna and in London with the Anglo-German Fellowship, Philby was under Moscow's orders when he next traveled to Spain posing as a journalist to cover the civil war. Eventually he landed a job as a correspondent with *The Times* (London) covering the war from Franco's side. He wrote glowing descriptions of the antidemocratic forces, describing Franco majestically entering a village "on a chestnut horse . . . the enthusiasm of the populace lining the street was unmistakably genuine."[38]

Within weeks of his February 1937 arrival in Spain, as in Vienna, Philby moved in with an older woman he had barely met. Frances "Bunny" Doble was ten years his senior, a sometimes actress, and a Royalist camp follower.

One day a car he and three other journalists were in took a direct hit from an artillery shell. As the sole survivor, Philby was decorated and embraced by Franco. Writing about this episode approximately thirty years later, British journalists insisted that the ceremony forced Philby to summon all his strength to repress "his real emotions when he found himself congratulated and embraced by the Fascist leader." According to Doble, however, who was there, this was not true at all. She remembers Philby's being so genuinely exhilarated by Franco's gesture that he arrived home "exhausted with emotion because of the high honor done him."[39]

In late March 1939 the Republicans hoisted the white flag as Franco's Nationalist troops took Madrid without firing a shot. In July, Philby left Spain. Weeks later the Nazi–Soviet Pact was signed making war inevitable and causing devastated communists the world over—unwilling to serve this unholy alliance—to renounce their faith. Philby was not among the afflicted.

Indeed, it is an astonishing fact that in Philby's world the Nazi–Soviet Pact, the event that made the Second World War inevitable, and came as a cataclysmic shock to communist idealists, never occurred. That is, it is never mentioned in his book; nor is it examined in three major biographies on his life. This would be tantamount to writing about the Civil War without ever mentioning the Emancipation Proclamation, or the First World War while omitting the incident at Sarajevo involving Archduke Francis Ferdinand.[40]

So completely did Philby accept the Hitler-Stalin alliance that he was cheerfully indifferent to the Nazi blitzkrieg, and, when he covered the British Expeditionary Force in northern France, he found it impossible to write with the same gusto about the Western forces fighting Hitler as he had about Franco. "The idea of writing endlessly about the morale of the British army at home appalled me," he later explained. With his call-up fast approaching, and bereft of any desire to actually fight Nazis, he looked around for a hole in which to hide. Thanks to Guy Burgess, he found one.[41]

Burgess, following his return from visiting Michael Straight in Washington, was able to hire Philby into Section D, then part of the Secret Intelligence Service (SIS). Because Burgess, who had been in SIS since January 1939, had also been a member of the Anglo-German Fellowship, he was not troubled by Philby's pro-Nazi associations or his meetings with Third Reich officials. Presumably, no one objected either to the awkward fact that, as Philby was being commissioned to wage war against Germany, his father was about to be jailed as a Nazi sympathizer.[42]

British officials were not impervious to such risks. At about the same time Sir Robert Bruce Lockhart, a legendary name in British intelligence with all the right family, school, and social ties, was being considered for a wartime intelligence organization. The appointment was nearly derailed when a senior official objected that Lockhart "was a fascist with [British fascist leader Oswald] Mosley wasn't he?" Lockhart was not, and eventually he got the appointment. But he was astonished that someone would plant such a reckless rumor.[43]

In addition to his scandalous political past, Philby's personal life was still a mess. In September 1939, as the world went to war, Philby moved in with Aileen Furse. She was only a year older than he, though she looked far older. Underneath her pleasant smile and common but attractive features was a tormented person who lacked confidence and was given to self-destructive behavior. In July 1940 the couple had a child, but they were not married because Philby was not yet divorced from Litzi. Finally, in September 1940, while still legally married to Litzi, Philby informed his approving superiors at Section D that he and Aileen had married.[44]

Section D had a brief and inglorious life. But Philby did sufficiently well that by September 1941 he had been transferred into SIS proper (also known as MI6 even though it was under Foreign Office rather than military authority). Trevor-Roper, the future Lord Dacre and Oxford historian, was already in SIS by the time Philby joined. He had heard from a mutual friend that nearly eight years earlier Philby had declared himself a communist. Although SIS's leaders were thought to be "lunatic in their anti-communism," this was hardly cause for concern. After all, before the war was over, SIS would also embrace Muggeridge, who once moved his entire family to the Russian Garden of Eden and pledged never to return to the West; Graham Greene, who was a card-carrying, dues-paying member of the Communist Party; and James Klugman, who was known as the Party's chief pitchman in Cambridge if not in England. Philby's "mere juvenile illusions" were comparatively small beer.[45]

At last Philby had found his niche. In this closed world of time-servers, skeptical amateurs (like Muggeridge and Greene), former stockbrokers, retired Indian policemen, middling former naval officers, and eager adventurers, Philby "seemed an exceptional person: exceptional by his virtues for he seemed intelligent, sophisticated, even real." A born bureaucratic politician, both the Old Guard, to whom he was correctly deferential, and the young Turks, who seemed to detect a knowing twinkle in his eye, thought of him as one of their own.

"The most general reaction," according to Trevor-Roper, "was simply to idolize him." He had the cachet of being the son of a great explorer, and a war correspondent for *The Times*. His tanned good looks, his casual dress, his melancholy eyes and stutter, all combined to give him, at the age of twenty-nine, an air of weary cynicism, the "pose of the unhurried, sophisticated, worldly politician. Men liked him, women wanted to mother him. And those who did not actually idolize him relied on him."

But Trevor-Roper also admitted that he found it nearly impossible to engage Philby in any substantive discussion, realizing only later that this was because "his critical spirit, his intellectual purity, his moral conscience, were dead—sacrificed not to faith or truth but to Stalin's politics."[46]

By the summer of 1943 Philby had become the head of SIS's Iberian Section, with responsibilities for Spain, Portugal, and Gibraltar. Although this area was far removed from the war in Europe, Philby—the CIA later suspected—may have been able to use information to which he had unique access to help drive several decisive nails into Poland's coffin.

The obliteration of "the bastard of Versailles," as Molotov contemptuously called Poland, had been the cornerstone of the Nazi-Soviet Pact. After the German invasion of Russia in June 1941, Moscow signed a friendship treaty with the Polish government-in-exile in London. But Stalin had no intention of either handing back eastern Poland, part of his booty from his alliance with Hitler, or restoring Poland's independence. This awkward and testy friendship ended after thousands of Polish officers "packed closely around the edge, head to feet, like sardines in a tin" were found in mass graves in the Katyn Forest near Smolensk in April 1943. The Germans accused the Soviets of the slaughter.

"The German revelations are probably true," Churchill told General Wladyslaw Sikorski, the widely respected prime minister of the Polish government-in-exile, over lunch at No. 10 Downing Street on April 15, 1943. "The Bolsheviks can be very cruel." The next day the usually restrained Sikorski issued a statement "implying strongly that the blame for the murders lay with Russia," and called for the International Red Cross to investigate, a proposal the Germans quickly endorsed.[47]

This was the opportunity Stalin had been waiting for. Suddenly it was the Soviets who were the victims. Stalin protested to Churchill and Roosevelt that the "Polish-German proposal" proved that the two were colluding in "an anti-Soviet slander campaign launched by the German fascists." He immediately terminated recognition of the London Poles as the nation's official government and installed a puppet government in Soviet-occupied Poland.[48]

London and Washington were caught in the middle. They were not about to break with the Soviets, who were still doing the bulk of the fighting against the Germans. Yet they knew that only Sikorski had the stature to lead the postwar Poles to independence. So they played both sides, publicly unsympathetic to the evidence that Katyn was Stalin's handiwork, while resisting the Soviet demand to withdraw recognition from Sikorski and his pesky London Poles.[49]

Early on Saturday evening July 3, 1943, a Royal Air Force Liberator with General Sikorski and a traveling party of ten, including his daughter and two members of parliament, landed on the runway at the fortress of Gibraltar. Having just inspected the Polish army-in-exile, Sikorski was returning to London for an important conference with Churchill.

Stepping off the plane, Sikorski looked every bit the war hero and statesman—tall, with straight white hair, and warm open face dominated by a thick white mustache. As he was greeted by the British Governor Mason-Macfarlane, British soldiers, bayonets fixed, surrounded the plane, which a huge floodlight set off from the more than two hundred others parked near the runway.

Macfarlane had an awkward request. A cable from the Soviet mission in London had arrived requesting that Ivan Maisky, Soviet ambassador to the United Kingdom, be allowed to make a refueling stop en route to Moscow. He was due in at seven o'clock the following morning. Would the General ask his staff to remain in their quarters until Maisky resumed his trip? Sikorski agreed, certainly aware of the irony. Russo-Polish diplomatic relations had been restored via the Sikorski-Maisky Agreement in July 1941. Now, two years later, it would have been considered a major diplomatic blunder if the two men laid eyes on one another.

When Maisky's plane arrived, it was parked next to Sikorski's. Shortly before 11:00 A.M., a British officer—according to a prearranged signal—interrupted Macfarlane, who was playing host to the ambassador, and warned of shifting weather conditions. Macfarlane cautiously urged the ambassador to resume his journey, and the Soviet vessel was soon airborne.

That night, as the Liberator was being loaded, Poles stationed at Gibraltar were embracing and bidding farewell to the traveling party. After Sikorski boarded, the twenty-five-ton plane began its runway sprint with loud bangs and showers of flashing sparks, the Liberator's take-off signature. It kicked up sand and dust as it passed Macfarlane and the British actor Major Anthony Quayle, assorted officials, and saluting Poles. The plane lifted effortlessly off the runway, and began its ascent over the Mediterranean and into the clear, star-filled night.

It leveled off to gain speed before climbing again, the usual pattern for Prchal, the Czech pilot, in his early thirties and one of the Royal Air Force's best. But the airplane did not climb. Instead, it seemed to stall; then, suddenly, the nose began to head down. Those on the tarmac froze, waiting for Prchal to pull up. Instead, the plane continued to head toward the black water. Within seconds it had disappeared below the runway. Suddenly there was only silence. While others ran hysterically toward the end of the runway, several Poles standing next to Quayle began to sob, "This is the end of Poland, this is the end of Poland!"

Sikorski's body was eventually pulled from the wreckage; his daughter's remains were never found. Only the pilot survived.

A British Court of Inquiry was established with an unofficial mandate, much like the Warren Commission's approximately twenty years later, to rule out the possibility of conspiracy or sabotage. It dutifully concluded, "the cause of the accident was due to the aircraft becoming uncontrollable for reasons which cannot be established."

Although the plane had been heavily guarded, it was particularly vulnerable prior to take-off when the plane's armed guards were relieved and baggage, maintenance, and ground crews were attending it. The least-checked crews in the entire cycle were the baggage handlers, which included indigenous and low-level personnel.

Maisky later observed that it would not have been difficult for an agent to have been smuggled in "among the thousands of Spaniards who daily come to Gibraltar." Nor would it have been difficult for a first-rate espionage organization to see to it that the agent had the proper uniform and badge to join in the last minute frenzy to load and check Sikorski's plane. [50]

In its rush to judgment, the Court of Inquiry chose to ignore evidence that, in violation of all regulations, mailbags had been jammed into the Liberator's nose cone which housed vital gears and cables. It would not have taken more than a few seconds to stuff the pouches into the nose cone—or even to cut a cable—so that operations would have seemed normal until the plane tried to climb. [51]

Maisky was not as sanguine as the Court of Inquiry. The possibilities for sabotage were fairly obvious. And, although he "had no facts to confirm my idea at the moment," he was sure that the Germans had done precisely that.

Three years after Maisky's memoirs were published, the CIA, assuming the plane had been sabotaged, had another suspect. "Did Philby assist the NKVD in the assassination of General Sikorski at Gibraltar?" It is not farfetched to believe that it was Philby who had supplied the Soviets with "the information essential to the success of the operation; it was the kind of operation that needed inside assistance." [52]

The important element was knowing Sikorski's itinerary which, as with those of Churchill and Roosevelt, was a closely guarded secret. It is possible that Maisky's plane carried a saboteur, or that necessary IDs, uniforms, or other essentials were on board. If so, it was imperative that the Soviet plane not arrive *after* Sikorski had left. Philby would have routinely received cables on Sikorski's journey as he cleared Teheran, Cairo, and a British refueling stop—the last one before "the Rock"—in the North African desert. The Soviets could have known before Maisky departed from England that Sikorski was about to land in Gibraltar. [53]

If Philby had a hand in arranging Sikorski's death, it would have been by far his greatest wartime coup. Not only was Sikorski greatly admired by Churchill and Roosevelt; even Stalin, whom Sikorski did not fear, treated him with respect. He was also the only one who could hold together the faction-ridden Poles. His death was as disastrous as it would have been had England lost Churchill in 1940 or had the United States lost Roosevelt in 1942. Once he was eliminated, Poland's fate was sealed.

CHAPTER 4

We therefore request all those whom it may
concern, to receive and acknowledge Our Said
Trusty and Well beloved Donald Duart
Maclean . . . and freely to communicate with
him upon the things that may appertain to the
Affairs of Our Embassy . . .

Maclean's Royal Commission as Second
Secretary bearing the signature and seal of
King George VI, February 1941.[1]

MACLEAN: THE POLITICS OF SELF-LOATHING

What was there about Donald Maclean that first attracted Moscow to him? And how could a twenty-year-old transfer his loyalty to a country he had never visited, and whose language he did not speak?

His friend Cyril Connolly, the British writer, concluded that the roots of Maclean's treason lay buried in his subconscious. "Politics begin in the nursery," he observed. No one is born predisposed to the political Left or Right, patriotic or unpatriotic. "It is the child whose craving for love is unsatisfied, whose desire for power thwarted . . . [who] eventually may try to become a revolutionary or a dictator." There exists, Connolly adds,

the typically English brand of psychological revolutionaries who adopt left-wing political formulas because they hate their fathers or were unhappy at their public schools, or were lectured about sex.[2]

Perhaps. But too Freudian an interpretation—poor toilet training, an inability to resolve the Oedipal complex—suggests a fatalism that eliminates individual choice and responsibility.

Besides, Maclean did not hate his father, although he may have had a certain ambivalence about him. Sir Donald Maclean, a somewhat reserved but extremely formidable man, with handsome, kind features, was one of the most widely respected public figures of his day. He was the embodiment of the incorruptible Victorian liberal—free trader, social reformer, and devoted family and church man, who abstained from alcohol and rarely smoked. First elected to Parliament in 1906 and knighted in 1917, he led a spirited and unbending crusade to keep liberalism in England's political mainstream.

The apex of Sir Donald's career came in the summer of 1931 as his son was preparing to go up to Cambridge. Prime Minister Ramsay MacDonald's Labour Party, badly fractured over the economic crisis, could no longer rule. Instead of resigning, however, MacDonald formed a national government with Liberals and Conservatives, and then, in an act that smacked of betrayal, led an assault on Labour's traditional social welfare programs. In late August he invited Sir Donald to join his Cabinet as President of the Board of Education. The government was powerless to slow the tide of events, and Cabinet meetings were frequent and long. By June 1932 the strain was proving too much for Sir Donald. When he was unable to attend a Cabinet meeting on June 10—the day after his sixty-eighth birthday—his colleagues became alarmed. Five days later, he suffered a heart attack at his home and died. Only the intervention of family friends enabled Lady Maclean, with only "scant financial resources," to provide for her five children (four sons and a daughter), thus enabling Donald to continue at Cambridge.[3]

Donald Maclean was the antithesis of his father. He smoked heavily, drank excessively, scorned the idea of church and religion, and embraced political viewpoints as extreme as Sir Donald's were measured. He had declared himself a communist at Gresham's, a small public school with a radical tradition. This behavior was hardly unique, however, because so had the sons of at least four other prominent Gresham families. One, James Klugman, who was Donald's best friend, may have captured their spirit best when he said years later that he became a communist "in order to annoy the school authorities."[4]

Donald took pride in carrying a nationally known name and being the son of a Cabinet minister. But Sir Donald's politics—he strenuously opposed the General Strike of 1926 and had consistently voted against loans to Soviet Russia—were out of fashion with Donald's youthful peers. In fact, the father of Cambridge's best-known student communist had long been a parliamentary antagonist of the more conservative Maclean. By the time Sir Donald joined MacDonald's government, the prime minister was a despised figure among the leftist Oxbridge crowd. This certainly included Donald, who "devoured the newspapers each day and complained bitterly of the betrayal of the Labour rank and file through the perfidy of their leader."[5]

Maclean had not been particularly athletic at Gresham's and there was a flabbiness to his rangy height. He had a tendency to bend at the hips, and that combined with thick wet lips gave him an almost effeminate look. He was not a homosexual, and he seems to have been less experienced than many of the young men who spent years isolated in all-male institutions. Nor was he successful with women. Opportunities were rare, and, although he had the blond Aryan looks then much in demand in Germany, he seemed "a perpetual adolescent," spoiled and self-absorbed. Connolly thought Maclean "too shy and clumsy to succeed" in any amorous conquest.[6]

During his first year at Cambridge, Donald's voice had been muted, perhaps inhibited in part by his father's ascension to the Cabinet. But, by his second year, he had gained "a distinctive profile not just in his own college, but in the University as a whole," as a political and social critic. The shrillness of his comments, rather than any ideological slant, may have been what first caught the attention of the Soviet recruiters assigned to Cambridge.[7]

"The economic situation, the unemployed, vulgarity in the cinema, rubbish on the bookstalls, the public school, snobbery in the suburbs, more battleships, lower wages," were all intolerable, he wrote early in his third year. The whole "cracked-brained economic mess," he predicted, would soon come crashing down.[8]

Maclean's anger was not unusual among Oxbridge undergraduates. One historian described it this way:

Those on the tower were acutely aware of their exalted position. They suddenly became conscious of their middle-class families and upbringing. This realization resulted in discomfort and self-pity that turned into anger at the tower—at the society that had elevated them. But they faced a dilemma. How could they legitimately condemn the society by which they had so greatly profited? The solution was the discovery of a scapegoat that symbolized society, for example, the capitalist.[9]

Maclean's discovery of his middle-class guilt led to predictable excesses. British capitalism was condemned with a ferocity exceeding that directed at Hitler's Germany. Donald's wrath did not dissipate there, but continued in full force toward all British institutions. The government, the cinemas, the publishing industry, and the suburbs—all had failed him. So had Cambridge, which suffered from "reactionary valueless teaching on every faculty" and school authorities who were trying to stifle free speech, censor antiwar articles, oppress women, discriminate against Indians, and exploit all students.[10]

What characterized Maclean was not original thought, but the intensity and breadth of his fury and his need for revenge. Even his professed attachment to communism was a weapon, a means by which he would (as had the Bolsheviks) become part of a self-constituted ruling elite settling old scores. Maclean was neither intellectually nor emotionally capable of living the life of a dedicated communist, but he reveled in the thought that everyone he knew would suffer under a communist regime. As with other British intellectuals, communism was for him "a ready-made instrument of action to be wielded in their nihilistic attack upon bourgeois values."[11]

As a third-year student, he underlined and initialed a quote from Lenin in *A Brief History of Russia:*

For we repeat that, like the bourgeoisie, the intelligentsia lived on the surplus product that was extracted by force from the peasant and the workman. A Communist Revolution would mean that *it would have to give up its advantages, renounce all its privileges, and join the ranks of manual labor.* And this prospect could be accepted only by a small number of the most sincere and devoted revolutionaries of the intelligentsia.[12]

Not that Maclean was willing to give up any of his privileges or had any intention of working in a factory. In his scheme of things, he would never have to relinquish his pampered existence, but he rejoiced in the vision of his rich, powerful, wealthy, and well-connected fellow students, stripped of everything and consigned to the factory's drudgery. Meanwhile, Donald demanded all of the privileges due him from a society he wanted to destroy—confident that under a communist regime, he would be among the jailers, not the jailed.

Maclean was never persuasive as a communist. Robert Cecil—Cambridge classmate, Foreign Office colleague, and eventual Maclean biographer—visited Donald one day in his Trinity Hall digs. Between drags on his expensive Balkan cigarettes, Donald decreed that he was a communist. Cecil said nothing, but later admitted thinking, "this elegant young man in his leather armchair was not my idea of a communist." He seemed too trendy, too superficial, and too condescending and arrogant. "It never occurred to me that he was doing more than pursuing a young man's legitimate pastime of trying on a mask to see how it fitted."[13]

After Maclean defected to Moscow, Cecil concluded that he had misjudged the depth of his commitment. Not at all. "His was the intellectual's Communism, iconoclastic, derisory, cynical, a wishful-fillment fantasy of mastery over and vengeance upon a world and a society in whose material benefits he revelled, but whose spirit he hated and despised," is how British journalist John Connell more accurately described it. Maclean's "commitment to his country's enemies was total—simply because they were enemies."[14]

Had Maclean's ideological ardor been greater, the Soviets would never have recruited him. They were not interested in the hard-core communists, the working-class agitators, and middle-class prosely-tizers who spread the communist gospel through pamphleteering and debating. They lacked the spy's capacity to dissemble and to adopt a repugnant value system. Further, Soviet recruiters, particularly in Britain, considered communists dangerously spontaneous, capable of blurting out their revolutionary catechism at precisely the wrong moment. And worse, dedicated communists might let their beliefs inhibit implementing Moscow's edicts.[15]

If Soviet intelligence had any use for communists, it could not have done better than Maclean's friend, Philip Toynbee. Although his historian father, Arnold Toynbee, was then greatly enchanted by Hitler, Philip was the first communist president of the prestigious Oxford Union. "I would have considered it the highest honor to be asked to perform any service at all for Soviet Russia," he admitted later. Yet the Soviets never even approached him.[16]

Nor, so far as is known, were Donald's contemporaries at Gresham's, Brian Simon and James Klugman, ever approached by Soviet intelligence, although both dedicated their lives to communism. Klugman was one of the Communist Party's most eloquent and effective propagandists at Cambridge. His loyalty to the Party's cause was beyond question. But he would have been useless to Moscow as a spy. He was too open, too committed; he believed in Marxism and the class struggle, and enjoyed publicly debating his views, unlike Maclean who never spoke at the Union, preferring instead to conduct and resolve his debates within the friendly arena of his own mind.[17]

As the editor of Trinity Hall's student magazine, the *Silver Crescent,* Donald wrote a doggerel that glorified those who "dared to leave a herd they hate," and ridiculed the "panic-herd with frightened eyes, [who] know they've chosen the losing side." These themes—escaping the herd, and being on the winning side—obsessed Maclean for the rest of his life. His "sinking ship psychology" about capitalism was common among those who "unquestionably believed that it was only a matter of time before communism was everywhere calling the tune." Donald's rage and contempt pushed him a decisive step further. Certain that Britain and the West were finished, and determined to be "on the winning side," he secretly enrolled in Soviet intelligence.[18]

The exact circumstances of his recruitment are unknown. Moscow probably opened a file on him shortly after he began to gain prominence for his vicious denunciations of British society. Such attention, when he was finally told about it, would have flattered Donald greatly; he had a monstrous ego that puffed up at the slightest breeze. He was recruited by no later than his third year, because it was then that he redirected his somewhat aimless studies toward a goal he had summarily rejected in his first year—an appointment to the Foreign Office. This change, as Krivitsky had revealed and his younger brother Alan confirms, was made under orders from Soviet intelligence.[19]

When Maclean informed his mother that he no longer intended to teach in Russia following graduation, as he had once told her he would, Lady Maclean was exhilarated. But, she wondered, what about his communist ideals? "You must think me a weathercock," he replied, "but the fact is I've rather gone off all that lately." His decision to go to work for the Soviets was the catalyst that turned "an irresolute, mildly silly and underdeveloped lad into an imposingly brilliant young man."[20]

The board members who interviewed him as part of the exhaustive and demanding written and oral exams required for the Diplomatic Service were also curious about his political beliefs. Afterward, Maclean told some friends about it:

> All went well, and I got on famously with the examiners at the *viva*. I thought they'd finished when one of them suddenly said: "By the way, Mr. Maclean. We understand that you, like other young men, held strong Communist views while you were at Cambridge. Do you still hold those views?" I'm afraid I did an instant double take: Shall I deny the truth, or shall I brazen it out? I decided to brazen it out. "Yes," I said, "I did have such views—and I haven't entirely shaken them off." I think they must have liked my honesty because they nodded, looked at each other and smiled. Then the chairman said: "Thank you, that will be all, Mr. Maclean."

Of the seventy-five to one hundred who took the exams, only seven passed. Maclean ranked fourth, and joined the Diplomatic Service as a Third Secretary in October 1935.[21]

As Maclean entered the grim and forbidding mid-Victorian Foreign Office building across from No. 10 Downing Street, Cecil believes he carried with him the certainty that he would prevail "because history was on his side, as it was on the side of Marxists everywhere." It was a notion he could never completely abandon. Thirty years later, living in the drab gray emptiness of Moscow, Donald and his wife would pass the time in frigid winters fantasizing about the good times they would have in Italy and Paris "once the revolution comes."[22]

In the early autumn of 1938, on the eve of the Munich Crisis, Maclean won a prestigious posting to Paris. The assignment ended abruptly when France fell in June 1940. As the city was being abandoned, his seven-month on-again off-again courtship of Melinda Marling, a dark, thin, attractive girl, originally from southern Illinois, who had lived many of her twenty-six years in New York and Europe, culminated in marriage.

Maclean may have received the jolt of his life when he returned to London. Once back at the Foreign Office, he discovered how close Krivitsky had come to unmasking him. Some have attributed Krivitsky's mysterious death eight months later to the danger he posed to Maclean. It seems probable that Moscow knew as early as February 1940 the details of Krivitsky's Foreign Office visit. But even if they had only learned the details from Maclean in June, it is worth remembering that it was only weeks later that Burgess flew to Washington and met with Straight, and that Straight then began his campaign to rejoin the State Department.[23]

The Macleans spent most of the war in London. Since Donald had gone into the Foreign Office only because the Soviets had ordered him to do so, he never reconciled himself to being a member of the "herd" of drab gray diplomats. Yet his younger brother Alan believes that both Donald and the Soviets may have been surprised at how "exceptionally good he was at it." Indeed, "one of our most famous diplomatic representatives" told Connolly that Maclean was "a white hope, a *puer aureus* of the Service whose attainments and responsibilities were well beyond his years." His future almost certainly included a knighthood—Sir Donald—ambassadorships to France and the United States, and eventually Permanent Under Secretary of State, the highest possible position for a career diplomat.[24]

In the spring of 1944 he was posted to the British embassy in Washington, "the most important of all the functions outside this country," maintained Churchill, "that can be discharged by any British subject."[25]

* * *

Most observers agree that Maclean's four years at the Washington embassy marked the high point of his career, both as a British diplomat and as a Soviet agent. Even as a Third Secretary in Paris, he had seen every important incoming and outgoing cable, including those the Foreign Office instructed the ambassador to "decode yourself." In Washington he was a First Secretary for most of his tour and acting Head of Chancery—the traffic cop for all of the embassy's activities—for a critical period in 1946 when the world seemed constantly on the brink of war. Maclean did not merely have access, he controlled access.[26]

What was most remarkable about Maclean's performance as a Kremlin spy, however, was his reach beyond the embassy's walls extending, within three months of his arrival, into the White House. On August 29, 1944, Admiral William Leahy, Roosevelt's top military aide, and the senior officer of the Joint Chiefs of Staff (JCS), wrote a top-secret memorandum to Secretary of State Cordell Hull, briefly outlining the military strategy that would be used to drive the Japanese out of Indochina. More important, it established that the region's political spheres of influence would be decided by a Chinese-British-American committee.

The JCS had already concluded that "we should recognize, insofar as they are consistent with our national policies, the French desires concerning Indo-China." Similarly, the British were to be given the lead in their old colonial possessions, starting with Burma. This was contrary to Roosevelt's stated intention of preventing the European powers from reclaiming their former colonies. The Joint Chiefs, however, were much more interested in constructing a chain of global air and naval bases as forward basing positions for their long-range bombers, a task they preferred to negotiate with grateful European powers rather than unpredictable and possibly unwilling emerging nations.[27]

What Stalin would have found most revealing about the Leahy memorandum was Washington's intention to exclude the Soviet Union from playing any role in the Asian subcontinent, and a concomitant American willingness to impose a status quo ante bellum in the region. This fact would also have been of great interest to the region's burgeoning nationalistic movements, which Moscow hoped to influence. What is most noteworthy about the document, however, is simply that within hours after it was written in the White House—and before it reached the "action office" of the State Department less than one hundred feet away—it was in the hands of a Soviet agent.

Within a year increasing pressure on Maclean would cause him to start unraveling. In these early days, however, he seemed capable of recklessness. He immediately called H. Freeman "Doc" Matthews, the Department's deputy director of European affairs, whose responsibility it would have been to "staff-out" Leahy's message. Maclean's questions embarrassed Matthews. He had not seen the memo, was unaware of its existence, and had no idea what Maclean was talking about. Finally Matthews cut the conversation short to consult with Leahy.

It never would have occurred to Matthews to suspect Maclean of anything untoward. They had worked together in Paris before the war and the special Anglo-American camaraderie had only strengthened since then. Still, it was so unusual for a Second Secretary of a foreign embassy to come into possession of a top-secret memo from the head of the Joint Chiefs to the Secretary of State only hours after it was written that Matthews did make a record of it, noting that Maclean "did not say where it had been obtained."[28]

In December Maclean displayed a reach that went all the way to Moscow, concerning an issue that had its origin in Stalin's xenophobia. The Soviet tyrant considered any contact by Russians with foreigners to be treasonous. Not even senior Party officials were permitted to socialize with Westerners. Therefore, diplomats found it impossible to get any idea of what was going on in the country except from Tass and *Pravda,* and the resulting isolation not only added greatly to the drudgery of serving in Moscow, it ensured that those who did returned home with a hardened anti-Soviet attitude.[29]

British diplomats did manage to meet secretly with a few intrepid Muscovites desperate for contact with the outside world. Their discussions, which had little political significance except for the fact that they took place, were written up in a report called "Casual Sources," which the embassy provided to the Foreign Office. To protect the Russians, who risked death or exile, the report was kept under the tightest secrecy. Reference to it, however, was made in an exchange between the Foreign Office and the embassy in Moscow. The exchange had been routinely copied to Washington, where it was noticed by John W. Russell, a press attaché who had previously served in Moscow and was now supervised by Maclean. Russell quickly sent London a cable, likely cleared by Maclean, asking that he and Isaiah Berlin (who ended up serving in Washington after the aborted assignment to the Moscow embassy in the summer of 1940), be provided with a copy of the Casual Sources report.

"We make this request partly out of idle curiosity, partly out of a genuine need to keep abreast of developments in the U.S.S.R.," the cable pleaded. But both the Moscow embassy and the Foreign Office refused because of a "positive danger of it being seen by people other than those who are in fairly constant contact with what is going on in Moscow."

Then Maclean became directly involved. Initially, he too was turned down. But he and Russell persisted, assuring London that nothing would leak from the embassy. Maclean promised to "take steps to ensure that no item of information contained in the series is indirectly requoted to the Americans." (The Foreign Office had an almost irrational fear that, once the reports were received on American soil, the State Department would learn of them and begin badgering British officials in Moscow for a copy.) Finally, the Foreign Office relented.[30]

For Stalin, obtaining news about malcontents from his man inside the British embassy must have been an unexpected bonus. Although it is impossible to tell from Foreign Office files whether the information that Maclean passed to the Soviets was sufficient for Moscow to take reprisals against any Russians, it is certainly possible that dozens or more could have suffered punishment or death once they were compromised by Maclean. As the American diplomat Charles E. "Chip" Bohlen pointed out, "Any attempt by a foreigner to get in touch with a Soviet citizen was the equivalent of signing an order for his arrest if not his execution."[31]

★ ★ ★

On April 17, 1945, just weeks before Germany's surrender, Maclean was promoted to First Secretary. Shortly thereafter, Britain began calling home many of the top diplomats posted to Washington during the war emergency. This left Maclean as one of the embassy's most senior, capable, and experienced diplomats, at a time when

England's dependency on Washington was growing and East–West tension was building. One of the first crises to hit after his promotion was the very issue that had ignited war nearly six years before—Poland.[32]

CHAPTER FIVE

It would no doubt be a tactical mistake vis-à-
vis the Russians and of [sic] world opinion,
when the news comes out, to give the
impression publicly that the Polish question is
solved.

Churchill to Truman
June 4, 1945

THE SMOKING GUN

In the early morning of June 5, 1945, Donald Duart Maclean, dressed in a somber pinstriped Savile Row suit, stepped through the door of his whitewashed brick house in northwest Washington. The sun filtering through the silver maples highlighted his youthful head of swept-back blond hair, which, combined with his trim build, made him look even taller than an already imposing six feet four inches. The summer's dreaded heat and humidity had not yet arrived, and the air was crisp as he began his ten-minute walk along Thirty-fifth Place, crossing Wisconsin Avenue to Whitehaven Street, past the National Observatory to Massachusetts Avenue and the British embassy.

The adolescent flabbiness, which had been both physical and mental, and his effeminate look had disappeared with youth. The bad teeth, so common to his generation of Englishmen, had been fixed. At thirty-two he was lean, with a strong chin and a decisive authority. He seemed, the diplomatic community could agree, "the very picture of a British diplomat."[1]

As John "Jock" Balfour (Sir John after being knighted while in Washington), the embassy's Political Minister, described him:

> To all appearances he was the pattern, almost the too perfect pattern, of the trained diplomatist—efficient and conscientious at his work, amiable to meet, imperturbably good-tempered, elegant, exceedingly self-possessed, and with a cynical outlook which betrayed no particular ideological bias.[2]

In the year Maclean had been posted to Washington, his career had prospered. He had an excellent relationship with Lord Halifax, the wiry, self-effacing, and aloof ambassador, whose descent from one of England's most aristocratic families had not spared him the humbling experience of being born with a deformed left hand. Had Halifax not found ambition unseemly, he could have been prime minister in May 1939. Churchill had no similar reservations, and soon dispatched Halifax, who had been tarnished by serving as Chamberlain's foreign minister, to what most considered political exile in Washington.

Halifax's tour got off to a horrendous start—he was pictured disdainfully shoving a hot dog under his seat at a baseball game and then riding in a Virginia hunt—but he recovered and became a tremendous asset to the Anglo-American relationship. Carping about the British not doing enough of the Allied fighting receded after one of Halifax's sons was killed in the war, and a second had both his legs blown off.

Halifax and Sir Donald had been friends, in large measure because their profound religious beliefs contributed to austere habits, an incorruptible performance of their duties, and a lack of personal ambition. When Sir Donald died, Halifax took his place as president of the Board of Education. When word of Donald's assignment to Washington came through, Halifax took the unusual step of writing him a charming letter of welcome, "saying how glad he was that Donald was joining his staff."[3]

Included on that staff were several of Maclean's friends from earlier days including: Sir Ronald Campbell, later ambassador to Cairo when Maclean was assigned there; the chain-smoking Michael Wright, a brilliant and intense diplomat, later knighted and appointed ambassador to Norway and Iraq; and Paul Gore-Booth (later Lord), who entered the diplomatic service a year ahead of Donald and would rise—as many predicted that Maclean would—to the rank of Permanent Under Secretary. (When Maclean first came to Washington, he used Gore-Booth as a reference; later, he helped save his career.) Arriving in April 1945 was Robert Cecil, a Cambridge contemporary and later his deputy in the American Department.

It was "a team of almost fabulous distinction" according to one description, making the embassy "a center of political life rich in intellectual talent." Not only did Roosevelt and Churchill use it as the fulcrum of the special Anglo-American relationship, but other American officials such as Wisconsin Senator Arthur Vandenberg, the Republican Party's foreign policy leader, found it a more reliable source of information than the State Department.[4]

His rank, the fact that he had been there over a year, his excellent relationship with Halifax, and his snap-brim efficiency conspired to make Maclean nearly indispensable in conducting the embassy's rushed and demanding daily business. He was usually one of the first to arrive at the N-shaped chancery building and often did not leave until 10:00 P.M. or later. "No task was too hard for him; no hours too long," according to Robert Cecil, who had also served with Maclean in Paris. He was always willing to "take over a tangled skein from a colleague who was sick, or going on leave, or simply less zealous."[5]

Since late May the embassy had been a swirl of activity. With the always fragile Grand Alliance in danger of being shattered, President Harry Truman had dispatched Harry Hopkins—in frail health himself—to Moscow for negotiations over Poland with Premier Joseph Stalin.

At the Teheran Conference in November 1943, the Allies ceded to the Soviet Union those parts of eastern Poland it had taken by conquest over four years before. At Yalta in February 1945, Stalin gave vague promises to hold "free and unfettered elections." But a month later, the Soviet secret police lured the emaciated Warsaw underground government out of hiding with a false promise of safe passage to London. When the plane landed, however, the sixteen Poles found themselves not in London, but in Moscow, where they were thrown into prison.

In this one well-planned act, Stalin had removed from Poland's blood-drenched soil the nation's political leadership, something the Nazis had failed to do during six years of war. Stalin initially denied any knowledge of the Poles' whereabouts; finally he proclaimed that they were being held in Moscow as war criminals to be tried for "terroristic acts of diversion" against the Red Army.

A storm of international protest followed. Even *The Tribune,* a left-wing British labor weekly, condemned the Soviet action as "provocative and strikingly unjust." Churchill cabled Truman that "I have never been more anxious than I am now about the state of Europe."[6]

Truman was exasperated by the entire lingering European mess. As vice president he had met with Roosevelt no more than a half dozen times between the November election and the president's death five months later. Excluded from every important war-related meeting, bereft of foreign policy experience, the one-time court-house politician believed that his only chance to gain the nation's confidence was by tackling the mounting domestic crises. But first he had to get the Grand Alliance back on track. With no other rabbit to pull out of his hat, he resorted to a distinctly Rooseveltian move by sending Hopkins, who inspite of long absences due to illness was still on the White House staff, to confer with Stalin.

Once the Hopkins-Stalin talks began, a torrent of top secret cables kept the embassy's wires whirring as Maclean and his colleagues operated like a huge switchboard, frantically decrypting, analyzing, and relaying reports and swapping messages between London (No. 10 Downing Street and the Foreign Office); Washington (the State Department and the White House); Moscow (Sir Archibald Clark Kerr, British ambassador to the Soviet Union); and San Francisco (where Foreign Secretary Anthony Eden was attending the founding conference of the United Nations).[7]

It was the sort of activity Maclean thrived on. "In all the history of the British Embassy at Washington it was probably never so exquisitely efficient, so impeccably organized, as when Maclean was its First Secretary," a senior diplomat later told Dame Rebecca West. "He had the watchmaker's mind," she went on to explain, "which understands the workings of a complicated machine and is not repelled by complication and feels pride as the shining cogs and wheels perform the process that runs parallel with time."[8]

When Maclean arrived in the mornings all the urgent overnight cables would have been "unbuttoned" (decoded) by Wilfrid Thomas, the acting senior staff officer. On June 5 these included Churchill's Numbers 72 and 73 to Truman brooding over Poland. He conceded that Hopkins had made some progress, but insisted that it was only "a milestone in a long hill we ought never to have been asked to climb." Concerned that part of Stalin's tactics were to test Truman's mettle, and unsure that he would meet the challenge, the prime minister implored the president that "we must not cease our efforts on behalf of the Poles."[9]

The embassy did not receive copies of Hopkins's cables to Truman, but the White House did provide it with summaries that Maclean or other senior officers transmitted to London. They were not very encouraging. Hopkins, who had been Roosevelt's special wartime emissary to Churchill and Stalin, advised Truman that the Soviet ruler would not budge on Poland. He refused to release nor even promise clemency for the arrested Polish leaders, and any further talks on Poland's future would have to take place in Moscow (even Germans, some officials noted sardonically, were tried on German soil, while the country's future was debated in Berlin).

Averell Harriman, the American ambassador in Moscow, and Chip Bohlen, who acted as interpreter, accompanied Hopkins to the talks. Stalin was emphatic that he would not release the Poles, Harriman recalled. "Outright release was out of the question." Bohlen realized that for the jailed Poles, "there was no possibility of a just solution." In fact, Bohlen, who had originally suggested the Hopkins mission, concluded that it had been a mistake. He thought that, in the end, Hopkins did too.[10]

Certainly Maclean did. Anglo-American policy at this time, he would later write disapprovingly from Moscow, was dedicated to little more than establishing "positions of strength against the Soviet Union." As for Churchill, what he really feared, according to Maclean, was "that Washington would prolong into the post-war period Roosevelt's policy of cooperation with the Soviet Union."[11]

So it is likely that, as he left the embassy that night, Maclean had tucked away in his briefcase a present for his Soviet control: copies of Churchill's cables Numbers 72 and 73 to Truman. Number 72 contained the warning that "it would no doubt be a tactical mistake vis-à-vis the Russians and of [*sic*] world opinion, when the news comes out, to give the impression publicly that the Polish question is solved. Renewed hope and not rejoicing is all the more we can engage in."

Exactly eight days later, however, millions of Americans learned that Poland was a cause for rejoicing. "Unless something unforeseen happens to upset it, Harry Hopkins has won a resounding victory for improved relations with Russia by ironing out the main points of the Polish dispute," columnist Drew Pearson trumpeted in the seven hundred newspapers that subscribed to his *Merry-Go-Round* column.

"The details of the Hopkins-Stalin conversations inside the Kremlin," Pearson boasted, "can now be told." He did so with an accuracy that jarred official Washington. Pearson recited, in the exact order that they had been considered, the main points discussed by Hopkins and Stalin. He knew the names of those who would be representing various Polish factions—which had been hotly debated—at the Moscow conference, as well as the arrangements that had been agreed to for the upcoming Potsdam Conference.[12]

How had Pearson gotten hold of such secret information, rattled administration officials wondered? "It could only have originated from the messages sent by Mr. Harry Hopkins in Moscow to the President of the United States," Harry Vaughan, Truman's naval aide complained to the FBI's Hoover. "Pearson's information must have come from the Russian Embassy or Russian sources," acting Secretary of State Joseph Grew countered, "because the statements appearing in the Pearson article were only those favorable to Russia." Truman appeared to agree. "Propaganda seems to be our greatest foreign relations enemy," he wrote angrily in his diary, "Russians distribute lies about us."[13]

"For goodness' sake don't muddy things up!" the President implored aroused reporters on June 13, after the front page of that morning's *Washington Post* repeated Pearson's claim that Stalin had agreed to the release of the sixteen Polish prisoners. "Just say that we have made some progress and that we hope to get some results." In London, Churchill, who had foreseen the clamor if expectations were falsely raised, warned the press against concluding that "the settlement of the Polish issue is imminent." But the genie promising

Grand Alliance harmony and a beneficent Stalin was out of the bottle, and it would not be easy to put back.[14]

"At last [an agreement] has been reached on what the Yalta formula means" the influential columnist Walter Lippmann applauded the day after Truman's caution. No one could still maintain "that Marshal Stalin is insincere" or that "Poland's independence must be a sham."[15]

That same morning Truman ordered J. Edgar Hoover to investigate how cables to the president of the United States had fallen into pro-Soviet hands. But not even Truman, who detested Pearson even more than did Roosevelt (who had once publicly branded him "a chronic liar"), would have suggested that the columnist deliberately distorted information to further Stalin's tyranny.[16]

Yet, although some of Pearson's statements were lifted verbatim from Hopkins's cables, at least as much was in direct contradiction to the information those cables contained. For instance, according to Pearson "Stalin admitted that not all [the arrested Poles] were guilty [and] agreed that not all would be tried and that some were to be released." Hopkins's cables made clear, however, that throughout their talks Stalin had "insisted that the men must be tried" and that "he at no time retreated from his position that he intended to try these prisoners."[17]

The "leak" could have involved several steps. Certainly Maclean did not hand Pearson a copy of the cables, or anything else.[18] It is more likely that after he passed copies of what he had to his control, the Soviets came up with a doctored version mixing highly classified information with fabrications intended to portray Stalin as a reasonable and compassionate man. Then, through a trusted intermediary—such as David Karr, his "legman" around Washington—the new document was passed to Pearson.[19]

However it happened, someone with access to America's greatest secrets was leaking them to a source whose purpose was to twist and distort. But who? The FBI started at the White House. By comparing the Pearson column with Hopkins's original cables and the White House summaries of those cables, the FBI established that all of Pearson's accurate information was contained in the summaries and that none of the information omitted from the summaries as too sensitive was included in the article. Taken together, these two findings suggested that Pearson's source had access only to the summaries, not to the original cables.

Next they examined the White House transcripts of telephone conversations between Hopkins and Truman. This revealed that none of the information contained exclusively in those transcripts and omitted from the summaries was contained in the column. Thus, Pearson's source probably did not have access to the telephone logs. In other words, it meant that the "mole" only had access to the summaries. This was a good news-bad news situation. The good news was that the White House was eliminated as a suspect because anyone who had access to the summaries would also have had access to the cables, the transcripts, or both. But the bad news was that the summaries had been so widely distributed that three other institutions with thousands of employees were suspect—the State Department, the British embassy, and, because of the pro-Soviet slant, the Soviet embassy.

The Soviet embassy had three strikes against it. First, it never officially received the summaries. Second, even if Stalin provided his Washington embassy with Kremlin summaries of the Hopkins talks, it was impossible that when the Russian version of the talks was translated into English the wording would have been identical to that of Hopkins. And third, the Soviets absolutely would not cooperate with such an investigation, so it was a dead-end from the start.

The State Department was not so much eliminated as held in abeyance, because, if it was the only probable source, the list of suspects could run into the scores or even hundreds. It still had the image, which Hoover delighted in fanning, of being notoriously unreliable—full, as Hopkins put it, "of leaks and creaks."[20]

So for the moment the spotlight shifted to the British embassy. Hoover did not concur with the general esteem in which it was held. His dislike stemmed from Britain's role in supporting the creation of the Office of Strategic Services, which Hoover had implacably opposed.

Because Hoover had a visceral dislike of diplomats, it was inevitable that the FBI would turn up a suspect inside the embassy. In this case it was John Russell, the tall, thin, balding press attaché whose job, the FBI darkly noted, was "to keep the press happy." He had also hand-delivered several Hopkins-related cables to the State Department and, most portentously of all in the circuitous Hoover logic that would one day be ridiculed by his critics, Russell worked closely with Isaiah Berlin, who was a friend of Felix Frankfurter, known to be a source for Drew Pearson.

Still, however illogical the route by which they got there, arriving at the door of the British embassy could have paid off handsomely. During the investigation, Russell rotated back to London. To follow through, the FBI would have had to talk to his supervisor, Donald Maclean. It would not have been the only item to discuss with Maclean because his responsibilities also included embassy security, and he was as knowledgeable as anyone about the embassy's inner workings.[21]

Although six years later, the mere prospect of being questioned sent Maclean fleeing to Moscow, it is unlikely that in 1945 he would have become similarly unnerved. It will never be known for sure, however, because as Bureau investigators were about to knock on the embassy's door, Hoover blundered and called them back.

Having determined the source of Pearson's correct information—the White House summaries of Hopkins's cables—this left unanswered the more intriguing question of where he had obtained his incorrect information. For instance, the FBI noted Pearson's assertion that at one point "Hopkins agreed to send a personal message to Churchill," and, on another occasion, he "told Churchill" about a conversation he had had with Stalin. These passages indicated that Hopkins had been in direct communication with Churchill. But had he? It was a crucially important question.

For the answer, FBI went to the White House Map Room, the communications nerve center of the American war effort and through which all presidential messages passed. A thorough check of all the logs, however, found no trace of any Hopkins-Churchill exchanges. "Hopkins sent no messages to Churchill," the Map Room and the Bureau concluded. Pearson's assertions to the contrary were, Hoover ruled, "in error."

Hopkins and Churchill, however, had been in direct contact—at least five times in three days. The Map Room had no knowledge of these exchanges because Hopkins had not bothered to report them to Truman nor had he sent copies to the Map Room.[22] It was Hoover who was "in error." Had he conducted a more thorough investigation, he would have realized that there was only one place in Washington that both had the White House summaries and knew about the Hopkins-Churchill exchanges—the British embassy.[23] This fact could have been quickly ascertained if only Hoover had instructed Assistant Director Mickey Ladd, the Bureau's liaison to the embassy, to ask MI5's Peter Dwyer, his British contact, if there had been any exchanges between Hopkins and Churchill (MI5 was the military intelligence cover designation for the Security Service, Britain's counter-intelligence organization). But Ladd was never ordered to do so.[24]

The British would have jumped at the chance to take a whack at Pearson. Throughout the war, he had maligned the valor of the British people, the integrity of British leaders, and the courage of the British fighting forces. He had hinted at murky prewar ties between Churchill and Mussolini, and attributed the deaths of American soldiers to the timidity of British forces. So the embassy would hardly have been reluctant to cooperate.

Hoover had other problems to settle, however. Unable to pinpoint the source of the Hopkins leak, and with "Amerasia," another major espionage case about to blow up in the FBI's face, Hoover went on the offensive. Both the Hopkins leaks and the "Amerasia" case, he maintained, were proof that the problem was not foreign spies; it was careless government workers. "Until such time as there is a general tightening up of the handling and dissemination of highly confidential government documents, such leaks of information will continue," he reported to Truman, "and originals or copies of such documents will be available for perusal or will actually be delivered to unauthorized individuals."[25]

With that piece of gratuitous advice, the investigation into the Hopkins leak was closed. Not forever, however. Although he had no idea of it, Maclean was doomed by two clues connected with this case. The first came about because during 1944 and 1945 he was reporting to his Soviet control in New York. The secret cables and other documents he passed would be encoded and dispatched by the Soviet mission and cabled to Moscow. The Soviet intelligence either did not know or was not concerned that the U.S. Army Security Agency (ASA) was intercepting its transmissions. At the time, this was not threatening, because ASA had not succeeded in breaking the Soviet code, so for years the "intercepts" were stacked up unread.

Within four years, however, a mistake by a Soviet cipher clerk was to give American cryptographers the break they needed to crack the Soviet code and go back and decipher the intercepted but unread "mail." Among their most astonishing discoveries was that someone had provided the Soviets with copies of messages between Churchill and Truman. It is almost certain that these included Churchill's Numbers 72 and 73. One of the reasons for believing so is that during an investigation carried on in conjunction with this book, it was discovered that Numbers 72 and 73 were missing—the only two out of hundreds—from the National Archives's master files of all messages between president and prime minister for the years 1939 to 1945. The only possible explanation Archivist John Taylor could offer was that they had been removed by another federal agency for investigative purposes.[26]

Eventually, William Lamphere, the FBI agent in charge of the effort to break the Soviet code, acknowledged that during the critical part of the investigation, "I managed to provide [the senior crypt-analyst] with copies of telegrams from Winston Churchill to Truman," and to be able "to obtain the original materials greatly enhanced his work."[27]

When it was first discovered that Numbers 72 and 73 had been passed, Maclean was doomed because in their intercepted transmission to Moscow, the Soviets even included the Foreign Office identifying numbers of the cables. Investigators realized this meant that a Soviet spy had been operating from inside the British embassy in the summer of 1945. Soon they learned the Soviets' nom de guerre for their spy was "Homer."

The clue that would seal Maclean's fate originated the day he and Melinda arrived in the United States on May 6, 1944. As part of the wartime Foreign Travel Control Program they were routinely interviewed by the FBI. It did not occur to Melinda to check with Donald about what she should put down as her U.S. address. She thought she knew. After a two-week stay at her mother's farm in western Massachusetts, she and Donald would proceed to Washington and stay at a hotel until they found a place to live. So she gave her address as "the British Embassy, Washington." But Donald told officials her address would be "277 Park Avenue," her stepfather's New York apartment. Both repeated this conflicting information on their Customs and Immigration forms.[28]

The discrepancy was not enough to arouse any suspicion, but it did signal that Melinda was in for a rude surprise. It was not until he was packing for Washington that Donald told her she was not going with him. She was stunned. What was he talking about? Of course she was going to Washington. It was only temporary, Maclean explained. He would go down first, find a place to live, and then she could join him; it would only be a matter of a few weeks.[29]

Melinda was not placated. She was extremely close to her mother, but she had left home for Paris eight years earlier as a twenty-one-year-old college dropout to declare her independence and escape from her stepfather. During the war she convinced herself that her rocky marriage would improve once the war and the stress of living in London ended (twice they had been bombed out of their apartment). Now Donald wanted her to live at home again. He had not been with her four years before when their first baby was stillborn. She was five months' pregnant; this time she wanted Donald with her. Moreover, their fourth anniversary was just a month off. But none of this, she angrily concluded, seem to matter to Donald. He did not want her in Washington.

She can not be faulted for missing the point. Maclean's problem was not to keep Melinda from coming to Washington. It was that the Soviets wanted him to report through New York, the headquarters for their North American espionage operations, and Maclean needed a cover story to travel there. Melinda's pregnancy, the Soviets decided, was the perfect alibi. They did not anticipate that in several years, when British security authorities were tracking down "Homer," this perfect alibi would become the smoking gun that proved Donald Maclean was that spy. During the next nine months, Maclean traveled to New York as frequently as twice a week. Although Melinda was his alibi, he rarely saw her. To get away from her stepfather, she spent the entire period at the farm in western Massachusetts. Donald did make occasional trips to the farm, but usually no more than once a month for three days.[30]

His travel routine never varied. He would catch the train from Washington's Union Station to Penn Station in New York, take the subway across to Grand Central, and then walk the few blocks to 277 Park Avenue. No one ever traveled with him to New York, and no one from the family ever met him at the train or saw him off.

Melinda's stepfather, a forty-five-year-old business executive named Harold Dunbar, liked Donald and, as he was often at home when Maclean came to spend the night, the two of them frequently had cocktails. Maclean never once accepted an invitation to stay for dinner, however, always declaring that he had "business to attend to," which was to deliver documents to his Soviet control and receive instructions on areas of pressing interest to Moscow.

Dunbar thought Melinda and Donald's living arrangements were odd, but then, he thought Melinda was odd. He never got along with any of his stepdaughters (he would divorce their mother in April 1945). This fundamental conflict was exacerbated by the fact that, although he was a wealthy man, he charged all of them rent when they lived at 277 Park Avenue. Melinda was the one who grated the most. Harriet and Catherine would do anything to avoid the parties Dunbar gave for his business associates, but Melinda would inevitably come—only to quickly announce that she was bored, and walk out.[31]

Dunbar had the last word, however. When it was assumed that Maclean had fled to Moscow, he volunteered to the FBI that he thought Melinda "would have been much more the type to furnish Russia with information than was Donald Maclean." He also told them she was a "social misfit . . . a very peculiar problem child who had practically no friends" because she "seemed to look down upon American social life." A conservative Republican, he also managed to get in a dig at Roosevelt, when he described Maclean as "no more liberal" than FDR.[32]

During the nine months that Donald reported through New York, which ended when his Soviet control was transferred to the Soviet embassy in Washington, Melinda visited Washington only once. However well this served the Soviets, it did little for the Macleans. Donald's petulant "the-world-owes-me" attitude led him to all but abandon responsibility for his wife. He did not even send her money, no doubt rationalizing that it was unnecessary for him to make such sacrifices because her mother was well-to-do, and Melinda had a small inheritance. His inability to accept the responsibility of husband and father perpetually undermined their marriage.

His journalist friend Geoffrey Hoare later wrote that Maclean had "a mother complex." There is plenty of evidence to support this conclusion, chiefly that from routine household chores—such as hiring and dismissing maids—to moments of great family crisis, Maclean usually receded into the background, and let Mrs. Dunbar take over the management of his family.[33]

He did not, of course, let her get involved in solving the Washington housing problem. His excuse was plausible. When he arrived in Washington, it was still "a wearying, worrying city with too many people, and too many lines. It has too little time and space for the big job at hand," according to *Life* magazine. For most people life consisted of "an endless, wearying succession of waiting—waiting for a place to live, waiting for something to eat, waiting for a taxi or a bus, waiting to get into an office, a store or a movie and then waiting to get out again."[34]

Yet, Maclean suffered few of these indignities. For housing, he simply moved into Michael Wright's four-story luxury house at 6 Kalorama Circle in the heart of Washington's most exclusive neighborhood. Wright, with whom Maclean had worked closely in Paris, and his wife, Alice, (the daughter of Dwight Davis, formerly Calvin Coolidge's Secretary of War), bought the six bedroom, four bathroom house in 1943 for $65,000; it would sell in 1988 for $3,250,000. Little wonder that Donald made the decidedly non-Marxist comment to his sister-in-law Harriet Marling that "There's nothing I like so much as the comfortable houses of my rich friends."[35]

Melinda gave birth to a son, Fergus, on September 8, 1944. But she did not move to Washington until January 1945, after Donald signed a lease at 2710 Thirty-fifth Place. She never liked Washington, and eventually would regard the years they spent there the worst of her far from happy married life. She seems to have never guessed at what was locked inside Donald. Hoare, Cecil, and others found her bored by and uninterested in politics, too candid and too lacking in the quality of deceit to be her husband's co-conspirator.[36]

Donald was so rarely around the house that in frustration she complained to embassy wives that "Donald often seemed moody and preoccupied." Now that the war was over, his career was established, and he was a father, why was he unable to spend more time with his family? Why did he have to drink so much? To the Cecils, her complaints seemed endemic to diplomatic families. Cecil's own opinion when he arrived in April was that Donald's "quiet efficiency inspired confidence among his embassy colleagues."

> Working with him at this period, I was less conscious of strain and tension than I had been in Paris ten years before. He was uncommunicative, but this was nothing new. He consumed a good deal of whisky, but he was never the worse for drink when it mattered. He played a vigorous game of tennis.[37]

Melinda had always found Donald's drinking threatening. "If you do feel an urge to have a drinking orgy," she irately scolded him before they were married, "why don't you have it at home so at least you will be able to get safely to bed?" By the time he had arrived in Washington, that is precisely what he was doing. In the summer of 1945, the drinking had not progressed to a point that aroused suspicion among colleagues. But in the privacy of his home it brought out an increasing hostility towards America that at times became "savage and unrestrained."[38]

CHAPTER SIX

> . . . there are, at present, seven [Soviet] agents,
> five in British Intelligence and two in the
> Foreign Office. I know, for instance, that one
> of these agents is fulfilling the duties of Head
> of a Department of British Counter-
> Intelligence.
>
> Soviet defector Konstantin Volkov
> August 1945[1]

STALIN'S LOYALISTS

After ten years as a diplomat and a Soviet agent, Maclean still was not reconciled to being either, and his alienation from his surroundings was becoming more manifest. As a diplomat, he was part of the herd he despised. As a spy, he could no longer rail openly about the government's failed economic policies. Drink converted these feelings of arrogance, contempt, and rage into a self-loathing poison. His consumption always worsened when Melinda was away, as she was almost every summer when she abandoned Washington and its intolerably humid weather for the farm in the Berkshires. In August 1945, the combination of his being a "summer bachelor," his drinking, and his growing anti-Americanism nearly caused a diplomatic row.

The episode began just after the Potsdam Conference. A friend suggested to Joseph Alsop, the influential and socially prominent columnist, that he should meet Donald Maclean, one of the most promising stars in the British Diplomatic Service. Maclean was worth getting to know, the friend continued, because one day he would return to Washington as the British ambassador.

Alsop, bon vivant, a man of old world charm and education, cousin of Franklin Roosevelt, and one of Washington's most imposing intellectuals and frequent entertainers, invited Maclean to attend a dinner party. Actually, to say Alsop entertained is like saying that Mozart wrote music or Picasso painted. Invitations to his dinner table were among the most sought after in Washington. There was never anyone inconsequential at an Alsop gathering. Forty years later, he could not remember who else was there that night, but typically grandees from Washington's diplomatic, political, and journalistic establishment would have attended.[2]

The evening started pleasantly enough—until Maclean aggressively turned the discussion to the crisis in Iranian Azerbaijan. Iran was still occupied by 75,000 Red Army troops, even though at the Teheran Conference the Allies had agreed that all troops would be removed once Germany had been defeated. Stalin claimed that his troops were protecting Russia from a possibly belligerent Iran. The real issue, however, was Iran's fabulously rich oil fields in the Azerbaijan region. This oil, which Truman's military advisers told him "may be the only large reserve left in the world," was more productive than all the other Arab nations combined, and was only one hundred miles from Russia's equally vast Baku oil fields. Stalin's troops were the exclamation point to his earlier edict to the Teheran government that it must cede the Azerbaijan region to Russia. Although he called it a defensive buffer, what the Soviet ruler was really proposing was to slide the Soviet border two hundred miles south so that all the region's oil would fall within Stalin's domain. The more Iran protested, the more Soviet sabers rattled, leading to the crisis that Maclean injected into the conversation.[3]

Maclean had been drinking steadily throughout the evening, and started his attack against a vulnerable target—the timid and hesitant young Shah who had been installed by the Allies after they first deposed his Nazi-leaning father. Then he turned on American policy, ridiculing it as amateurish and ineffectual. A stir was beginning. Alsop was annoyed that a senior British official would openly ridicule America's refusal to let Stalin grab so strategic a target when it was the very policy being promoted by the Foreign Office.

But he said nothing. Then Maclean homed in on James Byrnes, who only weeks before had become secretary of state. "Jimmy Byrnes happens to be a very close friend of mine," Alsop snapped in his clipped Groton accent, "and I find your comments grossly offensive." Alsop was extremely conservative and forbiddingly eloquent and witty. Even sober, Maclean was no match for him—few in Washington were. But Maclean tried a rejoinder by again insulting Byrnes. Alsop rose from the table, fixed Maclean with a withering glare and, in a frigid voice, ordered him to "Please leave this house at once."

When the story reached the State Department's John D. "Jack" Hickerson, deputy director of the Office of European Affairs, he did not believe it. "I knew Maclean and I liked him," Hickerson later recalled. "He was intelligent and dependable . . . If I had called Central Casting and said, 'Send me someone to play the quintessential British diplomat,' they would have sent me Maclean." The story, Hickerson concluded, must have been embellished as it made its way around the diplomatic circuit. There is no indication that it got back to the embassy at all.[4]

Unlike Philby, Maclean never took that subtle pleasure in deception for its own sake. He was sustained instead by "a vision of himself as a statesman and a diplomat whose life had been dictated by his convictions." In the summer of 1945 he could still feel confident that he had chosen the winning side. The Red Army controlled all of Central and Eastern Europe. It was assumed that communists would triumph in France and Italy. Britain had gone socialist. And Moscow-supported insurgencies were threatening to topple the governments of Greece and Iran.[5]

Before Maclean could cast off his secret life and emerge as a member of the new ruling elite in a Soviet-controlled Europe, however, there was the problem of America. In the immediate postwar period, it seemed an even bet that the United States would wash its hands of Europe's intractable problems and revert to isolationism. But as Truman's resolve stiffened, Maclean developed a deepening hostility toward the United States. Each challenge to Moscow's expansion prolonged the need for him to maintain the highly pressurized and distasteful undercover life. "I could criticize

America," Melinda told Hoare later, "there's lots to criticize. But I do so with love and affection; Donald did so with hatred."[6]

Nor could Maclean abide Whitehall. "British diplomacy," he maintained, "bent itself to the task of persuading American opinion that a Communist take-over in Europe was imminent, of pushing the U.S. Government into the leadership of an anti-Soviet alliance, and of consolidating London's position as Washington's chief partner within it." Because he viewed his Foreign Office colleagues as the instrument of that policy, he felt further alienated from them.[7]

"I get utterly sick of the game of personalities within our own circle; everything has been said and laughed at fifty times over," he wrote Melinda late that summer. He believed his embassy colleagues had an advantage over him because they did not suffer introspection "and are in that sense *freer in their choice of view of the world*." He signed the letter, "Yours in hope, charity, and trust in the middle middle classes."[8]

★ ★ ★

Not long after the Alsop dinner party late in the summer of 1945, Konstantin Volkov marched into the British consulate general building in Istanbul and offered acting Head of Chancery John Reed information that he was sure would be of great interest to England, including keys to a Moscow flat where a suitcase was stashed with documents detailing Soviet activities directed against the British. When he returned to the embassy several days later, he handed Reed a lengthy document in Russian, which Reed translated that night.

> There are, at present, seven [Soviet] agents, five in British Intelligence and two in the Foreign Office. I know, for instance, that one of these agents is fulfilling the duties of Head of a Department of British Counter-Intelligence.[9]

Volkov was no Krivitsky. He had grown fond of the West, and he did not want to return to Russia. He wanted £27,000, a hefty sum, for his information, and he gave the British three weeks to accept his offer. He had one other demand. Moscow's British agents enabled her to "read" intercepted British government cables. All communications between Istanbul and London concerning his proposition, Volkov insisted, should be sent by diplomatic pouch.

Although Reed had no background or connection to British intelligence, he recognized the importance of what Volkov was saying. His boss, however, did not. Ambassador Sir Maurice Peterson "was one of those who nurtured a mistrust of everything connected with secret intelligence," according to Cecil, and he was not interested in allegations about Foreign Office spies. He found it distasteful that such negotiations were going on in his embassy.[10]

Besides, he had another problem. He did not want anything to do with Sir Alexander Cadogan, Permanent Under Secretary at the Foreign Office. In 1940 Peterson had been suddenly and unceremoniously removed as ambassador to Spain to make way for one of Prime Minister Chamberlain's discredited advisers. Peterson still believed it was Cadogan who had orchestrated the humiliating episode, and he now circumvented him whenever he could. If he reported Volkov's allegations and offer through the proper channels, he would have to send them to Cadogan.

Reed finally persuaded Peterson to sign a cover letter to Sir Orme Sargent, Cadogan's deputy, insisting the whole matter be turned over to the Secret Intelligence Service (SIS). Peterson agreed, and Sargent apparently complied without troubling Cadogan on the matter. Once that happened it was inevitable that Volkov's statement and Reed's notes would land on the desk of Kim Philby, who was now the head of Section IX, the anti-Soviet division of SIS. He understandably took a greater interest than the others in Volkov's allegation about Soviet agents operating inside British intelligence.

Some, but not all, of the ensuing events that led to Volkov's death can be laid at Philby's feet. But Peterson's animus toward Cadogan was certainly a contributing factor, as was the pristine attitude of Peterson and Sargent toward intelligence issues. Together they permitted Philby to take a matter that had the profoundest national security implications and convert it into a personal vendetta.

Twelve days elapsed between Volkov's first visit to the embassy and the time Philby received the envelope containing Volkov's offer. After alerting his Soviet control to this dangerous development, Philby delayed his departure from London to give the Soviets more time to grab Volkov. It was not until Monday, September 3—

eighteen days after the initial contact—that Philby was in Ankara and Reed was finally authorized to call Volkov and tell him that his offer had been accepted. The Soviet embassy, however, insisted that no person by the name of Volkov had ever been assigned to the Soviet embassy.

Years later, Reed, recalling Philby's flippant attitude, would tell British journalists, "I finally made up my mind that either Philby was criminally incompetent or he was a Soviet agent himself." But at the time he shared that sentiment with no one else. Nor was Peterson "sufficiently interested to pursue the matter."[11] It was not until after Maclean had escaped that Philby was finally questioned about the Volkov matter.[12]

★ ★ ★

On the same night that Philby returned to London from Istanbul, September 5, Igor Gouzenko, a twenty-five-year-old Red Army lieutenant in the secret cipher department at the Soviet embassy at Ottawa, was preparing to make a break. For weeks he had secretly gone through the steel safe in his office, marking cables. Now, on this hot and sultry night, with the thick lead door to Room 12 locked (not even his superiors could enter without his permission), he began to carefully stuff over one hundred documents in his shirt. Some were entire cables; others mere scraps. All chronicled the Soviet Union's spying activities directed against Canada and the United States. The airless room and jitters combined to make his body so soaked with sweat that he worried the documents would be ruined before he got outside.

To get from the second story to the main entrance on Charlotte Street, he first had to pass through checkpoints on both sides of the double steel door that sealed the secret cipher department from the rest of the embassy. If he walked too rapidly or moved too slowly he might draw the attention of a guard trained to be suspicious. Or what if there was a slight bulge in the back of his shirt? "Come here Comrade Igor," he could almost hear a jocular voice ordering. "What is that in the back of your shirt? Let's have a look." Or "Why are you sweating so much this evening Comrade? Come here and let's talk about what is bothering you."

But he drew only glances before clearing the last checkpoint.

Then, as he stood at the top of the long straight staircase, terror struck. He could hear the voice of the head of Soviet espionage operations for all of Canada coming from an office at the bottom of the stairs. Why was he there that night? Did he know? It was too late to turn back.

Gouzenko began his descent down the stairs like a condemned man. Sweat was dripping from his forehead, running off his nose. He could not reach for his handkerchief, the whole load might shift. Each step jarred the documents. He could begin to feel his shirt tail starting to fall out. He feared he would black out from sheer terror. A piece of paper was about to fall from his pants leg.

As he reached the bottom of the stairs he stared straight ahead and tried to move neither too fast nor too slowly on legs that had long since turned to jelly. At the bottom he could hear the intelligence official talking in an even voice. Gouzenko reached the door. No one had challenged him yet. He stepped outside and gulped for air.[13]

Then his real troubles began. The Canadians wanted nothing to do with him. In the first hours after he made his break, Gouzenko took his story and his documents to newspapers, the local police, Parliament, and the Justice Department. "No one wants to say anything bad about Stalin these days," Lesley Johnstone, an attractive blond journalist with *The Ottawa Journal* explained. An editor said he was too busy; the police said it was not a matter for them. This was the same outlook, according to Reed, that permeated Whitehall. "The official attitude was that we must, at all costs, accommodate the Russians and do nothing to precipitate East-West hostility." To do otherwise was to display "fascist tendencies."[14]

When Canadian Prime Minister Mackenzie King arrived at his office at 10:45 A.M. on Friday morning following the opening of the 20th Parliament, Norman Robertson, the Permanent Under Secretary of Canada's External Affairs Department, was waiting for him. In an anxious voice he described a bizarre tale about a self-proclaimed Soviet defector. That night King wrote in his diary, "I don't believe his story of their avowed treachery." By then the Soviets were charging that Gouzenko was a disgruntled employee who fled after stealing money, and the seventy-two-year-old prime minister was prepared to hand him back as a goodwill gesture.[15]

Before that could happen, however, the Royal Canadian Mounted

Police set about translating Gouzenko's documents. Saturday morning, September 7, Robertson was again waiting for King. "His voice
betrayed a tremendous concern," King later recalled, "Everything
was much worse than we would have believed." The translated
documents verified that "the Soviets have come right into our own
country to a degree that we could not have believed possible." They
had penetrated the cipher room at the Department of External
Affairs as well as Canada's atomic research laboratories, and had
stolen everything from engineering blueprints and weapons to sam-
ples of enriched uranium 235—all of which had been shipped back
to Russia.

Canada's trust was mocked. Soviet officials belligerently predicted
that "today they are our allies, tomorrow they will be our enemies."
Even U.S. Secretary of State Stettinius "had been surrounded by
spies," Robertson went on, "and the Russian government had been
kept informed of all that was being done from that source."

The prime minister no longer considered Gouzenko a crank. "It is
all very terrible and frightening," he wrote that night. It could mean
"a complete breakup of the relations we have depended upon to keep
the peace. There is no saying what terrible lengths this whole thing
might go to." Then he added, "I can see that from now until the
end of my days, it will be with this problem more than any other
that, in all probability, I shall be most closely concerned."[16]

The FBI was alerted, snapping J. Edgar Hoover out of his lethargy.
"This is our No. 1 project," he told his two top assistants, Clyde
Tolson and D.M. "Mickey" Ladd, "and every resource should be
used to run down all angles very promptly." On Monday, September
10, special FBI agents were dispatched to Ottawa. Two days later,
Hoover told the White House that Dr. Alan Nunn May, a British
nuclear physicist who had graduated from Cambridge University in
the 1930s and was sent to Canada during the war to work on the
atomic bomb project, was part of the Canadian spy ring.[17]

It was utterly appalling news. The Manhattan Project, which
designed and tested the atom bomb, successfully exploded in a test
by the United States only a month before, was one of history's
largest, most expensive, and most secretive undertakings. Yet it was
now apparent that the Soviets had succeeded in penetrating it as
early as 1943.[18]

On Saturday, September 15, Hoover notified the State Department that some evidence had surfaced in Canada suggesting (as Chambers had told Berle six years before) that a Soviet agent was at work inside the Department. No name was mentioned.[19]

Two weeks later, King flew to Washington to brief Truman and Undersecretary of State Dean G. Acheson on what his investigators had learned after twenty days of debriefing Gouzenko and studying his documents. First, Alan Nunn May, the British physicist, was very knowledgeable about some aspects of the atomic bomb project. At one time he even provided the Soviets with a sample of enriched uranium 233/235. Second, Moscow repeatedly demanded from its agents information on "the true strength of America's army" and its combat readiness. It was as if Soviet leaders regarded "the possibility of war" as certain.

Finally, there was the matter of "an assistant," who had been very close to Secretary of State Edward Stettinius. According to Gouzenko, the assistant was still able to report on high-level issues to the Soviets even after Stettinius was replaced by Byrnes in July. Truman turned to Acheson and made a comment that King interpreted as meaning that he was not surprised by what he had just heard. Acheson, who had seen Hoover's reports, corrected the prime minister. The man in question "was actually an assistant to an assistant secretary." No name was mentioned, but Acheson seemed to know to whom Gouzenko was referring. Any doubt was removed when Hoover met Acheson at the State Department on October 9. Acheson asked if Hoover "had any suspects." Hoover replied he had "no direct evidence," but that the name he had was Alger Hiss.[20]

All this came at a time when Maclean was the right-hand man of Paul Gore-Booth, the acting Head of Chancery. Because the embassy was relaying Gouzenko's information from Ottawa to London, Maclean would have been fully informed. The realization that the authorities knew about Alan Nunn May must have been a shock to Maclean second only to his discovery five years earlier of Krivitsky's revelations.[21]

Maclean and Nunn May had been contemporaries at Trinity Hall, where both had been friends of Guy Burgess. It is unlikely that Maclean had known that Nunn May was also working for the Soviets. But what if Nunn May started naming names? What if he somehow mentioned Burgess or dragged Maclean's name in as one of the radicals he had known at Cambridge? Moreover, what other information might be contained in Gouzenko's 109 messages? What if Maclean's name was mentioned? Reference was made to at least twenty-five or more spies. After all, Nunn May, like Maclean, had reported through New York.

Suddenly, for Maclean, the thrill over deceiving one's colleagues and friends and working secretly for a foreign power must have taken on a darker side. It is little wonder that his nighttime drinking sessions were becoming longer and longer.

CHAPTER SEVEN

The future spheres of three great Allied
nations meet in the triangle between the
Dardanelles, the Suez Canal and Baluchistan.

The New York Times
May 20, 1945

DRAMA AT THE DARDANELLES

Maclean performed as both saboteur of the West and adviser to
the East. As a saboteur he operated behind enemy lines,
fouling the machinery of Western foreign policy and sowing confusion and distrust among Anglo-American diplomats.[1]

As an adviser he could tell Stalin which cards the West held and
how they intended to play them during the high-stakes geostrategic
poker game that took place in the immediate postwar years. It was
in this role that he earned Moscow's unprecedented respect. The
Soviets generally held their spies in low esteem if not outright
contempt. Personal requests, mood swings, guilt, doubt, or pleas to
be released, were not tolerated. The Soviets assumed that Western
agents operated only out of fear that they would be exposed or
perhaps even liquidated if they refused to do as ordered.

"What specially impressed me at the beginning, and became later
a source of revulsion for me," a Soviet defector told a Senate
subcommittee in 1956, "was the complete lack of humaneness and
consideration by the Soviet system towards the agents of its own
intelligence service. Agents employed by the Soviets were always in

97

a position of milk-cows, once they ceased producing milk, they were sent to the slaughterhouse."[2]

Not only were Maclean's opinions on global strategy tolerated, they were solicited and received with the utmost respect. Philby knew how rare this was. During the "Homer" investigation he would see some of the reports Soviet espionage headquarters in New York sent to Moscow by or about Maclean. They "dealt with political problems of some complexity, and on more than one occasion Homer was spoken of with respect." In part this was because of his rank within the embassy where he was, according to his colleague Cecil, "admirably placed to throw light on the main question which, above all others, must have been exercising the mind of Stalin: was the post-war era to be one of American [or Soviet] hegemony . . . ?"[3]

Maclean's actions as saboteur and adviser can be clearly seen during one ten-day period in the autumn of 1945. Appropriately, his two roles were fused together during "the war of nerves" for control of the Black Sea Straits which divide East from West.

As a saboteur, Maclean created mayhem among British and U.S. diplomats, which contributed significantly to the continued erosion of the once special Anglo-American relationship. In the end, the Soviets failed to capture the Black Sea Straits, largely because the Kremlin seems to have underestimated Harry Truman's resolve. If Maclean was among those who misjudged the president, he was not alone, especially in Washington. What is ironic about his role in the showdown over the Straits, however, is that Maclean may have helped avoid a war.

The Straits have been considered a strategic prize since the Trojan War, and Stalin sought them with an obsessive frenzy. He first tried to acquire them in partnership with Hitler, who, infuriated with Stalin's insatiable territorial demands, ordered his general staff to begin planning Operation Barbarossa—the invasion of Russia. Next, Stalin pursued them as an ally. Because the Straits were still regulated by the 1936 Montreaux Convention, which included Japan as a signatory, he taunted Churchill at Yalta that surely Great Britain did not intended "to strangle Russia with the help of Japan."[4]

Why did Stalin covet them so? Passage through the Bosphorus leads nowhere except to the so-called Black Sea powers of Rumania and Bulgaria, and, of course, to Russia's shores. Even if he were allowed to build the air and naval bases as he insisted he must for protection, they would be useless against American airpower. The Straits could be blocked indefinitely by sinking commercial or war vessels (as would be demonstrated during the 1956 Suez Crisis). Therefore, although it would have been convenient to control the Straits militarily in 1945, it was hardly essential.

To appreciate Stalin's real interest, however, the Straits must be viewed from his Kremlin office. It is from here, where Russia's future was being charted, that it is possible to imagine the Russian generalissimo thinking:

Hang the Straits as a gateway to Russia's "soft underbelly," of course this is preposterous. The point is not to swing the gates closed. That would only keep Russia bottled up as it has been for centuries. No, the gates must be swung open, and the Straits will then act as the link between the arch of Russia's land mass and Europe's. And they represent access to the Northern Tier—Greece, Iran, and Turkey—and the means by which the Mediterranean and the Persian Gulf can be converted into Russian lakes. If I can force Turkey to her knees, the floodgate will be opened. Greece, Syria, Lebanon, Iraq, Palestine, and Jordan—none will be able to withstand the pressure if Turkey cannot. Britain will howl once I start. But she is finished as a power. The only issue is, will Truman try to stop me?

London and Ankara wondered the same thing. Washington seemed infuriatingly indifferent to even the most egregious Soviet efforts to intimidate Turkey into submission. The problem, however, was not so much with Truman, as it was his secretary of state.

James Byrnes had gone to the 1944 Chicago Democratic convention expecting to be Roosevelt's running mate. But opposition by labor and liberals had resulted in the last-minute nomination of a compromise candidate, the surprised and largely unwilling Truman. Byrnes felt cheated, and, after Roosevelt died, he could never accept that Harry Truman, and not he, was president. Much of official Washington felt the same way. When Truman finally yielded to public, press, and political pressure to appoint the South Carolinian secretary of state—and first in line for succession to the presidency—a relieved Senate did not hold hearings or cast a dissenting vote. With the confidence in him in such stark contrast to the low regard for Truman, Byrnes came to believe that he, not the president, was the supreme authority for the conduct of U.S. foreign policy. Dismissing Truman as an intruder, he ignored the issues he took a strong interest in, such as the Black Sea Straits.[5]

Yet, although Byrnes was a veteran of twenty-five years in Congress, as well as a former Associate Justice of the Supreme Court and Roosevelt's Director of War Mobilization, he had little experience in foreign affairs. He also had an exaggerated notion of his negotiating skills, boasting to friends that he would use the same arm-twisting techniques with Molotov as he had with Republicans in the Senate cloak room. As it turned out, Molotov toyed with him.[6]

Both before and after Potsdam, the Soviets turned the screws directly on the Turks, demanding that they inform the Allies that the Straits issue would be resolved exclusively between Russia and Turkey; that they cede to the Soviet Union two ancient Turkish provinces; and that Ankara permit Soviet air and naval bases on the Straits, essentially surrendering their control to Moscow.[7]

The Turks refused all such bullying. For centuries the Straits had been a bone of contention between sultan and czar, and Ankara was prepared to go to war, or so they claimed, before acquiescing to Soviet demands. What Ankara could not comprehend, Foreign Minister Saracoglu complained to American Ambassador Edwin C. Wilson, was Washington's impassivity and naive hope "for mutual Turkish-Soviet understanding."[8]

Wilson agreed. "The question of the Straits as raised by USSR is mere pretense behind which lies real Soviet objective namely domination of Turkey," he warned Byrnes in a September cable. The Soviets were trying to convert Turkey into a satellite, control the Straits, end the Anglo-Turkish alliance, and extinguish "western liberal influences in the Middle East."[9]

The State Department's aloofness soon vanished. On October 9 Byrnes received a cable from George Kennan in Moscow that the British, French, and American embassies all had reports "from Soviet and other contacts to the effect that Russian people are being told by internal party agitators that the USSR may go to war with Turkey." Kennan and his fellow diplomats viewed the rumors as "part of refined war of nerves designed to soften up Turks."[10]

The next day an aroused G.L. McDermott—who had finished

immediately behind Maclean in the Foreign Office exam in 1935—
told his Foreign Office colleagues, "We first must try to clear up the
question of how the American minds are working." "Perhaps," a
colleague minuted forlornly, "Mr. Truman will have a further word
to say."[11]

Indeed he did. Where the Straits were concerned, Truman was like
a dog with a bone; he would not let go. He had seized upon the issue
at Potsdam with a singular passion. As Churchill fidgeted in embarrassment and Stalin looked on in silent mortification, the former
haberdasher, court house politician, senator, vice president (for all
of eighty-three days), and amateur historian unveiled his theory that
to prevent wars from breaking out over disputed waterways—like
the Black Sea Straits—they should all be internationalized. This
proposal so rattled Stalin that without waiting for the translation he
burst out "Nyet! No, I say no!" Amazed Westerners realized not
only that Truman had hit a sore spot, but that the pockmarked old
dictator could both understand and speak English. "Stalin wants the
Black Sea Straits for Russia," Truman observed at the end of the day,
"as have all the Tsars before him."[12]

Aware that the State Department was doing little, on October 13
Truman reproached Byrnes with a handwritten note. "I am of the
opinion if some means isn't found to prevent it, the Russians will
undoubtedly take steps by direct action to obtain control of the
Black Sea Straits." He instructed Byrnes to come up with a plan to
keep the Soviets at bay.[13]

Truman's note caught Byrnes off guard. In a further insult, he also
discovered the next day that the president's foreign policy antennae
were more intuitive than his own. A cable from Wilson in Ankara
reported that large numbers of Soviet trucks, tanks, and planes were
being concentrated along the Russo-Turkish border. Villagers on the
Turkish side of the ancient fortified town of Kars—one of the areas
that the Soviets were demanding be ceded to them—voiced the
opinion that the area "would not be part of Turkey much longer."
The Turks, Wilson cautioned, were as defiant as the Poles had been
in August 1939. "We would rather die on Turkish soil," one normally
staid diplomat told him, "than be deported to Siberia."[14] On October 19 the State Department rushed a plan to the White House that
Truman approved and returned the next day with the admonition to

"keep pushing the program so as to prevent Russia from taking over the Straits."[15]

The British also had a plan. Clement Attlee—who became prime minister after British voters unceremoniously swept Winston Churchill off the world stage in the middle of the Potsdam Conference—still harbored notions of maintaining the Mediterranean as a British lake. But, determined to avoid any conflict, he did not want to play his hand until the Americans showed their cards.

His Foreign Minister Ernest Bevin—who, in the best Churchillian fashion, forewarned that "the Russians are reaching across our throats [trying] to sever the British Empire's jugular at the Suez Canal"—looked to the Washington embassy to ensure Allied unity. "I think we must make another determined effort to discover how the American minds are working," he cabled Ambassador Halifax on Sunday, October 21. "Please try to persuade the United States Government to agree to the principle of consultations with us on this matter and to obtain their reaction to my views."[16]

On Tuesday, Halifax, pleading that "Bevin was very anxious about this," pressed Byrnes to allow the British to review the American plan unofficially before it was submitted to the Turks. Byrnes reluctantly agreed. It was a decision that Maclean would cause him to bitterly regret.[17]

A sense of urgency gripped the department the following morning after a cable arrived from Ambassador Averell Harriman in Moscow warning Byrnes that:

> Soviet policy toward Turkey will continue to be result of Moscow's estimate of need for expansion into Turkey as calculated against probable resistance such expansion would encounter from Turkey and degree of support from Britain and USA.

Hours later Loy Henderson sent the American policy statement to Michael Wright at the embassy. Now the director of the Office of Near Eastern and African Affairs, Henderson had previously told Halifax that "I attach great importance to our working completely hand in hand" on the Straits.[18]

Maclean's task for the Soviets was to separate the noble rhetoric championing Turkish sovereignty from the West's underlying willingness to go to war to deny Russia the Straits. With access to the cables of private conversations taking place in Ankara, London, and Washington, he was excellently positioned to do this. But he was also to play the role of the saboteur.

When Maclean joined Wright in analyzing the American proposal, they quickly discovered a conflict. The Americans envisaged the Straits being governed by the so-called Black Sea Powers—Turkey, Russia, Bulgaria, and Rumania. This would isolate Turkey, which would be outvoted by the Soviet Union and her two satellites, while Washington and London would be excluded from any meaningful role, even in time of war.

Maclean and Wright immediately telephoned Henderson to ask that he refrain from sending the paper to Wilson and the Turkish government for several days so that they could alert Bevin to the problem. Henderson and then Byrnes both agreed. At 1:17 P.M., as Russian troop trains were moving into Rumania toward Turkey and Red Army troops were massing on the Bulgarian-Turkish border, Maclean dispatched the American proposal to Bevin at the Foreign Office, where it was received at 7:30 P.M. London time. But Maclean, in violation of the agreement Henderson thought he had with the embassy, also sent a copy of the American proposal to the British embassies in both Ankara and Moscow.[19]

The following Tuesday, in an article datelined from London, *The New York Times*'s C.L. Sulzberger reported learning "on excellent authority" that the British and American governments were collaborating on a proposal for the Straits so that, in combination with the Turkish government, they could confront the Soviets. The very next day Molotov, citing *The New York Times* article, angrily blasted Britain and America for anti-Soviet collusion. These accusations were still reverberating through the State Department the following morning when Byrnes faced a packed press conference that quickly turned into an inquisition. Did Molotov have a legitimate complaint? *Were* Britain and America ganging up on the Soviets? How did U.S. interests in the Straits differ from Britain's?[20]

Byrnes kept digging himself in deeper. He said with only the smallest grain of truth that "the American government is without information concerning the plan of the British or Soviet governments in this connection." He further insisted that "it was a mistake to suppose that the U.S. government and His Majesty's Government had put forward a joint proposal." This, again, was true. But Byrnes then denied that there had even been "joint consultations with the British"—which was not true.[21]

Fuming, Byrnes stalked out of the press conference to his office and called Halifax. In a frosty southern drawl, the Secretary pointed out that events had "borne out his fear of sending [Bevin] his proposed communications in advance." Not only had the leak given Molotov immediate ammunition, but the story and Molotov's reaction had aroused the would-be foreign policy experts on Capitol Hill and the White House—antagonists such as Henry Wallace and Senator Claude Pepper and many others to whom the "danger of appearing to the Soviets to be endeavoring to make common front is taken seriously." Halifax, shaken, stammered an apology and promised that His Majesty's government would investigate the leak.[22]

Later that same day George V. Allen, Loy Henderson's deputy in the Near East Bureau, called Maclean ostensibly to advise him that the State Department had adopted British revisions for "Principle 3." This had been at the heart of British-American differences because it defined access to the Straits by warships of non–Black Sea powers, including in time of war. But Allen's real purpose was to echo Byrnes's complaint about "the very unfortunate" *New York Times* leak. It had occurred, he likewise emphasized, only because of "the British request to see our proposals in advance." Unfazed, Maclean solemnly decreed the leak "could not have occurred in the British Foreign Office." Why? Because it was "Mr. Bevin's policy to not give the Russians any basis for feeling that they are being confronted by a united Anglo-American position." And since no one at the Foreign Office would disobey Mr. Bevin's wishes, none would have provided a leak—let alone a false one—that would give the Russians such suspicions. But, Maclean grimly continued, if the leak did come from the Foreign Office, the State Department could be assured that "strong disciplinary action would be taken."[23]

To the thin, intense Allen, about to be named ambassador to Iran, Maclean's response may have seemed a puzzling non sequitur. But it was more an expression of Maclean's private scorn. Years later in Moscow he and Philby would sit around "swapping stale anecdotes about their past and laughing at how they had fooled everyone."

Maclean was often the instigator. "Remember old so-and-so?" he would ask Philby, and "They would laugh heartily over the tricks that they had played on him."[24]

Stonewalling Allen on the leak, however, was nothing compared with the grief Maclean brought Wilson. As has been noted, Maclean not only sent the American proposal to London—as had been agreed—but, contrary to the ground rules Henderson assumed were being observed, he also sent a copy to Sir Maurice Peterson, the British ambassador in Ankara. Peterson in turn flaunted it in front of Wilson at a meeting that was painfully awkward for the American ambassador. He had not been consulted on the plan and had never even seen it; besides, he did not like Peterson.

After their meeting, Peterson almost gloated to London, "I showed a knowledge of the American position that Wilson did not himself apparently possess." Wilson, a man of calm, unflappable dignity, composed a stinging cable to Washington. In the most acid terms he expressed his resentment at "receiving from the British Ambassador my first information concerning important proposals made by my own government."[25]

When Wilson finally did receive the proposal on the afternoon of Tuesday, October 30, he was told he would have the final word on it before it was transmitted to the Turkish Foreign Office. Convinced that it had some major flaws, he began to draft alternative language. But four hours later he received an urgent telegram from Byrnes instructing him to immediately deliver as drafted the proposal to the Turkish Foreign Office. It was only later that Wilson, alarmed and discouraged by the confusion emanating from the State Department, learned that panic over the leak in *The New York Times* had accounted for the second cable.[26]

But Wilson's roller coaster ride did not end there. On Saturday November 3, Byrnes instructed him to present the American proposal to Soviet Ambassador Sergei A. Vinogradov. Times were tense. Three more Red Army divisions had recently moved from Czechoslovakia into Rumania towards Bulgaria, and Turkey was rushing to get troops into place, fearing that "transportation facilities could be disrupted by initial bombing."[27]

Wilson expected a very brief and formal session. Under Stalin not even Molotov would respond to a Western proposal until the two of them had sniffed at it like bloodhounds, trying to find the foul odor of concealed traps, hidden ramifications, and unacceptable advantages for the West. Only then would the Kremlin line be set and an ambassador instructed on precisely what to say, what to ask, and how to follow up. Until then, a diplomat "would rather have bitten off his tongue than say something he had not been authorized to say." And, because the American embassy had been instructed not to deliver a copy to the Soviet Foreign Office until after Wilson had finished with Vinogradov, there was little to do now but hand the proposal over and wait for Moscow to react.[28]

Vinogradov took the document and immediately began scanning it. After only moments he looked up at Wilson and demanded to know the intent of Principle 3—the very point that Maclean had raised several days before. "What would be the situation in time of war?" Vinogradov demanded. Before Wilson could respond, Vinogradov blasted the whole proposal. It placed Russia's security in Turkey's hands, he sneered, when "Turkey is too weak" to carry out its obligation under the plan. How could Turkey prevent the passage of warships of non–Black Sea Powers through the Straits in time of war? Then with "bitterness and hostility" he "denounced" Turkey's war record. This was dismaying. If Moscow had not seen the proposal how could the Soviet ambassador be so completely familiar with its contents and already instructed on what to say?[29]

Wilson returned to his office unnerved. In all his years in the diplomatic service he had never seen such bizarre and incomprehensible behavior as he had in his recent exchanges with Peterson and Vinogradov. How had both obtained advance copies of what should have been a sensitive and closely held document?

Wilson, chosen by a *Fortune* magazine survey as America's ablest ambassador, responded in what, particularly for him, was a highly unusual fashion. He took out a sheet of plain white writing paper and a fountain pen and composed the first of two personal and confidential letters to Henderson intended to bypass all official channels. Something had gone seriously wrong with the once reliable machinery of British-American foreign policy, and he wanted to know what. Everything seemed rushed, ill-conceived, vague, sloppy. The net result was that the Soviets' advantage had been enhanced. How, Wilson asked, had an issue so fundamental to

American security interests become such a fiasco? Whence did *The New York Times* leak come? Was Anglo-American foreign policy as strained as it appeared from Ankara?[30]

Henderson placed Wilson's letters, but not his reply, in the department's files, so there is no way of knowing what explanations he offered. But he, like Byrnes and Acheson, placed the blame for all the confusion on the trust they placed in the British embassy. No one was mollified by Maclean's assurance that Bevin was "having the leak investigated."[31]

A rigorous follow-up would have found Maclean's fingerprints all over this case. He sent Peterson the American plan; he discussed with the State Department all the points raised by Vinogradov; and most grating of all, he handled the cable that was the basis for much of the Sulzberger article.

For Washington the leak ended any possibility of a united Anglo-American position. It left Whitehall paralyzed. "I do not propose to make any communications to the Turkish Government," Bevin advised Halifax. This meant the only Western proposal on the table was the American one, which the British and the Turks considered ill-conceived.[32]

The distrust resulting from the mishandling of the American paper and the subsequent leak were more hammer blows to Anglo-American relations. The leak "will certainly increase American reluctance to share their intimate thought with us," a demoralized Halifax admitted to Bevin. It caused the British to doubt themselves. "I naturally cannot tell if we are to blame for this leakage," Halifax continued, "but on such evidence as I have got it rather looks as if Sulzberger must have got it from us."[33] Halifax's despair was justified. As one historian pointed out years later, "the leak had been one of many which created doubts about the reliability of the United Kingdom to share secrets."[34]

Not that Maclean had to worry about any Foreign Office follow-up. His colleagues had come to resent American insinuations that the leak was their fault—despite the fact that Halifax agreed. Cadogan told Sargent on November 7 that "even if we were to know how it occurred, I do not see that we should say anything to Byrnes." After all, he snidely added, "We told him we would investigate the matter, but not that we would tell him the result."[35]

The Foreign Office regarded Byrnes as a weak and insecure man, who, to satisfy American public opinion, could be relied upon to be anti-British. According to Kennan, Bevin saw Byrnes as "another cocky and unreliable Irishman" who was "negligent of British feelings and quite unconcerned for Anglo-American relations." Many inside the Foreign Office chortled over his tumultuous October 31 press conference. If Parliament were to similarly press the government over the issue of British-American collaboration on the Straits, Assistant Under Secretary Neville Butler delightfully mused, "We shall either have to show off Mr. Byrnes's lie or tell one ourselves."[36]

★   ★   ★

Turkey and Iran would continue as the major crises through the awful year of 1946—when the world seemed constantly on the brink of war. Moscow's harangues and troop movements forced Turkey to remain on constant war footing, which—as Moscow hoped—caused such economic hardship that it threatened a collapse from within. This strategy was outlined in an aide-mémoire that Maclean delivered to the State Department as the crisis entered its second year:

> Soviet leaders probably appreciate that a most effective means of exerting pressure with Turkey is by the promotion of economic difficulties within the country. It is, therefore, in the Soviet Union's interest to force the economic burden of continual mobilization on Turkey and to continue the nerve war.[37]

He argued forcefully at State Department meetings that "we can hardly tell the Turks in view of Russia's attitude to go ahead with demobilization. We should therefore propose to them they should keep up their present degree of mobilization."[38]

Before long, the per capita amount of Turkey's national budget spent on defense was the highest in the world—one-third of the government's total expenditures—and managed only by cutting sharply such departments as Public Works and Hygiene. The "Kremlin is not unaware," the American embassy in Ankara concluded, of the "effect [of] heavy strain placed on Turkish economy by maintenance of armed forces in heavy mobilized condition."[39]

Truman refused to stand down. During a scolding he gave Byrnes in January, Truman again warned that "there isn't a doubt in my mind that Russia intends an invasion of Turkey and the seizure of the Black Sea Straits." And Bevin warned the House of Commons in February, "It is said that we are drifting into war with Russia." He hoped it could be avoided, but "I must really be frank and say that I do not want Turkey converted into a satellite state."[40]

Ultimately, because both Turkey and the United States stood stronger than Moscow anticipated, the Soviets received a setback. And perhaps a case can be made that if Maclean helped Stalin to realize that Truman was absolutely not bluffing when he vowed the Soviets would not be allowed to grab the Straits by force, he may have played a role, albeit an unknowing and unintentional one, in helping to preserve peace.

The final word on this episode comes from Loy Henderson. When he realized five years later that Maclean had probably been a Soviet spy while in Washington, he reacted with a bitterness he carried to his grave. In an interview months before his death in 1986, the ninety-three-year-old patriarch of America's foreign service was asked if he recalled Maclean's actions at the time. Pale, emaciated, hardly able to speak, he struggled as he searched his failing memory. Finally in a frail voice he answered, "Maclean . . . Maclean . . . the name has a foul odor."[41]

CHAPTER EIGHT

The formula . . . if published, will be
misconstrued by both the people of the United
States and by foreign countries, particularly
Russia.

Brigadier General Lincoln about a formula for
air and naval bases which was given to Donald
Maclean[1]

TRAGICALLY HARMFUL NEWS

During their December 1989 weekend meeting at Malta, Soviet President Mikhail Gorbachev stressed Kremlin anxiety by presenting President Bush "with a map showing the Soviet Union surrounded by U.S. military bases." The point, according to a Kremlin spokesman, was that "the Americans must understand that we feel a bit insecure surrounded by all these bases." The map, observers say, was drawn up by the KGB.[2]

Some things do not change even under *glasnost*. Joseph Stalin was even more anxious about those bases than Gorbachev, and the KGB map given to Bush was probably not that different from the one Maclean provided to Soviet intelligence some forty years before. In February 1946 Maclean spent over a week on the British island of Bermuda negotiating Atlantic base rights with U.S. officials. Hamilton's climate proved much more hospitable than was the case for Gorbachev and Bush. But the sessions at the Belmont Manor Hotel were held much more frequently, lasted much longer, and lacked the camaraderie of the "seasick summit." In fact, though Melinda, five months pregnant with their second son, could spend her days at the beach, Donald was closeted for eight days in a hotel conference room for the long and frequently stormy negotiating sessions over military and civilian base rights.[3]

Maclean had to return to Washington as soon as the conference ended on Friday, February 15. Michael Wright, the Head of Chancery and the embassy's point man on base negotiations, was about to take two weeks leave before being reassigned to Southeast Asia. Maclean had been designated acting Head of Chancery, with a special writ "to keep a watch" on the base negotiations until the Foreign Office sent out a permanent replacement, which turned out not to be until December.[4]

In the intervening ten months, Maclean's influence was felt in almost every phase of the embassy's operations, including copying, assigning, and distributing all incoming and outgoing cable traffic, conducting security briefings, and overseeing the renovation of the cable room.[5]

He represented Halifax at the highest levels, not only drafting but also signing cables in the ambassador's name to the Foreign Office and even the State Department. On March 9, 1946, for instance, he sent a "Top Secret/Immediate" British aide-mémoire to Byrnes and signed it, "D.D. Maclean, For the Ambassador." On another occasion, a worried Halifax called Maclean to rescind his order to send some top-secret papers on the U.S. military to the British Joint Supply Mission. Maclean followed through with such swiftness it seems impossible he had ever intended to carry out the original order.[6]

The most pressing items on the embassy's agenda at the time were efforts by the British to obtain from the Americans a desperately needed loan, while resisting relentless American pressure for British base concessions on the far-flung islands, territories, and colonies that constituted Britain's fading empire. Initially, the two issues proceeded on separate tracks. After impatient American lawmakers put them on a single path, Maclean tried to manipulate the base and loan negotiations to force a collision between the two.

The issue of bases had been a festering wound in the Anglo-American relationship since Roosevelt and Churchill had haggled over them during the grim days of 1940 and 1941. When the Prime Minister insisted that the acquisition of fifty World War I-vintage destroyers was "a matter of life and death," Roosevelt was equally emphatic that insurmountable legal and political barriers made the transaction impossible. Finally, Roosevelt suggested that the deal could be swung if America received ninety-nine-year-leases on British possessions in the Atlantic and Caribbean for the construction of U.S. military bases. Churchill reluctantly agreed, but, for the remainder of the war, a current of suspicion ran through Whitehall that the United States was exploiting Britain's dire situation to pick up an empire on the cheap.[7]

By 1944, the British possessions were becoming an American preoccupation. As Marines were fighting island by island toward Japan, Texas Congressman George Mahon warned "those bases have been bought with American blood and money; the American flag should never be hauled down from them." And Roosevelt's top military adviser, Admiral William Leahy, told the Congress that conquest of the Japanese-controlled islands was being accomplished by the United States and "there appears to be no valid reason why their future should be the subject of discussion with any other nation." America's Manifest Destiny "is bigger than we are," the once isolationist *Chicago Tribune* chimed in. "If we are to accept the responsibility Destiny has thrust upon us, we must have those naval and air bases."[8]

The Leahy memorandum that Maclean intercepted in May 1944 confirmed a Joint Chiefs of Staff (JCS) decision, with or without Roosevelt's concurrence, to "go after bases world wide." FDR either did not know about or did not object to the JCS recommendation that Southeast Asia remain under British and French influence in anticipation of more generous base concessions.[9]

Nor was Truman any shrinking violet on the issue. When Secretary of War Stimson asked what he intended to do with the strategically important British-administered, American-occupied Pacific islands, Truman replied without hesitation, "We will keep them."

"Forever?" Stimson asked.

"That depends," the president answered. "As long as we need them."[10]

That could have been for a long time because, at the end of February 1946, Navy Secretary James Forrestal sent a top-secret memo to Byrnes advising him that "the Joint Chiefs of Staff considers it essential to our national defense that the United States has exclusive control of a number of bases in the Atlantic and Pacific." This perception was shaped by the military strategy used to defeat Germany and Japan, and by the political assumption that, in the next year, the Soviets would be the enemy. This meant that Pacific islands, along with such Atlantic outposts as Greenland and the Azores, would serve as forward bases from which long-range American bombers could strike Russia, as well as "stepping stones" for getting relief supplies to Europe.[11]

The State Department was equally aggressive. At a Council of Foreign Ministers meeting, Byrnes rendered Bevin almost speechless after turning and asking with a trace of annoyance, "Why do you wish to retain the Bahamas?"[12]

Maclean's instructions from London were to "find out from the Americans what sort of use they propose to make of each of these bases, Naval, and Air," and what their "broad Politico-military policy" will be. And, because London had decided in October "to take up the matter of bases through the embassy at Washington," Maclean had even greater latitude than usual.[13]

On the morning of March 13, 1946, he led a delegation of senior military and diplomatic officials from Britain, New Zealand, and Australia to meet with an American team led by Jack Hickerson, deputy director of the Office of Europe Affairs. The diminutive and feisty Hickerson always made London nervous. As the European Division's indispensable man and its institutional memory, he preferred to use banter and wit rather than the obsequiousness of diplomatic conventions.[14]

A British colleague later described how Hickerson, "perched forward on the edge of his chair would dispose of difficulties, drastically, like a man swatting flies, and when confronted with new suggestions he would welcome them eagerly in the manner of an auctioneer receiving bids."[15] "It would be better and would create a good public atmosphere," he had recently explained to a startled Sir John "Jock" Balfour, minister at the British embassy, "if without exchanging claims and counterlcimas" over several British islands in the Pacific, "the United Kingdom were to agree to forgo their sovereignty and just hand them over." Because he was so close to Acheson, all Hickerson's remarks were reported back to the Foreign

Office, which was rarely amused. They feared the banter reflected a serious chasm between U.S. and British policymakers—and they were right.[16]

The next several days were a bonanza for Maclean and the Soviets. Once the preliminaries were over, R.L. Dennison, the assistant chief of naval operations and head of politico-military affairs, "read the full list of the desires of the Joint Chiefs of Staff with reference to base rights in the Pacific Islands." At another session "actual post-war plans with respect to [bases] were covered in detail."[17] Finally, it was agreed that Maclean and Hickerson would continue the negotiations alone. It was during these sessions that Hickerson, who for fifteen years had dealt with some of the West's ablest diplomats, got to know Maclean. "Donald was one of the best of the British diplomats," he recalled wistfully years later. "He would have been an ambassador, maybe to Washington. He would have been knighted."[18]

Maclean set the pace of their meetings with a steady drumbeat of questions. What were Washington's overall needs? What terms were they prepared to offer for which bases? What would be the U.S. response if any base arrangements were challenged as violating the U.N. Charter? How would joint Anglo-American control work? Which nation would have which rights in time of war? He was not deterred, even when it became apparent that his endless questions were beginning to exasperate the action-oriented Hickerson.[19]

Hickerson, however, appreciated Maclean's efforts at wit—though they often fell wide of the mark—and he always assumed that Maclean was just doing his job. So he was surprised years later to discover that, throughout their talks, Maclean was filing reports with London that imputed an unfriendliness to their meetings and a hostility toward Hickerson's responses. "They say there would be joint control," Maclean complained, yet "in the same breath [they] say we cannot exercise these rights except under the direction and regulation of the Americans. This seems an absurdity."

Whether or not it was calculated, the effect of Maclean's gloomy assessment was to fuel Foreign Office resentment. "The U.S. is treating us like a country which has suffered a decline from its former position," one official complained, "and which can be ignored or patronized when convenient."[20]

Of course, England had declined, and Whitehall was already recasting Britain's postwar role as an Athens exercising a calming influence on Washington's inexperienced, muscle-bound Rome. Joint control of bases, for instance, could require British permission before America could launch its bombers to strike the Soviet Union. It was a restraint Moscow was eager to see applied. Maclean consequently homed in on joint base control as he had "Principle 3" during negotiations over the Black Sea Straits. "The problem" he complained to London, "is that [the American position] does not say who would have control if both sides felt—*as was likely*—a state of hostility existed."[21]

As negotiations between Maclean and Hickerson dragged out, more was being affected than merely America's resolve to acquire a global string of strategically connected air and naval bases. England was bankrupt, unable to provide fuel or food for her battle-weary citizens. Since September, Britain had been almost begging for what John Maynard Keynes initially termed a $6 billion dollar "grant-in-aid" to jump-start her torpid economy. But America—racked by labor strikes, layoffs, insufficient consumer goods, high wartime taxes, and frequent price increases—was not interested.

Bernard Baruch, the self-promoting "adviser to the presidents," expressed popular sentiment, if not sage wisdom, when he said that America should first take care of its needs and then, if there was something left over, consider a loan. Why, the argument went, should an American soldier who fought the Germans or the Japanese have to pay higher interest rates for a house than England would for a loan? Jobs and prosperity, not more charity, dominated American minds. Besides, the American public had built up an abiding affection for Churchill, who had been unceremoniously dumped from office by unappreciative British voters, lulled by the Socialists' utopian promises. And Congress was loathe to subsidize socialism.[22]

"The idea that America is used as a Santa Claus by an ungrateful and largely undeserving world still flourishes luxuriantly here and in the present Administration," Isaiah Berlin cautioned from Washington. Gone were Morgenthau, Hopkins, and others who had an admiring gratitude for Britain's courage in standing alone against Hitler. A new get-tough-with-the-British attitude pervaded the Truman crowd.[23]

In December Washington finally agreed to a $3.75 billion loan at 2.5 percent interest. This does not sound like much today, but 2.5 percent would require the British to pay $200 million a year just to service the loan. Yet, her exports in the prewar years averaged only $150 million per year. Not only were there almost no exports after the war, but England was importing virtually everything.[24]

The British public was inflamed. Had they not given disproportionately in the fight against the Nazis? Lend-lease began in March 1941. What about England's contribution, they asked, beginning in September 1939? Roosevelt had always talked about giving her a chance to get back on her feet before trying to settle accounts. Charging interest smacked of war-profiteering.

The papers called it "an economic Munich." Its "harsh terms" treated Britain "like a defeated nation" made to "grovel like a beggar." Prime Minister Attlee was accused of "selling the British Empire for a pack of cigarettes." In Parliament the agreement was called "niggardly, barbaric and antediluvian." "The Americans," the Foreign Office reluctantly concluded, "have at last produced a formula which bears every sign of being unacceptable."[25]

The problem, however, was not in producing an agreement acceptable to Whitehall, but to Congress. And much more than England's economic health was at issue. If either Britain or America turned down the loan, the whole Bretton Woods agreement, including establishment of the World Bank and the International Monetary Fund, would collapse. "It was clear grave matters hung in the balance."[26]

American lawmakers, however, were not cowed by the high stakes. The debate on the loan was conducted in an "atmosphere of defeatism and pessimism." America, they complained, was once again being asked to pull British chestnuts out of the fire, to come to the rescue of a "decadent Empire."[27]

"The problem with the British loan," Senator Arthur Vandenberg, the ranking Republican on the Senate Foreign Relations Committee whispered to Ambassador Halifax at a White House ceremony, "is that then we would have to make loans to a lot of others including the Russians." What "gadgets" the Wisconsin senator wondered, "could make the British loan look different from" requested loans for France, Russia, China, or the Philippines?

Before Halifax could respond, Vandenberg, the staunch isolationist turned crusading internationalist, answered his own question. "What about converting the ninety-nine-year military leases America holds on British territories to 999-year leases as a 'sweetener' for the loan?" Under this formula Britain would give America the islands as a gift, or at least cede unrestricted military rights. Any hesitancy would be taken as a sign of British ingratitude for the $14 billion in lend-lease aid, and dampen all enthusiasm for further financial aid.[28]

The British had little choice. Another crushing setback might so exacerbate the grim domestic scene that an eruption of violence "of a kind unknown" to the island nation might result. "Many precious features of our civilization might be lost," Keynes's biographer added. There was no time to waste. If the loan was going to jumpstart their feeble economy it would have to come fast. Finally, on January 30, 1946, Truman sent the $3.75 billion loan request to Congress loaded, as Assistant Secretary of State Will Clayton phrased it, "with all the conditions the traffic would bear."[29]

Not enough so far as the Senate was concerned. A gaggle of lawmakers started drafting competing amendments to force ever greater British base concessions. This gave Maclean the opportunity to score a double whammy for the Soviets. From Stalin's viewpoint the best outcome would be no bases for the Americans and no loan for the British. Even better would be a militarily thwarted America and an economically paralyzed England, with each blaming the other for their condition.

Maclean did his part. Over the years Cecil thought he had become "hardened," and Hoare saw a side to him that was "cold." Those are the qualities he needed for this assignment. Britons were enduring great hardship and suffering deprivations in their daily lives. A drought had led to crop failures, and, a year after the war had ended, there were shortages of wheat, rice, sugar, fats, and starches; food was still being rationed. Food supplies and ships were plentiful, but Britain could not pay for them. Everything depended, said the Minister of Food, himself a target of intense public criticism, "on whether we get the loan from the United States."[30]

However much he despised the abstraction of the British nation, Maclean could not have been oblivious to the fact that his mother, his sister, and his surviving brother (Ian, the oldest, was killed in the war) were among those who were suffering. Yet he worked to undermine the loan that would have provided them relief.

He did this by continuing to drag out the base negotiations. At one point he even asked if the United States was prepared to grant the Royal Air Force reciprocal rights to American bases in the Pacific. Hickerson cringed. "It would be embarrassing if such a request were made." Finally, Byrnes had had enough.

"It would be of great assistance to the cause of the British loan," he wrote to Bevin directly on April 19, if an agreement on military bases could be signed "in the next two or three weeks." He was urging this "solely because of the present state of the British loan negotiations," by which he meant that the loan was still languishing. As a somewhat miffed Hickerson explained to Maclean, "We're just trying to get you to take your bows now for something you're going to do anyway." Included in the April 19 communiqué was an American "wish list" for bases that Hickerson handed to Maclean.[31]

As both the official responsible for day-to-day base negotiations, and as acting Head of Chancery, it was Maclean's responsibility to see to it that London responded promptly to Byrnes's pronouncement. Perhaps it should not be surprising that it was never answered. Considering the circumstances, however, it seems extraordinary that a direct personal appeal from the American Secretary of State to the British Foreign Secretary could be ignored without alarms being set off.

Perhaps the British later attributed it to an understandable lapse given all their other problems; in any case, the Senate and the State Department were not the only ones growing impatient. A week later, at the Conference of Commonwealth Prime Ministers, Herbert V. Evatt, Australia's Minister for External Affairs, decided to by-pass the foot-dragging British, and proposed "an Australia-New Zealand-U.S. defense board." This came as a shock to the British, who were still trying to enhance their bargaining position by claiming to represent Commonwealth interests as well as their own. But the obstinate Evatt had not even consulted Britain, let alone included it in the proposed pact.[32]

The Americans were even more horrified than the British by this turn of events. The Australian proposal called for nothing less than the integration of their military forces into a binding military alliance with America. Since the time of George Washington it was a sacred feature of American foreign policy to never enter into peacetime alliances. The administration had no intention of enduring the political paroxysm that such a suggestion would cause on Capitol Hill even if it were interested in the proposal, which it was not.

The formula, if published, Byrnes's military adviser Brigadier General George A. Lincoln warned, "will be misconstrued by both the people of the United States and by foreign countries, particularly Russia." Not only was the Australian scheme political folly, it was "strategically unsound [and] contrary to the accepted military concept of the Joint Chiefs of Staff." It had "inherent dangers" that would weaken the United Nations and accelerate "the generation of two world regions—one Russian and one U.S.-British."[33]

Byrnes, in Paris for a meeting of the Council of Foreign Ministers, was so nervous that word of Evatt's plan might leak out that he implored Bevin to take all possible precautions. Bevin, one of England's most security-conscious foreign secretaries in years, "immediately telephoned London to prevent this."[34]

The next morning, May 2, Maclean went to Hickerson's State Department office to brief him on Evatt's proposal. (Britain's communications always worked swifter than America's.) Hickerson was not surprised. He had hinted before that the United States and the Commonwealth nations might decide to bypass Britain. But his usual humor deserted him when Maclean demanded to know whether the United States would abandon its traditional bias against peacetime military alliances as the price for acquiring bases.

"No," the usually unflappable Hickerson snapped. "Who are [Australia and New Zealand] worried about?" he demanded in return. "We'll make sure Japan isn't a threat. Who's left? Do they think Siam is going to launch an invasion?"

"Perhaps," Maclean calmly replied, "Mr. Byrnes should go to London and sell the United States proposals to the Dominion's Prime Ministers."[35]

When he returned to the embassy, Maclean sent Hickerson a copy of Evatt's plan:

Washington, 2 May 1946

TOP SECRET

Dear Jack:

As agreed at our conversation this morning I send you forthwith, for your personal information, the text of the formula about Pacific Bases which Paul Mason handed to Doc Matthews in Paris on 1st May.

Mason made an explanatory statement to Doc who said he would refer the matter to Mr. Byrnes. Mr. Bevin hopes to discuss it with Mr. Byrnes at an early opportunity.

As our approach was made in Paris and as further discussion is to take place there you were kind enough to agree to regard our conversation this morning as entirely informal.

Yours ever,

D.D. Maclean[36]

With a Senate vote on the loan nearing, Whitehall implored the U.S. government to say nothing further about Britain's attitude toward base concessions. Harriman reported from London that "the British decided no public statement could in dignity be made" as the Senate prepared for debate. A misstatement might "arouse passions" on either side of the Atlantic that could prove "fatal" to the loan.[37]

The apprehension was well founded. A number of amendments were offered during a turbulent ten-hour Senate night session, all of which required various concessions from the British. Finally, at 10:45 p.m. the MacFarland Amendment was called. It would have required the British to relinquish several Atlantic bases. A packed gallery "to the point where visitors crowded against the back walls and filled the aisles," watched as the roll was called. When it was over, the amendment was defeated 45 to 40.

If three senators had voted differently, the British government would either have had to surrender their sovereignty to the Senate, or reject the loan altogether. Once the MacFarland Amendment was defeated, the loan passed by the still underwhelming margin of 46 to 34.[38]

Now it had to survive in the House of Representatives, where emotions were running even higher. Both the White House and Whitehall were determined that nothing should be said that might agitate the situation. Then, on the late afternoon of Tuesday, May 14, Averell Harriman, now ambassador to the Court of St. James, cabled Byrnes "tragically harmful news." The London morning papers were carrying reports about U.S.-U.K. negotiations that "had gone far beyond anything given out by the Foreign Office." The information was so detailed "it could only have come from the Prime Minister's office."[39]

"JOINT DEFENCE PLAN" shrieked the *Daily Express*. "Authoritative reports say that the United States has been informed that if it is willing to take part in a regional defence system in the South Pacific," the *Manchester Guardian* added, "it will get base concessions." According to the *Daily Telegraph* "Discussions are in progress between the United States and British Governments about the use and ownership of some island bases in the Pacific. Ultimately France, Portugal, and Holland would be linked up in the regional security pact."[40]

The loan seemed doomed as the stories touched off a new round of accusations and suspicions in both countries. House members were furious to think that they were part of a charade, making payoffs for secretly negotiated alliances. Emotions in England were so inflamed that it was possible that, even if the House approved the loan, an aroused British public would not allow the government to accept it. To try to calm the situation, Washington and London agreed to suspend further base negotiations.

Byrnes was seething. The leak was another obvious British security blunder. His ire was increased by the embassy's infuriating failure to respond to his April 19 letter asking for the British to give him a "sweetener," as Vandenberg had called it, to take up to Capitol Hill as an inducement. "The next move" he told Hickerson, "is up to the British." His clear implication: the United States could survive longer without the bases than Britain could without the money.

Hickerson called Maclean. The House of Representatives, he warned, was drawing up a crippling amendment which, if passed, would contain provisions intended to make it impossible for Britain to accept the loan. "It was precisely to forestall such an amendment," he pointed out, "that the Secretary made the proposal set forth in his [April 19] letter to Halifax."[41]

As Head of Chancery, it was Maclean's responsibility to see to it that a direct personal letter from the secretary of state to the foreign secretary was answered, and to badger the Foreign Office and placate Byrnes until it was. There is not another instance in British or American records where Maclean "fumbled" such a major policy issue. He did not seem distressed. As Hickerson reported to Acheson, Maclean merely promised to "send another telegram now to the Foreign Office." But Byrnes never received a reply.[42]

The leak in the London press had the same blend of remarkable detail and wild inaccuracies that characterized the leaks on Poland and Turkey. And, as with those leaks, it can be traced to information that Maclean had, namely Byrnes's April 19 "wish list" and the Evatt formula.

What is fascinating, if not brazen in this instance, is that on May 15 Moscow's newspapers printed the list of every base on Byrnes's list and a detailed account of the Anglo-American base negotiations, including segments of the Byrnes-Bevin meetings in Paris (which Maclean, as his May 2 cover note to Hickerson confirms, knew in great detail). The Soviets maintained that their stories—which ran over twenty column inches—were taken from the British press. In fact, they were even more detailed than the British accounts.[43]

With the base talks suspended, the House refused to take up the unpopular loan for another two months. By then, a year had passed since Keynes had first informed the British government that it was bankrupt and urgently needed at least $6 billion from Washington, and eight months since he had signed the $3.75 billion Loan Agreement. In the meantime, Britain was living on imports—largely from America—which depleted precious dollar and gold reserves, and added to its already staggering debt. When and if the loan won approval, 25 percent of it would immediately be used to pay off that debt.

Interest charges and soaring prices during the intervening year would reduce the purchasing power of the remaining $2.8 billion, by perhaps as much as one-third. Only $2 billion—one-third the amount originally sought—would be left to create jobs, oversee economic conversation, and stimulate the listless economy.

It was only thanks to an impassioned plea in July by Speaker Sam Rayburn that the loan passed the House at all. By then it was too late to avert an economic crisis, which in turn led to one of the most dramatic moments in postwar history—the British decision, at a time both were imperiled by the Soviets, to abandon Greece and Turkey.

Passage of the loan did not get the Anglo-American base negotiations back on track. As a result, the United States did not obtain the strategically placed forward basing positions for its long-range bombers. This failure, as will be seen, played a crucial role in shaping American military strategy for years.

Maclean's reports on America's designs for a string of global bases encircling Russia helped to fuel a debate that was raging through the Kremlin. It pitted Molotov, the Foreign Minister who until 1941 had never once traveled outside Russia, against General Zhukov, the defender of Moscow, conqueror of Berlin, and possibly the greatest war hero and most popular figure in Russia.

According to reports reaching American intelligence through Copenhagen:

> Molotov insists that pressure be exerted to the point of war in securing military bases. Zhukov has been trying to restrain Molotov from extreme measures which may precipitate war as he (Zhukov) insists the Army is not prepared to fight now.

Zhukov lost out, in part because Stalin wanted all Red Army war heroes eclipsed so that the Communist Party and its apparatchiks could be restored to preeminence. Stalin wanted the bases on the Straits—in Tripolitania and on the Dodecanese islands, but not, as Harriman predicted, to the point of war, though as the war of nerves over Turkey showed, he was willing to take it to the brink.[44]

By the middle of May, Maclean had helped to bring the loan and base negotiations to a jarring halt, but any glee from again fouling the machinery of Western diplomacy had to be mixed with increasing worry. Only hours before Maclean's plane touched down at Washington National Airport from Bermuda, the Royal Canadian Mounted Police—acting on information provided by Igor Gouzenko—staged a series of carefully prepared raids throughout Ottawa.

Twenty-one men and women were arrested on charges of betraying state secrets to a "foreign power," a euphemism for the Soviet Union. On March 4, just before Maclean began the series of meetings at the State Department with Hickerson, his Cambridge friend, Alan Nunn May, had been arrested in London as a Soviet spy. On May 1, the day Maclean received the Australian base formula that was later leaked to the British and Soviet press, Nunn May pleaded guilty and was sentenced to ten years in prison by a judge who savaged his "crass conceit . . . wickedness . . . and degradation."[45]

A study of the British loan and base negotiations by the economic historian Richard Gardner concluded that at the end, "the British predicament seemed worse than ever. So much had been promised—so little had been achieved. Who was responsible for the failure?"[46]

Years later, Jack Hickerson would try to answer that question. Retired, still dapper and impish, he grew solemn when asked about Maclean:

I was astonished when he went to Russia. I was never so completely fooled in all my life. I talked to Dean [Acheson] about it. He felt bad. We all did. He hurt us in more ways than one. After that, I found myself involuntarily being more suspicious about foreign diplomats, sometimes even my own colleagues. I would think, "but he seems like such a good fellow." And then I would say to myself, "but that's what I thought about Maclean too."[47]

CHAPTER NINE

> Perhaps a document might come to light.
> Bureaucrats tend to hoard documents. I know,
> I've been one.
>
> Alger Hiss, 1973[1]

ALGER AND DONALD

They had so much in common. Both were scholarship students at prestigious universities and studied Romance languages. They started their diplomatic careers within six months of each other, and, although both were regarded as somewhat cool and aloof by their colleagues, they were promoted by older professionals who esteemed their considerable skills. Both were tall, thin, and handsome, and had married women from the same part of southern Illinois. After living in the same neighborhood, for a brief period they lived only blocks apart on P Street in Georgetown. Each had received a promotion as recently as May 1944. Most important, each represented his respective government on some of the postwar's knottiest problems.

Yet for all this, Alger Hiss would later claim that he had never met Donald Maclean. Not only is this untrue, but both men would have been shocked to know that, for nearly a year, the FBI listened in on many of their phone calls. At the time of their first known meeting in December 1945, what most distinguished Alger Hiss from Donald Maclean, and what made so improbable their work together on highly sensitive foreign policy issues, is that for six years people had been telling U.S. authorities that Alger Hiss was a Soviet spy.

Whittaker Chambers had been first with his visit to Adolf Berle on the eve of the war. The following year, 1940, French authorities told Ambassador William C. Bullitt, according to his sworn statements, that "two brothers named Hiss" (Alger's younger brother Donald also worked in the State Department) were Soviet agents.[2]

When the FBI finally confronted Hiss in February 1942, it had nothing to do with either Chambers or Bullitt; the Bureau did not get Berle's notes until June 1943 and Bullitt did not reveal his information until 1948. They were acting instead on tips provided by informants appearing before the House Un-American Activities Committee (HUAC).

The FBI's interview with Hiss was mechanical. He denied being a communist, and they refused to reveal the source of allegations that he was. After the FBI sent the Department of State a copy of its report, Assistant Secretary of State G. Howland Shaw sent Hoover the following perfunctory note:

> Mr. Alger Hiss is well and favorably known to various of the higher officials of the Department and is a valued employee. The report of investigation affords no basis for administrative action and it is believed you will wish so to report to the Congress.[3]

Hiss seemed to have little to worry about. He had been a standout at Harvard Law School where New Deal talent spotter Felix Frankfurter steered him to clerk for a legend, Justice Oliver Wendell Holmes. He had done well in several New Deal agencies. But it was at the State Department that he began his rise to prominence.

"It was like a club," he still recalled with unfeigned melancholia fifty years later. "A very fine and exclusive club." When he walked down one end of the long, spacious, high-ceilinged corridors, he knew by the time of the day, the distinctive walk, or any number of other idiosyncrasies which office someone at the other end was coming from or on his way back to. But Hiss's continued membership in that club, once pregnant with possibilities, was about to become untenable for both club and member.[4]

The State Department's smug confidence in Hiss began to wilt in the face of a thickening cloud of unallayed suspicions and continuing accusations. In the autumn of 1945 two defectors, Gouzenko and Elizabeth Bentley (who had taken over as a courier for Chambers—whom she did not know) both implicated Hiss. Hoover needed little convincing. He loathed the State Department. Further, Hiss represented a social element which, because it was inaccessible to him, Hoover scorned. The possibility that Hiss was a Soviet agent was not only conceivable, it was delectable.[5]

The State Department, particularly Acheson, was having a harder time with it. The Hiss brothers were his protégés; both worked with him closely at the State Department, and he and Donald Hiss were members of the same law firm. If Acheson did not know at the time of Mackenzie King's White House visit that Alger Hiss was the likely Soviet agent fingered by Gouzenko and his documents, he made a point of investigating the matter shortly thereafter.[6]

At half past four on the afternoon of October 9, the squat, bulldog-faced Hoover was sitting across from the tall, trim, Acheson. What a pair! Acheson's Old World habits included testifying before the Senate with a handkerchief tucked in the cuff of his broad pinstripe suit, in the style of British nobility. Hoover's idea of sartorial elegance was to dress like a dandy—from staw hat to spats. His proudest accessory was a gun; Acheson's was a rolled umbrella and homburg. Hoover liked the gaming tables and the race track; Acheson enjoyed starting every morning by walking to work with his neighbor and friend Felix Frankfurter—a permanent fixture on every Hoover enemy list. The two men shared only an intense dislike of each other's profession.

Do you have any information, Acheson asked Hoover "concerning the identity" of the person referred to "as being a Soviet agent . . . in the State Department?"

Hoover normally sowed scandal the way Johnny Appleseed did trees, sprinkling people's names wherever he spotted fertile soil. On this day, however, perhaps sensing a tenseness in Acheson's voice or just knowing how personally important and potentially devastating the answer could be, Hoover was the paradigm of discretion.

"We have not been able to establish the identity of this man," Hoover responded patiently.

"Do you have any suspects?" Acheson probed.

"We have one party in mind as a possible suspect, though there is no direct evidence to sustain this suspicion."

"Who?"

"Alger Hiss." But, Hoover quickly added, there is no direct proof and "now is not the time to make accusations."

When he returned to his office, Hoover told his lieutenants to keep on the trail of the Soviet agent loose inside the State Department. "It should be made very special," he wrote in what became a prescient admonition.[7]

In November (shortly after Elizabeth Bentley had walked into FBI headquarters with her story of Washington espionage) Hoover sought and received authorization from Attorney General Tom Clark to place Hiss under surveillance—that is, to tap his phone, open his mail, and monitor his State Department activities. Clark agreed to the plan in early December. Among the first to be caught in the net thrown over Hiss, an embarrassed Hoover would discover in 1951, was Maclean. But for the third time (including his arrival interview in May 1944 and the June 1945 Hopkins investigation), Maclean aroused no suspicions.[8]

Although no record has been found of a meeting between Hiss and Maclean prior to December 13, 1945, the "Dear Hiss" salutation on a follow-up note Maclean sent two days later suggests a familiarity greater than would have existed after one meeting. It is important to establish here that all their meetings, as the FBI acknowledged, "on the surface would appear to be official business between two important members of the United States and British Governments."[9]

What the FBI did not appreciate was that all the issues they discussed were also matters of pressing urgency to the Soviets. For instance, on December 13 the two met in Hiss's office in Room 164 of the State Department to discuss the civil war in Greece and how the Military Staff Committee (MSC) should be structured. This was the proposed military arm of the United Nations that would advise the Security Council on its options in enforcing United Nations decisions against aggressor nations. The Soviets, who wanted a United Nations with no enforcement authority, were fighting the establishment of the MSC, and eventually they prevailed.

The Soviets were also fighting to gain control of some former Italian possessions, most notably the strategically positioned Dodecanese Islands in the Mediterranean, and Tripolitania in North Africa. The Anglo-American position was that all former possessions should be placed in a collective United Nations trusteeship. Moscow wanted them divided among individual nations. These and other items related to the upcoming United Nations session in London (which Hiss, suspected spy or not, would attend) dominated the phone calls, letters and memoranda, and visits that Maclean and Hiss exchanged throughout December. But their closest and most important session would not come until months later, by which time the State Department knew, or at least believed, that Hiss was a Soviet spy.[10]

The problem was that Byrnes did not know what to do about it. After Hoover finally mentioned Hiss by name to him, the Secretary became consumed with indecision. At first he vowed to discharge Hiss and several others that Bentley identified, but nothing happened. By March 1946 Byrnes was complaining to Hoover that he had not fired Hiss because "he cannot do this without giving him a hearing as he is a Civil Service employee." Byrnes thought about "sending Hiss to the attic," but worried that if he did he would be criticized by those on Capitol Hill who knew that Hiss was a suspect. (They knew because Hoover told them, so they, in turn, would pressure Byrnes to do something.) In his desperation, Byrnes looked upon Hoover as his confidant; together they would navigate their way through these terribly difficult and treacherous rapids. Hoover played the role to the hilt, assuring Byrnes that his indecision was the wisest course. But behind his back the FBI director mocked and ridiculed Byrnes's impotency. He helped turn Attorney General Clark (whom Byrnes also believed was an ally) against him and suggested to key congressional figures that the State Department was giving aid and comfort to a Soviet agent.[11]

Finally, feeling hemmed in by "four or five Congressional committees" that were "barking at him," and apparently believing that he could shame Hiss into resigning, Byrnes called the State Department's once rising star into his second floor office on March 20 and asked point blank whether he was a communist.

During the eighteen years that Hiss would be directly confronted with such charges, he never lost his capacity to respond with a fresh sense of confused disbelief, as if hearing it all for the first time. It had been more than three years since he had been first questioned by the FBI. Yet with Byrnes he acted astonished, as if struck by a thunderbolt from the blue. He denied all the charges. If that were the case, Byrnes advised, he should go see J. Edgar Hoover and tell him. Hiss responded that "he would like to do this, and would like to invite [Hoover] to cross-examine him, and then check upon his statements." But Hoover swatted Hiss away to one of his lieutenants with the instruction that when Hiss came "he is going to do the talking and we are going to do the listening."

Byrnes, clearly unnerved by the confrontation, immediately called Hoover for reassurance. He had been influenced, he said, in part by Whittaker Chambers's written statement. "What kind of a man is he?" Byrnes wanted to know. "He is a very good man," Hoover responded, pointing out that he was "a senior editor for *Time* magazine." Hoover then called Clark, who feared that Byrnes's actions might "alert [Hiss] and ruin an important espionage investigation," (an idea planted by Hoover). Clark denounced Byrnes's confrontation with Hiss as "an outrage."[12]

Byrnes did order that Hiss "was to be given no further consideration for promotion or assignment of responsible duties in the State Department." On March 22 in a memorandum to Assistant Secretary of State for Administration Donald Russell, Robert Bannerman of the State Department's security office—who also had read Chambers's statement to Berle about Hiss, as well as Bentley's revelations to the FBI about a Washington spy network—recommended that Hiss "be terminated from the Department."[13]

When Byrnes still took no action, Hoover kept up the pressure with leaks, not only to Capitol Hill supporters, but also to Walter Winchell, the influential radio personality. In his broadcast of September 29, 1946, Winchell reported:

> The so-called peculiar leanings toward foreign nations permitted by the Secretary of State James Byrnes have passed from a national scandal to a national danger. It can be categorically stated that the question of the loyalty and integrity of one high American officer has been called to the attention of the President.

Byrnes knew whence the valentine had come.[14]

It has been assumed that the Truman administration took steps "to deny [Hiss] access to confidential information and neutralize him within the State Department," but there is scant evidence that this happened. In fact, during the period of closest collaboration between Hiss and Maclean, there was no apparent diminution in Hiss's responsibilities, his access, or even the trust reposed in him by both Byrnes and Acheson.[15]

Alger Hiss and Donald Maclean resumed their frequent meetings in September 1946. According to Chambers, Moscow's standing order to Hiss "was to mess up policy." The result of his collaboration with Maclean was, at least temporarily, an Anglo-American policy in disarray. The real point of this episode, however, is that it renders absurd Hiss's later claim that he never met Maclean.[16]

As the Second World War was ending, few circumstances obsessed Stalin more than America's preparedness to fight another war. To Mackenzie King, the most alarming of all Gouzenko's documents were Moscow's orders in 1944 that its Ottawa embassy "give them a report on the strength of the American forces." Gouzenko's colleagues talked with casual certainty about the West as the enemy for the inevitable Third World War. While he was a Yugoslavian diplomat in Moscow during the war, Milovan Djilas attended several of Stalin's all-night drunken dinners:

> At one point he [Stalin] got up, hitched up his pants as though he was about to wrestle or to box, and cried out almost in a transport, "The war shall soon be over. We shall recover in fifteen or twenty years, and then we'll have another go at it."

At Potsdam, Stalin lectured Churchill that the proper catalyst for foreign policy is "a calculation of forces."[17]

Shortly before 9:00 P.M. Wednesday, August 28, 1946, Andrei Gromyko, the thirty-seven-year-old dark, square-shouldered, Soviet permanent representative to the United Nations, rose to speak to the Security Council. The delegates, exhausted from an eleven-hour tension-filled day, at first paid little attention. But, as the French translation began, word went around that the tough, shrewd Gromyko, without a word of warning, was demanding that England and America in effect submit their military forces abroad to the scrutiny, if not the eventual control, of the Security Council.

The problem, Gromyko insisted, was that British and American forces were occupying not only the former enemy nations of Germany and Japan, but also non-enemy nations such as Egypt and Greece—which had thousands of British troops—and China and the Philippines, where large numbers of American forces were stationed:

> The presence of Allied troops for so long a time after the end of the war, a presence which is not called for by military necessity, must provoke natural uneasiness in the peoples of those countries in which foreign troops are still stationed.

It was a crime without a victim. That is, no "non-enemy state" had protested to London, Washington, Moscow, or the United Nations about the presence of Allied troops on their soil. Indeed, other countries such as Egypt and Iraq, where large numbers of British troops were based, wanted them to remain as a deterrent to any Soviet ambitions. The only related complaint came at the January 1946 opening session of the United Nations, when Iran protested vehemently against the continued presence of seventy-five thousand Soviet troops.

Moscow had ridiculed the legitimacy of the United Nations during the Azerbaijan crisis. But now Gromyko, whose meteoric career included being ambassador to Washington at the age of thirty-four, and who, in addition to his United Nations post, was also Soviet deputy foreign minister, proposed that all member states be required to file detailed reports with the Security Council. The reports were to contain their troop strength outside every former enemy territory—those countries never allied with either Germany or Japan—as well as the position and strength of all their air and naval bases. Each country would have two weeks to comply.

By the time Gromyko finished, there was confusion bordering on pandemonium. He successfully hampered Allied communications and coordination by timing his bombshell when Bevin and Byrnes were at a meeting of the Council of Foreign Ministers in Paris, and when United Nations diplomats were already preparing for the weekend.

Still, Washington reacted with uncharacteristic swiftness. The next day word was passed unofficially to James Reston of *The New York*

Times that the United States not only would support and comply with the Gromyko Resolution, but intended to expand its application. Under the headline "U.S. Expected to Welcome U.N. Study on Units Abroad," Reston, whose sources included Alger Hiss, reported that American officials were convinced that:

> The Soviet Union was seeking to embarrass the Western Powers and make propaganda out of the fact that the United States and British troops were scattered all over the globe in occupation of more territories than those occupied by the Soviet Union.

Washington's countermove would be to expand Gromyko's resolution to include the same detailed reports on foreign troops in former enemy nations. "The Soviet Union would have an embarrassing time explaining," Reston pointed out, "why it had so many troops in countries such as Poland, Czechoslovakia, and Yugoslavia" which, while occupied by Germany, were never Nazi allies.[18]

The size and placement of the Red Army (and even Russian war casualties) were enshrouded in great secrecy. Its peak wartime strength was between 12 and 15 million men. By June 1946 American experts estimated that the Kremlin had settled on a permanent force level of 4.5 million with another 1.5 million divided equally among the secret police, the navy, and the air force. Both British and American experts estimated over 3 million Red Army troops were stationed outside Russia's borders, including 960,000 in Germany, 650,000 in Rumania, 550,000 in Hungary, and 500,000 each in Poland and Manchuria.[19]

While Stalin ordered a halt to further Soviet demobilization, the U.S. government was beseiged with demands for faster action. Demonstrations to "bring the boys home," which included near mutiny among some American units overseas and marches on Congress organized by the wives, mothers, and children of the "Bring-Daddy-Home-Clubs," exerted immense pressure on the U.S. government to demobilize rapidly. Five months after V-J day, the War Department announced that demobilization was occurring at twice the rate after First World War.

This compelled a group of senior American and British officers meeting in London in March 1946 to conclude that "any Anglo-

American policy of 'talking tough' to the Soviet Union on any of the various points on which the Western Allies and Russia differ is for the time being pointless and might be extremely dangerous" because of superior Red Army strength.[20]

The United States Army, which had a wartime high of 8.3 million men, was discharging more than 1 million men a month, leaving just over 2 million still in uniform by May 1946. Of these, 750,000— about one-fourth as many as Russia—were stationed outside the United States: 375,000 in Europe and 140,000 in Japan.[21]

The State Department, believing that the Soviets could deduce the size of U.S. force by extrapolating from the newspapers "detailed information about the size and location of United States forces," viewed Gromyko's resolution as little more than propaganda. This surmise was an instance of a stopped clock's being correct twice each day. The Soviets' move was propaganda, and Stalin did have the data. But if the belief was that Stalin began his morning—as they did—with a cup of coffee and *The New York Times,* it reflects an almost stunning naiveté among America's senior foreign policy advisers about the inner workings of the Soviet Union.[22]

Stalin fervently believed that the Western media were a mirror of his own, a government-controlled propaganda tool. Certainly any Soviet intelligence officer who stood before him and recommended action based on an item in *The Times* of London or *The New York Times* would quickly find himself bundled off to Lubiyanka prison or Siberia's gulags.

Stalin definitely had the precise information that the resolution required, but it came from a source he trusted—Donald Maclean, who was then serving as the reporting channel between the British Joint Supply Mission (JSM) and the Foreign Office. This entitled him to a special pass to the War Department (where the JSM was housed). In this role he could obtain what Stalin prized most— original documents that the government did not intend for either the public or the press to see.[23]

For instance, on September 11, less than two weeks after Gromyko's speech, the British Military Attaché Colonel Molloy sent Maclean a thick top-secret report that was far more detailed than the Gromyko Resolution required. "Latest Developments of the American Army" included a *month-by-month chart of Army and Air Force*

strength at every U.S. and overseas base, and a detailed description of
the sizes, types, and capabilities of every weapon used by various
units—signal, rifle, armored, and so forth—of a U.S. infantry division:

> Each has 32 twin 40mm M19 and 32 Multiple Guns M16; 54 105mm
> Howitzers; 32 multiple guns; 50A M45 on G.M. Carriage M. 16–81,
> 60mm Mortars.

The firepower and range of an American infantry unit engaged in
a field of battle are the kind of data that could help an enemy
overpower an adversary or stay out of its range. To know, for
instance, the range of mortars must have been useful when fighting
took place four years later between U.S. and Soviet-equipped forces
in Korea.[24]

Anglo-American strategy for the Gromyko Resolution was discussed by Hiss and Maclean during a meeting on September 14—a
meeting that years later would ignite speculation about whether they
knew each other. They agreed that the Security Council posed no
problem; they assumed the Soviets would veto the American amendment, and that the United States and the United Kingdom would
veto the original resolution.[25] That is what happened, shifting the
battleground to the General Assembly, where it was likely that the
American position would prevail. Some within the Truman administration and the British government, however, questioned whether
this would be a victory.[26]

"Because they are a police state with no monitoring in Eastern
Europe," let alone in their own country, Secretary of War Robert
Patterson (who had replaced Stimson in September) counseled Truman, the Soviet Union would be free to build ground forces and
develop atomic weapons "behind a facade of international agreements." Furthermore, sympathetic members of Congress, private
disarmament groups, and the American press would rigidly monitor
American adherence to any agreement, while the Kremlin would be
free of any internal pressure to comply.[27]

This was also Foreign Secretary Bevin's argument. "Molotov
would jump at this offer and provide figures whose accuracy," he
had complained from the start, "we should have no means of

checking." Yet the Soviets would learn precise Allied troop movements.[28]

Patterson and Bevin had reason for concern. Washington was losing the public relations battle for the moral high ground in the first postwar disarmament debate. According to the State Department press office, an "impressive number" of U.S. newspapers supported the Gromyko Resolution. Why did the West, they asked, oppose the Soviet vision of the United Nations as an instrument to demilitarize the world through collective action?

"The U.S. principle that the Security Council should never suppress a complaint went by the board like a rocket" the moment America's self-interest was threatened, CBS's Charles Collingwood charged. *The Washington Post* warned that if the United States did not find a way to support the Soviet initiative, America's "pretensions" would be evident, which would "lend substance to the charge of an Anglo-American bloc." Any further U.S. foot-dragging, the *Post* lectured, would be "unwise." A popular left-wing Latin American newspaper, meanwhile, harangued that "it is not the Soviet Union, but the imperialists who are inviting slander on the matter. They are really engaged in an expansionist and interventionist program."[29]

Finally Byrnes and Acheson decided that the United States would have to go it alone. America had nothing to hide and could not allow either the Soviets or the British to convince the world otherwise. Accordingly, on the evening of Friday, October 18, Acheson called Hiss and told him that if the Gromyko Resolution came before the U.N. General Assembly after it convened on October 23, the American delegation would be instructed to break with Britain and push for the passage of an amended version. Maclean, Hiss cautioned, should be informed.

Acheson agreed and added that he would withhold the change in plans from U.N. Secretary General Trygve Lie and even the American U.N. delegation until after Maclean had notified the Foreign Office. This would prevent any damaging leak from reaching the Soviets.

Early on Saturday morning—in one of a series of Maclean-Hiss conversations that the FBI taped between October 19 and October 30, Hiss called Maclean. If the issue came up next week, he warned, the United States was prepared to "make public our own troop dispositions." This would force the Soviets and the British to do likewise. "London would not welcome the news," Maclean predicted with considerable understatement. Indeed, as soon as his cable reached London, Attlee convened an emergency Cabinet session.[30] Maclean and Hiss talked at least twice more that day, including a call Hiss made to Maclean's home that evening. Early Monday morning, Maclean called Hiss with a pressing request. The Foreign Office was upset; Bevin needed more time. "Urgent" discussions were still taking place in London. "They regard [the Gromyko Resolution] as a joint problem since the Russian initiative, in their opinion, is aimed at both the United States and Britain." Would the United States hold off until the Foreign Secretary could meet with Byrnes in New York? "I assured Mr. Maclean," Hiss advised his superiors, that the United States would not move until after Bevin arrived in the U.S.[31]

On Wednesday, October 23, at 3:45 P.M. Maclean took a top-secret cable to Hiss from Bevin amplifying British objections to both the Gromyko Resolution and the American effort to amend it. "In no circumstances can we admit the obligation to disclose all our troop strengths and troop disposition abroad," it began. It would be "disastrous to reveal at the present time the exact strength and composition of our forces." Once such figures were provided, "There is nothing to stop requests for constant updating, eventually putting the Soviets in a position to demand that they be notified of every movement of every soldier, ship and plane."[32]

But that wasn't the real problem. The British Empire had always been ruled with far fewer troops than was popularly supposed. Now the war had left its famed Royal Navy depleted and widely scattered. Whitehall feared that if the Soviets knew just how feeble British forces were, Moscow would take it as an open invitation to promote armed insurrection in any number of Commonwealth nations, beginning with India, which was already in turmoil. Britain, as Maclean alone could appreciate, was risking a strain in the Anglo-American alliance to protect information that he had already passed to Moscow.[33]

Foreign Secretary Bevin pleaded with Byrnes to "make no move" until after he had arrived in New York on November 2. Because Bevin had an obsessive fear of flying, Maclean and Hiss were used to form a trans-Atlantic communication link between Bevin, steaming toward New York aboard the *Aquitania,* and Byrnes in New York. Maclean would decipher Bevin's cables and hand deliver them to Hiss for relay to Byrnes, and Hiss would do the same for the Secretary's.[34]

The State Department anticipated little difficulty in honoring Bevin's request. The major powers were girding up for a lengthy debate over the use of the Security Council veto, as well as debates over trusteeships, and the simmering problem of Austria. If the Soviet initiative came up at all it would be in committee where either the United States or Britain could keep it bottled up.[35]

On Monday, October 28, in a message that was routed from Hiss to Maclean, Byrnes assured Bevin that the United States "will take no action until you and I have an opportunity of discussing the matter further." He could not, however, completely surrender American fortunes to a ship tossing on the high seas, so a precaution was added. If, for some reason, the United States were pressed to state its position, it would have to do so. This would happen only "in the *unlikely* event that this issue is raised for discussion" before Bevin arrived.[36]

Molotov was scheduled to address the General Assembly the following evening. He would argue the Soviet position on the veto and trusteeships, the major agenda items. His speech probably was written at least a day or more in advance, but the Soviets, as usual, refused to distribute any advance copies. Because the Soviet positions on those issues were well known, a speech rebutting Molotov had already been written for Warren Austin, the American permanent representative. He would deliver it either that night or Wednesday morning, depending on the length of the Soviet speech. Only moments after he rose in the General Assembly, however, Molotov departed from his anticipated script. In a "violent attack" he excoriated the United States for its opposition to the Gromyko Resolution. "It is essential," he demanded, "that the General Assembly state its weighty opinion on this subject."

It was, James Reston reported, "the most deeply disturbing speech ever delivered before the United Nations." *The New York Times* also reported that the American delegation "still is without definitive instructions as to the position it will take about the Soviet resolution."[37]

As soon as Austin could get to a phone, he called Hiss in Washington. The United States could no longer straddle. He wanted permission to add to his speech America's amended version of the Gromyko Resolution. Hiss called Byrnes at his Washington home. The Secretary of State gave the go ahead. Hiss then called Maclean at home. As Byrnes had warned in the cable that Hiss himself had hand delivered to Maclean, "statements on the subject in Mr. Molotov's speech" were forcing the United States to break with the United Kingdom. Bevin would be denied his chance to discuss the issue directly with Byrnes. Britain was now on its own.[38]

"The United States has nothing to hide," Austin aggressively asserted the next day as he demanded that the Gromyko Resolution be expanded to include all armed forces at home and abroad for all fifty-four member nations. "The United States," he pledged, "will promptly fulfill that policy."[39]

★ ★ ★

Diplomatic records in the National Archives make it possible to track the hasty additions, mandated by Molotov's unexpected demands, inserted into Austin's speech. Although the Soviets do not oblige us with such records, clearly Molotov's remarks about the Gromyko Resolution were also added at the last minute.

His forty-five-minute speech dealt at length with the three scheduled agenda items: trusteeship, Austria, and the veto. In each case he described the historical intent, the commitments, and promises made about them at various stages up to the formation of the United Nations. But his comments on the Gromyko Resolution were simply accusatory, lacking any historical, legal, political, or even moral justification. Their inclusion seemed to serve no purpose other than to trigger the response Hiss and Maclean knew, based on Byrnes's warning, it would.

In the end the U.S. position prevailed against a series of British and Soviet amendments. The Soviet Union, unable to defend its need to retain troops throughout Central and Eastern Europe, was forced to backpeddle. Suddenly, in a move that "produced something of a sensation," the Soviets insisted that the troop census would be "useless" unless information were also supplied on "the manufacture of atomic weapons."[40]

This shifted the spotlight, as 1946 drew to a close, to a debate over nuclear weapons. Alger Hiss was eager to be a commander in that battle, but it was too late. Under continual pressure to resign, he finally arranged for a prestigious appointment as the head of the Carnegie Endowment for International Peace in New York, leaving the State Department on December 10, 1946.[41]

The enduring mystery of the Hiss–Maclean collaboration is Hiss's forty-year denial that he ever met or knew Maclean. In the mid-1960s, Robert Cecil met Hiss at a social gathering. Cecil could not resist asking him how well he had known his old colleague, Donald Maclean. Hiss replied tersely, "I know why you ask that question." Then he turned and walked away.[42]

Historian Allen Weinstein, who interviewed Hiss seven times between September 1974 and March 1976 for his definitive study of the Hiss–Chambers case, was aware that Hiss had written in his desk calendar for September 14, 1946 "McLean [*sic*], Brit. Emb." Yet "at no time has Alger Hiss ever mentioned either seeing or knowing Maclean."[43]

In the course of the research for this book, Hiss was asked again about Maclean. By then he was eighty, but his faculties were very sharp, and his recall in this and subsequent interviews was almost phenomenal. He was intimately familiar with nearly every detail of the Weinstein book. After preliminaries, the following exchange took place:

VN: In the Weinstein book [a hoot of laughter . . . "It is very unreliable"]. Well, perhaps so, but it did say that there was some reference to your having met with Maclean . . . Did you ever know Maclean or meet him?

AH: I never did. I understand there was an entry on my calendar for one day. I don't even remember which day it was, that his name appeared on my calendar.

VN: In September 1946.

AH: Is there a first name?

VN: Well, of course I haven't seen the actual exhibit, but the description I have read just says "Maclean."

AH: Well, I had a law school classmate by that name.

VN: It says, "Maclean, British embassy . . ."

AH: No? Well, if it says British embassy then it must have been that fellow. He may have come to see me, he may have called me, I have no recollection if he did. We certainly had no relationship of any significance if he did ever contact me.

Hiss's uncharacteristic memory loss is not about something that had happened forty years before (the time lapse relative to this book), or thirty years (with Weinstein), or even twenty years (with Cecil). It was less than five years, because Maclean's sensational 1951 disappearance made news that penetrated even prison walls (Hiss, by then convicted of perjury, was in an "honors" wing of Lewisburg prison where he had access to newspapers and radio). This means that although Maclean's name and picture were splashed across the front pages of every newspaper and magazine in America during the summer of 1951, it failed to stir any recollection in Hiss's mind of the meetings, phone calls, and urgent work they had done together between December 1945 and November 1946.[44]

Maclean was not similarly afflicted. As we will see in later chapters, Hiss's fall from grace had a profound impact on Donald. Cecil remembers that Maclean "heatedly championed [Hiss] on occasions when it would have been in his own best interest to have kept silent." At one time after knocking down his friend Philip Toynbee, who had publicly defended Chambers, Maclean shouted in a furious rage, "Don't you understand, I am the British Hiss?" A month later he was gone to Moscow.[45]

CHAPTER TEN

What is there that is secret? . . . In the real
sense there are no secrets.

David Lilienthal, the AEC's first chairman,
before he was privy to America's
atomic secrets.

I didn't sleep well last night, and little wonder.
I find myself in the midst of wholly strange
and fearsome things.

Lilienthal, after he had learned the same
atomic secrets that would later be
imparted to Maclean[1]

THE EXPLOSIVE SECRETS

Part One

Washington's cover-up of Maclean's activities was more singularly focused than Whitehall's and much less coordinated. It was less coordinated because it was conducted by lower-level officials, and it was more focused because it was almost exclusively concerned with his knowledge of atomic secrets. The Atomic Energy Commission (AEC), the State Department, and the FBI worked not only to deceive the Congress, the press, and the public about Maclean's true role, they also deceived one another.

It began as soon as the story broke in Washington on the afternoon of June 7, 1951. After seeing Maclean's disappearance splashed across the afternoon's front pages, Bryan LaPlante, the AEC's security chief, checked his records only to discover that during a ten-month period between August 1947 and June 1948, when Maclean was Britain's "atomic energy man in Washington," he had made at least twenty visits to the AEC headquarters. To make matters worse, he had attended a highly secret and rigidly controlled three-day conference in November 1947 to discuss which data, including those that had to do with the atom bomb, could be declassified.

The story could not have been more poorly timed. For two years the AEC and the State Department had been attacked repeatedly as a series of disasters overtook U.S. and Western policy. The AEC ineffectually defended itself in September 1949 against Senator Bourke Hickenlooper's charges of "incredible mismanagement" in guarding the nation's atomic secrets, after the Soviets exploded its first atomic device. The news shattered America's smug belief that it was both Armageddon's purveyor and the only people immune from its wrath. In February 1950, Hickenlooper's charges appeared almost prophetic when Klaus Fuchs, a top British physicist assigned to Los Alamos, confessed that he had been passing America's atomic secrets to the Soviets from 1942 to 1949. Then, in March 1951, the Rosenbergs were found guilty of being part of the same espionage conspiracy as Fuchs.

Meanwhile, the State Department, under siege over "who lost China" after that country fell to the communists (also in September 1949), became the object of a Red witch hunt launched by Senator Joseph McCarthy, a drunk and a bully with almost no redeeming virtue. The Wisconsin Republican fanned the prairie fire of Red hysteria already sweeping the country by announcing that he had the names of two hundred five State Department employees who were members of the Communist Party. It was unnecessary, therefore, to explain to LaPlante the potentially explosive nature of the report that he compiled on Maclean and sent to his superior, J.A. Waters. Nor did anyone at the senior levels of the AEC need to be coaxed to omit any mention of that report to the FBI officials who questioned them the following day.[2]

While the AEC was stonewalling, the FBI's L.B. Nichols was having better luck on Capitol Hill. William Borden, the executive director of the Joint Committee on Atomic Energy (JCAE), explained to Nichols that, during the early days of the Manhattan Project, Britain, America, and Canada had created the Combined Policy Committee (CPC), whose existence was as secret as the bomb itself. The purpose of the CPC was to resolve Anglo-American disputes over the bomb's development, to allocate precious uranium, and to coordinate the exchange of technical information.

The CPC, Borden continued, was run by a three-man secretariat, with one representative from each country. From February 1947 to September 1948, Maclean was the British secretary. The JCAE, Borden assured Nichols, had already requested the AEC to prepare "an estimate of how much information Maclean could have had." Realizing that he had just scratched the surface of potentially momentous information, Nichols urged that the Bureau make a "routine inquiry" at the AEC. "Liaison already has done so and didn't get as much information," Hoover responded brusquely. "It is obvious that AEC is not particularly cooperative in this matter."[3]

That turned out to be an understatement. On that same day, June 8, Sumner Pike, the acting chairman of the AEC, sent Senator Brien McMahon, chairman of the JCAE, the requested damage assessment. Clearly determined not to provide its Congressional critics with any more ammunition, Maclean's AEC visits, which actually numbered over twenty-five, were reduced to "several." It was emphasized that he was "only" a diplomat. "He is not a scientist and his duties in connection with these matters were of a procedural and British diplomatic secretarial character."

What could be more harmless than a confused diplomat in the world of arcane scientific data, and a mere secretary at that? The AEC was forced to admit that Maclean did know all the "procedural discussions and political aspects of atomic energy." But, in what became the centerpiece of the cover-up, doubt was expressed that Maclean was even a spy while he was in Washington. If he had been a Soviet spy in 1947–1948, the AEC conceded, the "classified Top Secret" data he had access to "would then have been useful to the Russian atomic energy program and strategic planners." But if he had not been a spy, it "would not now be of any considerable aid to Russia."[4] While officials at the top obfuscated, mid-level AEC officials who were familiar with Maclean's duties were peeling away for

FBI investigators some of the layers of mystery that enshrouded the story of the atomic bomb.

During the war President Roosevelt and Prime Minister Churchill signed a series of interlocking agreements governing the bomb's development and control. The most important was signed at Quebec in August 1943. It pledged that neither country would ever use the atomic bomb against the other, nor would either share any information about it with a third party except by mutual consent. And, in what became the most controversial element of all, the United States agreed never to use the atomic bomb unless it had Great Britain's consent. Nearly a year later at Hyde Park the atomic partnership was cemented as the two leaders pledged "full cooperation" on atomic energy matters even after the war. Quebec and Hyde Park were among the most binding commitments ever entered into by the United States. Yet, they had never been ratified or even shown to the U.S. Senate.

The partnership's instruments were the CPC and the later established Combined Development Trust (CDT). Maclean also represented British interests on the CDT which, as insiders explained to the FBI, would have been invaluable to the Soviets. At a time when it was assumed that the world's supply of uranium was finite, the CDT spearheaded an extremely secret preemptive buying program to secure the world's high-grade uranium deposits. If it were successful, it would virtually eliminate any threat of a significant Soviet atomic arsenal, because without uranium there could be no bombs.[5]

Roy Snapp, who joined the AEC after serving as an assistant to General Leslie R. Groves, the commanding general of the Manhattan Project, told the FBI "There was nothing that Maclean wouldn't have known at the highest levels regarding matters of policy." A.A. Wells, who, like Snapp, worked in the AEC's office of foreign liaison, found Maclean so knowledgeable "from the first day that I met him" that he was certain "the British must have spent a great deal of time grooming him beginning in 1946."[6]

On Tuesday, June 26, Admiral Lewis Strauss, a gruff-talking, cantankerous, and anti-British former AEC commissioner, called the Bureau's Mickey Ladd. For three weeks he had been digging through his papers. He finally found what he was looking for, and he wanted to make sure that Hoover knew about it. "Carroll Wilson, who was General Manager, had given a pass to Donald Maclean in November of 1947 which required no escort and permitted Maclean to go anywhere in the Atomic Energy Headquarters." Strauss had a copy of Wilson's written authorization. Although he had no copy of any documents to prove it, nor did the AEC produce any, Strauss claims that he bitterly objected to the pass for Maclean, but that he was overruled. He had not had any reason to suspect Maclean; they had met several times in agreeable circumstances. Strauss simply opposed sharing America's atomic secrets with any foreigner.[7]

The AEC's LaPlante had also discovered a copy of Wilson's order, but much earlier, on June 9. Not only did the AEC withhold this information, it had since assured the FBI that during Maclean's eighteen months on the atomic energy beat, "he was not cleared for classified information." In addition, on June 13, when the FBI interviewed Carroll Wilson—who had since left the AEC—he failed to mention the pass although he had led a review of all passes to "aliens" after Fuchs's confession only nine months earlier.

FBI Director Hoover was not focusing on these discrepancies, however. What infuriated him was that, as he wrote on a memo given him by Ladd, "I was always required to have an escort." So did nearly everyone else. Even members of the Cabinet and the Congress had to have an appointment to go to the AEC. Upon arrival, they would be escorted by armed guard to the appropriate office. They could go nowhere else. When the appointment was concluded, a guard would be called to escort them to the building's exit.[8]

Yet, Maclean's pass permitted him to enter and move around at will with no escort. The AEC understandably dreaded having members of Congress learn that, while they were kept on a short leash, a Soviet spy was allowed to roam around the AEC offices grazing for secrets. But Strauss forced their hand. Before he called the FBI, Strauss called LaPlante to let him know that he had a copy of Wilson's order and to make sure that his "strenuous objection" to it was part of the AEC's official record.

Anticipating the worst, LaPlante finally sent the FBI the memo—nineteen days after it had first been compiled—listing Maclean's visits to the AEC, as well as a copy of the order granting him a pass. Two weeks later, they also sent Hoover a damage assessment that was little more than a rehash of the one that they had provided over a month before to Senator McMahon. Hoover could not really complain, however, because, within a few weeks, the FBI would be a full participant in the cover-up.

Dissatisfied with the AEC's pro forma responses, McMahon demanded to know of the CIA, and the departments of Justice and State, "What information [do] you have that Maclean may have been involved in espionage during the time he had access to atomic data?" The Attorney General's response, prepared by the FBI, claimed that it had no specific evidence "that Maclean was engaged in espionage . . . from January 1947 to August 1948." A.H. Belmont assured Ladd that, "Our answer [to McMahon] is factually true." It was also completely misleading. For nearly three years the FBI had been searching for the Soviet spy that they knew had been operating from the British embassy in 1944–1945. Each Bureau report carried the heading, "Subject: Unknown" Espionage-R[ussia][9]

This changed immediately after Maclean's disappearance. The FBI was so sure that he was a Soviet spy they called off further investigation. As one Bureau official wrote, "In view of the identification of Maclean as the subject in this case, it will not be necessary for the New York office to conduct further investigation relative to [blacked out]."

Before the month had ended Hoover sent CIA Director Bedell Smith a report headed:

> Subject: Donald Duart Maclean
> Guy De Moncy Burgess
> Espionage-R

The Bureau hardly needed to establish again that the man they knew was spying in 1944 and 1945 was still spying in 1947 and 1948. Technically they were correct in saying that they had no evidence— because they were not looking for any—that Maclean was passing information in 1947. Hoover, however, was not eager to advertise that a Soviet atomic spy had been working in Washington right under the FBI's nose. Therefore, the Bureau helped to create the impression that Maclean, so far as it knew, had not betrayed America's atomic secrets.[10]

The State Department eagerly echoed the cry. "The Department has no information," their letter to McMahon stated almost defiantly, "that Maclean was ever involved in espionage during the time he had access to atomic secrets." The triumph of this campaign is enshrined in an October 1955 letter from Mississippi's Senator James Eastland, who conceded that "it is clear" that Maclean was a "minor employee in the British Foreign Office."[11]

What then is the truth about Maclean's role as an atomic spy?

First, although it was his most important role for the Soviets, it was one of the few that he did not have to seek out. For over two years Roger Makins, who had been personally selected by Churchill, was the embassy's "atomic energy man" in Washington. By the summer of 1946, however, London was eager for him to return as director of the Office of Atomic Energy. Because of the demanding nature of his Washington assignment, however, Ambassador Halifax refused to let Makins leave until his replacement had been named.

Halifax knew, as did the Foreign Office, that control and development of atomic energy and weapons were going to be a dominant issue in the postwar world, and that no individual would have the requisite scientific, political, and diplomatic skills, let alone the time, to follow and protect British interests. It was decided, therefore, that these responsibilities would have to be divided among at least three senior officials. But for weeks London and Washington could not agree on an appropriate combination.

Finally, on September 21, 1946 (at a time when Maclean and Hiss were working on the Gromyko Resolution), Neville Butler of the Foreign Office suggested Maclean for a pivotal role. He would work in tandem with Sir Gordon Munro, a British treasury official based at the embassy, to handle the critically important political and diplomatic work of the CPC and the CDT. Because the work was political in nature, Maclean "need not be technically qualified." Dr. Alex King, already in Washington with the British Scientific Office, would handle all technical duties. What was crucial, both Butler and Makins agreed, was that Maclean "lighten the load on Munro" by taking on as much of the work as possible.[12]

The new team took over on January 1, 1947, but within two weeks its impracticality became obvious. "The problem," D.H.F. Rickett in the Cabinet Office complained to the Foreign Office, "is that we have grown more and more dependent on Munro who is necessarily very largely engaged on other pressing work."

The British loan—thanks in part to Maclean—was too late to stanch England's hemorrhaging financial wound. The ensuing financial crisis of 1947 consumed Whitehall, which was forced to place its empire in receivership. Munro (who was already pressed with the activities surrounding the fledgling World Bank and International Monetary Fund) was in round-the-clock meetings with American treasury officials. The only practical solution was to have Maclean take over all the CPC and CDT work except for Cabinet-level meetings.[13]

Maclean's job, as London saw it, was to salvage a rocky marriage that the Americans believed had been performed under duress and had disintegrated into an embarrassment. England, the clingy, jilted partner, was willing to agree to a divorce, but only if it received an uncontested and equal share of the main asset that had accrued to the partnership—the secrets of the atomic bomb. The problem was that in September 1946, completely unaware of the "marriage," Congress had passed the McMahon Act forbidding such a union. To continue the metaphor, the U.S. government was to remain celibate; it was not—under penalty of death—to share its secrets with anyone.

The British considered this profoundly unjust. When the war began, British scientists were ahead of the Americans in the theoretical and experimental knowledge of atomic fission, and Britain's Maud Report greatly influenced Roosevelt's decision in October 1941 to commit to the bomb. It was FDR who urged the pooling of information by Anglo-American scientists, and then encouraged Churchill to transfer British efforts to North America beyond the range of German bombs. U.S. scientists and military experts "had been willing, even eager, to compare notes with their British counterparts" during this difficult research and development phase.[14]

By spring of 1942, however, the Americans, with superior manpower, money, and raw materials, inevitably began to pull ahead of the British. By summer they were ready to go beyond research and development to mastering the multitude of engineering and construction problems involved in the manufacture of a bomb. And by December a new attitude about interchange was taking hold and the

U.S. Military Policy Committee believed it necessary to reevaluate Anglo-American cooperation.

Churchill insisted that more was at stake than participating in the development of a potentially powerful weapon. England's destiny hung in the balance. It would be disastrous, he railed at Roosevelt's advisers during a stormy session at No. 10 Downing Street, if, by excluding Britain from information, Russia were "to win the race for something they might use for international blackmail." Europe's postwar security depended on an England equipped with the atomic bomb. It wounded him to believe that the United States was prepared to leave Europe to the mercy of the Russians:

> Great Britain would not agree to the United States claiming sole control of the atomic field at a peace conference and, therefore, if the United States thought it could not interchange fully, it would be necessary for the British to start immediate parallel development even though such action was a most unwise use of energies during the war.[15]

At first, FDR agreed with the recommendation of his advisers to sharply curtail exchange with the British. But soon a pattern emerged where Roosevelt would energetically agree to a get-tough-with-the-British-policy, only to turn around in a private session with Churchill and agree to virtually every demand of his. Churchill had one advantage: he got his concessions in writing.[16]

It was primarily to placate Churchill that Roosevelt agreed to the British prime minister's Quebec and Hyde Park initiatives. The very few White House aides who knew about these agreements—arguably the best kept secrets of World War II—cringed. After Quebec, Dr. Harvey Bundy, Stimson's special assistant for scientific affairs, warned that if FDR delivered "to the United Kingdom great power in the postwar world without due consideration by both the executive and legislative authorities," his political opponents would argue that he had used his war powers illegally.[17]

Having forged the partnership, Churchill insisted on observing its every ritual. It is, therefore, worth noting that the decision to drop atom bombs on Japan was not made by the United States and President Harry S. Truman. It was made by the Combined Policy

Committee. On June 30, 1945, Field Marshal Henry Wilson, acting on orders from Churchill, cabled Lord Halifax in Washington that when the issue was voted on at the CPC's July 4 meeting "you are to concur in the decision to use the weapon." And the CPC minutes reflect that "the Governments of the United Kingdom and the United States had agreed that T.A. weapons [Tube Alloys, the British code word for the atom bomb] should be used by the United States against Japan."[18]

As prime minister, Attlee followed hard on Churchill's path. On August 8, three days after Hiroshima, in his Cable No. 1 to Truman, Attlee solemnly declared that "*you and I* as heads of state which *have control of this great force,* should without delay make a *joint declaration of our intentions* to utilize the existence of this great power." Truman agreed to Attlee's request that they meet at the White House with Canadian Prime Minister MacKenzie King to issue a public statement on their plans to harness atomic power for peaceful ends. As a public relations gambit, the ensuing November 15 Truman-Attlee-King conference enjoyed limited success. Their public proclamations were largely drowned out by vehement protests from the excluded Soviets, which were echoed by a group of left-wing scientists assembled at Washington's Mayflower Hotel by Michael Straight.[19]

Behind the scenes the Allied leaders tried to conduct a secret agenda that proved even less successful than the public one. A discussion about Soviet atomic espionage bogged down over concern that nothing be done to offend Moscow. This meant keeping Gouzenko's disclosures from the public and not arresting Alan Nunn May, who was now back in England. This policy—characterized by a disgusted Hoover as "spineless"—convinced Prime Minister King that the other two nations were trying to isolate Canada as the troublemaker—the partner who insisted on disrupting wartime harmony by catching Soviet spies. Eventually, King mollified himself, America would discover that it too had an espionage problem, and when this became known, it would "come as a terrific blow to the Truman administration."[20]

Washington's efforts to break free of the Roosevelt-Churchill secret accords backfired. Not only did Truman fail to extricate the United States from the agreements that his science adviser Vannevar Bush warned Byrnes "could embarrass us all," he actually signed new ones. Although their language was slightly less binding, they gave Attlee every reason to believe that the Americans had just repeated the sacred vows.

The stage was set, therefore, for a spectacular collision between the White House and the Congress. The impact was further intensified when Republican Senate leaders Arthur Vandenberg and Bourke Hickenlooper, both of whom had been assembled to witness the signing of the Truman-Attlee-King Declaration, later discovered that they were mere props for a public event while being excluded from the secret diplomacy backstage.[21]

To complement this "Atoms for Peace" campaign Senator Brien McMahon, chairman of the Joint Committee on Atomic Energy, spearheaded a fight to transfer custody of America's atomic arsenal and her atomic secrets from military to civilian control. Just as it appeared that the civilians were about to prevail, General Groves and Senator Hickenlooper—both determined to maintain the Army's control of the bomb—conspired to "explode on the floor of the Senate" the sensational news that Alan Nunn May, a civilian, a foreigner, and a scientist, had stolen the nation's atomic secrets and passed them to the Soviets.[22]

An immediate counterattack was launched by politically active scientists, some of whom had worked at Los Alamos and now saw themselves as diplomats. Because they had discovered the key to unlocking nature's secrets, it was to be understood that they alone understood the immutable laws of human behavior. Scientists would henceforth have to dictate American foreign policy because only they understood atomic energy, the issue which would dominate the future. It even made governments obsolete; the earth would have to be ruled by one world government. "We must now work for world law and world government," Edward Teller, the otherwise brilliant Hungarian-born theoretical physicist, proclaimed at one point.[23]

With the same sagacity, scientists rushed to explain that all atomic information must be shared. Because scientists the world over knew the principles of fusion involved in the atom bomb, there were no atomic secrets in any event. If there were no atomic secrets, there could be nothing to steal. Thus, the whole notion of a Moscow-directed espionage operation using "atomic spies" was a hoax perpetrated by those who were reflexively hostile to the Soviet Union.[24]

This blatantly false syllogism was itself a hoax, and the scientists knew it—as did the Kremlin and No. 10 Downing Street.[25]

No one familiar with the rudiments of the bomb ever suggested that "the scientific principles of atomic fission" were secret or had been stolen. "There is no reason," Truman told a group of reporters in October, "for trying to keep the scientific knowledge covered up because all the great scientists know it in every country." He, Attlee, and King on November 15 had called for the "open exchange of the fundamental scientific aspects of atomic energy with other nations of the world." But, Truman also underscored, "the secret of the manufacture of the weapon would remain a secret with us."[26]

"The fundamental scientific discoveries," Attlee agreed, "are now common knowledge . . . the actual capacity for production exists only in the United States." When C.D. Howe, Canada's Munitions Minister, was pressed on the same point, he calmly replied that, although it was true that Canadian scientists understood the basic principles involved in splitting the atom, the industrial secrets to build the bomb "had never been known in this country, and Canadian military, political, and scientific authorities had always taken the attitude that they would rather not know them."[27]

"So far as Canada was concerned," Prime Minister King added, "it is not correct to say that we had the secret of the bomb because we had not had to do with its manufacture at all." Churchill made the same point in 1944 after his Foreign Secretary, Anthony Eden, grumbled about "needless" American secrecy. "I believe you underrate the lead which has been obtained by the United States," Churchill admonished, "There is all the difference between having certain paper formulae and having a mighty plant in existence."[28]

Yet the impression endured that the key to the bomb was a single scientific secret that only scientists could understand. This is the reason that the AEC and the State Department repeatedly stated that Maclean was not a scientist but a diplomat, with secretarial, not technical duties.

What were the atomic secrets? First and foremost they were the complex chemical, metallurgical, and engineering technology required to build the massive atomic plants necessary to complete all the stages involved in manufacturing a bomb. In 1945, England and

Russia had first-rate scientists, but lacked the critical mass of resources and engineering personnel to solve such problems.

The second category of secrets were political and diplomatic, such as the existence of the Hyde Park and Quebec agreements. Maclean's contribution to the Soviets in solving their engineering problems, while greater than popularly supposed, was certainly less than Klaus Fuchs and Alan Nunn May were able to provide. In the second category, however, he was invaluable. The difference was that the engineering secrets were essential for the Soviets to get a bomb; the political and diplomatic secrets could be used to impair Britain's efforts and even thwart America's atomic energy program.

This was particularly true where uranium was concerned. Uranium was the Achilles' heel of the American atomic energy program. Although it would lose its exalted position in later years, at the time geologists believed that the earth's supply of high-grade uranium was finite. The grayish metal was the irreducible First Principle without which there would be no nuclear fission, no plutonium, no isotopes, no chain reaction, and no atomic bombs. This meant that the inevitable atomic arms race between Russia and America would be won by whichever side could stockpile the largest share of uranium. But Nature's little joke was that it had blessed neither superpower with any known deposits of high-grade uranium. This left the United States, as Groves phrased it, in "the embarrassing position of having the plants, the knowledge and the skills, but no raw materials to work with."[29]

The world's greatest uranium deposit was found deep inside the heart of Africa, in the Belgian Congo (Zaire), where Union Minière du Haut Katanga's Shinkolobwe mines turned out ore so exceptionally rich in uranium that in 1937 the company, "having stockpiled sufficient ore to satisfy the anticipated world demand . . . for the next thirty years, ceased mining operations."[30] The few operating mines elsewhere in the world, unable to compete, had closed by the 1920s, when the known use went little beyond ceramics.

Once the war broke out, this source became inaccessible to the West, and in September 1942, with the Manhattan Project at a critical point, uranium became so scarce that the United States was in danger of having to halt the entire program. This disaster was averted when it was discovered that, just before German U-Boats would have made it impossible, the head of the Union Minière had managed to get out of Africa a last shipment of 1,200 tons of uranium, which he stored in a Staten Island warehouse. This fueled the Manhattan Project to its conclusion.[31]

America's dependency on foreign uranium ensured fidelity to her secret marriage to Britain. In 1944, after the Belgian government-in-exile flatly rejected American requests to reopen the flooded Shinko-lobwe mines, Groves was forced to turn to the British, who persuaded the Belgians to reverse their decision. The two nations shared deep historic ties; besides, the British owned a one-third interest in Union Minière. The purchase arrangements were all negotiated and signed in London.[32]

America got its uranium, but in the process it had been forced to rely on Britain, strengthening that country's claim to be not only an equal atomic partner, but an indispensable one as well. That partnership was spelled out unequivocally in the Belgian agreement, which gave London and Washington rights to jointly "purchase all Belgian Congo uranium." England aggressively exercised those rights by taking delivery of half of each uranium shipment, so that by 1947 Britain had the world's largest stockpile of high-grade mined uranium.

On the morning of February 3, 1947, Maclean entered the State Department and proceeded to the third floor conference room. Once his name had been checked at the door, he crossed the threshold to take his place among the elite fraternity of men who knew what were possibly the greatest secrets of the war—secrets that were still unknown to the Congress, Parliament, and the American and British Cabinets.

He must have been impressed with his own circumstances. Presiding over this top-secret meeting of the Combined Policy Committee was Secretary of State George C. Marshall. It is a pity that there is no record of Maclean's reaction, for surely even he would have felt Marshall's commanding presence. Churchill called him "the noblest Roman of them all." He was the only general with whom Roosevelt was not on a first name basis. Truman revered him. Acheson said Marshall's presence was "a striking and communicated force. His figure conveyed intensity, which his voice, low, staccato, and incisive, reinforced. It compelled respect." In five months, Harvard

University would proclaim that only one man in American history was Marshall's equal—George Washington.[33]

The other members of the CPC may have lacked Marshall's stature, but they were also distinguished and powerful men—Robert P. Patterson, who in September had succeeded Stimson as secretary of war; Vannevar Bush, science adviser to Truman as he had been to Roosevelt; Field Marshal "Jumbo" Wilson, the head of the British Joint Staff Mission located in the Pentagon; British Ambassador Lord Inverchapel; and Canadian Ambassador Hume Wrong (the first Canadian official to hear Gouzenko's story).

Joining Maclean off to the side of the room were Undersecretary of State Acheson, tall, aloof, impeccably tailored; Edmund Gullion, Acheson's special assistant on atomic energy matters (who years later would be known as "John Kennedy's favorite diplomat"); Thomas A. Stone, Canada's representative on the joint secretariat; Sir Gordon Munro; and Roger Makins, who delayed his departure for London to attend this meeting.

The atmosphere was tense. This was the first CPC meeting since Congress had passed the McMahon Act, which made it illegal to conduct the very business that the CPC had been created to transact. The British, who bristled at the mere mention of the Act, listened in silence as Acheson invoked its oppressive restrictions. It didn't take much imagination to know what was running through British minds:

The bomb should have been ours to begin with. We were ahead of everyone; we were the ones who convinced the Americans of its potential. Yet, once they caught up with us, they treated us like lepers. Winnie forced Roosevelt to acknowledge the debt and our entitlement to the full fruit of our joint labors. Truman agreed too. But now they're all trying to hide behind Congress's skirts, saying the agreements never should have been made to begin with. Well it's not up to us to question whether the President of the United States has the authority to enter into the agreements he freely makes.

Acheson's voice instilled a jarring reality to the proceedings. "If it becomes necessary to acquaint the appropriate committees of Congress," Acheson warned, "the United States Government would, so far as is possible, inform the other CPC" members so that they could prepare their governments for the inevitable political fallout.[34]

This provided cold comfort to the British. The Congress would demand to know the reason that the agreements had not been terminated. Parliament would demand to know the reason that they had not been fulfilled. The meeting ended with the Americans and the British still uneasy co-conspirators against other elements of their own governments.

While these developments were unfolding at the State Department, at the other end of Pennsylvania Avenue Bernard Baruch rocked an executive session of the Joint Atomic Energy Committee by testifying that he was certain that Russia had penetrated the inner walls of America's atomic fortress. For once he had no idea of just how prophetic he was.[35]

The year before, a group of advisers, with the Soviets clearly in mind, had warned Acheson that if the Kremlin ever learned that America was totally dependent on foreign sources of uranium "it took little imagination to conceive of a nation seeking to upset an existing compact or fomenting revolutions to gain control of uranium." But how would they know? The United States had faced uranium shortages since 1942 and the agreement with Belgium was nearly three years old; not so much as a whisper had leaked out.[36]

Then, only two days after Maclean's first CPC meeting, the State Department received a horrifying cable from Brussels. A Communist Party senator had recently confronted Belgian Foreign Affairs Minister Paul-Henri Spaak and asked him point blank "if a secret treaty between U.S. and Belgium concerning uranium existed." The Belgian Communists had suddenly learned—after five years of airtight secrecy—the source of America's uranium.

Spaak, who had signed the original agreement on behalf of the Belgian government-in-exile, warned Marshall in the cable that "I was able to avoid replying but question might be put to me publicly in such fashion that it would be difficult for me to reply."[37]

Four days later, another Communist Party senator, Van Hoorick, touched off an uproar when he rose in the chamber and publicly announced that he had discovered that Belgium "is furnishing great quantities of uranium to two Anglo-Saxon countries" for a price that was inadequate. It was the recipients, he insisted, not the price, that was important. With unerring accuracy—using the precise figures that were available to Maclean from the CDT—Van Hoorick charged that while thousands of tons of uranium oxide ore were being shipped to America, only fifteen kilos had been provided to Belgian scientists, while France (whose leading atomic physicist Frédéric Joliot-Curie was a communist) had received none.

"In practice," Van Hoorick continued, "the total production goes to Anglo-Saxon countries. We believe that we should not deliver it to any country which has not given us guarantees that uranium will be used solely for peaceful purposes." Indignation quickly spread.[38]

"Public opinion is now aware of fact that our entire uranium production is sold to the U.S.," Spaak warned Washington. Curie in France was urging Belgian scientists to join with him in the development of a French-Belgian bomb. He then "ingeniously suggests Belgian contribution should be uranium from their supplies in the Congo."

Spaak was under tremendous pressure. "I believe it really urgent that this question be examined and settled," he pleaded in another cable. For Washington, however, the problem defied a quick settlement, and by the late winter of 1947, Belgium's uranium (not even the Communists ever suggested that the uranium belonged to the Congo) had become the center of a national controversy.[39] The country's economy was extremely shaky. The nation had long been dependent on exports, but after the war there was no trade and Belgium was "going into her post-war depression with a bang, the first European country to do so." Communists claimed all of the nation's economic woes were a result of the odious uranium agreement that allowed the Anglo-Saxon capitalists to "rape" Belgium.[40]

The Belgian government, an uneasy and fragile coalition of liberals and communists, was without strong leadership, which made it extremely vulnerable to manipulation. Foreign Minister Spaak pleaded with Washington and London that the rumors about the terms of the agreement were much worse than the reality and that he must be allowed to publish them. His allies refused.

This was the string that, if pulled, could cause the entire cloak of secrecy to come unraveled. As Makins, now chairman of Britain's Atomic Advisory Committee put it, "If the [Belgian] Agreement were public it would be very hard to conceal the continued existence of the Trust." Britain knew that any chance it had of collecting on the agreements depended upon their continued secrecy.

CHAPTER ELEVEN

> Any publicity on our contracts with Belgium
> would strengthen the hand of the Communists
> and might easily make it very difficult for us
> to get the imports we vitally need to keep the
> [atomic] program running.
>
> Dean Acheson in a secret Congressional
> session, 1947
>
> There is nothing that we would have talked
> about in the raw materials area that we would
> not have shared with Maclean.
>
> CDT staff member, 1985[1]

THE EXPLOSIVE SECRETS

Part Two

By spring 1947 events were moving at a torrential pace. On March 12 President Truman stood before a joint session of Congress and made a sweeping pledge to help "free peoples everywhere," beginning with massive economic and military aid to Greece and Turkey. The initiative, which became known as the Truman Doctrine, was the culmination of a whirlwind three weeks following Britain's abrupt decision to abandon those two nations in their struggle for survival. Broke, unable to provide for its own citizens, Britain could no longer afford to maintain troops in the area nor subsidize a proxy war.

London's withdrawal forced Washington to stop vacillating about a retreat into isolationism. It also, however, increased the possibility of confrontation between the United States and the Soviet Union, feeding British fears, as Maclean explained them, that should the United States strike Russia an atomic blow, Britain, "but not the United States, presented a priority and wide-open target to obliterating counter-attack."[2]

The best, if not the only, way to deter Soviet retaliation was for Britain to have its own atomic weapons. To do that she would need to duplicate the Manhattan Project's billions of dollars and years of work to construct such plants as those in Los Alamos and the Clinton Engineer Works in Oak Ridge, Tennessee. But British engineers simply did not know enough about how America had done it.

In January, in an almost desperate effort to tap into America's atomic secrets, Roger Makins had paid a Saturday visit to Dean Acheson who was ill at home. The British needed help, he pleaded, to solve a dozen obstacles "related to the know-how rather than to basic scientific information" of trying to construct a large atomic energy plant. He spuriously claimed that the British could solve the problems on their own in six months. But could the Americans not oblige and tell them "how these specific obstacles had been overcome"?

Makins had picked "the Dean," product of Groton and Yale, because he was an unapologetic Anglophile who was known to be sympathetic to England's atomic claims. In fact, Acheson would confess in his memoirs, he found U.S. willingness to break its promise to Britain "repulsive." He had also, however, resigned as Roosevelt's Undersecretary of the Treasury after a "spectacular row" in which he accused the President of trying to get him to "sign illegal documents." Sympathetic though he may have been, and though he liked Makins personally, Acheson impatiently dismissed his blandishments to circumvent the McMahon Act.[3]

When that back-door approach failed, Attlee pressed Truman for "certain information relating to manufacturing and industrial aspects of atomic energy" which, he made clear, the United States "is under a commitment to supply."[4]

"The Joint Chiefs of Staff," Secretaries Patterson and Forrestal told Marshall in early March, believed that a plant in England would be "disadvantageous" to America's national security interest. If England were overrun by Russia, they reasoned, the Soviets would gain an atomic plant and large stockpiles of uranium. In fact, the existence of the plant and the uranium might be the incentive for a Soviet invasion of Great Britain. Therefore, instead of building a plant, England should recognize "the overriding importance" of sending all of her ore to America.[5]

The implication that, should the Soviet Union conquer Britain, Washington's only concern was the fate of a few tons of uranium offended the British almost beyond words. General Leslie R. Groves had been the first to talk about "the danger of storing uranium in Britain." Disgusted, Ambassador Halifax suggested to London that the Combined Development Trust be dissolved and America's access to Congolese uranium be terminated.[6]

The Soviets moved first, however. Using the information provided by Maclean, they continued to leech small doses of the uranium virus into the Belgian body politic, which resulted in wild accusations and inflamed passions. Finally, on March 11, after five weeks of relentless pressure, the Belgian government fell.[7]

During the ensuing confusion the Communists, who seemed well positioned to be a broker in any government, announced that they would not be part of any coalition ruled by Spaak. As Gullion, a native of Kentucky with Ivy League polish and good looks, told Acheson, "The [American] Embassy thinks the move was due to instructions from" Moscow. Because with the Communists "out of the Government, they are free to attack Government handling of uranium which is what we have feared for some time."[8]

The Soviets had scored a major coup. To hold together even a non–Communist coalition, Spaak had to swing way to the Left and agree to a Belgian atomic research project that Communists and nationalists alike hoped would lead to a Franco–Belgian bomb. This would also require diverting uranium from America to Belgium. Moreover, if Spaak could not halt the Communists' successes and their ability to rally mass public opinion against the Anglo–American "rape" of Belgium's national asset, the government might be forced to nationalize the uranium deposits.

This sent tremors through Washington's atomic energy community, which considered the upheaval in Brussels as "danger[ous] to our procurement program . . . and to [our] security." The Soviets, Gullion assumed, would have full access—through Joliot-Curie and other French scientists—to any research program. More appalling, if nationalization of the Katanga mines did follow and the ore production were sold on the basis of competitive bidding, the Russians would make an all-out effort to offer the best terms.[9]

U.S. policymakers were unaware of the worst contingency, however. If the ore were sold to the bidder offering the best terms, the Soviets—because of Maclean's knowledge of the details of any Anglo-American bid—would always be able to offer better terms. In the midst of all this tumult, Maclean was brought to London for consultations toward the end of March.

While Washington was preoccupied with continuing the flow of uranium to its atomic plants, England was equally absorbed with constructing its plant. Maclean had attacked the problem with robust intensity, as he did whenever Soviet interests were as important as Britain's. He had been badgering Gullion to the point that the American eventually sent a memo to Acheson advising him that "As he does *at frequent intervals,* Mr. Maclean asked me if any progress could be reported on the British desire to secure from this country information relating to the construction of a large-scale atomic energy plant in Britain."[10]

Maclean returned to London empty-handed, however. The JCS would not budge. And although General Dwight D. Eisenhower, chief of staff of the army, had assured Inverchapel that the JCS opposition "was not due to any misgivings as to the blemish in [Britain's] secret arrangements," Maclean knew there might be darker motives. As Inverchapel told Attlee, the real problem was Alan Nunn May, "who our people certified as being entirely trustworthy." The unspoken American implication was clear: How many more Nunn Mays are there beneath your cloak of establishment respectability? How many, indeed.[11]

The Foreign Office did have some good news for Maclean. London had decided that his work was far too critical to be interrupted. Therefore, instead of pulling him out of Washington when his tour expired at the end of May, he was to remain in Washington at least another year. In fact, his tour was extended for sixteen months. Only Halifax served longer in the Washington embassy during the decisive war and postwar era.[12] Maclean returned to the United States on April 6 in time for the atomic shockwaves that were about to reverberate through Washington.

The chain reaction began in January when David Lilienthal, the paunchy, sixty-year-old former Tennessee Valley Authority chairman and now chairman of the AEC, traveled to Los Alamos to inspect America's mighty nuclear arsenal. He was not prepared for what he found—a jumbled collection of contraptions, devices, and parts stored haphazardly behind some chicken wire. At a time when its critics were accusing America of flaunting its atomic might, there was not a single operative atomic bomb in its stockpile, nor did the capacity exist to assemble any.

"Probably one of the saddest days of my life was to walk down in that chicken-wire enclosure; they weren't even protected, what gimmicks there were," he told historian Gregg Herken years later. "I was shocked when I found out" that perhaps one bomb was operative. But a team of twenty-four highly trained technicians would require two days to assemble it, and the U.S. military did not have even one team in uniform. "The politically significant thing is that there really were no bombs in a military sense . . . We were really almost without bombs, and not only that, we were without people; that was really the significant thing . . . You can hardly exaggerate the unreadiness of the U.S. military at this time."[13]

At 11:15 A.M. on Wednesday, April 16, Truman convened an emergency White House meeting to hear Lilienthal's official report. Present were Secretary of War Patterson, Admiral Leahy, military chief of staff to Truman as he had been to Roosevelt, Secretary of the Navy Forrestal, and Lilienthal. The gathering was so secret that both the White House and the participants were instructed to keep it off their official calendars.[14]

The situation was grim. The crash demobilization program had thinned America's military personnel to fewer than one million. Bomber and fighter planes had simply been blown up on airways. Ships had been mothballed or sunk. Marshall characterized it not as the demobilization of the American military, but as its disintegration. With a peacetime draft politically unpopular, postwar U.S. military strategy relied entirely on its atomic weapons.[15]

Therefore, when Lilienthal reported to the President that there were no assembled bombs, no assembly teams, no tests even to determine whether the wartime devices were still good, "the shock was apparent on Truman's face." There was worse to come. The United States was also nearly out of uranium. Even if America's "bomb factory" were properly staffed and equipped, there was no fuel with which to run it; nor were prospects good. The Belgian political situation remained tense, and in Katanga the mines themselves had been affected by labor unrest and might be closed by either strikes or the need to sink new shafts.[16]

Patterson, grim, humorless, and intense as always, asked testily if the British were still getting 50 percent of the Congo shipments. Yes, Lilienthal replied. Leahy demanded to know why, insisting they were not entitled to it. This was a blind spot for the admiral, whose dark, bushy, and always furrowed eyebrows gave him the appearance of having just bitten into the world's sourest lemon. Although he pompously titled his memoirs *I Was There,* Roosevelt actually had excluded him from most of his and Churchill's highly secret atomic negotiations. Because he did not know of the Quebec and Hyde Park agreements, Leahy always insisted that they were figments of the British imagination, and when London produced documentation, he intimated they were a forgery. All this drove him, when he finally learned of the Manhattan Project, to assure everyone that the bomb would never work. Entitled to it or not, at a time when the United States had no uranium, the British had more than three thousand tons—the world's largest stockpile of mined high-grade uranium ore.

The military implications of Lilienthal's report were staggering. A little over a year earlier, the Joint Chiefs of Staff had declared that "The U.S. must for all time maintain absolute supremacy in atomic weapons, including number, size, and power." They were not permitted to know about the size of the arsenal, which they naturally believed was plentiful. The JCS would now have to be told that their contingency planning was based on nonexistent bombs and on phantom production schedules that could not be met for years.

Someone else also had to be told. If there was blustering and bombast about America's unchallenged military power it was not coming from the War Department, the State Department, or the White House. It was coming from Capitol Hill which, left in the dark, had sprouted dangerous assumptions and myths like wild mushrooms. They had not a clue about any secret diplomacy that gave Britain joint custody of the bomb. They had no idea that production had been virtually abandoned after the bombs fell on Japan. Their unspoken belief was that, with its "winning weapon" the United States could, if necessary, dictate the shape of the postwar world. Only one thing was certain. When the Congress had its cherished illusions shattered, there would be unshirted hell to pay.

Maclean understood all this, so what prevented the Soviets from blowing the whistle? By leaking proof that the West had engaged in sinister and secret wartime diplomacy in violation of its own domestic laws as well as the new U.N. Charter, Moscow could have touched off a civil war between the Republican Congress and the Democratic White House, jeopardized America's uranium supply, and scored a Soviet triumph in international public opinion.

Because of Maclean, however, Soviet interests were almost perfectly aligned with those of Britain. So long as Maclean was able to extract classified information from his CPC and CDT activities, it was in Russia's interest to become, quite literally, a secret partner to the wartime agreements. Once the wall of secrecy came crashing down, Maclean's access would vanish and with it the best—if not the only—source the Soviets had inside the West's atomic vaults.

This was particularly true once the Atomic Energy Commission was created and General Groves, the bête noire of the British, reluctantly yielded his once commanding role. Maclean found that the civilian staff of the AEC had a refreshingly open attitude. For years Groves had blocked visits by British scientists to America's atomic facilities, but Maclean was soon able to secure approval for British visits to the most restricted sites.

As a result, when British scientists visited the fifty-four thousand-acre Clinton Engineer Works at Oak Ridge, Tennessee, their hosts "expressed a desire to help in every possible way in their power." At the time, Clinton's electromagnetic plant was the only one in the world turning out the fully enriched uranium needed for an atomic bomb. "It is an astonishing place," A. K. Longair, a top physicist at the British Ministry of Supply, gushed after Maclean arranged for him to make a follow-up visit to Oak Ridge. In a report Maclean helped to draft, Longair marveled that this one visit "saved us many months of work."[17]

One day P.J. Eaton, British liaison to the AEC whose office was in its headquarters, showed Maclean a publication that AEC general manager Carroll Wilson had given him. "This is the sort of publication of which we should like to get hold of more copies," he told Donald as well as London, "but the circumstances are such that it is not possible to do so . . . being of a secret nature."[18]

Wilson, formerly an MIT professor and Vannevar Bush's wartime aide, also cleared British scientists to visit the Berkeley Radiation Laboratory, which Groves had blocked for years. This led to the greatest coup of all—for both the British and the Soviets. The AEC forwarded—through Maclean—the blueprints for the ninety-two-inch synchro-cyclotron being developed at Berkeley. This came at a time when the largest Soviet "atom smasher" was thirty inches.[19]

But the inevitable day of reckoning was nearing. Tuesday morning, May 6, Maclean received a call from Gullion telling him "The cat is out of the bag." The secrecy that Britain (and, through Maclean, the Soviets) were depending upon to get America's atomic secrets was coming unraveled. During secret testimony before the Joint Committee on Atomic Energy (JCAE) the day before, Lilienthal "had been closely questioned by Congress about arrangements for obtaining raw materials." When members of the JCAE assumed America's atomic energy program was fueled by domestic uranium, Lilienthal and Wilson felt compelled to disabuse them of such a naive belief.

"We were soon," as Lilienthal later told it, "in the middle of the Belgian Congo." Using a pointer and a series of maps, Wilson, to gasps of disbelief, explained that America received no uranium from domestic sources, and that half of the Congo's supply went to England. Lilienthal added that currently America did not have sufficient uranium to produce atomic bombs.

The committee was in near shock. They had no idea that England from the beginning had been so involved in the development of the atomic bomb. "You mean," Senator Tom Connally, the tall wavy-haired Texan asked incredulously, "that England knows how to make the bomb?" "The answer," Lilienthal inexplicably responded, "is certainly yes." With looks of indignation spreading around the hearing room, Lilienthal quickly explained that he and his AEC colleagues had opposed keeping Congress in the dark about "the secret agreements with England," but they had been overruled by the State Department.

Gullion predicted to Maclean that "Acheson may have to appear" before the JCAE, and that the State Department was "acutely aware of the difficulty this may cause Spaak." Maclean immediately rushed a coded top-secret cable to London. Within forty-eight hours Dr. J.D. Cockcroft, the director of Britain's Atomic Research Establishment at Harwell, was in Washington. If the door was about to slam on any British hopes, they were going to make one last charge to get whatever secrets they could. Their target was the affable Carroll Wilson.[20]

"He's a very live wire and a nice lad," Gordon Munro had cabled London after he and Maclean had a long session with Wilson back in March. This followed on the heels of a report by Dr. Alexander King, the third member of the British atomic troika in Washington, that he had received a number of encouraging signs "on the part of the Commission that they intend to help us in every way possible."[21]

On May 10 King and Cockcroft listened as Wilson outlined a loophole that he knew the State Department was considering as an emergency measure to try to prevent Communist efforts to guide Belgium into a go-it-alone program. Spaak had suggested that one way to placate the leftists was to incorporate Belgian scientists into American research projects. But the State Department said its hands were tied because the McMahon Act "makes it impossible for us to comply."[22]

As Wilson now explained it, however, the Act permitted the president to share classified information to "assure the common defense and security." If the administration was thinking about invoking that to avoid troubles with Belgium, why not Britain? And Congress would not be any the wiser.

King and Cockcroft understood the risk involved in this maneuver. Acheson had almost blown up when Makins suggested a conspiracy to evade Congress. And Truman was now antagonistic toward the idea that the United States had a legal, moral, or strategic interest in helping Britain in its arms race against Russia. But the two Britons liked the direction of Wilson's thinking and their communiqué provided London with "cheering news."[23]

The three met again two nights later for dinner at the elegant and exclusive Cosmos Club on Massachusetts Avenue. They talked of the status of the French program and the quality of Britain's atomic intelligence (Wilson was not impressed). Although they did not discuss specifics in their report to London, the two scientists reported that Wilson "outlined what he would do to help Britain."[24]

Wilson was playing with fire in a highly charged atmosphere. Earlier that day, Acheson had trudged up to the Hill. (By then Lilienthal, having primed the senators for Acheson's appearance, was on a Caribbean cruise writing that "[I] feel quite pleased with myself at the moment.") In a private meeting with Republican Senators Bourke B. Hickenlooper, chairman of the JCAE, and Arthur Vandenberg, chairman of the Senate Foreign Relations Committee, Acheson laid out the history and present circumstances of America's atomic energy program. The two men listened in stony silence; then they ripped into him.[25]

"I was shocked and astounded," Hickenlooper later told Secretary Marshall, while Vandenberg characterized the agreements as "astounding" and "unthinkable." Both were offended by what they considered White House audacity in entering into such binding commitments without even consulting the Senate. But the most loathsome requirement of all was that the United States could never use its greatest weapon—even if at war with the Soviet Union—without England's prior consent. That is, the prior consent of a second-rate, bankrupt nation run by a socialist government headed by a pacifist. (Clement Attlee refused to carry a gun in the First World War; he led his men over the top with a swagger stick.)

The full JCAE was only marginally less vituperative when, meeting in executive session, they listened to Acheson explain for two hours that the United States was utterly dependent on foreign uranium, and that the United States was neither the sole developer of the bomb nor the sole master of its use.[26]

Acheson may not have fully realized it, but the Truman administration had just acquired a new atomic partner—the U.S. Congress—more specifically, Vandenberg and Hickenlooper. They quickly proved to be jealous, demanding, tyrannical, and suspicious, and soon the State Department would long for the days when their greatest problem was rebuffing the compliant British.

What is most striking about Congress's machinations is that it regarded Britain, not Russia, as America's most threatening atomic rival. This was partly owing to the fact that Congress was the most voracious consumer of estimates, which, until August 1949 when the Soviets finally exploded their first atomic device, were often wildly inaccurate.

Bernard Baruch, America's atomic negotiator at the United Nations, authoritatively predicted that it would be another twenty years before Russia could manufacture its own bomb. General Groves, who was now a member of the Military Liaison Committee to the AEC, and Strauss dismissed the possibility of a Red Bomb in less than a decade. There were more reliable estimates, though the Congress was not getting them. In July Roscoe Hillenkoetter, the first director of the recently created Central Intelligence Agency, estimated that the earliest date for a Soviet bomb was the mid-1950s, probably mid-1953. Several months later, that was revised. It is "doubtful the Russians can produce a bomb before 1953," he assured the President, "and almost certainly they cannot produce one before 1951."[27]

The later the date, the greater the buildup of America's stockpile. But there was another consideration. Stalin had proven himself a ruthless and tyrannical despot, an international menace on the scale of the prewar Hitler. Washington believed that the best chance for avoiding an arms race or a nuclear war, would be if Russia did not have the atomic bomb until after Stalin had departed the scene. He was seventy, and the West could secretly hope that his years as a chain smoker and heavy drinker, not to mention the strain of a career as an unsurpassed mass murderer, might catch up with Stalin before his scientists finally solved the elusive atomic secrets. Had the CIA's estimate of mid-1953 been correct, it would have turned out that way. Stalin died in March 1953.

Scholars, however, would later estimate that in June 1947—at a time when the CIA was reporting "the highest Soviet authority [Stalin] was secretly disturbed by the lack of progress" and heads were rolling—Soviet scientists had actually achieved their first chain reaction. If so, this would mean they were then only four and a half years behind America, whose first chain reaction came at the University of Chicago in December 1942. At that pace, they would have had their first bomb by some time in early 1950. Using a different calculation, the State Department's Gullion believed they could have it even sooner. Reasoning that "it took the United States, with its almost unrestricted resources, three years to build the first atomic bomb," and assuming that since Hiroshima, the Russians had thrown all their resources into the project, they should, he told Acheson, have a bomb by the summer of 1948. Unless, he pointed out, they were having any one of several problems, including "their uranium availabilities."[28]

Gullion did not know how accurate he was. In their "frenzy to complete their first nuclear chain reaction, Soviet scientists utilized every last bit of uranium at their disposal," roughly forty-five tons (a U.S. reactor required only twenty-seven tons to achieve a chain reaction). By the summer of 1947, then, the Soviet and American atomic energy programs were dead even in one category—both were out of uranium.[29]

The difference was that while Maclean enabled the Kremlin to know the exact status of America's plight, Washington did not have a clue about the Soviet position. "It is essential that we know as soon as possible when the Russians have succeeded in developing atomic explosives," Robert A. Lovett pleaded with Marshall in July 1947.[30]

The Soviet Union had uranium but it was mostly low-grade deposits located on the fringes of its thinly populated borders near Afghanistan, or in the Caucasus where no suitable transportation was available either to haul labor in or ore out. A crash mining program begun in 1940 was abandoned after the German invasion in June 1941. By 1943 the head of the Soviet atomic bomb project railed "that they lacked even a microgram of pure uranium."[31] Moscow tried repeatedly to buy even small quantities from the United States, but Washington refused. In August 1945, when Alan Nunn May provided his control in Canada with 16 micrograms of uranium 233 and a sample of uranium 235, the Soviets were so elated that a high-ranking military attaché immediately flew them to Moscow.[32]

After the war, Red Army troops occupying Czechoslovakia, Bulgaria, Poland, and Hungary were presiding over slave labor camps where hundreds of thousands of civilians and former military personnel were being forced to extract low-grade uranium ore from open pit mining. The most intense effort was in the town of St.

Joachimstal, sixty miles southwest of Prague, where uranium had first been discovered in 1789. According to some reports, the miners of 150 years ago might have had it easier, because the Soviets made their laborers dig out the rock using only their bare hands. It was precisely these activities that made Moscow so determined to exclude their troops in Central and Eastern Europe from the U.N. troop census.[33]

By 1946 the total Soviet yield from all sources was still insufficient to support more than a modest atomic development program. One hundred tons of high-grade uranium was considered the minimum working stock for an atomic energy plant. Thousands of tons of Soviet low-grade ore had yielded but a few pounds of pure uranium.[34]

In December 1945 General Groves had completed a comprehensive survey which concluded that the Combined Development Trust (CDT) "controls 97% of the world's uranium output from presently producing countries." With access to the Trust's Restricted Data Reports, updated monthly, Maclean could provide the Soviets with the details of the Katanga mining operation—how much ore was mined, what its purity was, how much was shipped and to where, and how much Britain and America were paying Union Minière.[35]

"Maclean attended all meetings of the [Combined Development] Trust from March 1947 until he left us," Wilson told the FBI. In fact, during those eighteen months, he was the only official of the three member nations to attend every meeting of the CDT.[36]

The CDT's data was considered, Acheson had emphasized to the JCAE, "prime military secrets." Historian Richard Hewlett confirms that "global uranium sources were very secret at the time, very hush-hush. There were really a very limited few who were aware of information on raw materials." One American engineer assigned to the CDT later verified that "there is nothing that we would have talked about in the raw materials area that we would not have shared with Maclean."[37]

All three Trust nations were equally anxious to keep very secret all information about uranium movements, contracts and quantities. When asked if there was any laxness about security around when dealing internally with other staff members or representatives of their British allies, the same AEC engineer replied, "I certainly believed every document I handled was terribly, terribly important. We knew that the information about uranium was enormously important. We did not want the Soviets to know how limited our own supply was."[38]

In October 1945 Secretary of State James Byrnes had pointed for emphasis to a map on his wall as he insisted to a visitor that the Russians "were after" the uranium deposits in the Congo. With Maclean's help they had made a good try. By injecting the fate of the Katanga mines into Belgium's daily political life, they were able to manipulate the fall of the Brussels government. Although the Communists were able to keep the uranium issue on the front burner, however, the mines still had not been nationalized. Nor had their valuable ore been available for bids on the international market. The only real hope of severing the United States from the Congo supply was to further arouse Belgian national passions against the arrangement.[39]

On the morning of August 6, Ambassador Alan Kirk in Brussels awoke to discover the exact weights, prices, and other statistical data on Congolese uranium shipments to England and America plastered across the front page of *The New York Herald Tribune*. He immediately cabled Washington that "the Soviets can now deduce pretty closely how much active stuff we get from the Congo deliveries." "Communist wrath" in Belgium, he predicted with deadly accuracy, "will now be directed at United States deliveries." Kirk also guessed that "the Communists had these data for some time."[40]

The French-language newspaper *Le Drapeau Rouge* led the attack. America, it charged, was paying an inadequate price. It was suggested that "a proper price would pay for all war damages to Belgium," and that coal shortages would be irrelevant if the nation could use its own uranium for atomic energy. Uranium was portrayed as a panacea that would permit revolutionary science and medical breakthroughs, if only Belgium were "really master of her own fate." The villain in this piece was the United States; England was barely mentioned. Spaak maintained "his stony silence" for the recriminations that followed, but Kirk thought it was possible that "he might find himself obliged to yield to heavy internal pressures in order to remain in power."[41]

Meanwhile in Washington, Maclean was not only making recurrent visits to the CDT, the AEC, and the State Department but, according to later FBI reports, he was also "a frequent visitor" to the CIA's temporary offices around the Reflecting Pool. "The logs kept by the door guards at your 'O' Building [sic] located in front of the Lincoln memorial," Hoover advised in a memo to the CIA, "reflected that Maclean often entered that particular building after hours." The FBI also had reason to believe that Maclean was dating two CIA stenographers.[42]

Melinda Maclean might have found this news almost comforting, because, by the spring and summer of 1947, Maclean had begun what his drinking friend Philip Toynbee later diagnosed as "a state of sickening descent." Geoffrey Hoare, the British journalist who interviewed Melinda extensively after Donald fled, concluded that his "bouts of wild drunkenness seemed to have their beginnings around 1947." And, as he knew from firsthand experience, "if there was anyone who should not drink heavily, it was Donald." Increasingly, as he became drunk, he was prone to violent outbursts, often directed against Melinda.[43]

Although Gullion had no clue about the seamier side of Maclean's life, he did notice a strain surfacing sometimes over what seemed arcane business. One day he mentioned that the United States had received requests for atomic information from two Scandinavian countries. Agitated, Maclean demanded to know the reason that they needed any atomic capability. Surely the United States did not intend to comply, he asserted with more than a trace of anger. Gullion had never seen Maclean so wrought. This incident slipped his mind, however, and he never thought of associating their conversation with an item that appeared from Tass and in European communist papers several days later, alleging that "secret military agreements" were being arranged between "the United States, the United Kingdom and Scandinavian countries." It was not until June 1951 when he was in Vietnam (preparing a tour for a young Congressman from Boston, John F. Kennedy) and heard that Maclean had fled behind the Iron Curtain that Gullion recalled the incident. Then he realized the source of Donald's agitation—the Kremlin's fear of having neighbors within a short flight of Moscow armed with nuclear weapons.[44]

By late August Donald had taken charge of making arrangements for a British delegation to attend a three-nation conference to decide which atomic secrets could be declassified. He cannot, however, take credit for including Klaus Fuchs, the Soviet's premier atomic spy. That initiative came from Wilson, who early on recommended to the British Commonwealth Scientific Office that "three or four experts who participated in the work at Los Alamos . . . such as Dr. Klaus Fuchs . . . would be very helpful to the meeting."[45]

The AEC's security check of Fuchs noted that he was a German-born British-naturalized citizen who had been part of the original British mission assigned to the Manhattan Project in 1943. Like other members of that mission he was "never investigated by the U.S. government, their special investigation as conducted by the British government was accepted [as was Nunn May's] by General Groves." That clearance was again accepted.[46]

What none of those security checks showed, of course, was that not only had Fuchs been providing secrets of immense value to the Soviets since 1942; it was probably his reporting that alerted the Kremlin to the military significance of atomic energy. As a result, Soviet intelligence launched a massive espionage effort targeting Anglo-American research and development installations, beginning in early 1943. (As part of that campaign Igor Gouzenko, after special training, was assigned in June 1943 to Soviet military intelligence in Ottawa.)[47]

From Los Alamos, Fuchs later conveyed to the Russians information about the implosion method for detonating a plutonium bomb and a description of the bomb set off in the 1945 "Trinity" test. At the end of the war he returned to England to become one of the most important physicists at Britain's Atomic Energy Research Laboratory at Harwell.

Both the British and the Americans were heartened by the ease with which Fuchs and other British scientists were cleared for participation. "We may be over the worst of the crazy hysteria about 'loyalty'," Lilienthal enthused in his diary the weekend of the conference. London was encouraged because the conference was one of "the rare forums where British and American nuclear scientists could meet."[48]

On November 5, ten days before the conference, Maclean received his non-escort pass for the Atomic Energy Commission headquarters. (Coincidentally, the next day Molotov sent jitters through Western capitals by announcing that the secret of the atom bomb "had ceased to exist.") While Groves and Strauss reserved a special distrust for the British, who not only craved the atomic secrets but believed that they were entitled to them, someone of Maclean's stature was never a target of the usual security screens.[49]

In the United States as in England, it was assumed that only the low-born would accept Soviet bribes to steal. The AEC boasted to Congress that in the first six months of its existence, the Commission had received fourteen thousand applications for routine guard jobs and had rejected thirteen thousand of them. Further, by the summer of 1947, "considerable progress was made in reducing the number of construction workers who have access to restricted work areas."[50]

The preparations for the sixteen "non-citizen aliens" attending the three-day conference from Friday through Sunday reflect just how much freedom Maclean's pass gave him. The British and the Canadian delegations were assigned a private office near the conference room. A cabinet safe and a screwdriver were provided to both delegations so that each could set their own combination. Britain's and Canada's most prominent scientists were restricted to the conference room, their private meeting room, and an assigned restroom. To ensure that nobody wandered, three armed guards were posted at points from which they could see all three rooms. All "non-citizen visitors . . . were kept under rather constant security cognizance at all times," security chief LaPlante reported to Carroll Wilson afterward.

"At no time during the three-day conference were there any actions observed by either me or my assistants that would cause any reason to doubt the motives or actions of the visiting personnel." LaPlante's embarrassment must have been acute when he later learned that his elaborate security system had failed to prevent two of Soviet Russia's most accomplished spies from attending every session and being wined and dined at the Willard and Carlton hotels at the taxpayer's expense. It is fair to ask, as he must have, in what way did their presence help the Soviets?[51]

Fuchs, then thirty-six, "was not an inspired or original scientist but, rather, a highly competent and omnivorous worker with a remarkably good memory," according to Margaret Gowing, the official historian for Britain's atomic energy program. By 1947 "he was the one ubiquitous scientist at Harwell," and one of the few who had been deeply involved in the development of the weapon at Los Alamos.[52] His inclusion caused the British to hope that the Washington conference would go beyond health and industrial problems to the much more restricted information associated with atomic weapons. Although the AEC would later mislead the Congress about this, as Wilson admitted to the FBI, the technology associated with the atomic bomb was discussed.[53]

Everyone considered the conference a success. The Americans were happy to finally obtain from Cockcroft specifically which data the British needed to develop their atomic capacity. In his report to the Foreign Office, Maclean gloated that the British delegation "managed to get declassified a number of borderline documents." Furthermore, understanding the American reasoning behind their refusal to release certain information "provided useful clues as to the productive areas to pursue."[54]

According to one of his biographers, Fuchs "took a conservative line throughout, always on the side of keeping things classified; at times the line-up among scientists was seven against one." This echoes Maclean's reputation around the embassy as being relentlessly intolerant of breaches in security. In this case it is slightly surprising, because for Fuchs (and Maclean) if he were ever caught, his best defense would be that much of what he gave the Soviets was then or had since become declassified.[55]

Although three years of leaks never caused the spotlight of suspicion to shine directly on Maclean, the cumulative result was a loss of confidence in the embassy by the State Department. This is a complete reversal from circumstances at the time of Maclean's arrival. Then, it was the State Department and the American embassy at the Court of St. James that were bypassed by the White House and No. 10 Downing Street, both of whom vastly preferred to rely on the British embassy in Washington. Maclean's role in undermining trust in the embassy may have cost him and the Soviets one of the Cold War's most politically charged secrets.

One of the administration's newest partners to the atomic secrets, Senator Bourke Hickenlooper—a portly Iowan given to white suits,

panama hats, and frequent overseas trips that earned him the reputation for being the premier junketeer of his day—was so offended
by the notion that Britain could restrict America both in terms of its
ability to produce the bomb and its freedom to use it, he decided to
rectify the entire situation. His solution was simple—blackmail.

On June 5, one month after Acheson dropped his bombshell on
the JCAE, Secretary of State George Marshall, delivering the Harvard commencement speech, called upon the United States to launch
a massive economic aid program for Europe. Under Marshall's
leadership, and with the considerable help of Vandenberg, the improbable idea of America's once again coming to Europe's rescue
caught on, and by late summer a considerable segment of the
American public rallied behind the idea. Still, it would be a tough
sell to the Republican-dominated Congress and Hickenlooper's support would be crucial.

Aware of this, Hickenlooper decreed in a letter to Marshall that it
was time for the United States simply to take possession of Britain's
uranium stockpile. England did not need it, and with so many
problems in the Congo, and with no chance of the United States
finding new domestic sources, this was the best solution. Besides,
the size of her stockpile was so large, it might become "bait" for
Russia to invade and seize it first. Moreover, Britain must renounce
all further claims under the Quebec Agreement, which would have
to be rescinded. True, objections could be expected, but Hickenlooper was prepared for that. If Britain refused, "I shall oppose, as
vigorously as I can, and publicly if necessary, any further aid or
assistance to Britain." He was putting the Marshall Plan on the line.
England could choose between being a second-rate military power
and being economically destitute, or just being a second-rate power.
He called these actions a prerequisite for pulling "British chestnuts
out of the fire." Some might call it a quid pro quo; others came to
think of it as extortion.[56]

The State Department was appalled at the prospect. Lovett, Acheson's successor as undersecretary, told the American members of the
Combined Policy Committee that if such a linkage were known, it
would greatly damage U.S. foreign policy:

No British Government could be expected to sell uranium, or put it
up for collateral, for an amount in dollars which would make little

impression on its financial crisis but which would place the government in the position of surrendering an asset far more important in terms of political and national security value.[57]

"Uranium had acquired a symbolic value bound up with nationalism and defense," Lovett tried explaining to Hickenlooper and Vandenberg, and Britain would never surrender it.[58]

None of this interested Hickenlooper. Besides, he had won over Vandenberg without whose support the Marshall Plan was dead. In a series of meetings the two senators first got the State Department to succumb. Then they turned their sights on Britain. Vandenberg, if possible, was even more tactless and vengeful than his colleague, as Lilienthal's notes of a December 5 meeting make clear. "I don't recognize [the British] veto [on the use of the bomb]," he told Lovett. It is a "source of desperate embarrassment. Horrified and have been since I learned of it. Vitally essential wipe that off beyond any dispute, though I deny continuing authority of the agreement." Vandenberg was so upset about the threat to atomic bomb production caused by the uranium shortage and looming labor troubles in Katanga that he threatened to resign from the Joint Committee if it could not secure for America the uranium it needed to produce bombs and the sole right to use them.[59]

"It was inconceivable that we should go to pains to aid Britain financially" if Britain continued to "hoard uranium." Vandenberg wanted it explained to Ambassador Inverchapel that this all had to be settled before the Marshall Plan legislation came before Congress. He gave the State Department an ultimatum—get the British to capitulate by December 17 or else.[60]

Lovett recoiled at the suggestion of confiding in the embassy. The last thing he wanted to do was "to lay the cards on the table" for Ambassador Inverchapel. The aging ambassador had all but disappeared once he came to Washington. He was not up for this last assignment, and he never should have been offered it. Acheson charitably called him "eccentric" and was never sure "whose views he was representing, and how what one said in reply appeared in his telegrams to London."[61]

When this was added to the doubts about the reliability of the embassy, it was decided to bypass the British in Washington and communicate this ultimatum—couched, of course, in the most diplomatic terms—to No. 10 Downing Street through the American embassy in London.

The Soviets had declared war against the Marshall Plan. Decrying American efforts to subjugate Europe, Molotov tried to block plans for an integrated economic program at a June meeting with the foreign ministers of France and Britain. He failed and stormed out of the session. When Eastern European nations expressed an interest in receiving American aid, Moscow "promptly announced regrets" for all of them. When Czechoslovakia persisted, Stalin summoned Czech Foreign Minister Jan Masaryk to Moscow and told him to desist or be considered an enemy of the Soviet Union. Soviet-inspired "spontaneous demonstrations" against American imperialism broke out in a number of Western countries throughout 1947.[62]

Soviet actions were to no avail. But, had the Kremlin known that U.S. senators were using Marshall Plan aid to extort concessions from an ally in an imperialist move that Marx himself would have found breathtaking, they might have been able to strike a real blow at the Plan in its infancy. Kennan, the head of the Policy Planning Staff, the think tank for the Marshall Plan, predicted that the United States would be "subject to the severest criticism if it should become known that we were bargaining relief aid for rights to atomic materials."[63]

Bypassed, Maclean was in no position to alert Moscow. On December 4 at 7:00 P.M., Lovett sent a "Personal, Top Secret, NIACT, 'Eyes only for the Ambassador' " cable to Lewis Douglas in London. "Vandenberg and some others strongly feel that further aid to Britain . . . should be conditioned on Britain's meeting our terms with respect to allocation of atomic raw materials" and other considerations. If Great Britain could not be persuaded to meet the terms, the Marshall Plan could be endangered, he explained.

Lovett also made clear that although he had hinted to Inverchapel that something needed to be done about uranium allocation and that it must be kept free of the Marshall Plan legislation, he chose not to confide in the embassy. In a subsequent telegram, he confirmed that the terms America had to insist upon "probably will not be shown to the British at this time or in that form."[64]

George F. Kennan, who could become almost catatonic at the

sight of a loathsome politician meddling in diplomacy, warned that "we can be faced with a situation in Congress which could have appalling consequences" if the British government would not acquiesce.[65] Marshall put it in a quite different form directly to Bevin: "What we urgently need in THE NEAR FUTURE," he wrote in a cryptic note during a Council of Foreign Ministers meeting, "is more of such which you have."[66]

Whitehall had no choice but to give in. They complained bitterly, and, at the last minute, negotiations in Washington were interrupted so that Roger Makins could return to London and present the American ultimatum to the Cabinet, but the British knew they had their backs against the wall.

On December 10 the Combined Policy Committee met, with Maclean as the British secretary. Lovett said it was time to end "the anomalous wartime arrangements" which could threaten "the world political situation." The Hyde Park and Quebec agreements were torn up. In exchange the British got some vague promises for more information in the future. Britain agreed to ship two-thirds of its uranium stockpile to America, and, for at least the next two years, the United States was entitled to all the Congolese uranium.

All of this was contained in an agreement called the *Modus Vivendi,* whose "Principles of Future Cooperation" was drafted by Maclean and three others.[67]

This arrangement ended any British hope of winning the nuclear arms race against the Soviets. Maclean was in a surly mood before the formal signing took place on January 7, 1948. As British, American, and Canadian dignitaries gathered in the Blair House conference room, Maclean sought out Gullion to protest the name given to the document. *Modus Vivendi,* he pointed out, "was an agreement between two adversaries who have come to terms." This seemed a harsh characterization of Anglo-American relations. Gullion demurred. It was an accurate enough term, and besides, it was too late to change it. Maclean quickly dropped the point, almost apologetically explaining that he had been instructed by London to raise the objection.[68]

A shabby atmosphere pervaded the entire ceremony. If the often fiercely unhappy atomic partnership had ended with a messy divorce, this "new beginning" had all the characteristics of a shotgun wedding. At the last moment, "the State Department boys," as Lilienthal derisively called them, realized that green tablecloths, mandatory for any diplomatic event, had not been put out. Lilienthal, who characterized the entire event as "a day of torture," watched the officious diplomats get upset as the housekeeper explained that none could be found.

The AEC, which had pushed hardest to make the Anglo-American relationship "legitimate," did not even see the agreement that it was suppose to approve until the last minute—nor had any of the other agencies. "I have never felt more ashamed of the internal workings of an organization," Lilienthal confided to his journal. By the time the British and Canadian ambassadors stood and solemnly announced, "I have been authorized by my government to approve this agreement; this I now do," it was anticlimactic.[69]

CHAPTER TWELVE

If the Soviets know where the holdline is
drawn they will move on what isn't protected
like any predatory animal.

Note by Donald Maclean during top-secret
talks leading to NATO

THE HOLDLINE

As 1948 began, Donald Maclean's life, to all outward appearances, was a storybook existence. To most of his American neighbors he was "a typical British aristocrat," prone to absentmindedness (cats and dogs could be found sleeping in his car because he would forget to close the door) but "compassionate, cheerful, with splendid manners, and never cross." The head of a household that featured two robust sons, he played an invigorating game of golf, was a top performer on the tennis courts, at the top of the ladder at the embassy, and in constant demand on the diplomatic social circuit. The future held unlimited promise.[1]

When Maclean looked toward the future, however, he could see only the dark uncertainty of the abyss. His final nine months in America were actually an unrelieved torment. They began with his being forced to confront ugly truths that he had long tried to deny, and ended, as strong evidence indicates, with his contemplating suicide.

At lunch one day with Kim Philby in Moscow during the autumn of 1964, Melinda confessed that her marriage to Donald had virtually ended in 1948 (which was all the encouragement Philby needed, if he required any at all, to pursue an affair with his co-conspirator's wife). What surprised those who had witnessed the Maclean marriage at close range was not that it ultimately ended, but that it had lasted so long.[2]

Because Maclean refused to be interviewed in Moscow and never wrote any personal account of his life, we must rely principally on the descriptions of their marriage that Melinda provided to the British journalist Geoffrey Hoare. Since Hoare knew the Macleans as friend and neighbor in Cairo, he was in a good position to smooth some of her rough edges. Yet the portrait he draws is harsh and unsympathetic to Donald.

"Right from the beginning of their affair in Paris," he concludes, "right through their married life, Donald behaved with extraordinary irresponsibility towards Melinda." She understandably found "Donald excessively difficult to live with." His qualities made for neither a good husband nor father. He was "selfish and self-centered; he had a mother complex and he had been badly spoiled [and] he was far more dependent on [Melinda] than he cared to admit to himself."[3]

Washington, even more than now, was a rigidly stratified, work-oriented, male-dominated, company town that never held much promise for Melinda. Bored by politics, she never felt comfortable. "Melinda was not unintelligent," Cecil explains, "but she was in essence a non-political creature; great causes and international conflicts left her cold." When an invitation to a White House ball came, she ordered a "dazzling new creation" from her New York dress maker. It arrived, she tried it on, thought it perfect, put it in the closet, and left it there. On the night of the ball, she wore a frock borrowed from one of her sisters. She seemed almost to fear calling attention to herself.[4]

Melinda found the social pace both excessively demanding and personally unrewarding. At times she appeared breathless from trying to raise children and act as hostess, not only on planned occasions, but also to Donald's unannounced guests. Life in the diplomatic fast lane required her to appear witty and charming at the countless receptions that a First Secretary is expected to attend.

She considered herself a cosmopolitan and enjoyed living amidst strange cultures just as she had enjoyed her Swiss school. But she had become a bored, restless, and uninspired child once she moved to New York. As soon as she was old enough, Melinda had returned to Europe and flourished as a cigar-smoking bohemian expatriate, an habitué of Paris café life. And, tattered though her marriage may have been, she later prospered in Cairo, which was Donald's last overseas posting. In Washington, however, she was just another American housewife, and a very unhappy one at that.[5]

Her fragile, defenseless quality, Hoare thought, "made nearly all men feel they wanted to protect her, although against what one had no idea." There was also something elusive about her attractiveness:

> It is not easy to decide exactly where Melinda's charm lay, for she was changeable, and her appearance changed with her moods. She was attractive rather than beautiful, with a little oval face, pale skin, and dark eyes and hair, but could, when animated, look quite lovely . . . She had [a] kind of casual, effortless, elegance . . .[6]

Increasingly there were times when it seemed that Donald did not fit in either:

> Gradually he seemed to tire of the life he was living—of being endlessly social, endlessly entertained by people who, if they had different names and slightly different faces, were obviously cut from exactly the same pattern.[7]

These were the sheep that he had loathed since Cambridge, and he became increasingly driven to force them to admit their deficiencies. He once complained to Isaiah Berlin that "he was tired of meeting conventional and pompous officials." Berlin thought nothing of it. However, not long afterward, he invited Donald to a dinner party. "The evening was a disaster" after Berlin unintentionally set Maclean off. First, Donald attacked some of the other guests for being on the wrong side of the barricades. Then, he managed to turn them against their host's politics—moderate, reasoned, carefully considered. Says Berlin, they "attacked me passionately and unanimously." Several weeks later "I had a row with Maclean" Berlin reports. "After that I never saw or spoke to him again."

By February 1948 his work at the embassy, combined with growing global tensions, kept Maclean constantly on the go. He also, as Hoare delicately phrased it, "began to frequent a new milieu." Drinking sessions at the house might end in a spat, after which he often left. Melinda seemed to have little idea, and a dwindling interest, about where he went. It could have been, as may have often been the case, to meet with his Soviet control; or, if Hoover was correct, to date a CIA stenographer. It is also possible that he was beginning to experiment with homosexual liaisons, which he would pursue more openly in Cairo and London.[9]

Maclean's self-destructiveness stemmed from his inability to reconcile the demands of being a spy with the emotions that no amount of betrayal and anger could deaden. One side of him could be cold and pitiless, but the other side was filled with remorse and guilt. "It would have needed a far tougher, far more ruthless character than Donald," Hoare writes, "to be able to live and work among people who loved and admired him without having most grievously on his conscience the knowledge that—to their way of thinking—he was betraying them."[10]

★   ★   ★

The perception that the Soviets were prospering as 1948 began was more than just superficial. What *The New York Times* called "the Cold War declared by Russia against the Western Democracies" seemed on the verge of several major victories. Stalin's iron grip extended across all of Eastern Europe after he forced Rumania's King Michael—the continent's last monarch—to abdicate. In September he created the Cominform to succeed the Comintern, which had been abolished in 1943 as a goodwill gesture to the Allies. Like its predecessor, the Cominform's job was to control communist movements abroad.[11]

The Communists in France had suffered a setback at the polls in December 1947. The country was still volcanic, however, rife with labor and economic problems and divided by bitter social rivalries. Italy was even more promising. There, the Communists were deftly exploiting unemployment, inflation, and general misery. The Party had thousands of well-armed, paramilitary shock troops that were shifted around the country to influence elections. By the end of 1947, the Communists controlled more than three thousand of Italy's seven thousand municipalities, and they were given a good chance of winning the national elections that were expected to be held on April 18.

The war of nerves had not ended for Turkey, whose treasury continued to be drained by mobilization, as Maclean argued it should at State Department meetings. The Greek insurgents, supported by the communist regimes in neighboring Yugoslavia and Albania, would almost certainly take at least the northern half of the country. The Middle East appeared ripe for the taking, as Palestinian Arabs and Jews were both shooting at the British, while London and Washington would soon be bitterly divided over recognition of the new state of Israel. And in China, communist forces under the command of Mao Tse-tung and Chou En-lai were steadily gaining against the weak and corrupt Kuomintang.[12]

Only a few more pieces remained on the global chessboard and, as the Cold War intensified throughout the spring and summer of 1948, both sides were determined to grab them before all were frozen into place. The Soviets, as Acheson explained to congressional leaders, "did not need to win all the possibilities. Even one or two" could lead to "a breakthrough [which] might open three continents to Soviet penetration."[13]

It is now, of course, self-evident that Stalin failed in his grand global designs. Because Moscow failed does not mean that Maclean did, however. It is doubtful that any other Soviet agent in the postwar period—from those hair-raising spring days following the coup in Czechoslovakia to the June showdown over Berlin—served Moscow more ably than Maclean.

In strategic philosophy it is axiomatic that capabilities create their own intentions. The issues Maclean had worked on during the past three years—the Black Sea Straits, Iran, East-West troop levels, bases, and the West's atomic stockpile—formed an unsurpassed index to America's capabilities. First, he could send Stalin cables spelling out America's resources. Then, because he sat at the table with Western strategists, handicapped because they had only the flimsiest idea of Soviet capabilities and intentions (a gap they often tried to fill, pathetically, by thumbing through Marxist tracts), he could describe for Stalin Washington's political will to use those resources.

Yet during the critical year of 1948, with all these advantages, time and again Stalin blundered. Observing him from his Moscow vantage point in 1945 and 1946, George Kennan marveled at Stalin's "immense, diabolical skill as a tactician. The modern age has known no greater master of the tactical art." Stalin might begin an assault against an adversary with an opening move that could be "as innocently disarming as the first move of the grand master at chess, [which] was only a part of his brilliant, terrifying tactical mastery." Perhaps by 1948, however, Stalin was slipping into "the sterility and madness" that characterized his last years.[14]

Western policymakers also deserve credit for his failures, however. Although they are often criticized either for vacillating in the face of their own destruction or of an irrational fear and hatred of the communist "bogey man," Western strategists exploited Stalin's lapses expertly.

Disheartened by the failures of the London conference in December 1947, and exasperated by Moscow's effective use of pious platitudes to conceal a campaign of domination that rivaled Hitler's, the State Department began the year by stripping Stalin of his moral fig leaf. In January, ignoring British worries about antagonizing Moscow, Washington released captured German documents detailing the Nazi-Soviet Pact. Until then, even at Nuremberg, the West had conspired to conceal the Soviet government's squalid story from the public.

The sordid details must have made even Maclean wince. They included Stalin's spontaneous toasts to Hitler and the Gestapo; his denunciation of "vulgar anti-fascists"; Ribbentrop's rapture at discovering, as he cabled Hitler, that Stalin and Molotov are like "a bunch of good old Nazis"; and proof—contrary to every statement Stalin ever made—that Hitler turned *him* down for membership in the fascist alliance.

"Ideology has little to do with Russian foreign policy," *The New York Times* concluded after the documents were released. It is "merely a weapon which can be set aside at will, and can be revived or turned against new foes" when convenient. Although when making territorial demands Stalin had played on Western sympathies for Russia's horrendous war casualties, it was now evident that he had made the same demands of Hitler before a single shot was fired or a single Red Army soldier had fallen in battle:

The Russian expansion of today . . . is nothing new in itself, but only a rigid pursuit of the same aims . . . which he sought to realize first with Hitler, then against Hitler, then with the Allies and now against them.[15]

The shocked disbelief with Moscow almost rivaled that felt at the time of the Nazi-Soviet Pact nearly ten years earlier. The chagrined Soviets tried to rally by accusing the West of collaborating with Germany during the war to "bleed Russia white." Curiously, however, although the Soviets too had captured not only German archives but archivists, Stalin could produce no documents to substantiate his claims: he was forced to rely on crude forgeries.[16]

This minor propaganda skirmish, however, left Stalin with little more than a bloody nose. The year's first real showdown began with Soviet Deputy Foreign Minister V.A. Zorin's February 19 arrival in Prague. The following day, all the non-Communists resigned from the cabinet. A beaten-down and dejected President Benes—certain that he had been abandoned in 1948 as he had been at Munich in 1938—allowed the Communists to form a government devoid of pro-Western members except for the half-American, Harvard educated Foreign Minister Jan Masaryk.

On March 10 "the news came screaming out of Prague" that Masaryk, son of the nation's founder, was dead. The Communists said he had committed suicide by jumping out of his office window. Because his office was on the second floor, and the window too small to fit through, the better bet is that he was beaten, tortured (the heels of his feet had injuries from hammer blows), shot at point blank range (he had powder burns and a wound from a 7.65mm bullet in the back of the neck), and stuffed through the window (which had excrement on it) to the ground below, wearing pajamas with mis-matched tops and bottoms.

Although America had helped to precipitate the crisis by consigning Czechoslovakia to the Soviet bloc, "no witness to those times in the United States can forget the despair, the rage, and—justified or not—the loathing, for Communists behind the Iron Curtain, that welled up around the headlines and radio bulletins."[17]

There is no evidence that Stalin directed the takeover. But the ensuring crackdown, the suspension of human rights, the abolition of political thought and expression, the mass arrests, the show trials, and eventual executions—all accompanied by the obligatory Marxist rhetoric about enemies of the people—had that adroit Bolshevik touch. Czechoslovakia had been the most democratic and economically advanced of all the Central European nations before the war. "My country," said one Czech official, "is now a terrorized, silenced and enslaved people." A panicked Western Europe wondered aloud, who will be next?[18]

The events in Czechoslovakia and blustering moves in the direction of Finland and Norway helped change long rigid American attitudes against peacetime alliances. According to one account, Jack Hickerson "stumbled into the State Department on New Year's Eve, drunk on Fish House punch from the Metropolitan Club," and declared to his deputy, Theodore Achilles, "I don't care whether entangling alliances have been considered worse than original sin since George Washington's time. We've got to negotiate a military alliance with Western Europe in peacetime, and we've got to do it quickly."[19]

In mid-January British Foreign Secretary Bevin cabled Secretary of State George C. Marshall that because "the Soviet Government has formed a solid political and economic block," Western Europe must do the same. "I saw Marshall," Ambassador Inverchapel cabled the Foreign Secretary in his usual florid style on January 19, "who saw nothing but good in your proposal . . . your plan has filled the hearts of the senior officials at the Department of State with great joy."[20]

On March 17 England, France, and the Benelux countries (Belgium, the Netherlands, and Luxembourg) signed the Brussels Pact. The timing, one week after Masaryk's grisly death, was not accidental. After the events in Prague, France, for instance, abruptly ended its practice of distancing itself from the United States and Britain and rushed to join the Western union.

The administration (to get the Marshall Plan), the Defense Department (to get larger appropriations), and Western Europe (to form a binding military alliance) would all unashamedly manipulate the Czech crisis. This is not to say, however, that their initial fright was contrived.

"Will Russia move first? Who pulls the trigger? Then where do we go?" Truman asked Marshall on Friday, March 5. On Tuesday the chief of naval operations proposed steps "to prepare the American people for war," and by that Saturday the Joint Chiefs of Staff had produced an emergency war plan for Europe. On the morning of March 16, Truman told his White House staff that the nation must know the situation. "It was better to do that than to be caught, as we were in the last war, without having warned Congress and the people." The next day, Wednesday, while European nations were signing their pact in Brussels, Truman made a nationwide radio address before a joint session of Congress. "The Soviet Union and its agents," he charged, "have destroyed the independence and democratic character of a whole series of nations in Eastern and Central Europe."[21]

Even Walter Lippmann, a frequent apologist for the Soviet regime, pronounced the brutal seizure of power in Czechoslovakia, and Moscow's efforts to intimidate Finland and Norway, as clear "strategical actions planned by military men in anticipation of war." The United States, he argued, should declare a national emergency, institute a draft, and go on a war footing through immediate mobilization.[22]

Maclean was squarely in the middle of the swirling events. On Friday, March 12, Marshall—"fearing leakage if other members of the cabinet are admitted to the secret"—huddled alone with Truman after a cabinet meeting. Truman gave permission for highly secret talks to take place in Washington with British and Canadian officials to discuss a North American-Western European military alliance.[23]

Maclean handled the preparations for the British side. First, he drafted a note of congratulations to Marshall from Bevin and Inverchapel expressing delight "that we and you mean business and are prepared to see this thing [an Atlantic alliance] through, and not stop short at exhortations."[24]

Then, he began exploratory talks at the State Department to probe for information both Whitehall and the Kremlin would have been eager to know. How would the alliance work? Who would decide when it was activated? And who would decide whether or not to dispatch troops? In the midst of all this, he dropped by Gullion's office to officially notify the U.S. government that a special section of the British government—in "complete secrecy" from the public and the Parliament—was "engaged on research and development on atomic weapons."[25]

Indeed, throughout the next six months Maclean would be juggling so many policy balls that State Department officials later could not agree on his primary area of responsibility. Gullion saw him as Britain's atomic energy man. Hickerson held meeting after meeting with him on the Atlantic Alliance. But Edward T. Wailes, the chief of the Division of British Commonwealth Affairs, who had been to dinner at Maclean's house, told security officials that "he was of the opinion that Maclean was interested in Eastern European affairs." His deputy, Herbert P. Fales, however, thought that Maclean was primarily "interested in matters relating to the Near and Middle East."[26]

The talks that took place between March 22 and April 1 may have been the most secret ever held in Washington. They would lead within a year to the formation of the North Atlantic Treaty Organization (NATO).

Elaborate precautions were taken to conceal them from the Soviets. The French, though a party to the Western union, were considered such a notorious security risk that they were blacklisted. And, although the administration hailed the new era of bipartisanship in American foreign policy, Vandenberg, chairman of the Senate Foreign Relations Committee, was not informed. American politicians were considered second only to the French in terms of their unreliability.[27]

As a deception measure, cover stories were invented so that Sir Gladwyn Jebb's prolonged absence from London would not be noticed. After flying from London to New York, he made himself conspicuous at the United Nations. Then, he would slip to the airport, fly to Washington, and disappear into the Pentagon's fortified walls. After several days, he would resurface back in New York. The dodge was so successful that Jebb crowed to London that Dean Rusk, the director of the State Department's Office of United Nations Affairs and a future secretary of state under Presidents Kennedy and Johnson, "never suspected my true reason for being in the U.S." (It can be imagined that because all the arrangements were handled by or at least known to Maclean, after June 1951 the frequency with which Jebb regaled his colleagues about Rusk's gullibility diminished.)[28]

Finally on Monday, March 22—at the same time that the British government began a purge in London to remove communists from "work vital to the security of the state"—Maclean and the British delegation entered a thick, steel reinforced vault in the Pentagon basement. The sessions lasted into the early evening. Time was so precious that sandwiches were sent in to avoid a luncheon adjournment. Inverchapel's involvement was nominal, almost ceremonial. Yet Maclean, who drafted nearly all the reports back to London, had the grace to portray him as being in charge. "I led our side," Maclean's report written for Inverchapel's signature began, "and was supported by Hollis, Jebb and Maclean." Donald was being modest. Jebb later acknowledged that "the chief embassy advisor was the Russian spy Maclean."[29]

For Washington, more was at stake than just an unprecedented military alliance. For the first time since the Monroe Doctrine in 1823, America was trying to draw the "holdline," the line which, if crossed by the Soviets, would be considered an act of war against the United States. The difficulties seemed intractable. An Atlantic Alliance would naturally include Western Europe. But what about Italy? And Greece? And Turkey? And Iran? They could hardly be left out. But how could an Atlantic Alliance extend to the Persian Gulf? And even if it did, what about Afghanistan, India, and Pakistan, not to mention China, Korea, and Japan? It would be one thing to persuade Congress to enter into a peacetime alliance with the European countries that made up the nation's heritage. But they would never accept a global string of regional military alliances. The United Nations had been created to obviate any such need.

The entire situation made the American delegation, led by Robert Lovett, nervous. Therefore, when Inverchapel made a passing reference to a report he had sent to London, there was an immediate protest. The Americans insisted that the discussions were far too preliminary to be reported to the Foreign Office. To ensure no leaks, an extraordinary procedure was agreed to—no note-taking. The State Department did not want to take any chances that the Russians would know where the United States would fight and where it would not.[30]

Maclean, who was known for his retentive memory, still made notes at the end of each session. They must have made spellbinding reading in Moscow. When the risk of challenging the Soviets militarily was raised, Hollis replied that "it is far safer to risk war now than to acquiesce to the taking one by one of the Soviet strategic positions." Maclean's own handwritten notes record the common assumption that "if the Soviets know where the holdline is drawn, they will move on what isn't protected like any predatory animal."[31]

In a further note of irony, Maclean drafted a cable for Inverchapel admonishing the Foreign Office that the talks "are being regarded as highly secret, and I feel sure that you are giving [our reports] the most limited distribution in London."[32]

The six meetings over eleven days resulted in the "Pentagon Paper," which recommended that the Western Union be extended to Norway, Sweden, Denmark, Iceland, Italy, and Portugal. An armed attack against any of the signatories "would be considered an armed attack against the United States." Eventually, West Germany, Spain, and Austria might be included. It was also agreed that Moscow should be given a "hands off" warning over Greece, Turkey, and Iran.[33]

Several events shed light on how Maclean and the Soviets may have worked together. Toward the end of the talks, Maclean sent a cable to the Foreign Office complaining about "the problem of trying to persuade the Americans not to pursue Scandinavia" or put any pressure on Italy until after the elections. Bevin immediately registered his concerns on both points, as Inverchapel informed the Americans and the Canadians on March 29.[34]

Bevin's weighing-in clearly jolted the Americans. The issue was one of timing. The Americans had already agreed that Italy would not be approached until after the elections, and that matters were extremely sensitive with Scandinavia. "The talks were too tentative," Hickerson objected, "to merit official reaction at Mr. Bevin's level."[35]

The issues of Scandinavia and Italy were of more than passing interest to the Kremlin. They had great hopes for a Communist victory in the Italian elections. And after forcing the Finns to submit to an agreement, the Soviets were putting immense pressure on Norway and on Denmark, where there was "acute nervousness" and talk of preparing "against [a] possible Soviet invasion." At the same time, Sweden, which was fiercely proud of its own neutrality, was insisting that Scandinavia should be non-aligned. [36]

On April 4, just three days after the Washington talks ended, and after Maclean tried to drive a wedge between London and Washington on Italy and Scandinavia, *Zycie Warosovy,* a Warsaw paper, charged that Anglo-American leaders were planning a North Atlantic military bloc which Scandinavian countries were being pressured to join. This touched off angry outbursts in Sweden, making matters awkward for the governments of Norway and Denmark, which did want to join. [37]

Similarly, not long afterward, "for reasons that have never become clear," the Soviets threw a monkey wrench into the Austrian peace talks. Moscow apparently believed that Washington was secretly determined to pull Austria, once independent, into their new military alliance. In fact, while the status of West Germany and Austria had been discussed at the Pentagon, no final decision had been reached. But as Cecil points out, "only someone who was present or had access to the record would know" that their possible inclusion had been discussed. It would be seven years before the final treaty with Austria would be signed. The Warsaw story about an Atlantic military bloc did not appear until after the talks ended. Moscow clearly did not want to jeopardize the procedure that allowed them to have a man inside the Pentagon's vault. [38]

With the basic outline of a military alliance established, the issue, as Maclean pointed out to London, was whether "State Department officials (who are perfectly sound) can get the big idea across to their political chiefs and eventually of course to Vandenberg and other Congressional leaders." All the agreements so far were with the executive branch. After the ill-fated Hyde Park and Quebec agreements, the British were understandably dubious about putting all their eggs in the White House basket.

They were especially concerned about Truman, who was the most intensely unpopular president in modern U.S. history. Jebb was hardly alone in his prediction that "President Truman will, after all, probably disappear from the effective political scene after next November." A 1948 poll of recent public figures showed that FDR was still the most admired with 43 percent. Truman, who had been president for over three years, received only 3 percent. Members of his own party—led by Roosevelt confidants and his sons—organized the "Let's Get Rid of Truman" movement and the liberal Americans for Democratic Action endorsed General Eisenhower for the presidency. Freshman Senator William J. Fulbright—egged on by Lippmann—called on the President to resign even before the elections, while Truman's congressional friends merely refused to be seen with him on the campaign trail.[39]

But Maclean and the others also misjudged the increasing frequency with which Stalin's "divide and rule" campaigns were uniting the West. The Berlin crisis in the summer of 1948 is a good example of how Maclean's efforts came to naught because of Stalin's ineptitude. The defeated German nation and its capital Berlin had been divided into zones of occupation. Russia controlled eastern Germany, while the western half was divided among American, British, and French forces. Although Berlin was also divided among the four Allied powers, it lay totally within the eastern zone, so that overland access to Berlin was impossible without passing through Soviet-controlled territory.

By the end of 1947, the Western Allies decided that the burden of supporting millions of Germans was both untenable and unnecessary when their own countries were so needy. As a first step toward making Germany self-supporting, the Western powers decided to institute currency reforms. Stalin was appalled at the prospect of a possible oasis of Western pluralism and prosperity thriving in the midst of a Russian satellite that had been stripped bare of its material and human resources. He countered with a campaign to force the West to quit Berlin:

• On March 20, the Soviet representative to the four-power Allied Control Council (ACC) (to which Alan Maclean, Donald's younger brother, had been assigned) declared that currency reform, to say nothing of a separate West German state, would be illegal. He announced that the meeting was adjourned, and the Soviet delegation stomped out (the ACC would not meet again until the Soviet-installed East German government collapsed in 1989).

• Four days later, a shoot-out nearly occurred when the Red Army began boarding Allied military trains passing through East Germany en route to West Berlin.

• Beginning on April 1, every vehicle coming from the West into Berlin was stopped, and each individual was questioned.

• Even before Truman signed the Marshall Plan into law on Saturday, April 3, the Communist parties in France, Italy, and other European nations were inciting protests—often violent—against "Yankee economic imperialism."

• On April 5, a Soviet fighter that was harassing a British transport plane over West Berlin suddenly collided with the aircraft, killing all fourteen aboard the transport, including two Americans. Thereafter, U.K. and U.S. fighters were ordered to escort all unarmed planes over Soviet airspace.

The campaign intensified in June. The Soviets harassed all forms of surface transportation. Auto traffic was stalled for hours for emergency bridge and road "repairs." Trains were shuttled off to sidings indefinitely.

Soon there were encouraging signs that it was working. The nervous French and British reduced their Berlin garrisons, and began to evacuate women and children. French officials openly declared "that not a single Frenchman would vote to fight for Berlin," and some American military officers joined their allies in arguing for withdrawal from Berlin before suffering the humiliation of being forced out.[40]

Stalin's apparent willingness to take the world to the brink of war staggered Western strategists. Their assumption had been that war "would most probably come about as a result of a Soviet miscalculation." But these actions were so deliberately provocative that everyone from *The New York Times* to the National Security Council now assumed that Stalin, as did Hitler before him, had a timetable for world conquest. It was further believed that facing the specter of an independent West Germany, as well as an economically and militarily unified Europe, forced Stalin to accelerate that plan. Undoubtedly, there is something to all of this, especially given what Maclean was telling him about Washington's intention to order the Soviet Union to steer clear of, or risk war over, huge sections of the globe.[41]

Anxiety in Western capitals was compounded by Washington's refusal to rise to the challenge. Surely the moment that the United

States waved its atomic wand, Stalin would cease his reckless behavior. As Lippmann argued, Russia would be prevented from marching west not by an alliance of "weak and dubious allies," but from Soviet fears of American atomic retaliation. The bomb made saber rattling with conventional weapons obsolete. General Lucius Clay and Ambassador Robert Murphy, the ranking American military and civilian authorities in Berlin, rushed to Washington during the height of the crisis with a similar message. Stalin was bluffing, they argued; it was time to flex America's atomic muscle. [42]

The Kremlin, according to Nikita Khrushchev, was aware that Stalin's desperate gambles in Eastern Europe could have led to catastrophe. "America was conducting its foreign policy from a position of strength," the then First Secretary of the Ukraine and member of the Politburo later attested. "The Americans had the atomic bomb and they knew we didn't . . . I would even say that America was invincible, and the Americans flaunted this fact." [43]

Yet Washington did nothing. And "the lack of forceful American policy" British historian Paul Johnson suggests, was a contributing factor to "tempt[ing] Stalin further." Murphy, a career diplomat, was so discouraged by Washington's refusal to get tough with Soviet aggression, he nearly resigned. What most astonished him is that "nobody, either military or civilian, mentioned that the United States Government in 1948 possessed a growing stockpile of atomic bombs while Russia had none yet." [44]

"Could the West have flexed its military muscle in Germany?" Daniel Yergin also asks. The historian, he argues, "cannot avoid the conclusion that the Russians would either have backed down or been at a disadvantage in a larger confrontation. The United States was militarily stronger, and did have sole possession of nuclear weapons." [45]

That was not the viewpoint, however, of the handful of American political and military leaders who were responsible for crafting a U.S. response. Two weeks before the Czech crisis, as he surveyed the global hot spots and considered the Truman Doctrine's blank check, Marshall told the newly formed National Security Council, "We are playing with fire while we have nothing with which to put it out." [46]

Congress had turned down Truman's plea for universal military training, and the army could not fill its 670,000-man ceiling. The 552,000 men who were in uniform were insufficient to meet the first stage of the Pentagon's emergency war plan. The President had pledged to "help free people everywhere," yet were he to dispatch enough troops just to make a difference in Greece, the entire nation would have to be mobilized.[47]

Red Army strength meanwhile was estimated at between 2.5 and 4 million troops, with at least 1 million in Eastern and Central Europe facing 113,000 U.S. troops. Not surprisingly, if war broke out, the Pentagon's war plan called for an immediate evacuation of Germany, Austria, and the Middle East.[48]

"The limitations of our military power to deal with various potentially explosive areas over the world," Secretary of Defense James Forrestal had warned Truman in February, were "lamentably clear." A Pentagon study concluded that if the Soviets launched a blitzkrieg across Europe, the Red Army would "reach the Atlantic and the Pyrenees" so fast that the Americans would not have time to evacuate their forces from Europe—something even the enfeebled British had been able to do at Dunkirk in 1940. Marshall urged that the study be suppressed because its "hopelessness" would only "dishearten free Europe" and "reduce the will to resist."[49]

When Clay and Murphy were agitating for an immediate show of force over Berlin, the Joint Chiefs were telling Truman that the United States would need at least eighteen months to mount such a challenge. But Clay, Murphy, Lippmann, Congressional leaders, and European nations all believed that none of this mattered because the United States still had the bomb and the Soviets did not.

Actually, America's atomic arsenal was nonexistent. The British uranium had not yet arrived, and even after it did it would take time to get production to the military's required level. Further, the United States had only thirty-two B-29s "suitably modified for carrying an atomic bomb on a combat mission" and only three assembly teams in uniform.[50]

If, at the time that Stalin began his campaign to harass and intimidate the West in Berlin, he had been as completely in the dark about Washington's capabilities as the United States was about Russia's, then Yergin would doubtless be correct in believing "those summer months in 1948 were a time of considerable nervousness in the Kremlin. Stalin and his comrades needed all the bluff and nerve they could muster.''[51]

It is the thesis of this book, however, that, because of Maclean, Stalin knew he had nothing to fear from America. Indeed, Stalin's knowledge of America's military preparedness may have equaled or even exceeded that of the Joint Chiefs of Staff and the Strategic Air Command—neither of which were allowed to know anything about the size of America's nuclear arsenal. Therefore, Stalin was not bluffing; nor, from a military standpoint, had he miscalculated. He simply knew that the United States was incapable of launching either a conventional or atomic response to his aggressions.

Robert Cecil, a witness to the events, who worked at the embassy as a Second Secretary with Maclean throughout this crisis, was struck by how Stalin "was acting with marked self-confidence; he was in no way deterred by any fear of the US bomb from consolidating his hold on Eastern Europe and, at the time of the Berlin blockade, bringing the world to the very brink of war.''[52]

Yet, Cecil points out, "Stalin was never a rash operator in the international field." He was acting with the confidence of someone who knew his adversary's intentions because he knew their capabilities. "No candidate comes near to Maclean," says his former colleague, as the one who provided Stalin this critical information. That is the reason that General Clay may have been more correct than he realized when he predicted on June 25 that "if the Soviets go to war, it will not be because of the Berlin currency issue but only because they believe this [is] the right time.''[53]

Maclean could recite America's weakness as well as anyone who sat around the White House Cabinet Room during those gloomy days of February and March. America's strategic military problems were a composite of the problems that he had worked on for the past three years—troop levels, bases, and, most important of all, America's atomic arsenal.

"The number of atomic bombs in America's possession was perhaps the premier secret of the Truman Administration," according to historian Greg Herken. Truman, who once told his Cabinet that he did not know the number and "he didn't really want to know either," was not finally informed until Lilienthal told him as part of his disturbing report in April 1947. Truman later confirmed that as

long as he was president "no document 'anywhere in the government' contained such figures." It would be years before the Congress
was entrusted with such portentous information. "We do not know
how many atomic weapons we possess," Senator McMahon complained in January 1949. "Therefore I fear we lack perspective to pass
upon any major defense issue." The U.S. government did not finally
divulge the size of its atomic arsenal in the 1940s until 1982, and
then only because of the persistent efforts of historian David Alan
Rosenberg.[54]

Yet Donald Maclean knew, possibly even before Truman did, but,
in any event, not long afterward. Therefore, Joseph Stalin knew as
well, and not even the opaque verbiage of the government's cover-
up could conceal this fact. In its June 11, 1951, letter to McMahon,
the AEC conceded that Maclean knew the "requirements of uranium
for the atomic energy programs within the three governments," and
that this and other information "classified Top Secret [would] have
been useful to the Russian atomic energy program *and strategic
planners.*"[55]

Two months later, the State Department tried to convince McMahon that Maclean would not have had information on "stockpiles of
fissionable materials and weapons." But internal documents not
intended for Congress's prying eyes, told a different story. The
Department's Atomic Energy office concluded that Maclean had
been able to provide the Soviets "fairly reliable estimates of our raw
material [uranium] supply," which enabled Moscow to compile
"intelligence estimates of *the scope and scale of our program*" (that is,
the rate at which the United States was manufacturing and stockpil-
ing atomic bombs in 1947–48).[56]

In other words, as Rosenberg concludes, Stalin knew "that during
the critical year when the United States was entering the Cold War
with the Soviet Union" it had no atomic threat. As Rosenberg would
reveal in 1980, "the United States was producing less than one atomic
bomb every two months." Specifically, in June 1947 there were only
enough nuclear components for thirteen bombs, and by March 1948
that number could not have increased to more than thirty. This was
the capability at a time when the Joint Strategic Survey Committee
was estimating that as many as two hundred would be required in a

war with the Soviet Union, while others placed the number as high as five hundred.[57]

It makes little difference whether Maclean knew that there were precisely thirteen or thirty bombs. The point is that he did know that the number had to be pathetically small. He also knew that by early 1947 the United States was out of uranium, and he could advise Kremlin strategists that current production was proceeding at a snail's pace, if at all.

Stalin blockaded Berlin on June 24 by bringing all rail, autobahn, and canal traffic to a complete halt, and cutting off all power to the city. Two and a half million West Berliners were sealed off with only enough food to last thirty days. What was seen as a breathtaking gamble pushed the world to the edge of war when Truman countered four days later by announcing that the United States was dispatching sixty "atomic capable" B-29s to bases in England and Germany.

It was Truman, not Stalin, who was bluffing, however, and the Soviet dictator knew it.

Truman refused to say whether the planes actually carried atomic bombs. Everyone, including recent historians, assumed that they did. It seemed probable that, in a national emergency, the United States would play its trump card. Marshall, worried that Stalin would assume otherwise, delayed their departure until mid-July—which still would not have been enough time to assemble and load that many bombs.[58]

Maclean knew that the United States could not possibly have had enough bombs to equip sixty planes. Further, it is inconceivable that Attlee would have agreed to permit U.S. bombers to land in England without knowing in advance whether they carried atomic weapons. Maclean would have followed the cable exchanges closely. Either way, he was able to spare Stalin the anxiety felt throughout Western Europe. The point is made by Herken: "The Russians probably knew of the subtle deception being practiced in the skies over Europe and almost certainly knew by espionage that the U.S. arsenal remained small."[59]

★ ★ ★

Stalin failed in Berlin, not, as many eventually believed, because he was cowed by Truman's highly publicized launching of "atomic

Donald Maclean was Joseph Stalin's most important spy during the years he served at the British embassy in Washington from May 1944 to September 1948. (Courtesy of Michael Maude)

Gen. Krivitsky, Former OGPU Leader Who Feared Assassins, Shot to Death in Hotel Here

WALTER KRIVITSKY,

publishing an article by Krivitzer in April, 1939, said:

"Gen. Krivitsky, the one leading survivor of the great purge in the Red Army, served in the Soviet military intelligence department for nearly 14 years, until May, 1938. He was often sent abroad on highly confidential missions. He was then appointed director of the Soviet war industries institute, a post he held in 1933-34. The following year

Suicide Ruling Held Up After Friends Insist He Was Slain

(Pictures On Page 3.)

Gen. Walter G. Krivitsky, mysterious Stalin-hating refugee from Russia and former western European head of the Soviet Military Intelligence, was found shot to death yesterday morning in his room at the Bellevue Hotel, 15 E Street Northwest.

Coroner A. Magruder MacDonald first issued a certificate of suicide, then recalled it after acquaintances of Krivitsky expressed the belief that the former Kremlin agent was assassinated by the OGPU (Russian Secret Police).

Krivitsky was known to have lived in fear of the OGPU since his disclosure in 1939 before the Dies Committee and in Saturday Evening Post articles

While investigators first pointed the possibility of international intrigue, Curren said he would have all the available facts in his hands by morning and would decide then what action was to be taken.

The district attorney reported that three letters had been found on a table in Krivitsky's room, one in English, one in Russian and a third in German. None of them made a definite statement of suicidal intent, but all hinted at it.

Visit to Trotsky Revealed

One note, in English, was addressed to Louis Waldman, his New York Lawyer, and asked him to provide for Krivitsky's wife and son. Another, a long letter in Russian, was addressed to the dead man's wife. The third, written in German, was to "Susan Lafo," of New York City.

Waldman identified Miss "Lafo" as Suzanne La Follette, who, he said, is a cousin of Sen

Only months after Soviet defector General Walter Krivitsky warned British officials about spies in their midst, he was found shot to death in a Washington hotel. This *Washington Post* headline reflects skepticism of the suicide ruling.

Shown here, a copy of one of three "suicide notes" found in Krivitsky's room. Never before published, it was found along with the other two in 1989 among his lawyer's papers. (Waldman Papers/New York Public Library)

CHARLOTTESVILLE, VIRGINIA

Donald Maclean's father, Sir Donald, was a Cabinet member, head of the Liberal Party, and one of the most respected men in British public life. (Courtesy of the National Archives: 306-NT-169273)

British Ambassador Lord Halifax entering the White House. A friend of Sir Donald Maclean, he gave a special welcome to his son and frequently relied upon him. In the background is the Department of State, now the Old Executive Office Building. (Courtesy of the National Archives: 208-PU-87Y-1)

The British embassy staff. Maclean is directly in front of the pillar to the far left. Ambassador Halifax is to the right in the front row. On the front row far left is John "Jock" Balfour. (Courtesy of Sir Frederick Everson)

Alger Hiss, with whom Maclean worked closely. By the time their collaboration started in 1945, a number of sources had already warned American officials that Hiss was a Soviet agent. (Courtesy of the National Archives: 59-JB-523-1)

John D. Hickerson takes the oath as Assistant Secretary of State, while Secretary of State Dean Acheson (directly behind Hickerson) looks on. Hickerson knew Maclean well and later lamented: "I was never so completely fooled in all my life as when he went to Russia." (Courtesy of the National Archives: 59-JB-1718-2)

BRITISH EMBASSY,
WASHINGTON 8, D. C.

Ref: G28/-/46

9th March 1946.

TOP SECRET

IMMEDIATE

740.00119 COUNCIL/3-946

My dear Secretary of State,

      You will remember telling me on March 6th of
your proposal that there should be a meeting of Foreign Ministers
in Paris on April 15th and asking me to find out from Mr.Bevin
how he felt about it before you sent off telegrams to him and
Monsieur Molotov.

      I have now received a telegram from Mr.Bevin asking
me to thank you and give you the following reply.

      Since you spoke to me there has been a new
development in the form of the French proposal for four power
discussions on the question of central German administrations
and Western Germany.   Mr.Bevin feels that in view of the long
deadlock which has existed in Germany over central administrations
and the urgency of reaching decisions on the Ruhr and Rhineland,
it is necessary to settle these two connected questions at the

/ earliest

The Honourable
  James F.Byrnes,
    Secretary of State of the United States,
      Washington,D.C.

Maclean signed this urgent message for Secretary of State James Byrnes from British Foreign Secretary Ernest Bevin. It contradicts the British government's later portrayal of Maclean as only a minor official.

12

earliest possible moment and he is thus disposed to fall in
with this French proposal.   He would, therefore, be quite ready
to agree with your proposal for a meeting of the four Foreign
Ministers in Paris on April 15th.   But in his view the first
item for discussion should be the questions raised by the French
about Germany.   The meeting could secondly discuss the question
of the organisation and procedure of the Peace Conference, which
is due to start on May 1st, and also any important outstanding
questions connected with the draft peace treaties if any have
been left unsettled by the deputies.

       I am also asked to explain that the Dominion Prime
Ministers are likely to begin discussions in London on April 23rd
and Mr.Bevin would, therefore, have to go to London to attend
some of their meetings during the last week of April.

       I am to add that so far as Mr.Bevin is concerned he
would strongly deprecate putting to Monsieur Molotov any proposal
for a four power meeting until we have had some moderately
satisfactory reply to our remonstrances regarding Persia.

                 Yours sincerely,

                  S Maclean

               For the Ambassador

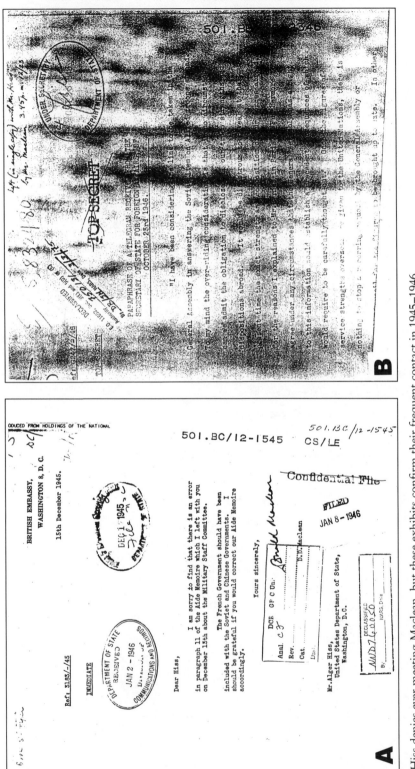

Hiss denies ever meeting Maclean, but these exhibits confirm their frequent contact in 1945–1946.

A. This Maclean-to-Hiss memorandum is the earliest record of their meetings. The salutation suggests a familiarity that Maclean did not express toward any other American official.

B and C. The October 23 marginal notation in Hiss's handwriting reads: "Left (in single copy) with Mr. Maclean 3:45 p.m. 12/23." The October 26 marginal notation in Hiss's handwriting reads: "Copy of Secretary's message to Bevin given to Maclean of British Em. 3:30 p.m. 10/28/46 a.h."

C

October 26, 1946

To: S - The Secretary

From: U - Mr. Acheson

Subject: Russian Proposal with Respect to Troops in Ex-Enemy Non-Enemy States

There is attached hereto the memorandum from Mr. Bevin which I mentioned to you on the telephone the evening of Wednesday, October 23, while you were still in New York. The British Embassy, in leaving it with us, emphasized that it was a personal message from Mr. Bevin for you.

Also on Wednesday, General Sir Henry Maitland Wilson of the British Joint Chiefs of Staff Mission left a similar memorandum at General Eisenhower's office (the General was not available). General Norstad immediately informed us of this and said that he was sure the General would wish to inform the British Joint Chiefs of the courtesy of hearing General Wilson's arguments. General Norstad said that as our Joint Chiefs would be meeting on Friday, October 25, he would see that the British representations were made by them and a Joint Chiefs of session reached this week. Meanwhile he knew that General Eisenhower

501.BB/...

D

D. Within 24 hours of learning that Maclean had fled England, the FBI discovered they had wiretaps of conversations between Maclean and Hiss. The uncensored portion of this June 7, 1951 memorandum to Hoover reads: "Wire dispatches on June 7, 1951, state Maclean and Burgess have defected behind the Iron Curtain. A Reuter's news dispatch dated June 7, 1951, reportedly stated the missing diplomats cabled their wives from Paris last night. . . . Our files reflect a contact between McLean and Alger Hiss on October 19, 1946. . . . Both contacts have related soley to official business."

o York Times.

LATE CITY EDITION
Cloudy, colder in afternoon, very cold tonight and tomorrow.
Temperatures Yesterday Max 38 Min 24
Sunrise today 7 01 A M Sunset 5 18 P M
Full 1 S Weather Bureau Report Page 1

YORK, TUESDAY, FEBRUARY 4, 1947.

THREE CENTS

)0 Employes)ed by U. S.

THE NEW YORK TIMES.
TON, Feb. 3—A re]
most a million and a
employes in a year
om 3,770,000 at the
.k on June 30, 1945,
at the end of 1946,
:ed today by the
Civil Service Com-

ires included em-
t home and abroad.
the United States
)85,000, falling be-
),000 mark at the
r the first time in
period. The Dec. 31
:0,475.
mployment of wo-
United States had
1,078,883 on June
497,719. Women's
vas still decreasing
en's at the year's
ember fall-off for
18,529 and for men,
cember. Full-time
nent in the United
year's end totaled

-CUT PLAN HOUSE ROW

All Conservatives on Bill—Truman 'eteran Funds

NEW YORK TIMES.
)N, Feb. 3—The in-
olican dispute over
uction was carried
or today. The brief
y bitter debate was
an appeal to all
o support "across
Noah M. Mason,
linois, a member of
Means Committee
regardless of par-
lan of the commit-
Harold Knutson of
n ungraduated 20
iction for high and
like.
acked Representa-
igel, Republican, of
d a revolt against
proposal on the
ffered small relief
great relief to the

JEWS IN PALESTINE RECEIVE ULTIMATUM IN FIGHT ON TERROR

Britain Gives Agency Seven Days to Cooperate With Troops and Police

REJECTS 'SPY' EXCUSE

Alternative of Martial Law Is Expected—Evacuation of Civilians Continues

By GENE CURRIVAN
Special to The New York Times
JERUSALEM, Feb. 3—The Jewish Agency for Palestine received
an ultimatum today from the Government to cooperate with the
police and bring terrorists to
justice within seven days. The
order was sent by the chief secretary, Sir Henry Gurney, on behalf
of the High Commissioner and replied to the agency's refusal yesterday to cooperate if, it said, Jews
had to be informers.
The ultimatum said that it was
the moral and legal duty of the
people of Palestine to cooperate
with the Government in ferreting
out terrorists and the question of
being informers did not enter into
it at this time. No indication was
given what would happen after
seven days if cooperation were not
forthcoming, but it is generally assumed that martial law in some
form will be imposed.

Government Warnings Cited
The letter, addressed to Mrs.
Golda Meyerson, head of the
agency's political department, said
that the Government had repeatedly warned Zionist leaders of the
growth and subsequent dangers of
terrorism. It said:
"In spite of the recent resolu-
tions purporting to condemn blood-
shed and terrorism, there have
been few signs that any action is
contemplated by the Jewish authorities or community to make
use of the only means available for
the enforcement of law and order:
namely, security forces. In effect,
the Jewish Agency has now openly
refused its cooperation with the
Government in this matter.
"I am now to invite your attention to the extreme gravity of the

---

OUR ATOM SECRETS TAPPED BY SOVIET, BARUCH BELIEVES; VALUE OF LEAKS DOUBTFUL

AT THE ATOMIC BOMB HEARING

Bernard M. Baruch before Congressional committee yesterday
The New York Times (by Tames)

Paris Urges Treaty to End Ruhr's Dominance in Steel

By HAROLD CALLENDER
Special to The New York Times.
PARIS, Feb. 3—The French Government will ask that the
peace treaty with Germany embody an international economic
regime for the Ruhr and that it establish a fixed basis for
division of Ruhr coal among
France and other coal importers.
This was disclosed today by
Hervé Alphand, chief of the economic section of the French Foreign Office. He added that it
would be "dangerous" to permit a
substantial increase in the Ruhr's

JARS CONGRESSMEN

Witness Says Russians May Not Know Worth of Knowledge Shown

SOVIET SPIES INDICATED

Revelations Suggested Linked With Ring in Canada and Briton Who Visited U. S.

By ANTHONY LEVIERO
Special to The New York Times
WASHINGTON, Feb 3 Ber-
nard M Baruch was reliably reported tonight to have told the
Joint Congressional Committee on
Atomic Energy that Russia evidently had tapped United States
atomic bomb secrets.
Clear indications of a penetration of some phases of the world's
greatest secret, it was said, were
unwittingly betrayed by Soviet
delegates to the United Nations.
In endless discussions within the
United Nations Atomic Energy
Commission, in which the subject
of international control was argued
in the greatest detail, the Russians were said to have used
phrases and asked questions that
could have been based only on inside information, classified secret.

Testifies in Closed Session
Mr. Baruch was chief of the
United States delegation that implemented American control policy
in the United Nations commission.
He testified on security in a closed
session after the committee had
heard him in an open hearing. The
committee is considering the appointment of David E. Lilienthal
and of his four associates on the
United States Atomic Energy
Commission.
Presumably the contact reach-

U. S. FLAILS RUSSIA IN GERMAN PRESS

On February 3, 1947, presidential adviser Bernard Baruch warned Congress about Soviet efforts to obtain America's atomic secrets. That same day, Donald Maclean attended his first meeting of the Combined Policy Council, the highly secret body that determined Allied atomic policy. Its existence was unknown to both the Congress and the British Parliament.

Loy Henderson, the patriarch of the American Foreign Service, often worked with Maclean in 1945–1946. On his deathbed in 1986 at the age of ninety-three, Henderson searched his failing memory when asked if he remembered Donald Maclean. "Maclean . . . Maclean. . . ," he agonized, "the name has a foul odor." (Courtesy of the National Archives: 59-JB-646-2)

H. A. R. "Kim" Philby arrived in Washington in September 1949 to assist the FBI in its search for "Homer," the Soviet spy whom the Americans had discovered was operating from inside the British embassy. A Soviet spy himself, Philby already knew that "Homer" was Donald Maclean. (UPI/Bettmann)

In August 1950, Guy Burgess, another British diplomat and Soviet spy, arrived in Washington. He lived in the basement at 4100 Nebraska Avenue, next to Philby's secret photo lab. (UPI/Bettmann)

GREEN REG〉

el. No.   3603

August 10th, 1950

CYPHER:OTP

COPIES TO:
H.E.
Sir F Hoyer Millar
Head of Chancery
Capt. Coleridge
Mr. Greenhill
Mr. Burgess

From   Foreign Office

To   Sir Oliver Franks

d.   3.25 PM 10th August, 1950

r.   2.00 PM 10th August, 1950

SECRET

Following received from Peking. Begins

Addressed Foreign Office telegram No. 1194 of August 8th, repeated for information to HongKong and Singapore.

Please pass following to War Office from Assistant military attache.

Following information received from a single source who is considered reliable.

(A) Moving of troop trains north along Pin-Han Railway over last two months has been continuing.

(B) Numbers not known but a large proportion of these troops are going to Korean border.

(C) Railway stations north of Shanhaikuan have had all name placards etc. removed and now only display numbers.

(D) Tatung coal has for the last two months been going to Russia. Peking stocks of this coal are now very low, in the past this has been the principal source of supply for Peking.

(E) All Russians in Peking south of airfield Nan-Yuan have left during the last ten days.

(F) In outer Mongolia Russians have moved out every man woman and child for a radius of 100 Li (thirty miles) from a very large mountain. (Unfortunately the name of this mountain was not known by informant). This occurred very recently and is common talk among Mongolian traders.

(G) Korean wounded are arriving in Mukden hospita

2.   All the above information is considered as probably true and the grade is therefore B 2.

3.   European travellers on Tsinan-Tientsin Railway saw 11 troop trains north bound between 17th July and 21st July. Comments: This might be part of 1(A) above and due to congestion on that railway.

F.O. asked whether we should inform S.D.

G.G. F416

Clubb (State Dep) informed 1/9 G.G.

Though the British government would later insist that Burgess had no important duties during his nine months in Washington, this August 1950 secret message, with Burgess's handwritten notes, suggests otherwise.

On present U.S. form such support seems more
likely than not. One can only hope it is
not being extended or organised via Hong
ng. (c.f. Past tendencies of U.S.
attaches there).

6.   The third reason for the
military attache's optimism was that in
spite of State Department announcements to
the contrary, the actual course of events
in Formosa indicated a real change in
U.S. policy in the direction of increased
military support being in fact available
from MacArthur in spheres other than that
of the 7th Fleet. Recent Taiwan telegrams
seen subsequent to writing the above
appear to go some way towards confirming
this last point. I enquired whether
Chinese M.A. appeared to have obtained
his information on this question from his
own government or from U.S. sources.
Source said that while Chinese M.A. had not
been specific it was clear that he had
received a cheering communication from
his own government and had probably obtained some
confirmation from sympathetic U.S. official contacts
outside the State Department.

X.

                    G. Burgess.
                    G. BURGESS

                    29th August, 1950
                    (Written
                    (Dictated on 25th August)

X. I have no comment on
paras 1-5. On para 6.
we have the recent State
Dept. memo on aid to
Chiang which indicates
the "real change" is in
fact only a modification
to help Formosa in self defence. Very strong representation
                        ... ... might, of course, with local

Philby's house at 4100 Nebraska Avenue in northwest Washington was the scene of a raucous dinner party that helped undo his career as a spy.

I, James A. Turck, of 998 Alexandria St., Carthage, New York,
being duly sworn, make the following statement:

On February 28, 1951, Mr. G. Burgess, Secretary of Embassy, of the
British Embassy of Washington, D. C., requested me to drive him to
Charleston, South Carolina. He advised me that he did not have to
be in Charleston until Noon March 1, 1951. We left Washington,
D. C. about 9:30 or 10:00 A. M. February 28, 1951, with Mr. Burgess
driving a 1941 Lincoln Continental with DPL174 license plates.

Just beyong or South of the Highway Department weighing station at
Woodbridge, Virginia, we were stopped by a Virginia State Trooper,
whose name I do not know, and he advised Mr. Burgess that we were
driving 90 mph. The Trooper recognized Mr. Burgess' immunity and
allowed him to continue on with the request that he stay within the
speed limit.

When we got about 8 miles North of Ashland we were passing an Army
Convoy and were stopped by another Virginia State Trooper and he
advised that he had checked us at 80 mph. Again Mr. Burgess' immunity was recognized and we were allowed to proceed with a warning
to stay within the speed limit.

We stopped at Ashland and had a Coco-cola and he requested me to
drive. I did, and we proceeded South through Petersburg on Route 301.
When we were about 10 miles South of Petersburg we were stopped by
County Officer S. H. Mellichampe, of the Prince George County police,
and being the driver I was charged with speeding at 80 mph.

All during the time Mr. Burgess kept on telling me to step on it.
On several occasions I told him that we were going too fast and if
we were caught I would have to take the consequences. He told me
each time that he would take the responsibility and he had Diplomatic
immunity, and all the police would do would be to ask me to slow
it down, and we would go on our way.

I am making this trip with Mr. Burgess at his expense. I have been
knowing him a long time, several years in fact, and I drive and tow
motor cars for Gilbert's Motor Sales, Patterson, N. J. I didn't have
anything to do for a couple of days and agreed to go with him on
this trip.

                              S/James A. Turck   (SEAL)

State of Virginia,
County of Prince George, to-wit:

Suscribed and sworn to before me this 28th day of February, 1951,
in my County and State aforesaid.

                              S/David R. Lyon, III
                              Justice of the Peace

Kim Philby later claimed that he and Soviet intelligence masterminded Burgess's April 1951
recall to London so that Burgess could warn Maclean he was about to be taken in. In fact,
this February 1951 affidavit by a homosexual drifter is what really triggered Burgess's recall.

Warren Chase

Telephoned - Def. has made no formal
investigation on Mcl-Burgess case. He talked with
Counter-Intel. people who felt that there might be
some substance to allegations and apprehensions of
Genl van Fleet and Ad. Joy that info had gone to
Brit., not only on Yalu but on other strategic
matters as well. McLean was only channel thru whom
such info might have gone that they can think
of.

Chase suggests that if anthoritive high level
info on this subject is desired Mr. Murphy would be
the one to go after it.

The British and American governments insist that Maclean was not able to endanger Allied lives in Korea. This note, found in State Department files, indicates that senior officials at the State and Defense departments privately thought differently.

After Truman threatened to use the atom bomb in Korea, a panicked Prime Minister Attlee (seated at right) rushed to Washington. For several days in early December 1950 he met with Truman, Secretary of State Acheson (standing behind Truman), and Secretary of Defense Marshall. Within hours of their meetings, a highly classified transcript of their talks was sent directly to Maclean at the Foreign Office. (Courtesy of the National Archives: 306-PS-50-16689)

A rare moment of happiness in Cairo: Donald, Melinda, Harriet Marling, and Michael Maude. (Courtesy of Michael Maude)

This June 6, 1951 FBI teletype confirms the American contention that the British had kept the FBI completely in the dark about the search for "Homer." When the FBI was finally alerted that Maclean (Homer) had vanished from England, they had no idea who he was. A requested "name check" misspelled his name and incorrectly assumed that he had lived in New York. The "DEFERRED" classification meant the message had the lowest priority. The uncensored portion reads: "NY SEARCH NAME DONALD McLEAN AND Mac-LEAN THRU FORTYTHREE TO FORTYFIVE TELEPHONE DIRECTORIES IN EFFORT IDENTIFY NY ADDRESS. CONDUCT IMMEDIATE DISCREET INVESTI-GATION VERIFY ADDRESS IF LOCATED AND DEVELOP DATA RE WIFE'S BACK-GROUND. WFO CHECK I&RS AND STATE RECORDS RE McLEAN AND WIFE."

...ington Post

JNE 8, 1951   WTOP AM (1500) FM (96.3) TV (Ch. 9)   FIVE CENTS

House Votes Cut in Cash For District

10 Percent Slash In $12 Million Allotment Facing Fight in Senate

A 10-percent cut in the Federal payment for District municipal expenses in the fiscal year starting July 1 was voted by the House late yesterday.

The reduction came on a 56 to 41 division vote along party lines. Most Republicans voted for the cut, while the comparatively few Democrats on the floor voted to hold the Federal sum to the full 12 million dollars which Congress authorized three years ago.

This was the only floor fight on the city's record-high $137,776,375 budget which the House later sent to the Senate by unanimous voice vote.

"We'll proceed without delay," said Chairman Lister Hill of the Senate Subcommittee on District Appropriations. He said public hearings on the House-approved budget will begin next week. The exact date will be announced within the next two days, "after we've had a chance to study the

Two British Diplomats 'Disappear' in Europe; Flight to Russia Feared

Both Served Here

Acheson Regards Desertions By Britons as Serious If True

Secretary of State Acheson agreed yesterday that it would be "quite aserious matter in foreign relations" if the two missing British diplomats prove to be Soviet sympathizers.

Acheson was questioned briefly about the pair during the Senate hearings on the ouster of General MacArthur.

He said in answer to questions by Sen. Owen Brewster (R., Me.) that he was not-acquainted with either of the two, Donald Duart MacLean or Guy Francis de Money Burgess, when they were stationed in Washington.

The secretary noted that he has met "most of the staff of the British Embassy," and may have met them at some time. He said he had no knowledge of their disappearance beyond news reports. Washington associates of the diplomats said that from their background it was more likely

department of the British Foreign Office at the time he and Burgess disappeared 14 days ago, was first secretary of the British Embassy here from 1944 to 1948.

Burgess served as second secretary here from Auguest, 1950, until May, 1951.

They were complete opposites in personality and demeanor, according to their associates.

Burgess was described by one acquaintance as a "neurotic intellectual type," attracted to heavy drinking and fast automobile driving.

His driving was his principal reason for being shipped back to England last month, the British Embassy said. A few weeks earlier, Burgess was arrested three times in one day in Virginia, en route to North Carolina, for driving at speeds of about 80 miles an hour. Burgess was educated at Eton

Foreign Office Gets Report Missing Men Have Been Located In French Capital

LONDON, June 7 (U.P.).— Two officials of the British Foreign Office have disappeared in Europe but the Foreign Office said tonight it was checking a report that they had been located in Paris.

Scotland Yard and continental police were alerted to watch airfields and "Iron Curtain" embassies in the French capital on the theory that the two men might be fleeing to Russia with top-secret information.

The Foreign Office said it also was checking two messages purportedly sent by the two diplomats to relatives in England. A spokesman said the messages had been received in the last 24 hours. **Missing Since May 25**

One of the two was chief of the Foreign Office section dealing

---

The *Washington Post* breaks the story. When Secretary of State Acheson arrived at his office that morning, he told his aide, Jack Hickerson, "That son-of-a-bitch Maclean knew everything."

An ebullient Kim Philby in November 1955 after the British government insisted he was not the Third Man who had tipped off Maclean. Behind him is American journalist Edwin Newman, whose efforts to question Philby about his ties to Burgess and Maclean were met with hostility by British journalists. (UPI/Bettmann)

bombers." Militarily, as Clay had suggested in June, Stalin chose the right time. His failure was not in underestimating America's military strength and its willingness to use it, but in underestimating, as did Hitler, America's vast economic strength and its willingness to use it—via the Marshall Plan and the Berlin airlift.

This miscalculation was compounded by Stalin's tactical blunder. In the early summer of 1945, both Truman and Churchill had requested "free access" to Berlin. Stalin had never conceded nor even acknowledged the requests, but, in the flush of the Allied victory over Germany, both London and Washington had assumed that such rights were implicit in the joint occupation of Germany. Therefore, Stalin's surface blockade was not a violation of any agreement. In 1945 however, Zhukov had signed an agreement that gave the West "incontestable" and exclusive rights to three air corridors. Stalin either did not know this or underestimated its significance. Either way, he left the West an escape hatch, which was used not in ignominious retreat from Berlin, but to hang a humiliating defeat on the Kremlin.[60]

The Berlin airlift was a spectacular Western propaganda victory where ingenuity, teamwork, and economic abundance triumphed over crude Soviet intransigence. It also signaled that the people in the Western zones of defeated Germany were now allies—and the Soviet Union was the enemy.

In addition, the United States again exacted long-term benefits from a crisis. One of the reasons that the American military advocated sending the B-29s to Britain (others went to France and Germany as well) was that "once sent they would become somewhat of an accepted fixture," as indeed they did. Britain conceded in crisis what it had previously been unwilling to negotiate—its role as a "carrier" from which the United States could launch a nuclear strike at the Soviet Union.[61]

The blockade also propelled Western Europe and the United States to expedite plans for an Atlantic Alliance. Maclean's role in this next stage was even greater than the spring talks because the British had finally pulled the plug on Inverchapel—described by *Time* magazine as "old and tired." This was precisely the image Britain was trying to shake in the American consciousness, so the seventy-one-year old dean of their Diplomatic Service was replaced by Sir Oliver Franks.[62]

The two men are a study in contrasts. Franks, forty-three, had not even been born when Inverchapel accepted his first diplomatic assignment. Whereas Franks was a moral philosopher turned economic technocrat, Inverchapel had little understanding or patience for the complicated financial issues that now dominated Anglo-American relations. Inverchapel had long been an ebullient party giver; Franks was an ascetic with the reserve of an Oxford don who wanted nothing so much as to return to the halls of academia, which he did in 1952, when his Washington tour ended.

Even before he arrived in Washington, Franks received "spectacular advance notices." After Inverchapel, the State Department particularly welcomed Franks's reputation as "the most unneurotic man in Britain."[63]

Although Franks did not develop strong personal ties to any of his staff, he did consider Maclean as one of the senior staff officers most knowledgeable about the workings of the embassy, and the one with the firmest grasp of the upcoming talks on the Western military alliance. The sessions that began on July 6 differed in several respects from those held in March.[64]

First, although the participants were secreted in the Pentagon, the military was excluded; only diplomats were present. This time, the French were invited, and, for their benefit, these were called "exploratory sessions" to mislead Paris into believing that these talks were the first, rather than the second, round. (Theodore Achilles, a March participant, feared as late as December 1955 that if the French ever learned about the March talks it would still cause embarrassment in Franco-American relations.)

Lovett, Bohlen, and Kennan led the American delegation; Franks led the British. At his side was Maclean, senior adviser to the delegation and the only one of the British team to participate in both sets of meetings. What is most fascinating now about these talks is the evidence they provide that the British had some reason to be concerned about their most secret communications.

The security arrangements imposed qualified these meetings as the most secret ever held in Washington. The State Department kept participants "to an absolute minimum." Any leak, it was feared, would "cast a cloud" over the whole effort at a Western pact. But even with this heightened sensitivity, by the second day of the meetings Franks announced he was imposing the "Metric System" on all embassy communications back to London and urged the other representatives to do likewise.[65]

This would require a complete telegraphic and telephonic blackout on all communication with London. All reports to the Foreign Office would be sent by sealed diplomatic pouch. The pouch could only be opened by the Metric registry inside the Foreign Office, where the contents would be recorded before being sent to the Foreign Secretary.

This should have set off alarms for Maclean. The clear implication was that London had reason to believe its telegraphic communications between Washington and London were being compromised. They clearly believed, however, that the problem was external,—that the Soviets were intercepting and reading their transmissions. Certainly, Maclean was in no way implicated. After all, he not only participated in the talks, but also wrote the reports that went into the pouch. British suspicion over the integrity of its telegraphic communications either coincided with, or was the result of, a dramatic breakthrough by American cryptanalysts in their effort to break the Soviet code.

During the war years, the Soviet mission in New York had to use America's private telegraph companies to send messages to Moscow Centre. The Soviets naturally would have assumed that the FBI was making copies of their messages, and they were correct. They also had every confidence that, given the complex coding system they used, the messages could not be "read," and they were again correct.[66]

For years the intercepted messages were stacked up unread. But by late 1947, Robert Lamphere, a former lumberjack from Idaho now in FBI counterintelligence, started working with the Army Security Agency's Meredith Gardner to decipher the Soviet intercepts. Gardner was one of the ASA's best. He was a brilliant linguist who knew a half dozen languages including Japanese—which he had taught himself in three months—and Sanskrit.

Assisted by the retrieval of a partially-burned Soviet codebook bought from the Finns, a careless mistake made by a Soviet cipher clerk in New York, and one of the world's first computers, by late winter 1948, as Lamphere put it, "We'd hit the jackpot." Gardner was able to present him "with completely deciphered messages," including, as we have deduced, Churchill's Numbers 72 and 73 addressed to Truman.[67]

Sometime in 1948 Lamphere tipped off British intelligence officers assigned to the embassy. It seems doubtful from his account that this happened as early as July 1948. If not, then Franks's use of the "Metric System" may be unrelated to Lamphere's breakthrough and something else—which remains a mystery—warned the British that they had problems. Either way, one thing is certain—Lamphere had pulled the string that would lead to Maclean's undoing.[68]

★　★　★

On Saturday, July 17, Melinda, Donald, and their two sons left Washington to join her family on Quogue, Long Island, for what he must have felt was a well-deserved vacation. The Pentagon talks had lasted until July 9. During that time the Combined Policy Committee also met, so that, for instance, on Tuesday, July 6, Maclean and Franks spent almost the entire day and evening inside the Pentagon. The next day, at 10:00 A.M., Maclean escorted Franks to the State Department for his first CPC meeting, and then the two had to bolt back across the Potomac for the afternoon Pentagon session.

During his two week vacation, Donald spent much of his time sailing and playing golf or tennis in male foursomes. He also went riding with Harriet—"Harry" he called her—Melinda's vivacious younger sister. She had left Paris the night before Melinda and Donald met and was in New York four years later to greet them when they docked at the West 57th Street pier. She was instantly taken with Donald's aura of casual authority and his inside and irreverent knowledge of political and literary grandees.

"He was a delightful person with a wonderful sense of humor. He knew everyone. Isaiah Berlin, Isherwood, Auden, just everyone." Yet, she also could recognize the arrogance that was so distasteful to some of his British and American colleagues. Harriet attributed it to "his ghastly Calvinist nature, he could be intellectually arrogant." And though she thought "he was a very tender father, cozy and warm with the children," she could also see how he pulled away from Melinda and at times disavowed or ignored his role as husband and father.[69]

Perhaps by the summer of 1948 Maclean was beginning to grasp that he could not continue the deception forever. Too many Soviets who knew too much had defected; too many Westerners had been caught. And he could no longer doubt that he was the one who had chosen the losing side. The Communists were routed in the Italian elections; efforts to derail the Marshall Plan had failed; the Berlin blockade was turning into a giant morale booster for the West; countries were falling over one other to be included in a U.S.-led, anti-Soviet military pact; and, finally, Yugoslavia, once the most ideologically zealous Soviet satellite, had unilaterally declared its freedom from Stalin.

Maclean was not so blinded by either his anti-Western venom or his adulation for Stalin that he could not recognize a pattern of Soviet ineptitude. If they had wanted to sabotage the Marshall Plan, the Soviets need only to have signed up for its largess. Congress would have choked before voting money to a Marxist regime. Instead, Molotov's temper tantrum and walkout in Paris only encouraged the European nations and Congress.[70]

Indeed, Moscow's refusal to apply for—or to let any of its satellites apply for—Marshall Plan aid, combined with the communists' needlessly brutal coup and repression in Czechoslovakia, provided urgently needed impetus to get the Marshall Plan through Congress. The same circumstances assured that Italy and France—the former aided by extensive covert CIA political activity—would rush to join the Western bloc rather than deliver themselves to the communist parties through elections. In addition, Moscow can take the credit for sweeping aside nearly two hundred years of history and clearing the way for the United States to enter into peacetime alliances and begin a massive peacetime military buildup.[71]

No member of Stalin's espionage service could have done more than Maclean to try to avert these disasters. Yet, his efforts had come to naught. If two weeks of Quogue's breezy beaches and cool evenings helped to alleviate the fear that the walls were closing in around him, it would only mean that his return to Washington would produce an even greater shock.

CHAPTER THIRTEEN

It was addressed "Dearest Melinda." It was
very grim. It sounded like he was either going
away alone on a very long trip, or was
contemplating suicide.

Description given to the FBI of a letter found
in Donald Maclean's house.

THE DEAD COLD HAND OF THE PAST

The convulsive aftereffects of a week that would shape the events of history and the destiny of men for years to come were still reverberating throughout Washington when Maclean returned to the city on Friday, August 6. Not until the Watergate scandal twenty-five years later would the capital again experience the drama that rocked Washington during the final weeks of the summer of 1948.

The curtain rose on July 31 when Elizabeth Bentley appeared as a witness before the House Un-American Activities Committee (HUAC). The former communist courier had first told her story to the FBI in November 1945. At the time, despite Hoover's efforts, her testimony had attracted little interest. Three years later, the climate had changed greatly. HUAC members were on the edge of their seats as Bentley described how between 1938 and 1945 she had worked in the communist underground transporting documents stolen by nearly two dozen government officials for delivery to Soviet agents. She mentioned several names including Harry Dexter White, a prominent Roosevelt-Truman Treasury official. She did not on this occasion, however, name Alger Hiss.

Having previously charged down too many blind alleys, HUAC staffers, many of them former communists, began scurrying around to find witnesses to corroborate Bentley's story. On the advice of Hearst columnist Howard Rushmore, a crusading ex-communist, they contacted Whittaker Chambers. Chambers, still disillusioned by his futile 1939 meeting with Berle and Krivitsky's violent death, agreed to appear before an August 3 executive session in order to avoid being subpoenaed.[1]

"His clothes were unpressed; his shirt collar was curled up over his jacket. He spoke in a rather bored monotone," first term Congressman Richard Nixon later recalled of the short and pudgy Chambers, now forty-seven. He "seemed an indifferent if not a reluctant witness," whose soft voice often trailed off. But HUAC, quickly recognizing that he had a sensational story to tell, adjourned its closed session, moved to a much larger hearing room, threw the doors open, and sounded the alarm for the press to listen to their "mystery" witness.[2]

The press's initial skepticism that this was just another publicity-seeking HUAC stunt quickly vanished as they listened to Chambers's statement. With the subdued voice of someone reading a grocery list, he sounded off the roster of underground communists with whom he had worked, including "Alger Hiss, who, as a member of the State Department later organized the conferences at Dumbarton Oaks, San Francisco, and the United States side of the Yalta Conference." According to *Time* magazine (his employer), before Chambers finished he was performing before "a jammed, floodlighted, Congressional committee room." His story made national headlines.[3]

Hiss, who had just returned from vacation on Sunday, August 1, the day after Bentley's testimony, immediately cabled a demand that he be allowed to appear before the Committee to rebut Chambers. The gauntlet had been thrown down; HUAC was delighted.

On Thursday, August 5, after a morning strategy session with his brother Donald (also named by Chambers) and Dean Acheson at their offices in the prestigious law firm of Covington and Burling, Alger Hiss walked into the old House Office Building's packed caucus room. Composed, handsome, confident, a study in dignity, candor, and authority—the president of the establishment-laden

Carnegie Endowment for International Peace gave a command performance.

Even HUAC members joined the stampede of press, public, and friends to offer Hiss a handshake in congratulation. They then retreated with their colleagues to curse the ineptitude that had led them to accuse publicly a man so obviously above the squalid activities of his accusers. Later that day, a buoyant Truman, in an uphill reelection campaign, denounced the "Capital Hill Spy Scare" as a "red herring."[4]

But Nixon, relying on his own dark instincts, was convinced that Hiss was lying. His expressions were too filled with innocent wonder, his sincerity—from repeating "so help me God" twice when he took the oath, to his bristling desire to confront Chambers—was too contrived. Like Dostoevsky's Raskolnikov, he was too eager to help investigators solve the mystery.

Driven to bring down the fair-haired boy of an establishment he both loathed and longed to be accepted by, Nixon stood his ground during this "crisis" of doubt. First he led an executive session grilling of Chambers—this time in New York and out of the public eye—to make sure that he had not led them down the garden path. Secure that with Chambers he was betting on the right horse, Nixon then insisted on recalling Hiss for a public session on August 16.

Hiss found the Committee's earlier respectful indulgence replaced by Nixon's aggressive and hostile questioning. As the grilling over apparent contradictions in his earlier testimony stretched into hours, Hiss's self-assured denials and amused condescension disappeared. When his claims that he did not know and had never met Chambers—a man who, as it turned out, had lived in his house, and to whom he had given money and his car—Hiss's answers sounded either evasive or implausible. Hardly a statement he made on that day was not then or later contradicted. It was Chambers, not Hiss, who was withstanding the Committee's scrutiny.

Hiss left the Capitol aware that the momentum was swinging against him. Then, he was hit by a thunderbolt. Harry Dexter White, who had cheerfully appeared before HUAC on August 13 and, to the spectator's rousing cheers, vociferously denied all charges, had that day died of a heart attack.

In desperation to deliver the coup de grâce to Chambers's credibility, Hiss bungled. He walked into a trap that Nixon had set for him in a New York hotel room where, suddenly face to face with Chambers, Hiss admitted that he did, indeed, know him. Then, agitated and having to be physically restrained, he dared Chambers to step out from behind Congressional immunity and repeat his accusations in a place where he could be sued for libel. "I hope you will do it damned quickly," Hiss snapped.[5]

From there it was all downhill for Alger Hiss. He apparently believed that Chambers, an introvert with no taste and even less aptitude for public spectacles, would refuse. Such a refusal could be waved by Hiss's supporters as a banner of vindication. It was a ploy Philby would use successfully seven years later. In Hiss's less skilled hands, however, it backfired, for not only did Chambers oblige him, he did so on the nationally syndicated radio program *Meet the Press*.

The nation then waited for Hiss to redeem his soiled honor by making good on his threat. He had another reason for doing so; he wanted the spotlight of attention to focus solely on Chambers as "the same single source" for the years of accusations against him. But this was not true. The French, based on information they likely obtained from Krivitsky, told Bullitt about Hiss. Gouzenko identified him with unmistakable accuracy, and Bentley also knew about him. And it is clear that in 1942, HUAC had more than one informer.[6]

For Hiss this was an embarrassment of riches. Why did so many people keep saying that he was a Soviet spy? Chambers—a former drifter, the object of rumors about mental instability and homosexuality, a former communist who had admitted to treason and lying under oath—was the most vulnerable of all Hiss's accusers. Therefore, Hiss portrayed him as his only accuser—a fiction that persists, and one of the few gambits that has worked for Hiss to this day.

Still, it was weeks before Hiss filed suit. Even then it was almost as though he followed through only because the media and his followers were making such an issue of the fact he had previously failed to do so.[7]

When Hiss appeared before HUAC on August 25, a Congressional hearing room for the first time in history featured television cameras. His audition as a matinee idol—unlike Oliver North's approximately forty years later—was a miserable failure. Now it was Hiss's voice that trailed off; he appeared hesitant and indirect. He seemed affronted that though he knew such luminaries as Felix Frankfurter, Oliver Wendell Holmes, Dean Acheson, and John Foster Dulles (what his detractors would refer to as "innocence by association"), the Committee appeared to have greater faith in an admitted traitor. Hiss's attitude seemed petulant and grasping.

Members of the Committee responded that Hiss was a "witness with a strangely deficient memory," and that every piece of "verifiable evidence" supported Chambers. Their interim report was even harsher. Hiss had been "vague and evasive," while Chambers had been "forthright and emphatic." It concluded that the burden of proof was upon Hiss. If he was unable to clear himself, then he must have committed perjury.

Newspapers that had once ridiculed HUAC, now acknowledged that Hiss's testimony had left "significant unanswered questions." They demanded that the Committee "get to the bottom" of the contradictions in the Hiss-Chambers case.[8]

Maclean found it understandably wrenching to witness the spectacle of Alger Hiss's humiliation. When Chambers described Hiss as a "rather romantic communist" who had failed to reconcile his underground life with the need to openly express his convictions, he could have been describing Maclean. When Hiss was shorn of his once impeccable coat of Establishment respectability, Maclean felt his own nakedness.

The vision of his being exposed must have been a nightmarish horror for Maclean. Hiss's brother and wife were said to have shared his life of deception and treachery. Melinda and Donald's families, as well as Melinda herself, were completely innocent, yet they too would be trampled. Maclean's father's reputation would be exhumed from its proud place in his country's recent history; Sir Donald would be remembered only as the father of a notorious Soviet spy. Maclean's sons would also be scarred for life with the brand of treachery.

Moreover, the statute of limitations had expired on all the "crimes" Hiss might have committed, even if he had done everything Chambers said he did in the 1930s. Maclean, however, might be prosecuted under a tougher judicial system than America's. He had stolen atomic secrets—a crime for which the McMahon Act prescribed death—because it was even conceivable that the Americans might insist on a sentence that went beyond those stipulated by British law. As it was, his Cambridge classmate Nunn May had been sentenced to ten years.

But no one suspected Maclean during his last two weeks in Washington; these were days to celebrate. His American and British colleagues—as well as his Soviet associates, if their opinion could be expressed—considered his American tour a triumph. He had served in Washington longer than any other senior British diplomat of the period except for Ambassador Halifax. The Foreign Office rewarded him by promoting him to the rank of Counsellor. Not only was he the youngest in the British Diplomatic Service to hold this rank, but, at thirty-five he was assigned to Cairo, his third Grade A embassy. (There were only five; Washington, Paris, Moscow, and Beijing were the others.)

The Americans toasted Maclean with going away parties hosted by the AEC (with all the commissioners present except Strauss) at the Mayflower and the Hay Adams hotels. They were unusually large and festive occasions. Maclean gave a large reception at his home for Western diplomats, and he and Melinda were guests at many intimate dinner parties.[9]

Only once did Maclean exhibit his testiness. As they were saying their farewells at the Hay Adams, Gullion congratulated him on his promotion and his assignment to a country so strategically vital as Egypt. Maclean did not see it that way. Egypt, he made it clear, was not commensurate with either his skills or status. He made disparaging remarks about the country, its people, British policy in the region, and about diplomatic life in general.

Gullion was taken aback. He had always thought of Maclean as the consummate professional. He felt, too, that they had their own special relationship because both were handed such senior positions in a critical field—atomic energy—at such a young age. Now, Gullion thought "how very unprofessional it was for someone of Maclean's caliber and attainment" to complain openly about his assignment and chosen profession.[10]

★   ★   ★

Maclean was not the only one unnerved by Hiss's ordeal. As Michael Straight watched Hiss's world crumble, he too felt the masonry of his own falsely constructed life start to crack. In the six years since he had left the State Department and started work at the family-owned *New Republic,* he had "thrust all thoughts of Guy Burgess, Anthony Blunt, and Michael Green from my consciousness." But in the summer of 1948 "those memories returned like the furies to pursue me."[11]

Actually this was not quite correct. In April 1947, when he was in London as part of former Vice President Henry Wallace's presidential campaign team, Straight met with Burgess. The trip, which Straight was instrumental in organizing, was to carry abroad Wallace's crusade to denounce America and depict Stalin as a guileless peasant revolutionary.

Wallace not only opposed the Truman Doctrine, but charged that Tito's break with Stalin was a fascist plot organized by the Americans. When he was unable to offer any evidence nor even his reasoning for such an allegation, some observers wondered whether Wallace was relying on his mystic for information. Eventually, Wallace would denounce the Marshall Plan, prophesying that it would start World War III.[12]

Understandably enthralled by Wallace's venomous attitude toward America, Burgess, accompanied by a Soviet embassy official, sought out Straight at London's Savoy Hotel to congratulate him. According to Straight, this time Burgess "had no messages to deliver, no questions to ask."[13]

Another whose life was coming apart in Washington's highly charged atmosphere was Louis Dolivet, Straight's mysterious brother-in-law. His participation in Wallace's campaign brought him to the attention of Straight's former State Department colleagues. He organized Wallace's Paris stop on the same campaign swing. Because no French or U.S. officials would meet with Wallace, he was greeted only by prominent Communist Party officials. Dolivet blamed the disaster on Pierre Cot, the former French aviation minister who had first directed Dolivet to Straight's house in 1940. Dolivet was upset because he feared that his own status in the United States would be affected.

He had cause for concern. According to information the French authorities provided Washington, if Dolivet was claiming to be a French war hero, he was an imposter. He was neither French nor a war hero, but a Rumanian, "a clever and well-known Comintern agent" whose real name was Ludovicu Brecher. Eventually, this and other damaging information appeared in *The Washington Star,* probably leaked by the State Department.[14]

The Straight family hired a private investigator, who confirmed the truth of all this and more. Dolivet and Straight's sister were soon divorced; Dolivet was forced out of the country, and refused reentry even to attend his son's funeral.[15]

As he saw Hiss and Dolivet hounded by their pasts, Straight was consumed with worry that he would be next. "Foremost in my mind was a sense of fear," Straight admits. And because he did nothing to turn in those he knew might still be harming Western interests, he was also "haunted by a sense of guilt." His anxiety was affecting his domestic life.[16]

His wife, Betty Compton Straight, had completed her medical training and was undergoing psychotherapy as part of her preparation for becoming a psychotherapist. Her therapist was Austrian-born Dr. Jennie Welder who took the name Welderhall after marrying H. Duncan Hall, an Australian diplomat then assigned to the British embassy in Washington.

During one of their sessions, Mrs. Straight told Welderhall that her husband, because of his past secret life, was living in terror. After Guy Burgess's "revolting" visit to their home in the summer of 1940, she was convinced that it was he who had started her husband on the path to his eventual association with Soviet intelligence. Part of the guilt her husband now felt, she explained, was that he could not bring himself to turn Burgess in, though he still occupied a position of responsibility in the Foreign Office.

As she remembers it, Mrs. Straight told Dr. Welderhall that she was free to give her husband this information so that he could report Burgess to the proper British officials. But Dr. Welderhall declined because "it would interfere with the work we are doing here." Yet, fifteen years later, Straight would tell the FBI that Welderhall not only reported Burgess but Anthony Blunt as well. It was the British government which chose to do nothing.[17]

Welderhall insists, however, that both of these versions are inaccurate. She does not recall Mrs. Straight's giving her permission to share this confidential information with her husband. "But even if she had asked me to give the story to him," Welderhall later wrote, "I could not have done it. My professional work cannot be shared with anybody."[18]

Although the pressures of exposure were tearing Straight's family apart, he claims to have had no sympathy for Hiss. The two had known one another at the State Department, so Straight called to ask what Chambers's story was all about. "I'm as baffled as you are," Hiss answered, once again feigning that he was hearing it all for the first time. "If he had been distraught," Straight later claimed, "I might have believed him." But instead he sounded as though "he had prepared himself for years for the moment when the story would break."[19]

None of Straight's Cambridge colleagues believed in Hiss's innocence either. Of course Hiss "was one of us," a joyous Guy Burgess confided to a close friend. "Only a communist would be capable" of fooling so many people at such high levels for so long. It was further proof, he boasted, of Soviet intelligence's high recruitment standards. And in his book, written in close collaboration with the KGB, Philby groups Hiss with a number of convicted or confessed Soviet agents. Only Maclean appears to have been so deeply affected by Hiss's plight.[20]

★ ★ ★

The Macleans departed America for England through New York, where they stayed at the Plaza Hotel. Maclean called up Valentine Lawford to join them for tea and strawberries at the famed Palm Court. The two had served together as Third Secretaries at Paris and had formed perhaps the truest friendship Maclean permitted himself in the Diplomatic Service.

Although it had been a time of great crisis and long hours, Paris was also a time when they were young and carefree and without, or so it seemed to Lawford, great responsibilities. Both were fond of riding; when things got too demanding around the Chancery, Lawford would joke that he was going to run off and join the Hungarian cavalry. At such times, Maclean would always insist that Lawford leave for the throbbing social life that characterized Paris until the moment that the Germans marched in. Maclean would stay alone, decoding and encoding top secret cables. He never complained.

"He was a young man who enjoyed his work and his status in life," Lawford recalled looking back:

> I always thought he was more serious and intellectual than I was. He was so young, so handsome, so promising, he could have had his pick of the social crowd. Years later, I puzzled over why Donald had such a different set of friends. He didn't like the diplomatic functions; he would not allow himself to be the eligible bachelor at the dinner party. He had different connections, different interests.

When they met at the Palm Court, Lawford was the British alternate representative to Sir Alexander Cadogan at the United Nations. "Donald looked a bit strange," Lawford thought, "sort of puffed-up and beaten-down simultaneously . . . But both he and Melinda were very nice to me, and we laughed at some of the good old jokes."[21]

Wednesday, September 1, 1948, was Donald Maclean's last day in America. It was a day filled with fireworks. The secret pact that Walter Krivitsky and Whittaker Chambers had forged in the early morning hours almost exactly nine years earlier suddenly came blasting into public view.

Isaac Don Levine, who had arranged the original Krivitsky-Chambers meeting, came on like gangbusters. First, the September issue of *Plain Talk,* an anti-Stalinist monthly that he had started in October 1946, appeared that same day. It contained the first public account of Walter Krivitsky's efforts in 1940 to expose Soviet spies inside the British government. And in that day's *New York Times,* Levine, who had also been present for the Berle-Chambers meeting, gave his account of the session. This was of great interest because Berle had just given HUAC the most curious and gratuitous account of that meeting, which also appeared in the morning papers on September 1.

It is uncertain how much of any of this Donald saw before the *Queen Mary* set sail for England that day. It is doubtful, however, that it could have depressed him any more than he already was. For as the ship taking him and his family back to Britain pulled out of New York harbor, an American family was moving into their newly rented house at 3326 P Street. The daughter found a letter that had been left behind. It was addressed "Dearest Melinda" and sounded very grim. It ended "I am going away, take care of yourself." As the girl read it she felt, as she later told her father, that the writer was very upset, "like he was either going away alone on a very long trip, or was contemplating suicide."[22]

CHAPTER FOURTEEN

Donald raises a large mirror above his head
and crashes it into the bath, when to my
amazement, and delight, alas, the bath breaks
in two while the mirror remains intact. It
was a disgraceful episode.

Philip Toynbee describing how he and Donald
vandalized an apartment in Cairo.[1]

MIASMA OF DESTRUCTION

The Macleans arrived at Cairo in October 1945 amidst violent
political turmoil. Seeking to avenge Egypt's crushing defeat at
the hands of the newly created state of Israel, the underground
Ikhwan El Muslimeen, Muslim fundamentalists, were attacking foreigners and blowing up Western stores. Explosions ripped through
the city's Jewish quarter as cars and even tricycles were rigged with
time bombs. In addition, cholera had broken out, and scores were
dying daily. It was Donald's first experience of the volcanic political
forces and grinding poverty of the "developing" world.

It was also the first time he had been in a climate where British
presence was deeply resented. The *Ikhwan* had publicly targeted both
the American and British ambassadors for assassination; in mid-
November police had stopped four youths as they approached the
two embassies in a jeep stocked with a submachine gun, twenty-
eight revolvers, twenty-seven hundred rounds of ammunition, forty-
eight hand grenades, two bombs, and maps of the American and
British embassies. It fell to Maclean to draw up a plan for evacuation

of all nonessential diplomatic personnel not only from Egypt, but also from all British posts in the Middle East.[2]

The region had become a new front in the Cold War when Truman beat the Russians (and the Republicans) as the first to recognize the state of Israel on May 14, 1948, the day a Jewish state was proclaimed. His decision clashed with Bevin's naive hope that Britain could harness Arab nationalism as a way of perpetuating the British Empire—a kind of Western union of desert tribes, a story line explored to excessive but unrewarding lengths by the Arabs in the First World War.

The day after the state of Israel had been proclaimed, the Arab armies, equipped with British-supplied weapons, launched their inept campaign to drive it into the sea. The margin of victory was provided for the Jews when the United States rushed in heavy equipment, including aircraft. Washington incorrectly assumed that London would halt its arm shipments to the Arabs once the United States became Israel's chief military benefactor.

Shortly after Maclean arrived, he found grounds for London's fear that Washington's ambitions included replacing Britain as the region's primary Western power. "Judging from the brashness and take-charge attitude of the U.S. mission," he cabled his old friend Michael Wright, now an Assistant Under Secretary at the Foreign Office, "America is ready to assume the dominant economic and military position in the Middle East." And indeed he was correct.[3]

The badly frayed relations between Washington and London were compounded in Cairo by the personal antipathy between their two envoys. Jefferson Caffery was one of America's most colorful, controversial, and politically conservative career ambassadors. "Caffery is not my type," the more liberal and decorous Sir Ronald Campbell cabled London after their first meeting. Sir Ronald was from the old school of British diplomacy, well schooled, gentle, and prone to regard American diplomats as amateurs. Around the British embassy they delighted in telling stories about Caffery, whom they called "J.C., Jesus Christ for short." According to press secretary James (later Sir James) Murray, at his dinner parties Caffery served his guests a white wine of mediocre vintage. He himself always served from a separate bottle wrapped in a towel. "Does J.C. have his own special reserve?" Murray finally asked Robert Simpson, his counter-

part at the American embassy. "Oh no," Simpson replied, "that's
not wine in those bottles, it's very dry martinis." Others wondered
aloud how the prudish Caffery, who vigorously denounced them,
knew in such detail the contents of King Farouk's pornographic film
collection.[4]

Maclean's relations with Campbell were excellent. Maclean had
impressed him both when they worked together in Paris, and later
when they overlapped briefly in Washington, where Campbell had
also worked in the atomic energy area. As the third ranking officer
in the embassy and Head of Chancery, Maclean's authority was
unchallenged. He not only determined who saw what within the
embassy; he also determined what would or would not be reported
to London. When the political officer wanted to report on the latest
round of violence in Cairo, Maclean overruled him. "There's no
need, the Foreign Office already knows about it." After Campbell
met with King Farouk, Sir Ronald drafted a cable which was then
sent to the Foreign Office over Maclean's signature.[5]

The most demanding adjustment for Maclean was not to the
region's turmoil nor to the embassy's personnel, but to the inevitable
difficulties in forming a relationship with his new Soviet control.
This is the spy's most intimate and important relationship. His
control is father figure, patron, and confessor, as well as boss. The
most dominant and complex part of Maclean's life was his career as
a spy. For fifteen years there had been only one person, his control,
to whom he could talk about his triumphs, frustrations, and doubts.
The quality of that relationship would be reflected in his overall
performance and stability. Considering the way in which events
evolved in Egypt, it must not have been a very good one.

Perhaps this was due to the fact that, in Washington, Maclean was
at the heart of Anglo-American decision-making and had reason to
believe that his reports were eagerly read in the Kremlin and might
be exerting influence on Soviet policy. But the Soviets were novices
in the Middle East, their policy hesitant and uncertain. Perhaps
Moscow's operatives in the area were not first rate; perhaps Stalin
did not consider Maclean's position that important. Perhaps Donald
knew this.

If so, this would only drive home what he must have realized: if
ever he were going to be discovered, it would be for the crimes he

had already committed in Washington. There was nothing that he could do in Egypt that would compare in importance to his four and a half years in America, which must have been one of the reasons why he resented going to Egypt. It was not because it was a lowly assignment in the British Diplomatic Service, but because it was held in such low esteem by the Soviets. In Cairo, he could do little more than wait to see whether his past would catch up with him. The tension became even more unnerving because of the Hiss drama.

In November Whittaker Chambers turned over to U.S. government investigators three rolls of undeveloped film that he had hidden in a hollowed out pumpkin on his farm in eastern Maryland. The "pumpkin papers" contained photostats of State Department documents that Chambers claimed Hiss had passed to him when they had worked together in the communist underground. Several weeks later, a grand jury indicted Alger Hiss for lying when he swore that he neither knew Chambers nor passed documents to him during that period.

Documents. That was the problem. Stalin always wanted documents. How many of the scores, if not hundreds, of documents that he had passed, Maclean had to wonder, were now in the hands of another potential or actual defector? It would require only one to hang him.

Maclean's doubts and fears were more accurate than he could ever have imagined, even in his darkest moments. The incriminating evidence was not hidden in a pumpkin patch, however. It was in the form of intercepted Soviet messages that American cryptanalysts and the FBI's Robert Lamphere were pouring over for hours every day as they attempted to unlock the secrets those documents could tell about Soviet agents operating in the United States.

In January 1949 the British government received official confirmation of what Ladd and Lamphere had told MI5 and MI6 representatives in Washington several months before—American security authorities had reason to believe that certain Foreign Office information had been leaked to the Soviets in 1944 and 1945 by someone working inside the British embassy.[6]

★   ★   ★

The Maclean's lived in the tranquil European section of Cairo, far removed from terrorist bombs and spy hunts. The wide streets were lined with brilliant orange and scarlet flame trees, and their large three-story colonial house had its own wave of mimosa and jacaranda washing over the veranda. Melinda sparkled in her new surroundings.

Once again she was an expatriate, and this time in the most exotic country she had known. The brilliant arid climate, and the gracious pace of social life nurtured a self-confidence in her that had been developing in Paris, only to be stunted by the oppression of wartime London and official Washington. Donald's promotion had been hers, too, and a domestic staff of four servants, a gardener, and a governess freed her from the tedium of daily housework. Having shed the inhibitions that made her so self-conscious and withdrawn, she now welcomed such chores as playing hostess for Ambassador Campbell, a bachelor.

Geoffrey Hoare, Middle East correspondent for *The News Chronicle* (London) and now a neighbor, noticed the difference at once. When he had sat next to her at a London dinner party in September, he was taken "with this delicate-complexioned, soft-voiced little American girl," whose fragility and defenselessness made him want to protect her. Six months later, she had emerged from her shell and was "on top of the world." He found her "as charming as ever, but I no longer felt any great need to protect her!"[7]

Donald noticed the difference, too. As Melinda was finding projects unrelated to the embassy and entertaining more at home, he became annoyed. He patronized her independence, mocked her new enthusiasms, and complained about the loss of his privacy. But Melinda suspected that what he really resented was her emancipation and the fact that her life no longer totally revolved around his.

"I have become more extroverted and enjoy gayer and simpler people," she later wrote to her sister Harriet, "but Donald will have none of that at all." Hoare spent many hours with Donald at their house:

A picture of him at that time would show a tall, fair, rather carelessly dressed man of thirty-six, slightly remote, a little too restrained, sitting low in an armchair, with one lanky leg crossed over the other and his free foot constantly jerking up and down, commenting with cynical humor on the stupidity and obtuseness of most of his fellows.[8]

Some time during the early summer Harriet came for a stay. Melinda began at once to organize a fifteen-mile jaunt up the river for a late dinner with friends. She rented a felucca, a narrow lateen-rigged vessel, designed to sail on the Nile's faint breeze. Several other embassy couples were included.

But the always stingy Nile breeze was particularly niggardly that day, and the felucca barely advanced against a four-knot current. It was a blistering hot day with neither shade nor food—only gin and wine. Donald began drinking. As the hours dragged by, he drained the gin. Drunk, menacing, loud, he first lit into the boatmaster. Then, as the tension among the passengers mounted, he turned on Melinda. After working himself into a rage over the stupidity of it all, he lunged and began to strangle her. He had immense latent strength that became uncontrollable when he was drunk. It took a powerful effort by two men to pull him off.

When they finally reached their destination at 2:00 A.M., they made such a commotion that the *ghaffir* (guard) came down to investigate, carrying an old single-shot rifle. Donald, unrepentant after his earlier outburst, leaped from the boat like some Hollywood swashbuckler, grabbed the rifle, and pushed the *ghaffir* down. Then he began to swing the rifle in arcs over his head at imaginary attackers. Finally Lees Mayall, a long-time friend and First Secretary at the embassy, grabbed him from behind and tried to wrestle the rifle away. They were on an embankment, and Maclean fell backward against Mayall, whose leg buckled and snapped as Donald came down on top of him.

When the vessel returned to Cairo the next day, its passengers could have been mistaken for the ragged survivors of a desert war. Donald gave Campbell a fabricated story when he showed up for work Monday, but the Ambassador must have been skeptical. When Mayall finally returned to work several weeks later, Campbell asked, "What really happened out there?" Mayall, along with the others, loyally advanced the cover story, and the incident was never reported to the Foreign Office.[9]

Maclean was increasingly irritable at the embassy. Unhappy with diplomatic pay and allowances, dissatisfied with British foreign policy, aloof to all but two or three of his colleagues, he hunted for opportunities to lambaste Whitehall. He never had to look far.[10]

When London promoted the expansion of British oil companies in the region, it cynically emphasized the advantages for local economic development. "It is a travesty to suggest that this is designed to further the interests and well being of the peoples of the Middle East," Maclean reported. "Unless some new and satisfying way of life is found for them, we shall sooner or later have a price to pay."[11]

In the summer of 1949, as the debate over the presence of British troops in Egypt raged on, Gallad Pasha, the influential editor of the French-language newspaper in Egypt, told Maclean that the "Soviet Threat" was not a valid reason for the British to maintain troops in the country. Only the two hundred wealthiest, most privileged, and powerful families feared the Soviets, he argued. Thus, the real purpose of approximately twenty thousand British troops was not to protect the masses—who were apathetic to such geopolitical concerns—but to protect the two hundred.

This struck a responsive chord in Maclean's 1930s mentality. He immediately composed a summary of Gallad's views for circulation to Campbell and other senior officials, noting, "Personally, I think there is a good deal of truth" to them.

His colleagues did not. They responded with a torrent of protest. Gallad was not popular at the embassy, where he was considered a self-absorbed radical whose only uncompromising principle was his elitism. *The Economist* had recently predicted that he would eventually "slither in his Packard to his doom."[12]

"I find it hard to comment on this astonishing statement," Alastair Maitland, the senior minister, wrote. To say that all but two hundred families were indifferent to whether they were ruled by a corrupt king or a Moscow-installed dictatorship was to ignore the professionals, the intelligentsia, the businessmen, and the students who were pushing for political reform and pluralism. Was Gallad (and by implication Maclean) ignorant of the middle class? He suggested that Maclean was remiss in not mounting a stronger counterargument.

Maclean tried to regroup by restating the argument, but it still sounded as though British troops were there to protect a parasitic oligarchy, while the vast millions would actually welcome the Russians to relieve their misery. One colleague chided Maclean, "Why doesn't Gallad come out of his despotic shell and mix with his own people?"

The debate went on for some time until it was summarily ended by Maclean. "I do not believe that the minutes so far have led to any conclusion worth reporting to the Foreign Office," he ruled imperiously.

This sort of thing created irritation toward Maclean. Some of his embassy colleagues eventually would express frustration about his style to their American counterparts. For all his brilliance, they complained that "he never made a clear statement, he was diffuse in his approach to things and he mumbled and hedged."[13]

None of these shortcomings impinged on his place in the embassy, however. As Anthony Eden later told the House of Commons, "All the reports I received confirmed that he was doing outstanding work." Maclean was entrusted with the job of drawing up a detailed Middle East Defence Plan to be used by Britain, America, and Egypt "in the event of war with Russia." Working closely with British and American military advisers, he laid out the organizational setup; mapped out the size of expanded Royal Air Force installations; itemized support facilities; fixed the numbers and placement of troops and headquarters staff; and estimated the requirements for radar, radio, and other technicians.[14]

★   ★   ★

The exercise soon appeared less theoretical. On September 5, 1949—exactly four years after Igor Gouzenko had defected in Ottawa with proof of atomic espionage—a U.S. weather reconnaissance plane detected large amounts of radioactive dust in the atmosphere. It had to have come from nuclear fission inside Russia. But was it from a weapon or a nuclear reactor accident?

Scientists in Britain, Japan, and America went to work. By September 15 the scientists were in agreement. Russia had exploded a nuclear device. They had the atom bomb. When Truman finally broke the news on September 23, the reaction was "shock and muted dread among millions of Americans." A tidal wave of insecurity—driven by predictions that within a year the Soviets would have enough bombs "to destroy fifty of our largest cities with 40,000,000 of our population"—washed over America. "This is now a different world," Vandenberg lamented, "the new problems are appalling."[15]

"It came at least three years sooner than expected," according to *The New York Times*. But *New York Times* Broadway critic turned war correspondent Brooks Atkinson, had warned against American complacency in November 1945. Although Russian natural and financial resources could not match those of the United States, he wrote, its scientific research and development "is one of Russia's most flourishing national enterprises. Of all modern nations," he predicted from Moscow, "the Soviet Union is in the best position to concentrate everything it has on one essential project involving security." But this assessment had been lost in the din of projections from Groves, Baruch, and others who had estimated ten to twenty years.[16] Gullion, as we have seen, had estimated 1948. Another leading American scientist, Arnold Kramish, also had predicted 1948, while Niels Bohr, the Danish scientist who had been at Los Alamos, told the World Bank's John J. McCloy that the Soviets would have the atom bomb between May and August 1949.[17]

Having lost the race to become Europe's first atomic power, Britain's calculations were along a different line. "How does it come about," Sir Henry Tizard asked on behalf of the entire British atomic energy establishment, "that knowing all that we did in 1945, we are still without the atomic bomb by contrast with Russia who starting from scratch has apparently now surpassed us?" What no British technician could believe, having tried to proceed without America's secrets, was that the Soviets had so quickly solved those same problems. This had to mean, as Tizard put it, that "to build and operate a plant of sufficient scale to give them material for a full-scale trial . . . [the Soviets] must have been able to acquire absolutely full details of the whole U.S. process." That is, they must have depended on spies.[18]

There was a silver lining for the British. Washington conceded that, because the Russians had the bomb, there was no longer any reason to withhold atomic information from the British. This proved James Reston's point that "the Russians have a genius for pushing things in the direction opposite from what they want." The Marshall Plan owed its quick success to the Czech coup, while the Berlin blockade gave NATO the critical boost it needed. Now the administration "will seek authority from Congress to pass on more information than in the past to Britain and Canada about the industrial process for producing atomic weapons." London could also expect "new financial and economic concessions" as well.[19]

For the first time in years London was bubbling with optimism about the future of the Anglo-American atomic "partnership." Then disaster struck. Lamphere had earlier come across "a startling bit of information in a newly deciphered" Soviet message containing verbatim sections of a scientific report written from Los Alamos. He had found the original of the report contained in the message in the AEC's files. It had been written by Klaus Fuchs.

In August 1949 Lamphere advised the British that someone, "probably a British scientist, had been giving information about the atom bomb to the Russians." When his report was received in London, Michael Perrin, one of Harwell's most senior officials, was called in. After reading the report, he looked up and pronounced solemnly, "it looks very much as if Fuchs at Harwell is working for the Russians."[20] Within a short time, Lamphere had what he considered the clinching piece of evidence. According to one intercept, the agent's sister had attended an American university. Fuchs's sister had been a student at Swarthmore.

The problem was to coax Fuchs into confessing, because, in the mistaken assumption that the Soviets did not know that their code had been broken, the British and American officials had agreed that the intercepts could never be used as evidence in a court proceeding. Fortunately for them, Fuchs, now head of the Theoretical Physics Division at Harwell, was something of a tortured man, who was having second thoughts about his long contributions to the Soviets, which had begun in 1942. It was Fuchs, a loner who had shunned intimacy of any sort, who initiated what turned out to be a series of peculiar and vague personal conversations with Harwell security authorities.[21]

Among the eventual participants in these sessions was William J. Skardon, the top British MI5 counterespionage interrogator. In late December, Skardon interrupted Fuchs during a rambling monologue about youthful indiscretions and accused him of being a Russian spy. Within a month, Fuchs made a full confession, leading to his formal arrest on February 2.

"The roof fell in today," David Lilienthal, chairman of the AEC, wrote after hearing the news. "It is a world catastrophe, and a sad day for the human race." He worked to keep "the top from blowing off things," but he also believed that "witch-hunts, anti-scientist orgies," and a new round of Anglo-American antagonism were inevitable. In contrast to how the AEC would deal with Maclean, by which time Lilienthal had departed, he insisted that a statement be issued making it clear that Fuchs knew "a wide area of the most vital weapons information," including his "attendance at a 1947 declassi-fication conference with the British." He pulled no punches with the Joint Committee. "I poured it on: there wasn't a bright light in the whole picture."[22]

Fuchs modestly assumed that his efforts had saved the Soviets one year, but the Senate-House Atomic Energy Committee later con-cluded that it was more like eighteen months. William Laurence, writing in *The New York Times* in 1951, estimated that Fuchs had saved them as much as three years, while both British and American scientific historians would simply say his role was "indispensable" to the Soviets, and the damage he caused "incalculably great." Others, writing much later, reported "it is conservatively estimated that [Fuch's] reports advanced the Soviet atomic bomb program by perhaps two years." And the AEC, long the champion of the "there-are-no-secrets" school, measured Fuchs's deceit by a yardstick other than time: "Fuchs alone has influenced the safety of more people and accomplished greater damage than any other spy not only in the history of the United States but in the history of nations."[23]

The Fuchs case tore open the barely healed Anglo-American wounds inflicted by the Nunn May case. All the proposals to accelerate atomic information sharing were abruptly shelved. Just as the British thought that the finish line might be in sight, they now had to struggle to get back to the starting line. "A technical program that was not working very well before Fuchs's arrest," Alex Longair, science attaché at the Washington embassy, would eventually inform the Foreign Office, "is now working badly."[24]

Whatever joy Maclean derived from witnessing the West's terrified reaction to a "Red Bomb" had to be tempered by the Fuchs case. How had they found out about him? Why had he confessed? Did Fuchs know about him? Would the fact that Fuchs was at the 1947 declassification conference trigger an investigation that might place him under scrutiny? (The AEC was in fact reviewing all "aliens" who had been issued non-escort passes.)²⁵

Then he received another blow. On January 22 jury foreman Mrs. Ada Condell stood before a packed courtroom on the thirteenth floor of the District Court Building in New York's Foley Square and broke a hushed silence by announcing Alger Hiss "guilty on both counts"—guilty of lying when he said he did not know Whittaker Chambers and guilty of lying when he denied passing State Department documents to him.²⁶

The combination of Fuchs and Hiss propelled Maclean to the first stage of his flagrantly self-destructive behavior. He may have railed against exploitation of the masses by day, but at night he had thrown in his lot with Cairo's decadent "fast group" (as one American diplomat referred to them) that swirled around the twenty-eight-year-old King Farouk and his two sisters, the Princesses Fawzia and Faiza, both world-class beauties.

The King had been handsome as a child, but by twenty he had gone to seed. He was insecure, petulant, and indifferent to his country's suffering. He was also a ceaseless debaucher, notorious for giving parties "of the most immoral type," which featured vast quantities of alcohol, exotic women, male prostitutes, drugs, and what Caffery described as the most "extensive and foul collection of movies and pictures."²⁷

Princess Fawzia, twenty-six, had the creamy complexion and auburn hair of an American debutante. At twenty she had married the Shah of Iran, but he divorced her after she gave birth to a daughter. Donald was closest to her younger sister, Faiza, who was married to an Egyptian army officer. James Murray, the press secretary who worked closely with Maclean, believes "they were not intimate," despite a persistent rumor to the contrary.²⁸

That was benign, however, compared with other rumors. According to a State Department report, which in most other details was accurate, at one party "Maclean was reported to have amused those present by completely undressing." On another night, after he had left one royal party, Maclean climbed over the wall of the exclusive Gezia Sporting Club, and fell asleep in a flower bed. The next morning, the police found him walking aimlessly through rush hour traffic in his stocking feet, shoes in hand, his white linen suit soiled.[29]

And where was Melinda during all of these episodes? There were rumors about her, as well. She had, as Hoare put it, "many admirers." According to some reports, she had formed a platonic relationship with Prince Ismail Daoud, a minor but wealthy royal figure some years her elder, who was married to an American. Initially, Melinda and the Prince were seen together openly in public, but that changed after they allegedly became lovers. Cecil speculates that Melinda's tryst "may well have been a contributory factor" to Donald's loss of self-esteem and self-control. Her sister Harriet, however, believes it was Donald's wayward behavior that drove Melinda to pursue companionship elsewhere.[30]

She was also a target of the vicious gossip mill churned by other embassy wives, many of whom were jealous that she, an American commoner, had been chosen to host an intimate dinner party for the Duke of Edinburgh which, according to Hoare, was "a high success." They cackled that Melinda "couldn't cope with her duties as the wife of a British diplomat." Not only could she not keep a proper house or her servants, she could not keep her husband. But these were all misdemeanors compared with the crime of "her American housekeeping."[31]

The embassy security officer, Major Sansom, did report some of what was reaching his ears about Maclean. George Middleton, head of the Foreign Office personnel department, was prompted to make a low-level inquiry of Campbell. As Middleton later told it, Campbell "replied sharply . . . that he disliked hearing tittle-tattle about an able officer like Maclean: such an enquiry would never have been made in the old days."[32]

Cecil believes that Campbell's motivation may have had more to do with sensitivity about rumors concerning his own life style than concern about fair play for Maclean. The Ambassador's long-time manservant was believed to be homosexual, and Campbell, a bachelor, was aware that there was speculation about their relationship. This may have, "predisposed him to ignore all stories about the private lives of his staff."[33]

Most staff members, however, were unaware of the darker side of Maclean's life. Murray found him "tirelessly conscientious. He demanded first class work, you could never let a shoddy telegram get past him. But," he added wistfully years later, "why he would go off and drink too much, I never knew." Another member of the embassy staff watched Maclean's ability to hold up under the embassy's crushing work load "while having the obvious appearance of one who was quite loaded" with grudging admiration.[34]

Slowly, the pall that was evident toward the end of his Washington tour was again clouding his life. Away from the embassy for a few days, he could relax over cards, play tennis, and show affection for his small sons. These interludes, however, could not forestall the inevitable. The spectacular end to his rise in the Diplomatic Service coincided with, if it was not caused by, the arrival of two of his favorite people, Harriet Marling and Philip Toynbee, in the spring of 1950.

Toynbee, whose appearance has been compared to a washed-up Gary Cooper, had just hit bottom—again. The great promise of his earlier years was fading. His writing projects went either unwritten or unread. When his marriage and the bottle collided, it was the marriage that broke. Finally, his father, the historian Arnold J. Toynbee, interceded to get him a job as a Middle East correspondent for *The Observer,* a job he was ill-prepared to fill. He had no training as a journalist, no knowledge of the Middle East, and no contacts in the region except for Maclean.

Although according to Toynbee's diary Melinda was as eager and accommodating about his stay with them as Donald, she told friends at the American embassy "she had no choice in the matter, it was all Donald's decision." She had discovered more than ten years earlier in Paris, even before she and Donald were married, that when he and Toynbee were together, the two of them drank like feckless teenagers.[35]

The next several weeks were a blur of parties and private drinking sessions. Many of the evenings began in a normal fashion—drinks at a diplomatic reception, dinner out, and a nightcap on the veranda. But few evenings actually were normal. Time and again Philip and Donald would disappear from receptions and end up "pub crawling." At other times, everyone would arrive home together from a night out, only to have Maclean and Toynbee sneak back out at two or three in the morning to search out Donald's royal friends.

The two often talked and drank through the night, toasting the dawn's first light. Toynbee was fascinated and delighted with Maclean's monologues: "His extreme gentleness and politeness—the occasional berserk and murderous outbursts when, so to speak, the pot of suppressed anger has been filled." As the pot spilled over, out came the malice. He loathed most of his colleagues; he detested the diplomatic service.

A State Department official who provided Washington with a summary of Maclean's last weeks in Cairo warned that "the picture which develops is not a very pretty one, and certainly leads one to the conclusion that the British were willing to put up with a great deal for the sake of having brilliant officers." He did not know the half of it.[36]

One night Maclean was completely out of control and careened from "disaster to disaster." He physically assaulted an embassy colleague at a bar, then started "throwing glass after glass at the wall." Several nights later, he and Toynbee became drunk to try to shock Melinda and Harriet. When this failed, Donald left a party with "a known homosexual, and did not reappear that night. . . . His bitterness became more savage and more uncontrolled." On another occasion he publicly insulted Harriet and then struck Melinda. In one all night session, he told Toynbee that he wished Melinda dead. "I really am getting to the point where I have to be shut up," he then admitted.[37]

On the night of May 8 the two of them never went to bed. Donald failed to report to the embassy the next morning, preferring a long drunken lunch with Toynbee and a journalist friend. Donald and Philip then went to an apartment building where Maclean knew several women. They found the door to an apartment of two American embassy female employees unlocked, and entered. But, after finding one of the roommates asleep and a servant in the kitchen, they left.

Maclean tried the door at the apartment directly across the hallway. It is not certain whether he knew who lived there, but, as it turned out, it was the apartment of two American women—one of whom was Ambassador Caffery's secretary. The husband of the other was an Arabian American Oil Company employee. The door was unlocked. The two men first raided the liquor cabinet in which they found more gin. Then, as Toynbee put it, they "went on a destructive orgy which surpassed everything that had gone before," breaking pictures, emptying drawers, ripping clothes, and smashing plates and glasses. In a grand finale, Donald lifted a huge ornate mirror and brought it crashing down on the marble bathtub. Toynbee watched, breathless, and "to my amazement, and delight, alas, the bath breaks in two while the mirror remains intact."[38]

The next day, while Donald was still at home too ill and incoherent to speak, Melinda went to see Ambassador Campbell. It was agreed that Donald would be sent to London at once for medical help. Campbell was forced to plead for understanding from Caffery, who, though he disliked Maclean as "a heavy drinker and somewhat offensive," promised not to make a diplomatic incident of it (when the Cairo press reported it as such, however, no denial was issued by the American embassy). No charges were pressed.

Donald, contrite, called the apartment dwellers. He also sent a note promising to pay for the damage and assuring them that he was seeking medical attention. The Marling sisters also called them, apologized, and promised to make restitution. The two American women agreed not to file any formal complaint.[39]

The Foreign Office finally realized that one of its most promising stars had become a severe problem. They were not the only ones who were surprised. It was a "miasma of destruction" (again, Toynbee's words) that Western diplomatic circles talked about for years to come. Jack Hickerson, who was now an assistant secretary of state, heard about the story in Washington, as did Valentine Lawford, after the story had circulated at United Nations headquarters in New York. Both were stunned.[40]

Early on the morning of Friday, May 12, almost six years to the day after he and Melinda had arrived in New York amidst such great promise, the career of the Diplomatic Service's youngest Counsellor seemed to be at an end. He was escorted to Farouk Field by embassy officials. Melinda's bright cheerfulness was replaced by taught grimness. Harriet looked shattered. Only Donald appeared composed.

Geoffrey Hoare, with a journalist's luck, was booked on the same flight. He had no idea of what had happened. Donald told him only that he was returning to England on business. Hoare was pleased to have a travel companion. The flight was delayed in taking off, and then stopped in Rome, so they were together for almost twenty-four hours. At no time did Hoare notice anything wrong with Donald "except possibly that he was rather more silent than usual. He had none of the external signs of a person suffering from a severe nervous breakdown."[41]

Robert Cecil, Maclean's Foreign Office colleague and biographer, has offered some fascinating speculation. Perhaps Maclean wanted to end his career as a Soviet agent, but the Soviets had refused to release him. So, desperate to be free of the forces that were destroying him, he engaged in the spectacular binges of April and May, aware that it was necessary to destroy his career to free himself from the Soviet grip; in effect, he engineered his own breakdown.

This theory is plausible, but there was nothing contrived about what happened to him once he returned to London.[42]

CHAPTER FIFTEEN

A purely internal Albanian uprising at this
time is not indicated and, if undertaken,
would have little chance of success.

September 12, 1949 CIA estimate before
Philby betrayed the Albanian mission.[1]

THE SEARCH FOR "HOMER"

K im Philby arrived in the United States aboard the Cunard Line's
Caronia, which docked its seven hundred and eighty-two passengers at New York's West 50th Street pier on Saturday, October 8,
1949. The East Coast was enjoying a resplendent Indian summer
with temperatures in the 70s and low 80s. Sun-worshippers dotted
rooftops and swarmed to the beaches and parks as if it were June;
only the explosion of red and gold leaves on the maples and elms
reminded them that it was not.[2]

"I found the famous fall," Philby wrote from drab Moscow nearly
twenty years later, "one of the few glories of America which
Americans have never exaggerated because exaggeration is impossible." He had also arrived at a time when both important changes—
Harvard Law School announced it would be the first to admit
women—and enduring traditions—the Yankees again beat the Dodg-
ers in the World Series—were dominating the news.[3]

Less than two years after the Secret Intelligence Service (SIS) had
sent Philby, one of its best and most promising intelligence officers,
as liaison with Washington, he would leave a ruined man. How he

functioned before the final cataclysmic months in the spring of 1951 depends upon who is asked.

Philby had two distinct jobs. With the CIA, he was "joint commander" of a covert operation to detach Albania from the Soviet orbit, and the operatives with whom he worked in the upper echelons of the Agency were enthralled with him. His second job was to coordinate with the FBI investigations, originating with the accumulated Soviet intercepts. The individual with whom he worked most closely, Robert Lamphere, an FBI supervisor assigned to counterintelligence work, thought that Philby was lazy and bordered on the unpresentable. Lamphere was not, however, very charitably disposed where the British were concerned.

Lamphere had become disenchanted with their truculent attitude even before Philby arrived. They were eager to devour all of the information that he and Meredith Gardner laboriously produced, but then it seemed to disappear into the void. The Americans never received anything in return. The Fuchs case had set the pattern. Britain gobbled up everything Lamphere had, but they became evasive and uncommunicative when asked what leads the information had helped them uncover.

The situation was exacerbated when British authorities decided that they had wearied of being spoonfed crumbs of information from the large pie of intercepts. They wanted their own pie. So, in what Lamphere saw as "a classic flanking maneuver," London invoked an agreement obligating the United States to "a full exchange of all cryptographic and other forms of technical surveillance." The United Kingdom's cryptographic service merely contacted the Army Security Agency directly and requested all copies of the decoded intercepts.[4]

Still, Britain failed to produce any helpful information. For more than a year, Peter Dwyer had promised Lamphere detailed biographical data on British diplomats assigned to Washington in 1944 and 1945. This was a minimum first step to enable the FBI to match the clues that they had developed with possible suspects. But Lamphere had received nothing.[5] He was in a skeptical mood, therefore, when Dwyer brought his replacement by for a courtesy call in mid-October. Lamphere's immediate thought when he first heard Dwyer was being pulled out—since he blamed him for British inaction and end-runs—was "perhaps I'd get along better with this new man." Based on the glowing reports that preceded Philby's arrival, this was not unrealistic, but that hope was quickly dashed.[6]

"I can't believe it when I first meet this guy," Lamphere later recalled. "I didn't like Dwyer, but I respected him. He was clever, witty, shrewd, engaging. Philby doesn't say hardly anything, and when he does he stutters." Lamphere, whom Philby later described as "a nice pudgy native of Ohio," was actually from the northern panhandle region of Idaho, son of a miner, a no-nonsense Westerner with gentle eyes, thick black hair combed straight back, and a dignified bearing.[7]

"I could hardly believe that this unimpressive man was being spoken of as a future chief of MI6, in line for a knighthood." He looked seedy and rumpled. His clothes were undistinguished and loose fitting. Philby signaled "his lack of friendliness" Lamphere thought by saying nothing when the other two spoke about the spy inside the British embassy. Perhaps, the American thought, "his sterling qualities were hidden, and he'd be warmer when I got to know him better."[8]

Lamphere did not have much room to maneuver. He had been ordered by Ladd, the number three man in the FBI behind Hoover and his companion and deputy Clyde Tolson, to maintain good relations with the British. It was not that the FBI's command structure was filled with Anglophiles, but merely a tactic in the life-and-death bureaucratic wars that consumed Hoover.

After failing to prevent the birth of the CIA, Hoover was determined to strangle it in the crib. This would be possible, he believed, if the FBI made its relationship with the SIS so rewarding that they would not jeopardize it by becoming too friendly with the embryonic CIA. Ladd implemented the plan with a zeal that might have exceeded even Hoover's own diabolical wishes.

Everything was done by the book in Hoover's shop. Each request from another U.S. government agency had to be submitted in writing and reviewed by Hoover before a written response was issued. With the British, however, there were no rules. Dwyer could graze the counterintelligence department, poking his nose wherever he pleased.

Lamphere was uncomfortable with the absence of any clear-cut rules in dealing with the British. They could get anything they wanted, while "we were getting nothing back from them. If the Department of State or Defense came around asking the questions that Dwyer did, they would have been thrown out," Lamphere insists. "But with Dwyer, if we didn't give answers, he would go to Ladd and I'd get a phone call."[9]

Philby made use of all of this. When he first moved to Washington, he and Ladd were neighbors on Nebraska Avenue just east of Connecticut Avenue. The two of them passed many nights in long drinking sessions. The short, paunchy, cigar-chomping Ladd was a veteran of the Chicago gang wars; when the shooting started, he was always the one who went in first. He never fitted into Hoover's rigid mold for agents. He loved whisky and women almost as much as he loved danger. "He was the sort of guy," said Lamphere, "who at a party would always grab your wife and have her sit on his lap."[10]

Ladd could get away with it because he was almost the only one in the FBI who could handle Hoover. When the Director erupted and fired an agent or vowed to exile him to the FBI office in Butte, Montana, it was Ladd who could later calm him down and get him to reverse himself. This commanded great loyalty among the agents who quaked at Hoover's footsteps.

In late October, Geoffrey Patterson, who had arrived in Washington the previous June as MI5's liaison to the FBI, provided Lamphere with a set of Fuchs's fingerprints, and the not terribly helpful acknowledgment that MI5 agreed that Fuchs was working for the Soviets.[11]

Whenever the opportunity came along, Lamphere would press Patterson again about what progress London had made on the embassy spy. Had the Foreign Office or MI5 not even compiled a possible list of suspects, or even a roster of who was in the embassy at the relevant time? "Gee, Bob, nothing new," Patterson would respond. "I'll have to go back to London and find out what the problem is." "Christ," Lamphere would respond, trying to hide his exasperation behind a jocular tone, "can't you guys just come up with some kind of list?!"[12]

Lamphere knew that "Philby's orders were to get close to the CIA, but to do it without antagonizing the FBI." Because Ladd often needled him about how he was getting on with the campaign to romance the British, Lamphere would also ask Patterson, "Hey, Geoff, where's Philby? He doesn't come around much." Lamphere just assumed, however, that Philby was not doing his job very well.

It was not that Philby wasn't interested, he knew perfectly well that Maclean was "Homer," the British embassy spy. And Maclean knew, because Philby had told him, that Kim was a spy. Any path that led to Maclean, therefore, could lead to Philby. He might not have gone to see Lamphere, but Philby was crossing the Potomac with some frequency to see Meredith Gardner. The tall, gangly, withdrawn American would later tell how "this pipe-smoking Englishman named Philby used to regularly visit him and peer over his shoulder and admire the progress he was making."[13]

Philby preferred the more informal companionship of the CIA. Many of its agents had met him when they were bumbling OSS recruits sent to London to learn at the knee of the revered British intelligence service. Not only were the British regarded as the old masters of the profession, Philby was considered one of their most promising, an up-and-comer.

James Jesus Angleton, then twenty-six, a Yale poet, Harvard Law School dropout, and later a CIA legend, had heard of Philby before he laid eyes on him. "He wrote the leaders, the number one story on the right side of the page, during the Spanish Civil War," Angleton still recalled with a trace of awe nearly forty-five years later. "This was great prestige for someone his age; The Times [London] was the gospel. He had great responsibilities at SIS, so he was looked up to, he was someone already with a reputation."[14]

Everything had conspired to bolster that reputation. Toward the end of the war Philby had instigated a major bureaucratic showdown, the leader, in American minds, of the Young Turks who had dared to take on the stodgy Old Guard and had won. Even the fact that his father was jailed as a Nazi sympathizer while his son served his country with such distinction that he was decorated by the king was seen as a measure of Philby's loyalty.

The CIA had no involvement, and little knowledge, of the Soviet intercepts. But SIS and the Office of Policy Coordination (OPC), a unit initially attached to the State Department but soon transferred to the CIA, were jointly running the highly secret Albanian operation to overthrow the anti-Western Communist regime of Enver Hoxha.

James McCarger, who worked with him closely on the Albanian operation, agreed that Philby "possessed a remarkable charm":

> He was witty. His smile, suggestive of complicity in a private joke, conveyed an unspoken understanding of the underlying ironies of our work. He was capable. Behind the modest, slightly rumpled exterior, there was no mistaking a quick mind and a tenacious will.

On several occasions, Philby arrived at McCarger's office with urgent reports on the Albanian operation that his American counterpart had yet to receive. The third time this occurred, Philby, "with an air of anxious helpfulness which had just the right degree of opacity asked, 'Well, look, in these circumstances, wouldn't you like us to handle your communications for you?' " Not even at its height did the Special Relationship permit such a merging of national interests. But "the offer of the poisoned apple was adroit," McCarger recalled admiringly. "In declining it, I laughed. The charm part was that so did he."[15]

The Albanian mission was the brainchild of some former Special Operations Executive (SOE) warriors who had served in the Balkans during the Second World War. Bevin wanted to participate, providing the Americans would collaborate and foot the bill. Anglo-American officials agreed in March that Stalin's long stream of failures, culminating with Yugoslavia's declaration of independence in July 1948, the formation of NATO in April 1949, and the Soviet dismantling of the Berlin blockade the following month, made the moment ripe "to liberate the countries within the Soviet orbit by any means short of war."[16]

Albania seemed the ideal target because Tito's defection meant that its borders were no longer contiguous to the Soviet empire. The Hoxha regime, or so Washington and London convinced themselves, was weak, unpopular, and isolated. It could be overthrown by Albanian exiles equipped and trained by the United States and Britain who would be smuggled back into the country. For Britain the operation had the advantage of portraying it as a bold and vigorous power capable of taking on the Soviets, even if only surreptitiously.

For the infant CIA—struggling to gain a chair at the table of the national security apparatus—it provided an opportunity to win kudos by beginning to roll back the Iron Curtain.

Philby betrayed the Albanian operation and it failed, but not because he betrayed it. The CIA's own research predicted the outcome before Philby had a chance to act. "A purely internal Albanian uprising at this time," the agency warned on September 12, "is not indicated and, if undertaken, would have little chance of success."[17]

The exiles had no political base of support, were unknown outside of their own remote villages, and had no means of communication to rally the population to action once they were inside the country. Philby had divulged the plan to the Soviets when he was still in London, and the first landing, conducted while he was sipping champagne aboard the *Caronia,* was wiped out. Although he was a "joint commander" of the operation, none of the opprobrium for its initial failures accrued to him. What is remarkable is not that the mission continued in the face of one disaster after another (or even the CIA's own prediction of doom) but that it continued even after suspicion had fallen on Philby and he had been recalled to London and expelled from British intelligence.

Until then CIA operatives were infatuated with him. Liquor was the holy water in this ritual of elite male bonding. For Philby, a two-fisted drinker well on his way to becoming an alcoholic, a better Trojan horse to penetrate the CIA citadel could not have been found. He would drop by Deputy Director Allen Dulles's office "knowing he would suggest drifting out to a friendly bar for a further round of shop talk." Sometimes he would go to Frank Wisner, Dulles's deputy and head of covert operations, to discuss political subversion abroad, knowing that the meeting would end with "Wisner or whoever producing Bourbon from his office bar, after which we would debate the wisdom of again abandoning our wives for a regular-guy evening on the town."[18]

Philby was a man's man, proper, but a regular guy. He was not stiff, aloof, and often arrogant like Maclean. "He had a stammer and a good stock of anecdotes—an excellent combination," attests Robert Low, a former OSS officer who the Agency brought aboard to work specifically on Albania. And, McCarger adds, "he had charm, warmth and an engaging, self-deprecating humor. He drank a lot, but then so did we all in those days."[19] That is, everyone in the CIA crowd drank. Philby made a faux pas before he even stepped on American soil by offering a stiff drink to the FBI agent who came aboard the *Caronia* to greet him. Hoover's G-men did not drink on the job, nor, so far as the Director was concerned, off it. But, says Philby somewhat snidely, the "CIA men flaunted cosmopolitan postures. They would discuss absinthe and serve Burgundy above room temperature."[20]

Actually, any discussion about wives would have been ill-advised for Philby. Nothing more reflected the interior mess of his life than his domestic arrangements. As we have seen, in September 1940, Philby lied to his employers in British intelligence by telling them that he had married Aileen Furse when he was actually still married to Litzi. They were not divorced until September 17, 1946. Nine days later he quietly and legally married Aileen. By then they had lived together for six years and were the parents of three children.

Fearing that he would be washed up if his SIS superiors ever stumbled across this shabby story, Philby came clean after he and Aileen were married. What happened next proves Sissela Bok's thesis that "the person who unveils a secret gains a measure of control over how others see it."[21]

The SIS discovered almost by accident in 1947 that Philby's real first wife had been living in Paris and Berlin with a suspected Soviet agent. But rather than considering the possibility that they had just scratched the veneer of a duplicitous man, the SIS threw its protective cloak around Philby and bundled him off to Turkey. A couple of years there as SIS station chief, they hoped, would prevent unknowing, not to say ignorant, outsiders unfamiliar with the Great Game's requirements from asking naive questions about why Philby had lied about his past.[22]

★ ★ ★

By 1950, Lamphere was making important breakthroughs. He established that the Soviets had codenamed their spy inside the British embassy "Homer." Further, Fuchs had finally confessed in late January, and on February 2, 1950, he was formally arrested.

Although the FBI modestly pointed out that "the case involving Dr. Fuchs was developed by the British on information originally furnished them by the FBI," London steadfastly insisted that they broke the case without any FBI assistance. This reflected not only the resentment and distrust of Hoover by British intelligence, but their paranoia in letting the Americans get near any case revealing British security lapses. Their sensitivity was understandable; after all, MI5 cleared Fuchs eight times. Only after the most protracted and unpleasant wrangling did British authorities finally relent and allow Lamphere—the one who had developed the breakthrough information on Fuchs—to interview him in Wormwood Scrubs prison.[23]

Lamphere arrived in London on May 19, exactly one week after Maclean had returned in disgrace from Cairo. But the lack of any information from the British ensured that even had Lamphere brushed up against Maclean in a bar or passed him in the street, he would not have recognized him as "Homer." For now, he had to concentrate solely on Fuchs.

Wormwood Scrubs prison, located in a suburb twenty minutes west of London, was not at all like the homes of Donald's rich friends. It was everything Maclean feared that prison would be— cold, dreary, bare. Even the interrogation room was unheated. It certainly was not agreeing with Fuchs. After two months he was thinner, paler, and more stoop-shouldered than he had been when he and Maclean had spent three days together in Washington less than two years before. His teeth were stained from smoking. The delicate features of his angular face were colorless, his thin straight hair had receded further from his high forehead. Fuchs was exceedingly polite, totally unanimated, and completely uncooperative. He hedged on every answer. But through patience and finesse, Lamphere finally got what he came for.

"My heart leapt," he later wrote, when Fuchs identified a picture of Harry Gold, a short, plump thirty-nine-year-old Philadelphia biochemist as "Raymond," his American go-between with Soviet intelligence. "Yes," he admitted after several sessions in which more pictures and film footage were provided, "that is my American contact."

Eventually the London press discovered that Hoover's G-men were in town, and, on May 24, the day before Maclean's thirty-seventh birthday, newspapers ran screaming headlines such as "Leads Given by Fuchs," and "More Data From Fuchs." On June 2, the day the FBI men returned to America, the newspapers blared the sensational headline: "ONE HUNDRED RED SPIES NAMED BY FUCHS". "Rumors flew that Fuchs had implicated entire networks of Soviet agents in Britain, America, and Canada . . . Gold was only the beginning."[24]

Actually, at the same time that Lamphere was with Fuchs in London, FBI colleagues were already questioning Gold in Philadelphia. Finally, they tripped him. "Raymond" had met at least once with Fuchs in New Mexico. Yet, Gold insisted that he had never been west of the Mississippi. But when FBI investigators searched his home, they found a map of Santa Fe in a book. "I thought you said you had never been out West," one of the agents noted. "Gold opened his mouth wide, then slumped down into [a] chair," and admitted, "I am the man to whom Fuchs gave the information."[25]

It was Gold, not Fuchs, who, as Philby later put it, formed the "chain [that] led inexorably to the Rosenbergs." He fingered David Greenglass, whose confession implicated his sister Ethel Rosenberg and her husband Julius. But the FBI issued wildly inflated reports that it was Fuchs who had unlocked the door leading to the Soviet underground. The intention was to throw fear into the likes of Michael Straight, Guy Burgess, Donald Maclean, and all the others who now would lie awake nights waiting for the knock on the door.[26]

The FBI's psychological shot in the dark hit Maclean with deadly accuracy. When he first arrived back in London, Donald wrote Melinda several thoughtful, witty, and determined letters. Arrangements had been made for him to see a psychiatrist—someone, as Donald put it, who acts as a consultant "when their employees' psyches miss a beat. I still have my lid off and I am prepared therefore to ask help":

> I am leery of making promises of being a better husband, since past ones have all been broken; but perhaps if some technician will strengthen my gasket and enlarge my heart I could make a promise which would stick . . . Don't feel sad about me as I will come back a better person and we can be happy together again I am sure.[27]

But when Dr. Wilson of the Foreign Office suggested something more than the tightening of a few screws might be required—

namely, being committed to a "clinic"—Maclean backed away. He could not allow anyone to probe too deeply. Instead, he went to Dr. Erna Rosenbaum, a Russian-born psychiatrist of his own choosing, whose "treatment was spread thinly over the six months sick leave" granted by the Foreign Office. It is a bit mysterious how, after being out of the country for six years and never having consulted with a psychiatrist before, he knew immediately where to find one. Stranger still is the fact that the Foreign Office allowed him to go to someone else and even paid for her.[28]

The letters to Melinda, and the determination to be healed, stopped in late May as the stories and rumors about Fuchs began sweeping London. It was about this time that his close friend Cyril Connolly ran into Maclean. Donald's "appearance was frightening": he had not shaved in days and had lost his aura of serenity. With the yellowish hue of his skin, sunken eyes, and hollow cheeks he "looked as if he spent the night sitting up in a tunnel." In conversation he would stop in midsentence and grimace, and then stutter and falter "as if," thought Connolly, "he had returned to some basic and incommunicable anxiety."

Geoffrey Hoare, who never saw Maclean again once they deplaned in London from Cairo, soon heard similar reports and concluded that "Donald's physical and mental condition had deteriorated since his arrival in London."[29]

Maclean realized the day was nearing when he would be faced with a Hobson's choice of either submitting to jail and ruin in England, or fleeing into the arms of Stalin's Russia. He had to wonder how he would react when they came for him. What if someone, a colleague, someone he trusted not even connected with MI5, asked him one day if he had ever been to a certain restaurant in Queens, or to Prospect Park in Brooklyn? How could he know whether it was an innocent question, or if someone had seen him with a mysterious looking man who might have been his Soviet control?

Five years before while a Second Secretary at the Washington embassy, Cecil, who had worked closely with the SIS, had approached Maclean and said that he wanted to talk to him about New York. Maclean's tension was palpable. He thought Cecil was about to interrogate him about his frequent New York trips. Perhaps they knew about his activities. Perhaps he was being tailed on his trips to New York. As it turned out, Cecil had only wanted to attend some lectures there. But even in those more rational times he could not be sure, and who could be trusted now?[30]

The answer is that he trusted no one. Never mind about MI5 or the FBI; Maclean was convinced that the Soviets were after him. This was not farfetched. He had been one of their best, and now he was fallow. Certainly he could not have counted on Stalin for sympathy. A prewar friend, Lady Mary St. Clair Erskine, spent an afternoon with him in a friend's garden. "He was seized by an attack of delirium tremens and would not lie still." He kept jumping to his feet and shouting "they're after me." "Who?" Lady Mary implored. "The Russians," he hissed.[31]

With Melinda gone there was no one to stop his drinking, and with no job, there was no reason to sober up. Not only was Maclean "drinking himself silly," as Cecil heard it, but he had imagined himself having achieved some level of catharsis with his insistence that he was a homosexual. He dragged this revelation around London like a dog with a bone to lay at the feet of all his friends. At one point, he announced that he had fallen in love with the black doorman at a London night club.[32]

"She is still baffled a bit," Melinda wrote to her sister Harriet about Donald's psychiatrist, "at the homosexual side which comes out when he is drunk and I think [his] slight hostility in general to women." Melinda had been overwhelmed with the mess Donald had left behind in Cairo. The domestics practically mutinied as they saw the Maclean family disintegrate. Melinda could not manage the house, preside over the staff, tend to the needs of her confused and frightened sons, or plan for her own life. She had to move out of their British-owned house. But where would she go? To return to England to be with Donald hardly seemed promising, and she had a more basic problem. Donald again had left her without money and sent none.[33]

Once more Melinda's mother, Mrs. Dunbar, came to the rescue. She had set sail on an Export Line ship from New York just before the days of destruction in Cairo had occurred; when she arrived at Alexandria on June 1, she was unaware of the calamity that had befallen Melinda's family. She immediately took over the household, paid the bills, disciplined the staff, and made arrangements for Melinda and the children to spend the summer on Spain's Costa Brava.[34]

As Melinda surely must have known, that was also where Prince Daoud was spending the summer. She may not have found it much of a respite. According to the story Dean Acheson received in Washington, "The Prince was reported to be violently anti-British and a heavy drinker." His American-born wife was also with him for most of the summer.[35]

Back in London, the person closest to Donald was his younger brother, Alan. He was twenty-five, thinner and slightly shorter than Donald, with a more athletic appearance, and every bit as handsome as his older brother. Despite an eleven-year age difference, they were extremely close; Alan thought of Donald as his best friend. He agonized over his brother's state. Donald's hands trembled as he reached for his first drink of the morning. His puffy and bleary eyes stared vacantly for long silent stretches. He seemed hideously tortured. Gone was the self-confidence, the near superhuman ability to recover from the most punishing night to resume his snap-brim efficiency the next day.

Alan adulated his brother to the point of wanting to become a diplomat too. Donald naturally could not tell him that had the decision been his, he would never have joined. Alan faltered a bit at the outset when he failed the competitive exam, but he managed to get a "temporary appointment" in the Foreign Office's News Department. Soon events would also take Alan away from Donald too, events which would eventually propel Donald to give his final and decidedly most deadly service to Joseph Stalin.[36]

CHAPTER SIXTEEN

What would Mao Tse-tung do?
What might the Russians do in the Balkans,
in Iran, in Germany?

President Harry Truman to his top advisers
after the invasion of South Korea[1]

WAR

It had been an exhausting week for Dean Acheson. First, there had been the Governor's Conference, and on Thursday the Harvard commencement speech. Friday morning began with a Cabinet meeting, followed by a press conference, and then a draining appearance before Congress. Even the weekend escape to his beloved Harewood Farm in rural Montgomery County was not relaxing.

Ugly passions had been unleashed by Senator Joseph McCarthy's communist witch hunt, and, among his cohorts, Acheson was a favorite target. Each day bags of hate mail arrived accusing the Secretary of State of being a communist dupe who had lost China and made the State Department a sanctuary for Soviet spies like the Hiss brothers. Now, Acheson and his wife had to live with four armed bodyguards who had difficulty being unobtrusive around the small farmhouse.

Still, on Saturday night, June 24, he had a satisfying meal, turned in early, and read himself to sleep.

While his boss was sleeping, Jack Hickerson, now the assistant secretary of state for United Nations Affairs, was relaxing with a book at his Cleveland Park home. Just before 9:00 P.M., the phone rang. Hickerson tensed. Even in Washington night calls were un-usual; this could only mean trouble. As he hurried to the phone, he grabbed his car keys. Because his home phone was not "secure," the duty officer could only tell him he must come to the State Depart-ment at once.

As he raced toward Foggy Bottom, Hickerson tried to guess which "hot spot" had ignited. For over a month, intelligence had been suggesting that military action by a communist power was imminent. Policymakers had convinced themselves that it would not be the Soviets because they were not expected to do anything until they had increased their atomic stockpile. Was East Germany creat-ing havoc in Berlin? Had conflict erupted again in Greece or Italy? Had the Arabs made another assault on Israel? He did not think so. It must be Formosa! Everyone knew that it would be simply a matter of time before the People's Republic of China made a move on this redoubt of Chiang Kai-shek and his Nationalist Chinese. As he parked his car in the Department's underground garage, Hickerson was convinced that the Communist Chinese must have invaded Formosa.

Although his guess had been close, as he rushed into the situation room, he was still unprepared for the shock of being told that the Soviet-installed North Korean dictatorship of Kim Il Sung had launched a sudden, unprovoked, and massive invasion of South Korea. How could this be? The CIA, the State Department, and G-2 (Army Intelligence) all had conceded that one day such an invasion might happen, but not in the summer of 1950. The Pentagon had assured analysts that the Republic of Korea's army was "the best damn shootin' army" outside of America; the problem was to keep it from picking a fight with the outclassed North Korean army. At 10:00 P.M. Hickerson called Dean Acheson through the White House switchboard to tell him that "the best damn shootin' army" in the world was "getting its ass chased" down the narrow Korean penin-sula.[2]

The news must have come like a thunderbolt to "the Dean." Even in his groggy state he surely could start to hear the shrill voices of his legion of critics casting the blame for this disaster on him. Just six months earlier, in a speech to the National Press Club, he had publicly declared that Korea was outside America's holdline, which he defined as running from the Aleutians to Japan through Okinawa and the Philippine archipelago, skirting but never touching the Asian mainland. As for the countries on the wrong side of that line, such as Korea and Formosa, he stated, perhaps more callously than he had intended, "No person can guarantee those areas against military attack." The fact that he had been too busy to travel to Asia the previous year, when he managed to make eleven trips to Europe, served as an exclamation point to the assumption that the Secretary of State had written-off mainland Asia.[3]

After he hung up from Hickerson, Acheson was connected by the White House to Truman at his home in Independence, Missouri. "Mr. President," he intoned. "I have very serious news. The North Koreans have invaded South Korea."[4]

The Foreign Office's Gladwyn Jebb was also spending the week-end at his country home outside London. He was working in the garden, trying to prune everything before he had to leave later in the summer for New York, to become Britain's permanent representative to the U.N. Security Council. Then, his phone rang too, and he was summoned to come at once to London. By the time he had arrived at the Foreign Office the news was grim. The North Korean army, trained and equipped by the Soviets, was one of the finest fighting forces in the world. The Republic of South Korea's army was little more than a constabulary force, completely overwhelmed by the first waves of North Korean invaders. Told that he must leave for the United Nations at once, Jebb ordered his private secretary, Alan Maclean, to prepare for an immediate departure. The next day, Monday, Alan was issued a diplomatic visa by the U.S. embassy. On Wednesday, he and Jebb were on a flight bound for New York.[5]

By then the Security Council, absent the boycotting Soviets, who were protesting the presence of Nationalist China, approved a U.S. resolution to repel the North Korean attack. It was the first time in history that the United Nations had voted to take collective action on behalf of a victim. At the time it seemed that the Soviets had committed an incalculable blunder—unless possibly Stalin had taken to heart General Douglas MacArthur's admonition: "Anyone who commits the American army on the mainland of Asia ought to have his head examined."[6]

Certainly MacArthur seemed to have forgotten it; moreover, he neglected to remind people that, even before Acheson, he had publicly declared that Korea was outside America's defensive perimeter. Characteristic of the General's admirers and the Secretary's critics—the two overlapped extensively—they only remembered Acheson's having said it. MacArthur had also been one of the first to push for the withdrawal of the U.S. occupation army in South Korea, a task completed in June 1949.

MacArthur had spent his entire life in the military after graduating from West Point with the highest scholastic average in twenty five years. He had served with Teddy Roosevelt, was decorated for extraordinary heroism in the First World War, and afterward was Superintendent of West Point. Although he hated Franklin D. Roosevelt (a sentiment he would transfer effortlessly to Truman), he was brought out of retirement and made commander of the U.S. forces in the Far East during the Second World War.

At seventy-one, credited with achieving miracles as the Supreme Allied Commander of Japan during the American occupation of Japan after the war, he was still viciously ambitious. He enjoyed, if he did not actually require, being treated as a demigod by foreign people. Once when Army Chief of Staff General George Marshall was in the Pacific for a conference, MacArthur began a sentence by saying, "My staff believes . . ." Marshall cut him off, stared him in the eye, and said: "General, you don't have a staff, you have a court." MacArthur was named Supreme United Nations Commander on July 7. He already had five stars, so the only additional honors were titles, of which he had no end including that of Supreme Commander of the Allies in the Pacific, Commander in Chief of the Far East, and, to some, "Alexander of the Orient." Controversy was as much a part of his career as were all of his titles and his cluster of medals and honors. During the next six weeks he would seem to justify every adjective that was ever applied to him, from genius to incompetent.[7]

The immediate concern for Truman, Acheson, and the Joint Chiefs of Staff was whether the outbreak of war in Korea was merely a Soviet-inspired feint—a diversion from the long-planned Red Army invasion of Europe and the prelude to the Third World War. A steady stream of intelligence reports provided fearful reminders of the frenetic but well-coordinated German activities in August 1939.

Russian blacked-out troop trains were moving throughout Eastern Europe; Soviet consular personnel billeted in Tokyo were seen preparing to leave the country en masse; a huge fire behind the Soviet embassy in Havana was assumed to be caused by burning files; and the Soviet ambassadors in the United States, France, Poland, Czechoslovakia, Japan, Turkey, India, and Syria-Lebanon had all been recalled to Moscow.[8]

"What," Truman asked his top political and military advisers, "would Mao Tse-tung do? What might the Russians do in the Balkans, in Iran, in Germany?" Had Stalin ordered the North Koreans into action believing that the West would never intervene? Or had he authorized Kim Il Sung (who had spent the war years in Moscow and returned to North Korea in 1945 as a major in the Red Army occupation) to grab South Korea so as to create a threat to the People's Republic of China, whose success Stalin had neither anticipated nor welcomed? Or were the Chinese in on the whole thing from the start? Without a spy like Maclean as a direct pipeline into the war councils of the Kremlin, no one knew.[9]

Stalin once told Eden, "You are wondering whether I shall know where to stop. But I am not Hitler—I know where to stop." There was some truth to this. As one biographer pointed out:

> Stalin had repeatedly halted at the very brink of armed conflict with his ex-allies. He had stopped at the Turkish Straits; he had stopped at Persia . . . he had stopped before turning the blockade of Berlin into ultimate disaster. It was not so clear how far he was prepared to go in the conflict engendered by the Korean War. 'Does he still know where to stop?' the men around him now wondered.[10]

For the next eighteen months, the Truman administration would be unable to shake off its consuming anxiety about the intentions of Peking and Moscow. It was dragged through every discussion like a ball and chain that hobbled each military and political consideration. There is no evidence to suggest that either Moscow or Peking suffered from any such concerns. And why should they? It was the other side that was trying to play poker with a mirror strapped to the back of its head.

Many years later, at Maclean's funeral in Moscow, three men

trailed his coffin carrying his Soviet medals atop red velvet cushions. None of the medals bore citations for specific missions, but if they had, they certainly would have singled out his service during the Korean War. It was his finest moment in his service to Stalin, although in June 1950, his capacity to sober up sufficiently to undertake one last mission must have seemed a dim possibility to Moscow.

The North Korean army overran the South Korean army all along the 38th Parallel, the demarcation line between the two Koreas, and, in four days, Seoul fell to a six-prong tank attack. Then, as the first U.S. forces were arriving in Korea, an uneasy calm prevailed at the United Nations. Alan Maclean took advantage of the lull to return to London in July to arrange for the shipment of his belongings. He spent what time he could with Donald, who must have been oddly envious to see his younger brother suddenly thrust into the thick of a world crisis as he himself had been in Paris in September 1938. When it was time for Alan to return to New York, this time sailing on the *Mauritania,* the two said their farewells. The next time Alan saw his brother was thirty years later, when Donald lay dying in Moscow.

Donald Maclean was not the only problem for George Middleton, the head of Foreign Office personnel in the summer of 1950. There was also the hopeless case of Guy Burgess. The Foreign Office solution was unique. They sent one of their worst men to one of their most important posts.

"I have a shock for you," Burgess wrote to Philby in July. "I have just been posted to Washington."[11]

CHAPTER SEVENTEEN

> When Guy found he couldn't be at the top, I
> think he decided to be at the bottom.
>
> Alan Maclean[1]

BURGESS: THE PATHOS OF TREACHERY

Guy Burgess fired people's imaginations. The descriptions of him are so poetic and artistically creative that they survive like works of art. But which to choose? Try that of a friend, Cyril Connolly, appropriately described as "the laureate of the disappointed." He wrote of Burgess that he had

> an inquisitive nose, sensual mouth, curly hair, and an alert, fox-terrier expression. He was immensely energetic, a great talker, reader, boaster, walker, who swam like an otter and drank . . . like some Rabelaisian bottle swiper whose thirst was unquenchable.[2]

Or, take that of an antagonist, Malcolm Muggeridge, one of England's most dominant literary personalities, who later wrote after meeting Burgess for the first time:

> He gave me a feeling, such as I have never had from anyone else, of being morally afflicted in some way. His very physical presence was, to me, malodorous and sinister . . . Etonian mudlark and sick toast of a sick society . . . a true hero of our time . . . hip before hipsters, Rolling before the Stones, acid-head before LSD. There was not so much a conspiracy gathered around him as just decay and dissolution. It was the end of a class, of a way of life; something that would be

263

written about in history books, like Gibbon on Heliogabalus, with wonder and perhaps hilarity, but still tinged with sadness, as all endings are.[3]

Or, consider Michael Straight, both admirer and adversary, who said of his fellow Cambridge Apostle:

> He derived an almost sensual pleasure out of any discussion of ideas. He craved the companionship and the physical love of other men . . . With his curly hair, his sensual mouth, his bright blue eyes, his cherubic air, he seemed at first sight to embody in himself the ideal of male beauty . . . Then, on a closer look, you noticed the details: the black-rimmed fingernails; the stained forefinger in which he gripped his perpetual cigarette stub; the dark, uneven teeth; the slouch; the open fly.[4]

Perhaps the most telling comment of all comes from his brother, Nigel, who in 1984 told the actor Alan Bates, "Guy was an extraordinary mixture of loathsomeness and charm."[5]

He also inspired debate. Writers cannot agree on whether he was the first of the Cambridge spies, or the last; the most dangerous or the least important. But whatever else may be debated, he was certainly the most complex of them all, and, in his own curious way, the most sympathetic and tragic.

The word "brilliant" is as inescapably fixed to Burgess's name as "charm" is to Philby's, and "efficient" to Maclean's. "Burgess when I first met him as an undergraduate was rather the most remarkable, one of the most brilliant, and let me make this distinction, one of the most intelligent people I have ever met," Anthony Blunt, his fellow spy, Cambridge contemporary, and former lover told *The Times* (London). If Blunt's veneration is suspect, then it can be pointed out that such luminaries as Felix Frankfurter, Isaiah Berlin, John Maynard Keynes, Anthony Eden, and even the great Churchill found Burgess's precocity—his brilliance—of an exceptional nature.[6]

At Cambridge he shared the Left's infatuation with communism, but he was never a very convincing prole. He was too much of a snob to spend time with workers, except for the "rough trade" he picked up at low-class bars. "As for his heroes," one friend put it,

Burgess "admired Churchill far more than Marx." He rarely invoked Lenin. Burgess "had no trace of idealism," according to Cecil, "[he] seemed quite at home at one of Hitler's Nuremberg rallies . . . he had no feeling of being an outcast, because he lacked all sense of shame."[7]

He was better known for "his seemingly inexhaustible supply of acid metaphors and devastating epigrams [which] could effortlessly reduce his critics to ashes." This "extraordinary self-confidence," the historian Hugh Trevor-Roper adds, enabled Burgess to "command his little Cambridge world." And it may have not been so small; Burgess, it is said, was the most well-known undergraduate of his day.[8]

By the time he arrived in Washington at the age of thirty-nine, however, the most charitable thing that could be said about Guy Burgess was that at least he had been spared the desolation of success. The promise had gone unfulfilled. His friend Connolly—who had to endure throughout his lifetime the curse of being called his generation's most gifted undergraduate—observed, "Whom the gods would destroy they first call promising."[9]

Rejection came quickly. He had hoped to become a Cambridge don like his friend Blunt. The quality of his work did not induce the needed offer, however, and in 1934 he was finally forced to abandon Cambridge for London. Not unlike the college football star who could never adjust to life without the adoring Saturday afternoon crowds, Guy had peaked at twenty-three.

Bereft of the discipline essential for professional success, he tried to get by solely on native ability. Though his wit, intelligence, and erudition surpassed that of those he tried to impress, it was not enough. Soon the once great promise was being squandered on the relentless pursuit of debauchery. Just as the great athlete, even after years of abusing his talent, can suddenly perform in a way that leaves people gasping in wonderment over what great abilities he must have once had, Guy's captivating charm and fascinating conversation could still open almost any door. As soon as he would be allowed in, however, his self-destructive impulse would reassert itself and get him thrown out again.

He wanted so much to be accepted, but he could never fit in, either socially or professionally. "He was trying very desperately to be one of the group," according to Christopher Isherwood, British-born writer of books, plays, and films and later a denizen of Hollywood. Isherwood, who with Auden and Spender became the most well-known of Britain's 1930s generation, felt pity for Guy. "He was a confirmed social climber and pretty obvious in his tactics," Isherwood later told the FBI from his Pacific Palisades office.[10]

Burgess floundered in an odd assortment of jobs during the prewar years, first as a financial consultant to the Rothschilds, and later as a BBC talk show host. By then he too was working for Soviet intelligence, and it was presumably on its behalf that he joined the Anglo-German Fellowship. It is maintained that he, like Philby, did this to fulfill some terribly clever Moscow scheme to hide his communist associations. If this is accepted as a plausible explanation for Philby, then certainly Burgess could get away with it, for although his communist footprints were shallow, they were deeper than those of his coconspirators.

If the Soviets were going to bother trying to smooth his rough edges, they should have done something about his ceaseless depravity, not his political views, which were the least of Burgess's problems. Of course, some have maintained that his persona, from reeling drunk and pouncing homosexual to pioneering drug user, was the perfect cover to penetrate Britain's decadent ruling class. Others ask the obvious—why would the Soviets ever rely on someone so erratic, unpredictable, and outrageous?

Except for his elitism and fondness for the exclusivity of secret societies, Burgess was wholly unsuited to secret work for either side. One must credit him, however, with what was doubtless his greatest undercover coup. When he finally managed to penetrate British intelligence in 1940 by joining Section D, he lasted long enough to pull Philby in after him.

He was also able to provide the Soviets with some valuable information—much of it supplementing what Maclean was providing from Washington—during eighteen months from January 1947 to mid-1948 when he was private secretary to Minister of State for Foreign Affairs Hector McNeil. McNeil, a Scot who had been a socialist since his student days, came to the Foreign Office as an outsider—the number two man in one of Britain's most powerful institutions. Cheerful, vigorous, and gregarious, he was captivated by Burgess's electric mind and considered him to be someone who would run counter to the prevailing bureaucratic views.

A rather provincial bachelor, McNeil was seduced by Burgess's facile urbanity and the place he seemed to occupy in London's literary and social set. In describing Burgess, Denis Greenhill (later Lord), a Foreign Office colleague, may have hit on this allure to McNeil:

> [Burgess] was at his most congenial slumped on someone else's sofa drinking someone else's whisky telling tales to discredit the famous. The more luxurious the surroundings and the more distinguished the company, the happier he was. I have never heard a name-dropper in the same class.[11]

McNeil took Burgess to Paris in the summer of 1948 for a meeting of the United Nations General Assembly where Susan Mary Patten, the wife of an American diplomat, saw them together. "They [McNeil and Burgess] are very different types. I should guess that Hector McNeil is an innocent man in the ways of the world; he seemed like a child at a birthday party at one of the Duff Coopers' lunches last Sunday at Chantilly—it was fun to see someone so enthusiastic."[12]

Actually, McNeil had several things in common with Burgess. He too was a heavy drinker and chain-smoker who was eager to explore London's seedier side, Burgess's natural habitat. And, if he was not possessed of it earlier, the Minister of State acquired Burgess's glee in using state secrets to monopolize dinner conversation.

"Hector McNeil," C. L. Sulzberger, *The New York Times* foreign correspondent, wrote in his journal during the same Paris visit, "dined at the house last night. He was indiscreet enough to indicate that one of his jobs is to serve as liaison between the cabinet and British Intelligence." He also "sneered at British and American intelligence services and diplomats for not knowing about Tito's fight" with Stalin. McNeil also assured Sulzberger—ironic in view of Philby's later career—that British intelligence "only hires [journalists] in the Middle East."[13]

Because of Ernest Bevin's frequent illnesses and travels abroad, McNeil often served as acting Foreign Secretary. He and his assistants later insisted that Burgess had no access to military secrets. There are, however, endless contradictions to this assertion, most notably Burgess's role as the chief notetaker for the McNeil-led British delegation for important meetings in Brussels in 1947 that led to the Brussels Pact.[14]

There came a point, however, even at the height of his Foreign Office influence, when McNeil could no longer protect Burgess. He was drinking whisky throughout the day from a flask kept in his desk, ate cloves of raw garlic as if they were slices of an apple, was perpetually dishevelled, freely passed around pictures of his various youthful conquests, and boasted of urinating on a statue in front of Buckingham Palace.[15]

For some inexplicable reason, none of this behavior was sufficient grounds for dismissal. Instead, he was shuffled off to several other jobs, ending up at the Far Eastern Department. Between November 1949 and June 1950—from shortly after the ascension of the Chinese communists to the outbreak of the Korean War—he managed to gain access to some of the most sensitive information that passed through the Department. He also continued to degrade himself.[16]

"Oh my dear, what a sad, sad thing this constant drinking is!" Burgess's long-time patron Sir Harold Nicolson wrote in his diary in January 1950. "Guy used to have one of the most rapid and acute minds I knew. Now he is an imitation (and a pretty bad one) of what he once was . . . I felt angry about it."[17]

What happened next makes no sense from anyone's perspective. The Foreign Office could not bring itself to fire Burgess, so it decided to send him to a "last chance" posting. Not to Kamchatka, Kathmandu, or Monrovia, or any of dozens of other places that would have forced Burgess to resign rather than accept—which is supposedly what his superiors prayed for daily. Instead, they sent this admittedly disgraceful individual to Washington, which was their most important and sensitive outpost.

"By any standards," the British writers Penrose and Freeman have observed, "the decision was incomprehensible. Burgess was proud of his anti-Americanism." This at a time Whitehall was still trying to recover its reputation after having sent over such dubious characters as Alan Nunn May and Klaus Fuchs.

Burgess was not excited about the prospect, either. In fact, he nearly refused to go. According to his brother Nigel, Guy had "a pathological hatred and fear of America," and detested the idea of leaving London and the support systems that he had established for his profligate life. He knew the restaurants, brothels, Turkish baths, pimps, prostitutes, bars, and bedrooms which catered to every possible taste and desire. He had never lived abroad before. What would he do in a land of rigid puritans and self-satisfied Philistines?[18]

There must have been something about Burgess that caused otherwise sane people to take leave of their senses. Simply because the British were willing to needlessly discredit themselves, there was no reason for Moscow to follow suit. Why did they not prevent Burgess from going?

Surely an elite institution that could order one of their vassals to join a cryptofascist organization should have had the wit to order him to stay clear of Kim Philby. Of what possible use could it have been to send a notoriously unreliable and indiscreet agent to the same city as one of their best? Not only did the Soviets allow Burgess to go to the place where Philby was operating, however, but, as if to insure disaster, they also let the two of them live together. Surely, if Burgess needed a job, the Soviets could have either fixed him up with one in London or simply subsidized him. What would a few thousand pounds a year matter in order to protect their most valuable penetration?

Perhaps Soviet intelligence, like other parts of Stalin's creaking state machinery, was becoming a decrepit and incompetent service, which, as Knightly would write about the SIS, must have been "run by a chain of command remarkable for its feebleness." They were allowing the Foreign Office to unwittingly threaten their most important operation. One can only conclude that Soviet intelligence deserved Burgess, and he devastated it.[19]

Refusing to save either the Foreign Office or Soviet intelligence from a compulsion for folly, Burgess set off for Washington, predicting to friends that he would take the city by storm and would soon be instructing Dean Acheson on the subtleties of a successful foreign policy.[20]

* * *

He too was delivered to America's distant shores by the *Caronia*. If ever there was a case of the wrong man in the wrong country at the wrong time, it was Burgess in America in the summer of 1950. The thick fallout from the Soviet atom bomb, the triumph of the Chinese Communists, the conviction of Alger Hiss, and the confession of Klaus Fuchs enveloped the country in a cloud of paranoia, fear, and distrust.

In early February, one week after Fuchs confessed to passing America's atomic secrets to the Soviets, Wisconsin Senator Joseph McCarthy told a Women's Republican Club in Wheeling, West Virginia, that America was losing the Cold War because Dean Acheson's State Department had two hundred communists guiding foreign policy.

McCarthy was a thoroughly despicable man. Pathologically ambitious, even his high school graduation picture looked like the portrait of a heavy. A drunk and a bully, he injected a particularly virulent form of poison into America's political veins. Many good people, but not enough, fought him; none more tenaciously than columnist Drew Pearson. McCarthy used to tell friends and Pearson to his face, that he could not decide whether to kill or just maim him. One night after a dinner at the Sulgrave Club, they arrived together at the cloakroom. McCarthy made an insulting remark that Pearson ignored as he reached in his pocket for his coat check. Suddenly, McCarthy, over six feet tall and nearly two hundred and fifty pounds, spun around, grabbed the pencil-thin Pearson, kneed him twice in the groin and then hit him with his open palm, knocking him to the floor. He would have turned him into a punching bag had not Richard Nixon intervened and pulled McCarthy off. "I won't turn my back on that son-of-a-bitch!" McCarthy yelled, insisting that Pearson leave the building first. When Nixon escorted McCarthy out, it took over a half an hour to find his car. He was too drunk either to remember where he had parked it or to recognize it.[21]

At the time of his Wheeling speech, the Republican Senator was forty-one, overweight, and an alcoholic whose midday stubble gave his dark features the proper shade for his sinister activities. Within six years, he would drink himself to death. Meanwhile, he gave his name to an era and ruined the lives of thousands of innocent people before finally being censured by the Senate.

Burgess had supposedly been warned about America's stultifying climate. An undoubtedly apocryphal story has it that he was admonished by McNeil to avoid discussions with Americans about communism, homosexuality, and race relations. Burgess's reply was, "What you're trying to say in your nice, long-winded way is: 'Guy, for God's sake, don't make a pass at Paul Robeson.' "[22]

After arriving in New York on Friday, August 4, Burgess headed to Washington. His new home was the large rambling brick house at 4100 Nebraska Avenue between Wisconsin and Massachusetts avenues, in the fashionable residential district near American University. The house, surrounded by tall elms (Philby complained that it was too dark and gloomy), was no more than a ten-minute drive from the embassy.

The addition of Burgess brought the Philby household to eight. From the outside, the house seemed large enough, an appearance that was deceiving. The rooms on the ground floor were enormous, but the bedrooms were all on the smaller second floor. At the top of the landing to the left was the master bedroom (including a bathroom) that Kim and Aileen shared with baby Harry. Adjacent to their room was the only communal bathroom. On the right side of the landing were three medium-sized bedrooms, two of which were shared by the three children. The Scottish nanny occupied the third.

Burgess lived in a makeshift basement apartment. The attic had been converted into a bedroom for Esther Whitfield, Philby's spinster secretary who had been with him in Istanbul. The retractable staircase that led to her quarters came down in the middle of the landing. This must have made for a hectic if not hazardous scene in the early morning, with the three children, Burgess, and the nanny all racing for the one bathroom, undeterred by the potential threat of Esther and her ladder suddenly crashing down on top of them.

None of this made Aileen happy. High-strung and tense at the best of times, she nearly had a nervous breakdown when Burgess came to Istanbul in 1948 for an extended visit. "Who do you think has arrived?" she wrote despairingly to friends in Turkey, "Guy Burgess. I know him only too well. He will never leave our house."[23] Unfortunately for her, she was the odd one out. As the CIA's James Angleton later attested, Philby took Burgess everywhere, and "constantly went out of his way to make his stay in Washington an enjoyable one," both at home and at work. The bond between them was not homosexual. Burgess simply venerated Philby with an awe bordering on hero worship, the only person he was genuinely proud to call a friend. When Burgess died in Moscow, he left Philby nearly everything, including what had to be one of the largest private libraries—said to contain approximately four thousand volumes—in Moscow, along with warm clothes and furniture that was difficult to obtain.[24]

Philby's fondness for Burgess could not be dimmed. That sentiment was a mixture of gratitude because Burgess had pulled him into British intelligence in 1940, and pity for Guy's squandered talents and unrealized ambitions. Burgess may have been the only non-Soviet that Philby could really talk to and relax with, because Burgess alone among his family, friends, and workers knew his true game. All this added up to a greater loyalty to Burgess than Philby ever displayed to any of his wives, to say nothing of anyone else.

As the promise of youth had given way to the promiscuity of the failed revolutionary, Burgess's once striking good looks had also surrendered into a heavier, though still handsome, face. The permanently rumpled clothes, the unkempt hair, the dirty fingernails (which everyone seemed to notice), contributed to his disorderly appearance. Initially, the added years might have seemed to suggest a certain weariness-of-the-wise aloofness. But this impression vanished upon meeting his dark furtive eyes, which flashed the message that he was hungrily looking for some illicit adventure that had miraculously eluded him.

Philby invented a lie, albeit not a very credible one, to explain Burgess's presence in his home. He told friends that he was playing matchmaker. It was time, the story went, for Guy to end his bachelor days, settle down, get married, and raise a family. To promote such mainstream virtues, Kim wanted to bring his friend into a domestic environment complete with a suitable companion—the quite average-looking, fortyish Esther Whitfield. He hoped, as Philby explained it to Angleton, "to ignite a romance between the two."[25]

This had to be purely for American consumption. The cable to the embassy announcing Burgess's posting acknowledged that he was a homosexual, and Guy made sure that no one was ignorant for very long about his preferences. Several years later in Moscow, when he came across a reference to himself as "a suspected homosexual," he wrote in the book's margin, "SUSPECTED!"[26]

At the embassy, Philby was the odd man out. Many of the senior officials such as Sir Hubert Graves, the Counsellor, Bernard Burroughs, the Head of Chancery, Sir Robert Mackenzie, regional security chief, First Secretary Denis A. Greenhill, and possibly even Franks, all knew Burgess from the Hector McNeil days. "Objections were not accepted by the authorities in London," Greenhill stoically reports. Mackenzie adds, "Hector McNeil was absolutely insistent that we take him."[27]

"My God," exclaimed Francis "Tommy" Thompson, the embassy's security officer, when Mackenzie, his boss, handed him the dispatch about Burgess's posting, "what lunatics agreed to send this man out here?" "I was furious and disgusted," Thompson wrote later. The Foreign Office acknowledged Burgess was a drunkard and a homosexual and that in Washington his behavior might get worse. "What do they mean worse," Mackenzie wondered, "goats?"[28]

Although Burgess was in the United States for a much shorter period than either Maclean or Philby, his tour is shrouded in greater mystery. What did he do at the embassy? More important, what did he do away from it? He zoomed up and down the eastern seaboard from plantations in South Carolina to New York's luxury hotels as though he were a man obsessed with a mission. But whose? Who paid for it, and who authorized his extensive leave time from the embassy?

The shopworn story is that he was nothing but a paper clipper and that everyone simply washed their hands of him, a specious claim at best. First of all, the embassy still had nearly nine hundred employees attached to it. Many were working from ramshackle temporary buildings erected on the embassy grounds during the war when nearly two thousand British civil and military servants were posted to Washington. Some were housed in other buildings around town such as the Joint Staff Mission, which was in the Pentagon, and two or three staffers had offices in the Atomic Energy Commission (AEC) headquarters.

The premium space, however, where only the most senior staff had offices, was the N-shaped chancery that faced Massachusetts Avenue. Burgess was given an office in the chancery. Although only a lowly Second Secretary in the junior branch of the Foreign Office (Maclean and nearly everyone else who has appeared in this story were in the senior branch), he was on the same corridor as Philby, Patterson, and the science attaché Wilfrid Mann. Their work—liaison to the CIA, the FBI, and the AEC, respectively—involved handling some of the embassy's most sensitive information.

What possible justification could there have been for putting a paper clipper, a reviled millstone around the neck of the embassy, in such treasured space? If they could not dissuade the Foreign Office from sending him, one would think they at least would have banished him to some remote office space.[29]

Almost as confusing are the issues of what Burgess did and who supervised him. "I abandoned any attempt to involve him in my work," maintained Denis Greenhill, officially the embassy's Middle East expert, who was also heavily involved in Korean matters. So was Sir Hubert Graves, who, like Greenhill, even though overburdened with work, refused to accept him.[30]

Although this is undoubtedly true, at 2:00 P.M. on Thursday, August 10, Burgess's fourth day in the Chancery, the embassy received a coded secret cable from Peking reporting Chinese troop movements. Such information was extremely revealing at a time when Washington and London were trying to divine Chinese intentions in Korea. Graves directed it to four people: Ambassador Franks, R. O. Coleridge (the military attaché), Greenhill, and Burgess.[31]

The Foreign Office permitted America's ambassador in London, Lewis Douglas, only to read the cable; he was not given a copy. He immediately dispatched what he could remember to Acheson. This truncated version did not arrive on the Secretary of State's desk until nearly two days after it had reached Burgess's.[32]

There is no indication that Burgess had continued access to high levels of information. This means one of two things. Either he actually did not have such access, or the Foreign Office has purged its files of evidence that he did, and merely overlooked the August 10 cable. Certainly his official duties were small beer indeed. Chief among them was to serve as an alternate member of the British delegation to the Far Eastern Commission, which had been established in 1945 to ensure that Japan fulfilled the terms of its surrender. MacArthur had ignored it, and the Soviets had resigned from it.

Burgess gamely put in appearance at the State Department where Greenhill originally introduced him as "my assistant."

Several State Department officials—all men—later told the FBI that Burgess's "poor personal appearance was in contrast to the usual type of person associated with the British Embassy." He would arrive for morning meetings with the smell of liquor on his breath, and came across to one as "high-strung, unstable, and a rather heavy drinker." Women, however, saw in him a certain vulnerability. "There was something about him that was likeable," one thought; he was "shy and did not enter into conversation readily." Another noticed "a delicacy to him, like an artist who required protection."[33]

After several meetings, another woman had the impression that Burgess's "primary interest appeared to be automobiles and motoring." Truer words have rarely been spoken. From the age of nine until his death over forty years later, Burgess never missed a copy of *Autocar* magazine. The one thing he treasured about America was its large cars, and, within three weeks of his arrival, he paid $1,195 in cash to purchase a 1941 Lincoln Continental convertible from Mayflower Motors on Fifteenth Street in downtown Washington.

He was soon a familiar sight roaring up and down Massachusetts or Wisconsin avenues, the top down, his collar pulled up, a cigarette dangling down from his lips, his hair blowing wildly. "He drove with the fury of a Mr. Toad," says Greenhill. He loved the car, and within weeks had spent more on "nonessential" gadgets and repairs than he had originally paid for the car. Even the men at Mayflower came to consider Burgess a "nut" and "a screwball" about cars. Indeed, Burgess's car became such a character in this drama, that the FBI compiled a thick report entitled, "Investigation In Connection With Burgess's Automobile."[34] The car was his ticket to freedom. By early September, he had begun a series of nonstop trips to New York. But his absences from the embassy preceded that. In fact, at the end of his first week, at a time when Saturday mornings were considered part of the embassy work schedule, he took a three-day weekend.

The letter inviting Guy Burgess to the Highlands estate of Emily and Nicholas Roosevelt outside Philadelphia arrived at the embassy even before he did. These were precisely the kind of people with whom Guy would want to associate. In her early sixties, with still a trace of her native South Carolina accent, Mrs. Roosevelt was related to the Whartons of Philadelphia and was the matriarch of a family known for its wealth and philanthropy.

Nicholas Roosevelt, sixty-seven, was a distant cousin of Franklin Roosevelt, but close enough that Franklin conferred upon Henry, Nicholas's brother, the position of assistant secretary of the Navy. This was not only a powerful position, but one of immense sentimentality because both Teddy and Franklin Roosevelt had held the office early in their governmental careers. After graduating from St. Paul's and Princeton, Nicholas had entered the investment banking business, made his fortune early in life, and retired to serve on the boards of several major corporations and blue-chip civic associations.[35]

The antecedents to Burgess's invitation can be found in a trip that Emily Roosevelt had made to Egypt more than twenty-five years earlier when Cairo was a popular place for wealthy American tourists. While there, she had met Lieutenant Colonel J. R. Basset, who was stationed with British forces. Several years later, Emily and Nicholas visited Basset in London, by which time he had married Eve Burgess, a widow with two chidlren, one of whom, Guy, was about to go up to Cambridge. The two families maintained contact, and when Guy was posted to Washington, Basset—who had a touching but unrewarded devotion and loyalty to Guy—wrote to the Roosevelts saying that he "would appreciate any courtesies" they could extend to his stepson.[36]

They extended many, for which they received considerable grief. The first visit went well enough. Although Burgess's constant drinking made them uneasy, he never lost control and charmed them with his dazzling conversation. After "three or four days" the Roosevelts bade him farewell with both an invitation to return and letters of introduction to Washington friends and relatives, including their cousins, the columnists Stewart and Joseph Alsop.

Burgess followed up with alacrity. He and Stewart got along fine over a drink, but a dinner with Joseph Alsop proved to be a disaster. Although Burgess might have been able to pass in other circles as a China expert, he was no match for Alsop, who had read *The Analects of Confucius* in classical Chinese, a language he had learned in a Japanese prisoner of war camp. Alsop had also served in the China theatre and had drafted Chiang's famous cable demanding Stilwell's recall.

As a young man, Alsop set for himself the personal goal of insulting at least one person each day. At forty, he had not yet abandoned that practice, and it may well be that he had not yet fulfilled his quota on the day when he and Burgess had dinner. They disagreed on everything from the Spanish Civil War to the Korean War. The evening ended with Alsop, in his frigid Harvard-accented voice, telling Burgess "how informative the evening had been." But he wondered, after having been urged to meet two of the Foreign Office's bright young lights—first Maclean and now Burgess—what sort of men Whitehall was promoting these days.[37]

Burgess also looked up Emily Roosevelt's niece, Grace Sinkler Lockwood, and, after a drink at her house, they went to a concert. Whatever happened next is uncertain, but, when she was asked her impressions of Burgess thirty-five years later, Mrs. Lockwood replied frostily, "Guy Burgess represents a very embarrassing episode for the family . . . I do not wish to speak to anyone about him."[38]

These were only the beginnings of Burgess's peripatetic search for companionship. After this initial and unsuccessful round in Washington, he not surprisingly decided that New York might be more compatible. He was warmly received by Robert Grant III, an American-born Eton classmate whose father had engineered the high stakes, secret, and often dramatic takeover of *The Times* (London) for John Jacob Astor. Young Grant returned to America, graduated from Harvard, and became a Wall Street stockbroker. He and Guy had seen each other in London during the war, and Guy now became a regular visitor to his home in Old Westbury, Long Island, or his New York City apartment.[39]

Burgess received a more chilling reception from Valentine Lawford, Maclean's Paris colleague. Since he had seen Donald and Melinda at the Plaza in 1948, Lawford had resigned his government position to take up writing. Guy drove out to the elegant estates of Oyster Bay, where Lawford lived with the fashion photographer Horst P. Horst, who took an immediate dislike to Burgess. In an attempt to rescue the situation, Guy took his hosts for a drive in the Lincoln, but his effort failed; Horst made a point of not inviting

Burgess to stay for dinner. As night fell, Guy drove back to New York alone.[40]

These visits could not have had any espionage significance, and were merely the driven and largely unsuccessful effort to find friendship in a new land by a man who could not bear solitude. The visits were, however, sandwiched between mysterious trips that clearly had some hidden purpose.

The puzzle is how Burgess was able to spend so much time away from the embassy. He often told friends that he was in New York to work with Gladwyn Jebb at the United Nations. Jebb steadfastly denies that Burgess was ever assigned or seconded to him, or that he even saw Burgess other than at a lunch in the early autumn of 1950. Considering that Jebb became one of the most well-known foreign diplomats during the Korean crisis, Burgess was probably merely name-dropping as usual.[41]

Whatever his purpose, however, Burgess did spend an inordinate time in New York. Did the embassy simply wash its hands of him? This seems unlikely in an embassy headed by the tough, businesslike Franks. He never would have permitted public funds and valuable embassy space to be wasted on a "no show." Besides, when Burgess traveled to New York on his own, he would stay at the apartment of friends, often sleeping on the sofa. Yet on other trips—presumably when someone else would pay for them—he would take a room at the Sutton, a luxury hotel on midtown Manhattan's East Side.[42]

Another indication that he had not been cast adrift is that Burgess was chosen to escort Sir Anthony Eden around Washington during an official visit. This was not a trivial assignment. Eden, fifty-three, was the Conservative Party's heir apparent to the seventy-six-year-old Churchill. The opportunity to ingratiate oneself with Britain's future prime minister was one which must have been avidly sought. The honor went to Burgess.

Still strikingly handsome, affable, and with a good humor and great self-confidence, Eden, as C. L. Sulzberger observed, was "suspended between a glamorous past and a still uncertain future." He had been dispatched to Washington by Attlee to represent the War Cabinet for the unveiling of a statue to Sir John Dill, the British head of the Combined Chiefs of Staff, whose close friendship with Marshall contributed greatly to the integration of Anglo-American wartime strategy and operations. Eden was to meet Truman at the White House on the afternoon of November 1 so that they could ride together to the ceremony at Arlington Cemetery.[43]

Before Eden and Burgess arrived at the White House, however, two Puerto Rican nationalists tried to storm Blair House, where Truman was then living, only to be cut down in a hail of fire. The President, calm and cheerful, arrived only a few minutes late where his unnerved Cabinet and Eden—and presumably Burgess—were waiting.[44]

The rest of his visit was less dramatic. Over the next several days, Burgess was constantly at Eden's side, including for a visit with Sumner Wells, once Roosevelt's powerful undersecretary of state—until he was forced out by a homosexual scandal. It should come as no surprise that Burgess, according to State Department officials, had already somehow gotten to know Wells.[45]

One of Burgess's proudest possessions—the existence of which many, including Aileen Philby, assumed to be another fabrication—was a book inscribed to him by Winston Churchill. Burgess had driven out to Chartwell in October 1938 during the Munich crisis to ask him to be a guest on his BBC talk show. Churchill declined, but the two had a fascinating exchange about the grave world situation. As Burgess was leaving, Churchill gave him a copy of his latest book, *Arms and the Covenant,* writing in the flyleaf "To Guy Burgess, in agreement with his views, Winston S. Churchill."[46]

Now, over twelve years later, Burgess handed the book to Eden, and asked him to write an inscription under Churchill's. Eden, who had resigned as Chamberlain's Foreign Secretary over the Munich humiliation, declined. "It would spoil it," he said. "He was wiser and stronger than I that week; but we *were* right."

Before he sailed from New York on the *Queen Elizabeth,* Eden wrote Burgess a note dated November 8:

My dear Burgess—

Thank you so much for all your kindnesses. I was so well looked after that I am still in robust health, after quite a stormy flight to New York and many engagements since. Truly I enjoyed every moment of my stay in Washington, and you will know how much you helped to make this possible. Renewed greetings and gratitude. Yours sincerely,

Anthony Eden[47]

CHAPTER EIGHTEEN

> Barclay gets information . . . in advance by an
> officer who should strictly speaking await its
> transmission via the warroom . . . this applies
> particularly to future operations.
>
> British Embassy to the Foreign Office on
> information affecting Korean War operations.[1]

PIERCING THE SCREEN

"Philby has admitted," British authorities later informed the FBI, "he knew that Burgess traveled to New York during this period [August 1950 to April 1951] to visit Alan Maclean." The FBI assumed that the purpose of these trips was to monitor Donald's progress—or lack of it—in London.[2]

Burgess had been a frequent guest in the Maclean home during Donald's last two years at Cambridge, and Alan had long regarded him as an old family friend. So when Guy would call or just appear at his New York apartment and ask whether he could sleep on the couch, the younger Maclean thought nothing of it. Alan later did not remember that it had happened very often, although Burgess's frequent presence in New York left Jebb with the impression that Burgess "shared a flat with my private secretary [Alan Maclean]."[3]

Alan traveled at least twice to Washington to meet with Burgess and Philby at the Nebraska Avenue house. "Kim was very impressive, I liked him," Alan recalled years later, his expression alive with the memory. "He made you feel that you were cleverer and wittier than you were. You wouldn't meet more than a half-dozen like him in your life." (Perhaps this is the real measure of Philby's charm.)[4]

But even the most pleasant lunch and a dose of good cheer could not overshadow the depressing news about Donald's unceasing self-debasement. He continued his homosexual infatuations (one report had it that the black doorman he fancied beat him up) and could be found stumbling drunk through London. One night a man opened the door of an empty taxi only to discover Maclean asleep on the rug. Awakened, he became angry, claiming to have hired it as his bedroom for the night.[5]

Drunk or sober, he denounced his career and renounced his marriage, telling friends that he could not bear the thought of living with Melinda again or going back to the Foreign Office. Then he openly began to court disaster. First, he accosted Gorowny Rees, a long-time friend of Burgess and Blunt whom Maclean (and later many others) believed had once been a fellow member of the Soviet underground. "You used to be one of us," he spat in disgust at Rees, "but you ratted."[6] Then, at a party in Chelsea, he capped a provocative conversation with Mark Culme-Seymour, an old and trusted friend, by bellowing, "What would you do if I told you I was working for Uncle Joe?" Seymour, embarrassed, fumbled for an answer.

"Well, wouldn't you report me?" Maclean demanded.

"I don't know. Who to?"

"Well, I am . . . Go on, report me."

After a silence, Maclean launched into a diatribe against the U.S. State Department and the Korean War. The episode unnerved Seymour. The next day, he went to see Connolly, and both decided that it was only Donald's macabre humor. As did most of his friends, they assumed that the demons inside Donald were personal ones associated with his marriage and alcoholism.[7]

Maclean, Cecil speculates, "half-hoped to end the suspense and the ordeal by finally bringing down upon himself the whole edifice of deceit and betrayal." No wonder, as Philby later wrote, "the development of the affair [the search for Homer and Maclean's condition] was giving me deep anxiety."[8]

He was not alone. The head of personnal at the Foreign Office, George Middleton, was convinced that one of His Majesty's most promising diplomats would be irretrievably lost unless some drastic action were taken. He contacted Melinda, who was alarmed by Donald's despondent letters, and asked her to come to London. She arrived in September, leaving the boys behind in Paris. Melinda checked into a London hotel, and met at the Foreign Office with her husband and Middleton. Middleton pointed out the obvious. The only way for Donald to support his family was by rebuilding his career. It was in everyone's interest that he do so.[9]

For Melinda the alternative was to become dependent upon her mother, and probably move back to the United States. Donald's only alternative was to drink himself to death. Discussions went on for two weeks, at the end of which the Macleans agreed to a reconciliation. For the first time in months they slept together, which resulted in another pregnancy (against her doctor's advice).

"Donald had grave doubts at first about our ability to be happy together," Melinda wrote Harriet, "but we decided to try it again." With his family providing the anchor he so badly needed, Donald began the long climb out of the abyss. He stopped drinking and decided that he was not homosexual after all. Eventually, they bought a house in the village of Tatsfield an hour outside London— Melinda made the down payment—in the somewhat naive hope that Donald's need to catch the 5:19 P.M. train at Charing Cross would force him to sprint past his favorite drinking haunts.[10]

By October, he and Middleton were discussing his return to the Foreign Office, but not because he was cured of anything; it was a matter of bureaucratic imperative. Although Donald had been free to diagnose his own problem, choose his own doctor, and monitor his own treatment, on matters of greater import, regulations had to be followed. And the rules clearly stated that an employee could receive only six months of medical leave at full pay. After that, the employee either had to return to work or was automatically cut to half pay. There were no exceptions.

"He is going back to the F.O. on November 1," Melinda again wrote Harriet, "poor lamb!" To the Soviets, as Cecil points out, "the leniency with which his misdemeanors in Cairo had been treated by the Foreign Office would have appeared incomprehensible." To have their man rejoin the senior ranks of British diplomacy was an unexpected bonanza; it meant that he was good for one last mission.[11]

Maclean returned to the Foreign Office's creaky lifts and drab halls as head of the American Department. When later forced to defend appointing a mental wreck to such a sensitive position, Whitehall predictably invented another of its patently absurd tales. The American Department was dismissed as dealing "principally with Latin-American affairs." Issues regarding the United States were limited to tourism and the welfare of British citizens in America.

The fact that this perversion of the truth was almost instantly shredded did not diminish the government's devotion to it.[12] This deceit was necessitated by Whitehall's determination to conceal from its American allies and the British public the nature and extent of the information Maclean had been receiving on the Korean War. The cover-up required that the Department's files for Maclean's tenure be purged before they were shipped to the British Public Record Office. The only ones intended to survive were to deal principally with Latin American affairs.

It should come as no surprise, however, to discover that, consistent with its handling of all other aspects of this case, the government's purge was bungled:

1. When purging the files, government document weeders neglected to also purge those preceding Maclean's tenure. So it is possible to track what was flowing to the American Department prior to his appointment. At the time Maclean assumed his new duties this included highly secret operational military information originating from the British mission in Peking, the British Cabinet, the American Joint Chiefs of Staff, and from General Douglas MacArthur himself.

The government would later claim that it withheld vital documents from Maclean once he was a suspect in the "Homer" case.[13] But, no one has suggested this occurred before March of 1951.[14] For example, an advance copy was found of a cable to Maclean (head of the American Department) from Ambassador Franks bearing the highest classification, "FO Immediate/Top Secret OTP" (one-time pad—a code never to be repeated), dated April 5, 1951.[15]

2. Moreover, the government's purge missed some files in collateral departments. By reviewing, for example, the files of the Far Eastern Department between November 1950 and May 1951 (which are also far from complete), it is possible to establish that during Maclean's tenure highly restricted war-related information was routinely copied to the American Department.

3. Finally, Cecil, one of Maclean's two deputies in the Department, acknowledges that Donald had "access to most of the important telegrams passing between the Foreign Office and posts abroad, as well as a selection of Cabinet papers," some of which Cecil found locked in Maclean's cabinet after he fled to Russia.[16]

★ ★ ★

"We can bring U.S. power into play [in Korea] only with the cooperation of the British," was the way Dean Acheson would eventually explain the facts of life to the National Security Council. Britain and her Commonwealth partners were crucial to Washington's fixation with wearing the United Nations's moral cloak in Korea. The troops provided by the twelve other allied nations never totaled more than just a small fraction of the 800,000 ultimately under the command of the U.S. Eighth Army. Their presence, however, particularly that of the Commonwealth Brigade, helped to preserve the fiction that the United States was not acting unilaterally in Korea, but as an agent of the United Nations.[17]

Thus, from the earliest days of the war, Pentagon leaders went out of their way to provide British military and diplomatic representatives with special treatment and access. Air Marshal Arthur Tedder, Britain's senior military representative in Washington, received special, private briefings directly from General Omar Bradley, chairman of the Joint Chiefs of Staff. And Sir Frederick Hoyer-Millar, Minister at the embassy and Maclean's replacement on atomic energy matters, reported to London in July that "my military advisor [Barclay], alone of all foreign missions here, has been issued one special pass to the Secret warroom of the General HQ and attends a briefing there twice daily." To top that, "Barclay gets information," Hoyer-Millar boasted, "obtained from U.S. Far East Air Force *in advance* by an officer who should strictly speaking await its transmission via the warroom . . . *this applies particularly to future operations.*"[18]

"Just seen Bradley and gone over bombing attacks," Denis Green-hill cabled the American Department in mid-August. "These include five North Korean towns . . . six of the targets are railyards, two are dock areas, and two are factories."[19]

Even MacArthur overcame his intense dislike and distrust of the Foreign Office and provided Sir Alvary D. Gascoigne, Britain's ranking political adviser in Japan since 1946, private briefings at SCAP (Supreme Commander of the Allies in the Pacific) headquarters in Tokyo. Gascoigne, who was soon to become Britain's ambassador to Russia, was able to provide London with information on proposed operations, bombing targets, and tactical decisions.[20]

Records surviving the government's purge show that in July, when the reports from Tedder, Hoyer-Millar, and Barclay started pouring into the Foreign Office from the embassy, the American Department was at the top of the distribution list ahead of the Prime Minister, the Ministers of Defense and State, and Michael Wright, the superintending Under Secretary. Those originating in Tokyo or with Britain's man in Peking went directly to the Far Eastern Department, which then copied them to the American Department.[21]

Dean Rusk, who had known Maclean in Washington and who was assistant secretary of state for Far Eastern Affairs during the Korean War, was not deceived by Whitehall's later description of the American Department. Based on nearly thirty-five years of experience in working closely with British diplomats and the Foreign Office, he later told historian William Manchester that, "It can be assumed, 1) anything we in our government knew about Korea would have been known at the British Embassy and 2) that officers in the Embassy of the rank of [Maclean, Philby, and Burgess] would have known what the British Embassy knew."[22]

This can now be refined. There is no evidence after his early August arrival that Burgess again shared in such top-secret information. In addition, for what it is worth, Philby claims to have reported "no significant information about the Korean War" to Moscow. Certainly anything he picked up from the CIA would not have been worth very much. Their role was largely limited to projecting, albeit rather abysmally, Chinese troop strength and forecasting the intentions of Peking and Moscow. Certainly, Philby may have been able to snatch copies of other reports circulating within the embassy, but it is inconceivable that he could have obtained anything more important than what Maclean was getting.

Rusk was correct. Maclean did know everything that the U.S. government knew about Korea and, it is worth emphasizing, he also had information the State Department did not. Washington had refused to recognize Red China, but Great Britain had done so, and was represented in Peking by John Hutchison (later Sir), the minister and chargé d'affaires. Hutchison provided London with a steady stream of reports on his conversations with Communist Party Chairman Mao Tse-tung, Premier and Prime Minister Chou En-lai, and leading military officials (it was his military attaché's report that Burgess received on August 10). These also went to the American Department.[23]

* * *

The punishing blitzkrieg launched in June 1950 by the North Korean Army sent the South Korean forces reeling backward, until they were huddled on the Pusan perimeter, clinging to the peninsula by their fingernails. Only superior American air power and United Nations reinforcements prevented the North Koreas from delivering the final push that would have driven the South Korea forces into the sea.

Then North Korea seemed to run out of steam. They could not deliver the death blow, which gave MacArthur time to plan one of history's greatest military surprises. In mid-September his bold and ingenious saber thrust at Inchon enveloped and isolated the North Korean army. On September 26, as its shattered remnants fled north of the 38th Parallel, United Nations forces retook Seoul. Days later, South Korean army officers, boasting that they would not stop until they had bathed their sabers in the Yalu River, led their troops across the 38th Parallel into North Korea.

The acting chief of staff of the People's Liberation Army had already declared that China would never permit American troops to advance to the Yalu (the river that served as a border between North Korea and China). "They may even drop atom bombs on us," Nieh Jung-chen warned Kavatam Madhava Panikkar, the Indian ambassador to the People's Republic of China. "What then? They may kill a few million people. Without sacrifice a nation's independence cannot be upheld."[24]

Neither London nor Washington wanted to pick a fight with the People's Republic of China, a point that they made repeatedly through public and private channels at every opportunity. Both considered the Soviet Union the enemy. There was even the view in Washington, advanced by George Kennan among others, that China and Russia were natural adversaries, because Stalin would try to thwart China's nationalist ambitions. "We hope in particular that the people of China will not be misled or forced into fighting against the United Nations and against the American people," President Truman pleaded in a nationwide radio broadcast on September 1.[25]

Some analysts, as well as Truman, considered China's threats a bluff. Surely if the People's Republic intended to intervene they would have done so in August when the North Korean army had the enemy on the ropes at Pusan, but needed help in delivering the final blow—not in October when North Korea's own defeat was inevitable.[26]

"Chou En-lai is too shrewd a statesman," Gladwyn Jebb was predicting from New York, "to take on the whole United Nations." There were other reasons for believing that China would not go to war. Recovery from the long civil war had not even begun, and the country's borders were not yet secured. Kuomintang brigands were still on the loose, famine was widespread, the cities were cauldrons of discontent, and Mao was trying to demobilize his army of five million men so that they could return to the fields and the factories.[27]

India frequently served as China's pipeline to the West, and its representatives soon reinforced Jebb's assessment. Sir Girja Bajpai, the Secretary General of the Indian Foreign Office, advised the British High Commissioner that China's leaders were under enormous pressure from Stalin to do what the Soviets "were not prepared to do, i.e., to take military action in Korea." The Foreign Office predicted that China's rulers would continue to resist because "their internal position is not yet consolidated, and they must know that in a war with the USA her cities and communications would be devastated, adding greatly to their internal difficulties."[28]

Yet, Peking warned of dire consequences if U.S. troops crossed the 38th Parallel, which they did on October 7. That same day, Washington pushed through a United Nations resolution calling for a complete military victory over North Korea, and the unification of the two Koreas under United Nations-supervised elections. Within two weeks General Walton H. "Johnny" Walker's Eighth Army took Pyongyang, North Korea's capital. Then, on October 25, South Korean forces encountered the Communist Chinese Forces, or "Chicoms" as MacArthur called them, and two days later, the Chinese halted the Eighth Army with stunning swiftness.

Once it was clear that the Chinese army had crossed the Yalu, Whitehall, which had initially applauded Washington's commitment to total military victory, became palpably nervous. As Peking became more belligerent, the Foreign Office began talking about the imperative of finding a political compromise acceptable to Peking and Moscow.

The West had assumed from the start that Stalin had authorized, if not directly ordered, Kim Il Sung to invade South Korea. But where did China fit in? Was she in on it from the beginning? If not, why would Peking want to pull Russia's chestnuts out of the fire now? Did Mao perceive hostility behind Stalin's effort to unify Korea as a Soviet client state? "Our bafflement," Acheson later wrote, "centered about the two principal enigmas of this situation: What were the facts about Chinese military presence in North Korea and what were their intentions?"[29]

It was at this time, when a fog of uncertainty enshrouded the councils of Western policymakers, that Maclean returned to the Foreign Office. The American Department, his new domain, had three rooms. The Third Secretaries, who did all the donkey work, occupied the large outer office. Maclean's two deputies, of whom Cecil was one, were in a smaller inner office; he occupied the inside private office.

The tables had turned since his Washington days when he was repelled by Britain's "sniveling dependency" on the United States. Now Britain was calling the shots in the Anglo-American relationship, and it was the United States—fearful of losing its United Nations mandate—that was pleading and cajoling to obtain British cooperation.[30]

George Kennan left the State Department in August, bitter and disillusioned with Washington's postwar foreign policy—particularly the inability of U.S. political leaders to grasp that "what people in Moscow decided to do might be a reaction to things we had done."[31] He should have remained, because eventually the West succumbed to the delusion that it was they, not Chou, who controlled the People's Liberation Army, just as it was they, not Stalin, who controlled the Soviet Air Force. It was as though the PLA and the Soviet MiGs were perched on powerful springs that only the West could release. Anglo-American strategists tormented themselves with worry that they might stumble over the string that would catapult Chinese troops into Korea, or unleash Soviet MiGs. For instance, once United Nations forces retook Seoul on September 26, London and Washington convinced themselves that, should MacArthur destroy the hydroelectric plants supplying power to China, Manchuria, and the Soviet Union, *that* would be the action that would propel the Chinese army into Korea.

"American Chiefs of Staff have ordered American Air Force now restrict their bombing only to targets that have immediate effect on tactical situation," Franks cabled the American Department on September 29. "Attacks on such targets as hydroelectric plants recently attacked will now cease."[32]

MacArthur infuriated Truman by publicly criticizing the order at the time. Later, in his ceaseless quest for scapegoats, he branded the order as "the most indefensible and ill-conceived decision ever forced on a field commander in our nation's history." Eventually it was broadened to include every plant in North Korea capable of furnishing electric power to Manchuria and Siberia, including the even more powerful Racin supply center.[33]

The British particularly were afflicted with the recurring nightmare that Stalin was searching for a provocation to commit the Soviet Air Force. When Foreign Secretary Bevin discovered that MacArthur was preparing to pursue Soviet MiG-15s conducting hit-and-run sorties back to their Manchurian sanctuary, he complained by cable to Washington that "the doctrine of hot pursuit not applicable to U.S. in Korea." He instructed Franks to make it clear that he refused to "endorse the U.S. suggestion that violation of Manchurian border may be necessary," because it carried with it "the great danger of provoking the Soviet Air Force." Soon all thirteen allied nations with forces fighting in Korea vetoed hot pursuit, even though it was an age-old concept in international law.[34]

At a time when the CIA was reporting that Chinese Communist troops were steadily infiltrating from the Manchurian border across the Yalu into North Korea, MacArthur ordered a massive bombing attack by ninety B-29s on five bridges spanning the river. Just as the pilots were suiting up, however, word came from Washington that no bombing raids were to be conducted within five miles of the Manchurian border. After protesting vehemently, MacArthur was told that he could bomb the one-half of each bridge that was on the Korean side.[35]

Bevin constantly worried that Peking did not "understand the pacific nature of our intentions towards Chinese territory." Not appreciating that one of his own senior officials could provide greater assurances on that score than anything said publicly by Western statesmen, Bevin vehemently opposed any action that Mao might construe as unfriendly. For instance, as the Chinese increased their infiltrations and ultimatums, the Joint Chiefs of Staff and the National Security Council suggested responding with threats of massive retaliation. Bevin immediately advised Washington: "No ultimatums to China would be supported by me." And none were made.[36]

MacArthur was of the opposite opinion. He believed that Peking "had shot its bolt" during the October skirmishes, and he told Truman at their Wake Island conference that if the Chinese intervened, he would annihilate them. In the meantime, he planned for an "end-the-war offensive" that would be the capstone of his career, equal to Inchon for tactical daring and brilliance.

On November 13 the General told Gascoigne that he would pursue and crush the North Korean army on the banks of the Yalu. Confidence was so high around headquarters of the commander in chief of the Far East that there was even talk about redeploying "surplus troops" from Korea to Europe. The boys, MacArthur boasted, would be home by Christmas. When Gascoigne alerted Bevin to MacArthur's plans, the Foreign Secretary became nearly paralyzed with anxiety.[37]

What could he do? As early as July, both Gascoigne and Sir Frederick Hoyer-Millar (later Lord Inchyra), Minister at the Washington embassy, had warned him that if London ever tried to use its special advance knowledge to obstruct MacArthur, the General would immediately terminate their special access to future operations. On November 22, Bevin complained to Ambassador Oliver Franks that he was in an impossible situation. Neither he nor Attlee could reveal to their Commonwealth partners, the Cabinet, or Parliament, let alone the public, what was about to happen. Thus once the offensive was launched, it would appear that either "we don't know what is going on, or MacArthur is acting outside of the UN scope." He ordered the ambassador to "speak to Acheson urgently of it."[38]

Acheson, who was in a perpetual state of agitation over MacArthur, listened sympathetically to Franks and promised that he would be happy to try to resolve Bevin's dilemma. But there had been a lull in the fighting for almost two weeks; the Chinese seemed to have pulled back from North Korea, and the next day was Thanksgiving. Could it wait until Friday? Franks agreed.[39]

★   ★   ★

Kim Philby and his family had their first Thanksgiving at the home of Jim and Cicely Angleton. Also there from the embassy were Miriam and Wilfrid Mann. With ten children, it was a festive if slightly chaotic affair.[40]

Halfway around the world, thanks to American ingenuity and determination, scores of thousands of American boys dug in along North Korea's frozen, snow-covered hills, valleys, and ridges, huddled in their foxholes with a Thanksgiving meal of turkey, cranberry sauce, buttered squash, Waldorf salad, mince pie, and after-dinner mints. The great challenge was to eat the gravy before it froze. As the meals were served, the troops were told, on orders from MacArthur, that "they will eat Christmas dinner at home."[41]

Later, MacArthur and a good many others would charge that thanks to Donald Maclean (and perhaps to a lesser extent Kim Philby and Guy Burgess), for an indeterminate number of these young Americans, this would be their last Thanksgiving meal.

The next day MacArthur's headquarters released a statement from the General that "if successful, this [offensive] should for all practical purposes end the war." The three-prong assault moved north with MacArthur's American forces making up each flank and South

Korean troops in the center. During the first two days their advance met only trivial resistance. Then, on the night of Sunday, November 26, catastrophe struck.[42]

Three hundred thousand howling Chinese Communist troops, seemingly propelled by their eerie, penetrating flutes, drums, whistles, and bugle calls, poured out of hiding places along a three hundred-mile front and descended upon the United Nations forces, who were outnumbered seven to one and, in some cases, twenty to one. (By way of comparison, during the first forty-eight hours of the D-Day invasion, a total of 107,000 Allied troops landed in Normandy.)

The fifteen thousand men in the 1st Marine Division at the Chosin Reservoir were hopelessly outnumbered and surrounded. "Men," one commander is said to have told his troops, "the enemy is behind us, he is in front of us, he is to our left and on our right. This time the bastards won't get away." The Marines began their inch-by-inch retreat down a narrow, steep, winding dirt road relentlessly swept by machine-gun fire and winds that dropped the temperature to thirty degrees below zero. One company, having used their ammunition and all their grenades, swung shovels like baseball bats to bat back enemy grenades. Another company with two hundred twenty-five men on Thanksgiving day was reduced to seven after the retreat.[43]

For the first time in history a communist power had defeated a Western army in a major battle. The recriminations began immediately. How could three hundred thousand troops have entered the country undetected? How could they have remained hidden until the perfect moment? Incompetence? Myopia? Delusion?

All of the above, most historians agree. Max Hastings, the British military historian, argues that China could not have made clearer its intention to enter the fray should American soldiers cross the 38th Parallel. By ignoring the warnings sent through Panikkar, the Americans "had created a fantasy world for themselves," and "blundered into" what The Guardian called "one of the supreme mistakes of history."[44]

There is much to this, but it is not quite that simple. No one thought that China wanted war; Washington and London broadcast, at least as loudly and earnestly as Chou, that they had no desire for war with China, and they took every possible precaution to avoid inflicting any damage on the Chinese, a policy that remained unaltered even after they massacred Western troops.

Moreover, the signals from Peking were not quite as unequivocal as was later claimed. On October 13, six days after U.S. troops crossed the forbidden Rubicon of the 38th Parallel, Hutchison was called to the Chinese Foreign Ministry. "Chinese seemed to back away from threat of intervening," he reported afterward, "there is now very little danger of extension of hostilities." Even Panikkar and Bajpai agreed that the message delivered to Hutchison "was real."[45]

It was also no secret that vast numbers of Chinese forces had crossed into North Korea, but in what force, and whether or not Peking intended to actually jump in with both feet, was uncertain. Throughout September, CIA reports on these two points "were so contradictory as to be meaningless." During October the CIA, *The New York Times,* and *Time* magazine all reported as many as seven hundred thousand Chinese troops poised along the North Korean border, with at least two hundred thousand having crossed under the command of Lin Piao. And John Hutchison, the British chargé in Peking, was reporting later that month that "the Dean of Peking National University believes there are large numbers of Chinese already in Korea."[46]

MacArthur's numbers were lower; G-2 (Army intelligence) estimated that four hundred thousand were amassed and one hundred thousand had infiltrated. That figure was later lowered to sixty thousand. Whatever the number, however, it was enough to make a believer out of the Mikado of Japan and Korea, as some referred to MacArthur. On November 4, he warned Washington that large concentrations of Chinese "threaten the ultimate destruction of my command," and a few days later that "a new, fresh army now faces us," operating from its "privileged sanctuary" across the Yalu. He finally received permission to knock out the bridges, but again was forbidden to hit the Yalu dams or power plants.[47]

Soon thereafter, Lin Piao's blue-coated troops had completely disappeared. The Chinese broke off all action; United Nations patrols could not flush out a single Chinese soldier. A daring air reconnaissance flight on the eve of battle in an unarmed plane along the Yalu at five thousand feet convinced MacArthur that the Chinese had withdrawn. Mao's bluff had been called.

"They really fooled us when it comes right down to it, didn't they?" Senator McMahon asked Acheson during a Senate investigation of the Korean debacle. "Yes, sir," was the "shattering honesty" of Acheson's response. MacArthur was fooled, as was Hutchison (who was reporting that, "In my opinion the Chinese Government hopes to localize the conflict"), and the CIA (which was assuring Truman that "there is no evidence that the Chinese Communists plan major offensive operations in Korea").[48]

MacArthur would later claim that he was a victim not of miscalculation but treachery—that Maclean and his cohorts Philby and Burgess had enabled the enemy to outmaneuver him. But MacArthur was a well-known paranoiac and could not be taken seriously. Others eventually chimed in, however, including General James van Fleet, who assumed command of the Eighth Army after Ridgeway replaced MacArthur as Supreme Commander of the Allies in the Pacific; Admiral C. Turner Joy, who left Korea in 1953 to become superintendent of the Naval Academy; and, most formidably, General James M. Gavin, a hero at the Normandy landing and later President Kennedy's friend, adviser, and ambassador to France.

In an interview Gavin asserted:

I have no doubt whatever that the Chinese moved confidently and skillfully into North Korea, and in fact, I believe they were able to do this because they were well-informed not only of the moves Walker would make, but of the limitations of what he might do.

He was convinced, "All of MacArthur's plans flowed into the hands of the Communists through the British Foreign Office."[49]

"The enemy would not have entered Korea if he did not feel safe from attack in Northern China and Manchuria," Van Fleet insisted. "My own conviction is that there must have been information to the enemy that we would not attack his home base."[50]

Are such charges credible? Cecil for one believes "this goes too far" because operational telegrams on the military situation were not distributed within the Foreign Office. But, as we have seen, the files of the British Public Record Office tell another story.[51] Once in place, Maclean was able to provide the Kremlin with both the policy and operational options and decisions being made in London, Washington, and Tokyo. The Foreign Office believed that the leadership of China "must know that in a war with the USA her cities and communications would be devastated, adding greatly to their internal difficulties."[52]

What if Mao knew, however, that such vital industrial and strategic resources were immune from attack? What if he knew that the only price would be a few hundreds of thousands or millions of what MacArthur called their "bottomless well of manpower"? And what if he was assured that his greatest worry—that the United States would deploy the atom bomb against Chinese targets—was groundless?[53]

As enemy forces increased, MacArthur had again asked for permission to hit the Yalu power plants, especially Suiho, the world's fourth largest generating plant, with its associated plants stretched in a grid system across North Korea. On November 7 (after Maclean had taken over as head of the American Department), Franks cabled that "MacArthur has been given instructions . . . not to extend operations in any way over frontier . . . [and] NOT repeat NOT to destroy the Suiho dam."[54]

When the Chinese assault was launched later that month, Chinese ground forces—-powerless against U.S. air strikes—hit hardest south of the Suiho Dam. Their defensive and offensive tactics indicated that they did not fear an air attack; they were confident that the only threat was from United Nations ground forces. Indeed, antiaircraft batteries had been moved from the dam to other targets of less strategic importance which had not been declared off limits to the U.S. Air Force.[55]

It is worth noting that between the time when MacArthur warned that Chinese forces threatened the destruction of his command (November 4), and the time when he was convinced that they had slipped back into Manchuria and China (November 26), Maclean had learned about all of the limitations on United Nations forces— no hot pursuit, no bridges, no strikes against dams or power plants, and that all targets in Manchuria and China were off-limits. And he knew one more thing—the date and the order of battle for the end-the-war offensive as cabled to the Foreign Office by Gascoigne.

As Manchester puts it, "Not until the UN rout reached disastrous proportions, and the General was improvising so fast that Washington and the Philby agents couldn't keep up with him, was he able to match the foe blow by blow."[56]

Maclean's service was still far from completed. At a November 30 press conference, Truman, still irritable and edgy from the disastrous turn of events in Korea, responded to a question by saying that use of the atomic bomb was under active consideration, and were it authorized "the military commander in the field would have charge of that weapon."[57]

Maclean received Franks's "EMERGENCY" cable alerting Attlee to the possibility that MacArthur, by now dubbed "the mad satrap" by many British officials, might have custody of atomic bombs. Personally horrified, confronted with a revolt in his own Labour Party, and faced with angry public protests, the Prime Minister immediately invited himself to Washington to pry "Truman's finger off the nuclear trigger."[58]

Maclean did not accompany the Prime Minister to the hastily and ill-advised Washington summit. He did, however, help to prepare the briefing papers delineating the political concessions that the British believed that the United Nations should be prepared to make to end the war. At the end of each of the five days, a written report was encoded in a one-time pad, designated "of particular secrecy," and sent to Maclean in London.[59]

On the first day, Monday, December 4, 1950, for instance, Attlee and Truman called a halt to their talks at 5:30 P.M. (so that Truman could attend his daughter's piano concert). At 7:56 A.M. on Tuesday an "unbuttoned" (decoded) copy of everything they discussed was placed on Maclean's desk. Purged though the official files may be, this transcript, along with those covering the next five days of the Attlee–Truman talks, could still be found in the British Public Record Office, complete with handwritten notations by Maclean (the first day at 6:06 P.M. he dispatched a copy to the Paris embassy).[60]

Truman came to admire Attlee; Acheson did not. The Prime Minister was small, thin, bald, and, at sixty-six years of age, withered in appearance. His speech came in halting bursts delivered, Acheson thought, with "all the passion of a woodchuck chewing a carrot." The Secretary of State found the talks "persistently depressing," and could not resist repeating Churchill's description that Attlee was "a sheep in sheep's clothing."[61]

For his part, Attlee considered himself a beacon of reason cutting through the murky thinking that was driving Washington to an inevitable and catastrophic war with China. A negotiated settlement must be reached, he insisted, speculating on what China would want in exchange for a cease-fire. A seat in the United Nations? Formosa? These were acceptable to the British.

Acheson sniffed the stench of defeatism. He rejected all talk of concessions with an oratorical barrage that left American, as well as British, participants dazed. The enemy, he emphasized, was Russia. China was merely a satellite. But China must not be allowed to shoot her way into the United Nations. Now was the least opportune time to make any concessions.[62]

Truman was at his feistiest. Allied troops would not be withdrawn from the Korean peninsula unless they were driven off the beaches as the British Expeditionary Force had been at Dunkirk. To abandon Korea, he allowed, would be to condemn to death the millions of Koreans who had placed their trust in the United States. "[We'll] fight it to a finish," he vowed.[63]

Yet, over the next several days, concessions were made. Any suggestion of bombing Chinese industrial targets Attlee said, "is fantastic and should be ruled out." After all, if China's capacity to wage war were impaired, she might commit even more troops than the three hundred thousand already in North Korea (no targets in China were hit; nonetheless, the Chinese army quadrupled in strength to 1.2 million troops).[64]

Washington had also been actively considering "a limited war with China by way of an economic blockade and stirring up internal trouble in China." At British insistence, however, all such plans were abandoned. Both sides also agreed that Stalin's wrath must not be aroused for fear that if the Allies were forces to withdraw from Korea, he might use his air force to slaughter the troops as they were huddled on the beachheads.[65]

By the time the talks had ended, the United States also conceded that military victory and a unified Korea—so boldly declared just two months before—were no longer possible. The best that could be hoped for now was to reestablish the territorial integrity of South

Korea. In other words, the United States was willing to settle for a status quo ante bellum.

Even to accomplish this, the Allied forces would have to retreat well to the south of the 38th Parallel and establish redoubts on South Korea's coasts. Such planning demanded complete secrecy. If the South Korean army discovered this strategy, the British feared, they would "almost certainly dissolve and perhaps form guerilla bands against us."[66]

On the night of December 5, approximately twelve hours after Maclean received the transcript of the first meeting, a wire service story written by Arthur Gavshon, the Associated Press's London correspondent whom the Foreign Office considered "tricky and unscrupulous," described the summit as taking place in an atmosphere of gloom and defeatism. Washington and London were so serious about "pulling a Korean-Dunkirk," Gavshon reported, that islands were being identified on which to resettle South Korean political and military leaders.[67] The Americans blamed the British for the leak; the Foreign Office accused the office of the press secretary of the Cabinet, which, in turn, pointed out that they had not even received a copy of the transcript—only the Foreign Office had.[68]

It was not until the fifth and final day, in a private meeting with the President, that Attlee raised the issue of atomic weapons. Truman assured him that he would not use the bomb without prior consultation with the British. Acheson—doubtless recalling the drubbing he took on Capitol Hill three years earlier after revealing the secret Roosevelt-Churchill agreements—blanched when Truman cheerfully imparted this news. The summit's public communiqué merely stated that the President would keep the Prime Minister "informed" of any developments or changes.[69]

"If a man's word wasn't any good," the President replied when Attlee suggested that they put their private agreement in writing, "it wasn't made any better by writing it down." It was a point that Attlee, who had copies of the promises made at Quebec and Hyde Park, should well have appreciated.[70] But Attlee had received all the assurance he needed, especially if he was also told, as the Joint Chiefs of Staff recommended, "that the United States had 'no intention' of using nuclear weapons in Korea unless they should be needed to protect evacuation of UN forces or to prevent 'a major military disaster.' "[71]

"The reassurance Attlee gained from Truman, that the United States was *not* actively considering the employment of nuclear weapons in Asia," and would not do so without British agreement, according to British and American historians, enabled him to "rightfully claim that . . . he had taken a big step toward resuming the [atomic] partnership."[72]

In addition to the uncensored transcript of their talks, Maclean received a copy of the report that Attlee made to his Cabinet upon his return. (Maclean expressed skepticism that the Americans were really prepared to abandon the idea of a limited war against China. "It is not dead yet," he predicted.) This underscores Maclean's real value. He allowed the enemy to "pierce the screen" of American intentions. He could tell Stalin exactly how far the United Nations allies were prepared to go, which threats most unnerved Washington and London, which rifts divided MacArthur from the British and American chiefs of staff, and what current of dissent ran between Anglo-American statesmen. He enabled Stalin and Mao to know not only which cards Truman and Attlee held, but how many chips Peking or Moscow would have to push into the center of the table to get London to insist that the West should fold its hand.[73]

The only way to gauge the value of this information to Stalin and Mao would be to imagine that the West had a similar source in the Kremlin. It is *believed* that Stalin held meetings of equal, if not greater, importance in Moscow with Kim Il Sung, Mao Tse-tung, and Chou En-lai. The primary source for this—the Soviets do not oblige us with even doctored, purged, or sanitized records—is Khrushchev's memoirs.

Kim Il Sung and his delegation arrived in Moscow in late December 1949, just six months after the last U.S. troops were pulled out of South Korea. Kim informed his host that he wanted "to prod the South Koreans with the point of a bayonet," and later returned to Moscow with a concrete plan, including an assurance that a popular uprising would greet the North Korean army. Still, Khrushchev reports, "Stalin had his doubts. He was worried that the Americans would jump in." He decided to consult with Mao, who had been in Moscow during the time Kim Il Sung's plans were being reviewed.

The Chinese leader was all for the action, and Stalin then gave his final approval.[74]

The West, of course, was ignorant of the meeting, but once the invasion began, they assumed something along such lines had taken place. "How could an army," Charles (Chip) Bohlen asked, "trained in every respect by the Soviet Union, with Soviet advisers at every level, and utterly dependent on Moscow for supplies, move without Soviet authorization?"[75]

Stalin approved the plan, asserts Strobe Talbott, editor of Khrushchev's memoir, with the almost "casual amateurishness with which [he] approached problems not immediately affecting the security of the Soviet Union as he understood it." And his great miscalculation, says Bohlen, who was called back to Washington from Paris after the invasion, is that "he never dreamed the United States would intervene."[76]

Mao sent Chou En-lai to Moscow (Khrushchev suggests that it was after U.S. troops crossed the 38th Parallel in early October). "At first, Stalin and Chou seemed to conclude that it would be fruitless for China to intervene." Both leaders resigned themselves to a Korea unified under Western control. But just before the Chinese prime minister was scheduled to return home, either Stalin or possibly Chou on Mao's orders—Khrushchev is unsure which—"reopened the whole matter." At the end of this review it was agreed that Peking should commit troops to Korea.[77]

It will never be known what risks the Soviets and the Chinese were unwilling to take, though it would surely be wrong to think that there were none. Instead, because of the information provided by Maclean, Peking and Moscow knew that they were fighting almost a risk-free war:

• The possibility of the United States using atomic weapons against targets in either Korea or China was almost nil. Chinese infrastructure—its industrial and power plants—was immune;

• There would be no direct retaliation, not even harassment—the so-called limited war—against China no matter what level of forces it committed;

• England was prepared to make almost any concessions to end the war, while the United States had abandoned thoughts of uniting the two Koreas, and neither country was willing to increase the level of forces in Korea even if China did.

"The avowed Chinese Communist military strategy," Hutchison explained, *"is not to attack unless success is assured."* Military strategists attributed the genius of the Chinese army to its ability to operate as "a phantom which casts no shadow. Its main secret—*its strength, its position, and its initiative*—has been kept to perfection, and therefore *it was doubly armed."*[78]

What if the situation had been reversed? What if the U.N. command had known the Chinese army's strength, its position, and its operational orders? And what if Lin Piao had not known his enemy's troop disposition? Even more important, what if someone had been able to inform the West about the extent of Stalin's commitment (as it turned out, not very deep at all), and what price—in terms of industrial and power plants—Mao was unwilling to pay, or, perhaps, that there was no limit on how far he would go?

Yet, at the very moment when Moscow could read the details of the December summit, Washington's best analysts were brainstorming to divine Chinese and Russian intentions. Their total intelligence yield was that Peking must have received "some assurances of support from the Soviet Union" before it intervened and that Peking intended "to make the U.S.-U.N. position in Korea untenable." On a slow morning, Maclean could have told the enemy significantly more than this.[79]

American lawmakers and others would later demand to know how many deaths could be laid at the feet of Maclean and his co-conspirators. In one response, *U.S. News & World Report* noted that in the week preceding his appointment, the United Nations had suffered its fewest casualties in seven weeks. U.S. war dead then totaled 5,300 and 31,000 casualties. Before it was over, 54,000 U.S. soldiers were dead and another 142,000 were wounded.[80]

It is little wonder that, to this day, Britain has wanted to conceal the extent of Maclean's information. Not only had he received intelligence that may have cost large numbers of lives, but he received it even after the Foreign Office later claimed he had been cut off.[81] The British government, however, may not have to bear the entire burden for allowing Maclean to operate at such dangerous levels.

During the spring of 1949, Lamphere and American cryptologists were groping in the dark to try to understand how classified information had been leaking to the Soviets. A breakthrough of some undetermined sort had occurred in April, however, that convinced the Bureau that Moscow's source must have been someone from inside the British embassy. Without knowing who the source was, the FBI could not be certain about whether he was still active, or whether he had moved to some other point in the British communications chain.

A prudent approach would have been to assume that the embassy had been compromised and to ensure that no vital information would be passed through it to Whitehall, or perhaps passed to Whitehall under any circumstances. The FBI, as its own internal documents suggest, realized that it had an obligation to advise the White House, the Pentagon, and the State Department that military or other secrets provided to the British might be flowing to Moscow.

Nevertheless, Hoover chose not to do this. Later, worried about recriminations, he constructed a defense in case he were ever held accountable. As late as 1965, the FBI was still polishing a response for Hoover to give if he were ever asked the reason that he had failed to warn the various national security agencies about the danger of providing secrets to the British. In a highly defensive section of the FBI Summary Report on the Maclean case entitled, "Why We Did Not Disseminate In April, 1949," the Bureau explains:

The information was not disseminated prior to the identification of Maclean in June 1951, as the Soviet agent who operated in the British Embassy in Washington [DELETED] for the following reasons:

1. The information was extremely sparse and contained insufficient data to identify the agent.

2. The information pertained to British matters and British subjects in the British Embassy [DELETED] prior to 1949.

3. An active investigation was launched by the British, most of which was carried on in London.

4. The information was furnished by [DELETED_____
[DELETED_____.

5. We were most anxious to discover any possible American angles prior to a leak that could have resulted from dissemination of the information.

"In retrospect," this section of the report concludes, "it would have been better to advise White House and State Dept. on a very high level most confidentially of this info *so that they could regulate their dealings with the British Embassy accordingly*."

Hoover, however, was never called upon to defend his failure to do this."[82]

CHAPTER NINETEEN

I was shocked at Burgess's behavior. He
practically accosted Franklin.

Kermit Roosevelt on the confrontation
between Burgess and FDR, Jr.[1]

SABOTAGE

Years later, because the temperature had reached sixty-five degrees that day, some who were there would remember it as
happening in the spring. Actually, it was Friday, January 19, 1951—
one of those balmy days during a brief thaw that Washington seems
to get every January. Philby intended for the dinner party to be no
more than a particle—though hopefully a sparkling one—in the
mosaic of social gatherings that took place throughout the nation's
capital that night; yet another milestone in his casual climb to the
top of British intelligence. Instead, it hastened his demise.

Aileen Philby had worked for days to make their most ambitious
Washington social event a success. No buffet "with those dreadful
cold cuts," which is the way Cicely Angleton remembered most
gatherings at the Philbys'. This was to be a formal dinner for twelve.[2]

Even Washington's most seasoned hosts may not have dared to
attempt the social mix that Philby did. Bringing together some of
the leading lights from both the CIA and the FBI was risky business—not merely because the rivalries between the two intelligence
organizations went beyond the sporting, but because of a deeper
chasm that bordered on class war. Hoover despised the upstart
Agency. He had come from extremely limited circumstances, and

he recruited his G-men from the Midwest's small towns and industrial centers. Many were high school graduates, village lawyers, or former policemen. Nearly all had to support themselves on their modest government salaries. Hoover expected his men to have as little contact as he did with the CIA.

The Agency's ranks were stocked with Eastern Establishment bluebloods and Ivy Leaguers, many of whom had either inherited wealth or married into it. Most of them had become fascinated with clandestine work when they joined the wartime Office of Strategic Services (OSS). Members and foes alike joked that the abbreviation stood for "Oh-So-Social." They remained with the CIA either because they could not bear to leave the world of secrecy, or because they had a sense of noblesse oblige (or, as one wag suggested, because their schools did not want them back). As the newest kid on the block, the CIA realized that although Hoover's style was déclassé, his power commanded respect, if not fear. Yet the Agency could rarely muster more than a patronizing recognition from Hoover's enlistees. For all of these reasons, the footsoldiers in both organizations rarely gathered to break bread.[3]

What made this evening particularly awkward was the presence of William K. Harvey. The thirty-five-year-old Indiana native had been forced out of the FBI by Hoover because of his reputation as a heavy drinker and a ladies' man (flaws that Hoover did not seem to notice in Mickey Ladd). Although Harvey lacked the usual prerequisites—an Ivy League degree, highly placed social contacts, and either a trust fund or a rich wife—he joined the CIA and brought with him a prized dowry: his encyclopedic knowledge of Soviet espionage. Several years later, Harvey would be introduced to President Kennedy as "America's James Bond." He shared Bond's love for guns, gadgets, action, women, and liquor. But the short pear-shaped man with heavy eyelids and a bullfrog voice more closely resembled the comedian Rodney Dangerfield than the dashing Agent 007.

The fact that Harvey prospered at the Agency only increased Hoover's disdain for both the man and the organization. When CIA chief Bedell Smith once attempted to extend an olive branch to Hoover, he asked, "Edgar, suppose you tell us what's wrong. Why can't we seem to get along?" Hoover replied, "The first thing wrong is all these ex-Bureau people over here sniping and proselytizing, and in particular Bill Harvey."[4]

Harvey had brought Lamphere into the Bureau and become his mentor. After he departed, the two men remained friendly, but any contact had to be discreet, almost surreptitious. "To Hoover, going from the Bureau to the CIA was almost as bad as going over to the Soviets," Lamphere later recalled. "It only missed it by a very few degrees." If Hoover heard that the Lampheres were "fraternizing with the enemy, there would be hell to pay."[5]

Among Philby's other guests were:

• Libby Harvey, a thin, darkly attractive native of Kentucky, who would unwittingly ignite the fireworks that night. She had never been at home in the social whirl of diplomacy, international intrigue, and great public issues. She, even more than her husband, was a proletarian operating in an environment that the upper class considered exclusively its own. Her way of feeling at ease in such company was to match the men martini for martini.

• James Angleton represented the more stereotypical CIA man. He was thirty-four and had lived in Italy where his father was an executive with National Cash Register. Angleton had graduated from a British boarding school (his Malvern played Philby's Westminster every year in soccer), and he had won recognition as an accomplished poet at Yale. Following graduation, he had attended Harvard Law School until his Yale literature professor recruited him into the OSS. He had excelled at his wartime assignments in London and Italy, and had survived the various postwar limbos until Truman finally created the CIA in 1947. Angleton had the nebulous title of liaison officer at a time when the CIA was so dependent upon finding bureaucratic allies that outreach was their main activity. He did not enter counterintelligence, which would eventually make him one of the Agency's most powerful and controversial officials, until 1954. Thin as a rail, he had a head of thick straight black hair, high cheekbones, narrow lips, and long arms which—combined with his stooped posture—gave him the appearance of a soaring eagle when he raised them in moments of animation.

• Cicely d'Autremont Angleton, "a vivacious and exceedingly bright" graduate of Vassar, was an amateur actress and considerably more outgoing than her husband. A native of Duluth, her wealthy and prominent parents had since moved to Arizona.[6]

• Dr. Wilfrid Mann, forty-three, the British science attaché, was a graduate of St. Paul's School and the Imperial College, London University. He first came to America in 1943 as part of the British atomic bomb mission. In 1946 he had been considered for appointment as the embassy's atomic energy man, but Roger Makins turned him down because he was not political enough. So, the job had gone to Donald Maclean.

• Miriam Mann came from Idaho, as did Angleton and Lamphere, and had graduated from the University of California at Berkeley with a degree in economics. An attractive, quiet woman, she seems to have been one of the few who found Kim Philby's charms resistible. She regretted the lack of support he extended to his "long-suffering wife."[7]

• Sir Robert Mackenzie, forty-four, an Oxford man, was the short, energetic, and good-natured regional director of Foreign Office security, whose duties extended to Canada and South America. Americans always found titles awkward, and Mackenzie seldom used his. Everyone called him "Bobby," but his official passport listed him as "Robert Mackenzie, Bart."—an abbreviation for the baronetcy he had inherited from his father at age thirty. One day at National Airport he was oblivious of the continual page for "Mr. Bart." Finally, the plaintive voice cried out, "Would Mr. Robert Mackenzie Bart please report to the Pan Am counter!" He was the only other person in the embassy besides Patterson and Philby who knew about the search for "Homer." All traffic about it came over the special cipher in Philby's office. Not even Franks knew about the case or saw the cables. The only bachelor among the group, Mackenzie that night escorted Canadian-born Geraldine Dack, another of Philby's devoted secretaries, to the party.[8]

As at all Philby gatherings, the cocktails consisted of pitchers of martinis and open bottles of scotch and whiskey. Philby poured the first, and then the guests were on their own. During the cocktail hour, two other officials from the British embassy stopped in for drinks but departed before dinner.

For a few uncomfortable moments, Lamphere joined a circle where Angleton was holding forth about intelligence systems, methods, and priorities. It struck Lamphere as a "bunch of crap. Blue sky stuff. It was theoretical, impractical. The West was getting its ass kicked in intelligence operations, but it wasn't because we lacked priorities." At the Bureau, Lamphere always referred to Angleton and his CIA staff as "spooks," because of their infatuation, not with winning or losing, but with playing the Great Game for its own sake.

If Angleton was like a soaring eagle, Lamphere was like a low-slung basset hound who hunts by scent and keeps his nose to the ground. He drifted over to talk to Harvey. Libby had already helped herself to a number of martinis, which reinforced Lamphere's apprehension that the cocktail hour had gone on too long.

Finally, they were called to the dining room. As they took their places, none of these spy-catching guests could have imagined that directly below their feet was a secret photo lab where Philby reproduced the documents that he filched at the embassy to pass on to Moscow.

The dinner conversation rambled amiably. A popular play had just opened in Washington written by one of Philby's former colleagues. *Seven Days to Noon* was a thriller about a demented scientist who threatened to hold London hostage until the British government pledged to stop making atom bombs. *The Washington Post*'s Richard Coe called Paul Dehn's play "the ultimate in its class."[9]

One of Mann's former associates had gained fame of quite a different nature. In September, Bruno Pontecorvo, a brilliant Italian-born atomic physicist, who had become an integral part of Britain's atomic energy community, had defected with his family to Russia. When the Manns had known him at Chalk River in Canada, he was "one of the best tennis players in the community, an amusing conversationalist, a quite popular local personality . . . [who was] not given to political views." At Harwell he was regarded as an even better physicist than Fuchs, and certainly more popular. His defection was another blow to the British and a boon to the Soviets, for whom he would play a leading role in developing the hydrogen bomb.[10]

The discussion about Korea was not much more encouraging. The Chinese had rejected two United Nations cease-fire proposals; General Johnny Walker had been killed in a jeep accident; and the Chinese forces had again crossed the 38th Parallel to begin a major offensive in the south.

It was almost 10:00 P.M. before Philby and his guests adjourned to the living room. Lamphere was relieved to have survived dinner without a major incident. Throughout the meal, Libby had been cursing in barely hushed whispers about this "typical goddamn British dinner party." "For chrissakes, Libby," he would hiss back, "be quiet." Having felt awkward during the entire evening and filled with a sense of impending doom, he was anxious to depart. As the others trailed toward the living room, the Lampheres excused themselves.

The others found places to sit on the dark, ornate stuffed sofa and chairs that were arranged around the fireplace. Another round of drinks was being passed when the irrepressible Burgess suddenly burst into the room. Mann shot a glance toward Philby, who looked surprised to see his friend. He may even have made the mistake of telling him to stay away, which would have been tantamount to an engraved invitation to an inveterate gatecrasher like Burgess.

Everyone there knew Guy except for the Harveys. As he was being introduced to Libby, Burgess, a caricaturist of some ability, swooned, "Ah, how remarkable to see the face I have been drawing all my life suddenly appear before me." Libby bit. She begged him to sketch her. The others, who knew that his drawings were primarily an outlet for Guy's savage imagination, braced themselves.

His eyes were a study in concentration as he went to work, his hands framing her face with a theatrical flair, as Libby preened. When he had finished he held up the result as if it were a placard. It was only of her head, and the hair, eyes, nose, and ears bore an identifiable likeness. But, when it got to her jaw—and, to be truthful, Libby Harvey's jaw did protrude—Burgess had drawn it "like the prow of a dreadnought with its underwater battering ram."

"I've never been so insulted in my whole life," Libby shrieked as she bolted out of her chair. She demanded that her husband, who looked to some of the guests as though he were about to punch Burgess, take her home. They headed for the door with Philby in pursuit. "It was just a bad joke," he pleaded. "Burgess meant no harm." But Harvey was having none of it. He saw in Burgess's

gratuitous insult an aristocratic contempt for his unadorned mid-
western background and that of his college dropout wife.

The rest of the guests were left behind in embarrassed silence.
Angleton glanced at Aileen. She looked destroyed. She had worked
hard to make the party a success, only to have it ruined by a man
whom she despised. Miriam Mann and Cicely Angleton followed
her into the kitchen to offer comfort. Angleton and Mann, seeking
escape from the highly charged atmosphere, slipped out to sit on the
red brick retaining wall. The evening was still beautiful. The full
moon silhouetted the two thin figures as they talked about what
Angleton later told CIA Director Smith was "a social disaster."[11]
Inside, the unrepentant Burgess helped himself to the liquor.

When Angleton and Mann returned half an hour later, they started
into the living room on the left side of the entrance when they heard
a muffled sound from the smaller sitting room to the right. They
looked inside. There, in the darkened room, sat Kim Philby with
his head cradled in his hands. The man who had never been known
to lose his self-control, the pride of the British service, was weeping.
In between his anguished sobs, he kept saying to himself over and
over, "How could you, how could you?"

One Soviet spy had, in the home of another Soviet spy, insulted
the man whose job it was to flush out Soviet spies. As Talleyrand
would have put it, it was worse than a crime; it was a blunder.

★   ★   ★

Philby might better have bleated, "How could I, how could I?"
His later claim that he had Burgess live with him because Guy "was
much less likely to make himself conspicuous in my household than
in a bachelor flat," was either another of his pathetic alibis or sheer
stupidity. The dinner party was only one in a series of hammerblows
that Burgess had landed to shatter Philby's career. It was not even
the first.[12]

In December he had made his debut in Georgetown society at a
Joseph Alsop dinner party for Pamela and Michael Berry. Berry was
the owner of the London *Daily Telegraph* and Burgess's Eton classmate. When Guy, who saw journalism as a ticket out of his failed
government career, heard that Alsop was hosting a gathering for the
visiting Berrys, he tried to invite himself.

"Sorry, Guy, there's no room at the table," Alsop responded. Burgess persisted to the point of pleading. Alsop finally yielded. "You can drop by for a drink later if you like." Burgess arrived drunk, unshaven, and unkempt, and soon started denouncing America's Korean War policy. Alsop, annoyed with himself for having agreed to let him come at all, ordered Burgess out, giving this admirable American the distinction of being, as far as is known, the only one to have ejected both Maclean and Burgess from his home.[13]

The following day Angleton was lunching with a friend near Martin's restaurant in Georgetown. Burgess suddenly approached and asked whether he could borrow a few dollars. Angleton was appalled. As he told the story later:

> He wore a peculiar garb, namely a white British naval jacket which was dirty and stained. He was intoxicated, unshaven and had, from the appearance of his eyes, not washed since he last slept. He stated that he had taken two or three days' leave and had "an interesting binge" the night before at Joe Alsop's house.

Burgess informed Angleton—after ordering the cheapest bourbon available—that he and a Long Island friend were going to make a fortune by importing thousands of the type of naval jacket he was wearing and "sell them for fantastic profits to exclusive shops in New York." He also pressed Angleton for a date so that they could "test the overdrive on the Oldsmobile [*sic*]."

When he returned to his office, Angleton called Philby and told him about the encounter. Philby, no doubt staggered by the image of Burgess begging from one of his most prized CIA contacts, was at a loss for words, confirming only that Burgess had taken some leave. Angleton was completely trusting of Philby. Years later, he would describe how Philby's friend and SIS colleague Nicholas Elliott, who had worshipped Kim, was filled with rage when he realized that Philby had betrayed him. Eliot told Angleton that he would shoot Philby if he ever saw him again. "I never felt that way," Angleton said dispassionately.[14]

His anger would eventually manifest itself in a paranoia so extreme that it not only consumed him, but also, many believed, destroyed the CIA itself. That situation was still several years away. Even in

December 1950, however, he thought it strange and unprofessional that Philby shared openly with Burgess the identities of his CIA and FBI contacts. Burgess was not part of British intelligence and had no need to know; what is more, he was completely indiscreet. But Angleton said nothing to Philby.[15]

Given Burgess's advance billing, it is difficult to understand the reason that the embassy gave him preferred office space, generous leave arrangements, and plum assignments such as escorting Eden. Even more baffling is that, once he started exceeding even his past uncouth behavior, the embassy continued to send official bouquets his way. In January, even after the Alsop dinner (where other embassy officials were present), the dinner party (when two embassy officials were present), and the begging incident involving the CIA and State Department officials, Burgess was chosen to represent the British nation at a conference on international affairs at the Citadel.[16]

For Burgess, it was an ideal assignment. The Citadel, a private military academy in Charleston, South Carolina, was home to two thousand teenage boys. Further, his friend Albert Fequant, Second Secretary at the French embassy, was also on the program. In addition, Emily and Nicholas Roosevelt, who owned a nearby plantation, agreed to send letters of introduction to all the town's leading lights.

On Wednesday morning, February 28, Burgess aimed his Lincoln in the direction of the historic old city, five hundred thirty miles from Washington. At some point, it is not clear when, he took on a passenger, James A. Turck. Not much is known of him. He was born near Carthage, New York, and had served in the air force. He was in his late twenties, of slight build, a drifter with no fixed address who occasionally worked for a used car dealer in Paterson, New Jersey. At various times, Turck and Burgess claimed that he was a hitchhiker picked up en route. But Turck also maintained that he had already known Burgess and had started the trip with him. There is convincing evidence that this claim is true.

Just outside Richmond, Burgess asked Turck to drive. They passed Sam Mellichamp of the Virginia State Police on Highway 301 near Petersburg at a speed of over eighty miles an hour (the speed limit was sixty). Mellichamp gave chase, and the Lincoln quickly pulled over. As Turck was handing Mellichamp his driver's license, Burgess intervened. "I am a diplomat," he said, passing his passport and driver's license through the window, "and Mr. Turck is my chauffeur; we are both protected by diplomatic immunity."

"That's nice, Mr. Burgess," Mellichamp, a ruggedly built man with handsome features said in his polite, southern accent, "but Mr. Turck is driving, not you, and he is an American citizen." Burgess started to argue. Mellichamp cut him off. "Mr. Burgess, if you'll have Mr. Turck follow me into Petersburg, you can explain all about your diplomatic privileges to Mr. David Lyon, the local justice of the peace." Burgess, apparently confident that someone who had dazzled Churchill, Eden, Keynes, and Frankfurter could surely dispose of some country bumpkins, agreed.[17]

While neither a lawyer nor a judge, David Lyon, a short man with great energy, was proud of his role in the judicial process. He had handled other cases involving diplomatic immunity, but he had never heard anyone claim that their "chauffeur" was entitled to immunity:

> I'm sorry Mr. Burgess, but I cannot accept your explanation. I am setting bond for Mr. Turck at $47.50. I will set a trial date before Judge Francis Binford. You may appear at that time and argue your case of diplomatic immunity if you wish. If Mr. Turck does not appear, the bond will be forfeited.

"Will you take a check?" Burgess asked. "No," Lyon replied, "I will not." Humbled by the American court system, Burgess, more flustered than angered, went out to try to find a bank or a hotel that would cash a check.[18]

Lyon went into the back room and picked up the phone. He was sure that he was correct, but he did not want to precipitate an international incident because of a speeding ticket. He called Judge Binford, who was also a friend and neighbor, to confer. Binford, it turned out, also knew something about immunity. On one occasion, Roosevelt's boys had been stopped for speeding through his county at more than ninety miles an hour. "We're on our way to Warm Springs to get ready for the President," they argued. "Mr. Roosevelt is counting on us."

"Is that right?" Binford replied, pretending to be impressed.

"Well, I'm just a two-by-four county judge. I don't know anything about that sort of thing. Why don't you go to that phone over there and call up the President. If he says to set you free, I will." The President was much too busy, they pleaded, to be called about such trivial matters. "Well, then, call Eleanor; call anybody you want." They didn't move. "All right," Binford offered, "you pay the fine, and when you leave here, you drive slowly. But, when you get back to Washington, if you can get the President to send me a note, I'll send your money back."

His eyes twinkling as he related the story over forty years later, Binford, a large man with soft features, added "I never had to send the money back."[19]

"You did the right thing," he now told Lyon. "If Mr. Turck can't post bail, lock him up." Lyon hung up with a sigh of relief.

Binford, however, was not eager to create a huge diplomatic row, either. He called his friend John Battle, the Governor of Virginia. "You're absolutely right," Battle thundered. "If they can't post bond, so far as I'm concerned you can throw 'em both in jail."

Meanwhile, after his conversation with Binford, Lyon went over to talk to the forlorn Turck. "You know," he began in a soothing voice, "You don't know that this fellow Burgess is ever coming back." Turck looked at him quizzically. Lyon spelled it out:

The summons is against you. If you can't post bail you'll be held until your trial. That could be five days, maybe more. After that you'll either have to pay the fine or serve time. You've got no money. The time could be thirty days or more. That's a long time for one speeding ticket.

Turck started to protest his innocence—Burgess had egged him on and told him to drive fast. Lyon swiveled his chair around to the typewriter beside his desk. It was then that Lyon learned for the first time that Burgess had been stopped twice before on that day. The first incident had occurred near Woodbridge, Virginia, twenty miles from Washington. (It is Turck's familiarity with this episode that suggests that he began the trip with Burgess). The second time he was stopped near Ashland, just north of Richmond, when he tried to pass an entire Army convoy at ninety miles an hour.

Each time, Burgess pleaded diplomatic immunity, and each time he was let off with a warning. No ticket was written or issued. When Turck had finished, Lyon read the statement out loud and then handed it to him. "Does this represent what you just told me?" he asked. "Yes," replied Turck, as he signed the affidavit. Just then, the phone rang. It was Binford. "Don't worry about anything. We've been backed all the way to the Governor."[20]

A short time later, Burgess reappeared with the cash and paid the fine. As he and Turck resumed their journey, Lyon got in his car and drove over to show Binford the affidavit. The judge decided that it made such good reading, he sent a copy of it to Governor Battle. None of this was known to Burgess, who spent the night in a seedy motel room outside of Charleston. Turck later admitted to the FBI that Burgess "made homosexual advances," which he rejected. Hoover believed half of that story.[21]

The next morning, March 1, Burgess put Turck on a bus back to Paterson and checked into the Francis Marion Hotel in Charleston's historic downtown district. In the course of the next twelve hours, he managed to insult and enrage people whose prominence and sheer numbers were impressive even for Burgess.

When Benjamin Kittredge, a relative of Emily Roosevelt and a pillar of the community, took Guy for a personal tour of the Cypress Gardens, which he had spent forty years and much of his fortune developing, Guy passed out drunk on the floor of his boat. By the time he arrived at the dinner in the Citadel's cavernous mess hall, Guy still had not sobered up. He was seated at the head table with a State Department official; professors from Duke, Princeton, and, of course, the Citadel; Féquant (Second Secretary at the French embassy); and General Charles Summerall, a former chief of staff of the Army and now President of the Citadel. Still remarkably vigorous at eighty-four, Summerall reflected southern pride in the 110-year-old military school whose cannoneers fired the Confederacy's first shots in what southerners still called the "War for Southern Independence."[22]

Sprinkled in the audience were friends and relatives who had been encouraged by the Roosevelts to attend to hear their brilliant and witty British embassy friend. What they and the other nearly two thousand five hundred listeners were subjected to, however, was a diatribe on the failures of American foreign policy, especially its refusal to recognize Red China (Britain did not escape unscathed; Burgess attacked her "classic mistake" in India). He said much more, but his speech was so slurred that most of it was incoherent. When he finished, there was only a smattering of polite applause.[23]

Summerall was incensed at "this highly contentious and unpopular speech." Burgess was indifferent. As the next speaker began his presentation, Guy rested his head against the back of his chair and went to sleep.[24] The Roosevelts' friends were appalled. The most shell-shocked of all was Josephine Pinckney. The years when the city thrived as an important commercial center in the British Empire were known as "Charleston in the Age of the Pinckneys." The most prominent landmark in Charleston Harbor was Pinckney Castle. Now, Josephine Pinckney was mortified by the spectacle of the man passed out on the dais. She had invited the upper crust of Charleston society to a cocktail party the next night in Guy Burgess's honor. It was too late to cancel.

Actually, the party was amazingly successful. Guy was at his best and most charming. There were only one or two glitches. The Kittredges refused to attend. And Emily Fishburne Whaley, Emily Roosevelt's niece, was caused some slight embarrassment. She had not been in the mess hall on the previous night, and had spent that day giving Guy a tour of Charleston that included a long lunch in one of its finest restaurants. She was completely taken with Burgess's erudition and charm, and could scarcely wait to introduce her new friend to her husband that night. Yet, when she came gushing up to him at the cocktail party, Guy stared blankly. He could not for the life of him remember who she was.

Burgess was back in Washington on Monday, March 4. Ten days later, Battle wrote a scathing letter to John F. Simmons, the State Department's chief of protocol, attacking Burgess's "flagrant violation of our traffic laws which might very well have resulted in a disastrous accident." Citing the previous use by other Western diplomats of immunity, he fumed that "I cannot and will not continue to countenance utter disregard of life and property on the highways." Enclosed was a copy of Turck's affidavit.[25]

Because Franks was in London from March 10 to March 28, the State Department did not bother to forward the Governor's letter and Turck's affidavit to the embassy until March 30. Meanwhile, Burgess, thanks to an introduction provided by Philby, was invited to a cocktail party at the home of Kermit Roosevelt, a senior CIA official. Philby was not present, although just two weeks earlier, on the very night that Burgess had spent with Turck, Philby had enjoyed a social evening at Roosevelt's Georgetown home.

Kermit, the grandson of Theodore Roosevelt, would eventually win fame for his role in plotting the overthrow of Iranian Prime Minister Mossadegh, in order to return the Shah of Iran to the Peacock Throne in August 1953. Among other guests on the night of March 16 were Franklin D. Roosevelt, Jr.; Colonel J.C. Windsor Lewis, the British embassy's military attaché; C.A. Gerald Meade, a First Secretary at the embassy; and a pleasant American woman named Mrs. W. B. Smith.

Guy immediately struck up a conversation with FDR, Jr., a tall and strikingly good-looking man of thirty-six who had, along with other members of his family, accused Truman of being needlessly antagonistic toward the Russians. He fully supported the decision to send American forces to fight in Korea, however, and soon he and Burgess were at loggerheads over the war. As their voices rose, conversation in the rest of the room trailed off. Finally it became so heated that Kermit and Lewis stepped in to separate the two.

"I was shocked by Burgess's behavior," Kermit Roosevelt later recalled, "he practically accosted Franklin." Guy predictably was oblivious of his host's wrath as well as the shocked reaction of the other guests. Not only did he remain, but he was one of the last to depart.

That night when she arrived home, Mrs. Smith told her husband about the unpleasant incident created by Mr. Burgess of the British embassy. Her husband happened to be Walter Bedell Smith, Eisenhower's wartime chief of staff, ambassador to Moscow, and now the director of the Central Intelligence Agency. A colleague once described Smith as the most even-tempered man in the world: he was always angry.[26]

The next morning, Kermit Roosevelt marched into Allen Dulles's office and shuddered with outrage as he recounted the performance of Philby's houseguest. As it happened, Dulles had already heard about it from Smith.[27]

Not surprisingly, news of Burgess's systematic and relentless sabotage of Philby's career finally reached MI6 headquarters. Toward the end of March, Colonel Valentine Vivian, an early patron of Philby's, flew to Washington "and told Kim he thought it was very unsuitable for Burgess to live with him." Philby supposedly replied that "he had told [Burgess] to get out" and that Burgess's mother had come to Washington to find him an apartment.[28]

Burgess's mother did come to America in late March or early April, although there is no evidence that Philby had told Guy to leave or that he or she ever looked for alternative housing. In any event, Guy took her to Charleston, where they arrived on April 5. Leaving aside the nagging issue of how he was able to get more leave, this trip involved other peculiarities. For instance, while his mother flew down, Burgess drove. Further, Turck claimed that he made the trip with Burgess (which would explain the separate travel arrangements for Mrs. Basset), and that Burgess told him that the reason for the trip was to take pictures of the Savannah River site where the United States was planning to construct plants to build the hydrogen bomb. In the back seat of the car were "a camera similar to those used by newspaper photographers and . . . a movie camera and a tripod." Finally, Burgess remained in close touch with Philby by phone and telegram throughout the trip.[29]

If Burgess actually made a photo reconnaissance of the area, he could not have seen much. Truman announced the decision to build the "Super" on October 10, 1950, and it was only in November that the Savannah River site, based on terrain and the mineral content of its water, was selected. Construction on the huge water-cooled uranium furnaces had not yet begun. Still, it may have been enough to earn Burgess the distinction of being the first hydrogen bomb spy in the West.[30]

While he was on this excursion, the embassy finally received Battle's letter and Turck's affidavit. The State Department was advised on April 7 that Ambassador Franks "is consulting the Foreign Office about the action to be taken."[31]

Burgess arrived back in Washington on Saturday, April 14, and was called in by Ambassador Franks on either Monday or Tuesday. The precise exchange is uncertain, other than that Franks told him to pack because he was being sent home. Unprepared for this sudden turn of events, Burgess immediately stormed into Greenhill's office "boilling with rage." How dare the Ambassador claim that he had exercised poor judgment and behaved irresponsibly! When he had calmed down a little, Guy admitted that it would be embarrassing to return to London under such inauspicious circumstances. He had told his friends that he would take Washington by storm, dine with Dean Acheson—Brigadier Brilliant telling the provincials how to conduct foreign policy. Now, he was being sent home in disgrace.[32]

On Wednesday, April 18, fifty days after the incident at Petersburg, Virginia, the embassy notified the State Department that "Mr. Burgess has been recalled by the Foreign Office. He will be leaving Washington very shortly and will not be returning to this Embassy."[33]

The embassy had finally done for Philby what neither he nor the Soviets had the wit to do for themselves—get Burgess out of Washington. But it may have been too late. Philby and his elite Soviet colleagues had placed his career in Burgess's hands, and Guy had smashed it with the craven delight of a child who has been handed a figurine and a hammer.

Burgess had become a one-man wrecking crew that had taken aim at the compliant Philby's career. In two months those known to have been hit by the flying debris included the son of America's most revered political figure (FDR, Jr.), the wife of the CIA director (Mrs. Smith), the head of CIA counterespionage (Harvey), the Governor of Virginia (Battle), and indirectly the director and deputy director (Dulles) of the CIA as well as another of its senior officials, Kermit Roosevelt.

Before he left Washington, Burgess had one last encounter. During his months in America, he had left no stone unturned in seeking out friends from his past life such as Grant, Lawford, and W. H. Auden (whom he had seen in New York the day after Kermit Roosevelt's party), among many others. But, he failed to contact one of the most obvious persons for him to have called, at least according to Michael Straight.

This omission is surprising, for once he had his claws into someone, Burgess never let go, and he had once had his claws very deeply into Straight and had exercised considerable influence over him.

Further, Straight represented everything that Burgess liked in friends. He was rich, well connected, and led a glamorous life.

Straight attributes the reason he was never called to a confrontation that he had had with Burgess and Blunt in 1949, during a chance encounter in London (according to Straight, after 1940 all his encounters with Burgess were by chance). These were the two men whose worldly brilliance once enthralled him, and for whom at Cambridge he felt, as he wrote his mother, a "violent love."[34] Aware that he could report their Soviet ties, the two now demanded to know whether Straight had already turned them in to the authorities. He assured them that he had not. (This was a lie that turned out to be the truth. For, as has already been noted, Dr. Welderhall had not, despite Straight's belief to the contrary, informed her husband at the British embassy that Burgess was a Soviet agent.)

Straight reminded Guy that at their previous encounter in 1947, Burgess had said that he was planning to leave government. Guy now replied that he had intended to, but had then received another offer. He assured Straight this time that "he was about to leave the government for good." Burgess and Blunt left the meeting satisfied that Straight had taken no action.[35]

Straight believes that Burgess never contacted him during his Washington tour because he did not want Straight to know that he was still in government. That is, the man who raised the concept of indiscretion and self-destructive behavior to new levels, who insulted war heroes such as General Summerall, tough intelligence cops such as Bill Harvey, and formidable political figures such as FDR, Jr. avoided the vacillating Straight out of fear.

If this were so, it would also mean that Burgess would have had to believe that Straight was capable of destroying his own very plush life; if he had betrayed them, he would also have had to betray himself. But Burgess had taken Michael's measure during those first days at Trinity. It seems unlikely he would have concluded that Straight was prepared to jeopardize his own considerable Washington reputation.

In any event, the two did meet on the eve of Burgess's departure. According to Straight, he had just completed an interview with a British official and was leaving the embassy grounds when he saw

Burgess standing on Massachusetts Avenue vainly waving for a taxi. Straight pulled over, Burgess hopped in, and without apparently registering much surprise, asked his once close associate to drop him downtown.

Although the distance they traveled was short, Straight apparently acquired a prodigious amount of information about Burgess's experiences in America including the trip to Charleston, Governor Battle's letters, the Lincoln, and Burgess's recall to London. Straight says he angrily reproached Burgess for breaking his earlier "promise" to leave government. And he again warned him to resign his Foreign Office position or this time, because of the threat he posed to the Korean war effort, Straight really would take action.

Burgess blithely replied that he was about to return to England and planned to resign as soon as he arrived in London.[36]

Straight places their encounter in mid–March, but this cannot be accurate. As has been noted, Battle's letter did not arrive at the embassy until March 30, and Guy did not know that he was to be shipped home until April 16 at the earliest. He finally left Washington on April 26. Because he spent several of those ten days in New York, there were only three, perhaps four, days on which this meeting could have occurred.

Whenever it occurred, it was at a time when, unbeknownst to Burgess, he was threatened by something more formidable than Straight's threats. By early March, the Foreign Office had developed a "short list" of suspects for "Homer." It read like a Who's Who of their most illustrious diplomats—Roger Makins (later Lord Sherfield and ambassador to Washington during the Eisenhower administration), Paul Gore-Booth (later Lord Gore-Booth and Permanent Under Secretary), Michael Wright (later Sir Michael and ambassador to several countries), and Donald Maclean.[37]

By early April the list had been narrowed to two—Gore-Booth and Maclean. Philby was doing everything in his power to confuse the situation. He tried to convince Patterson and Mackenzie that the culprit was Gore-Booth. "Homer" in its Russian form is "Gomer," a near anagram of Gore. "Homer-Gomer"—was Mackenzie unable to see the connection? According to Philby, later confirmed by Mackenzie, Sir Robert was taken in and gave "short-odds that Gore-Booth was 'Homer' "[38]

On Tuesday, April 17, however, perhaps within hours of Burgess's dressing down by Ambassador Franks, British authorities concluded that Maclean was "Homer." The clinching piece of evidence: "Homer" had traveled to New York twice a week to meet with his Soviet control. His cover story was that he was going there to see his pregnant wife. Maclean was soon put under surveillance in London and his phone was tapped.[39]

According to Philby, his Soviet control gave him permission to tell Burgess before he left Washington that Maclean was in a severe bind that threatened everyone in the Cambridge spy network. If he told Burgess, and subsequent events suggest that he did, it was just one more bad decision piled upon a mound of others by Philby and Soviet intelligence.[40]

Burgess had helped to plan a party in New York on the weekend of April 21 for James Farmer, an artist who was staying with Alan Maclean. Farmer, whom Alan considered his closest friend, had known the Maclean brothers since 1939, and had met Burgess at their home several times. He had come to New York from Brazil to show his paintings at the British-American Gallery. But Guy, despondent over his dismissal, did not go to New York that weekend.[41]

He did make one more trip from Washington to New York between April 16 and April 26, and then returned to New York on April 27, where he remained until his departure five days later. Those last days in America (more leave time at the British taxpayer's expense) were ones of parties and farewells. Burgess was filled with melancholy. "I'm very depressed," he wrote Emily Roosevelt the day before he sailed. At a bon voyage party given that night, he was uncharacteristically quiet and subdued.

"The memory of such an evening of music making among friends will never be forgotten," he told Norman Luker, an old BBC colleague in whose New York apartment he was staying. Then he asked Luker if he could use his "sound mirror," as tape recorders were then called. He wanted to make a record of the crowning moment of his life—his meeting with Churchill, when he tried to boost the spirits of the man who later rallied the Western world.

The following day, Burgess was so concerned that he might have recorded something "incriminating," that he rushed back to Luker's apartment to listen to it again, and almost missed his departure. His host offered to destroy it, but Burgess declined. Then he made a dash for the *Queen Mary*.

For some reason he also left behind his most treasured possession. When the FBI later searched Alan Maclean's apartment at 123 East 55th Street, they found the book from Churchill. It was inscribed to him just as Burgess had claimed.[42]

CHAPTER TWENTY

> NY search name Donald McLean and Mac
> Lean thru fortythree to fortyfive telephone
> directories in effort to identify NY address.
> Conduct immediate discreet investigation
> verify address if located and develop data re
> wife's background.
>
> Hoover's urgent June 6 teletype to the FBI's
> New York office

ESCAPE

The news poured out of the first floor wire service machines so fast on the morning of June 7 that they repeatedly ran out of paper. Dean Acheson, angry and impatient, finally ordered the press office not to waste time running "tear sheets" up to his fifth floor offices. Instead, Ruth Griffith, a secretary in the press office, read each new revelation over an open line to Barbara Evans, Acheson's secretary, who rushed them in to him as soon as she had typed them up:

- *Scotland Yard officers and French detectives are hunting for two British Government employees who are believed to have left London with the intention of getting to Moscow. All French airports and frontiers are being watched.*
- *According to a friend, they planned the journey "to serve their idealistic purposes." News of the plan was given by the friend who said they expected him to go with them. The friend backed out.*
- *The Foreign Office announced today that two members of the Foreign*

Service have been missing from their homes since May 25. One is Mr. D. D. Maclean, the other Mr. G. F. de M. Burgess.

- *Maclean was suspected of being an enemy agent and was about to be taken in for questioning when he disappeared.*
- *There is speculation in both London and Washington that a "Third Man" tipped off Maclean just as British authorities were about to take him in.*
- *Shaken State Department officials have expressed a lack of confidence in the Foreign Office and are turning away all inquiries with "This is a British matter—ask them."*
- *The largest manhunt in history has been launched to find the missing diplomats.*
- *15,000 Secret Service men, master detectives, diplomatic personnel, and policemen are combing Western Europe, peering into cafes, hotels, airports and bordellos looking for the vanished diplomats.*
- *British officials became alarmed when Maclean failed to show up for work on Monday, May 28. They kept the disappearances secret from the United States government and Parliament for ten days.*
- *Maclean was considered one of the Foreign Office's most promising officials and was well known and highly regarded by his American associates.*
- *The search is centering in southern Italy where it is thought possible they may be staying with the British poet W. H. Auden or Truman Capote, an American novelist.*
- *Authorities on several continents are flooded with reports that the vanished diplomats have been seen simultaneously in Florence, Istanbul, Detroit, the Pyrenees, Cyprus, Malta, Miami, Paris, San Francisco, New York, Warsaw and Prague.*[1]

Among the items not on the news ticker:

• In Saigon, former special assistant to Dean Acheson Edmund Gullion, who was about to receive a visit from Congressman John F. Kennedy, was so incredulous over reports that Maclean had fled behind the Iron Curtain that his initial instinct was to return to Washington and testify to Maclean's character and ability.

• In Chicago, Valentine Lawford was changing planes when he was spotted by a colleague who told him that two friends from his Cambridge days were assumed to have bolted for Russia. "How could they?" Lawford demanded. "They know too much about it."

• In Philadelphia, Nicholas Roosevelt "was so goddamned mad at Burgess when he heard the news he wanted to shoot the bastard." He was reportedly a very good shot.

• In Sao Paulo, James Farmer was drinking whiskey in a bar and told D. J. Darling he had received a cable from Donald Maclean in Helsinki.

• In Washington, a proposal to improve atomic cooperation with Great Britain was stricken from the National Security Council's June 18 agenda.

• In New York, Robert Grant, Burgess's old Eton classmate, told FBI agents that to find Guy they should "search the sewers of Paris."[2]

★   ★   ★

Over the next several days the State Department was able to piece together the following story:

• On the morning of Friday, May 25, Foreign Secretary Herbert Morrison authorized British security authorities to question Maclean about suspicions that he may have been passing information to the Soviets. The interrogation was not to take place until the following Monday at the earliest, and possibly even later to allow for more time to strengthen the case against him.

• That night, however, Maclean fled the country with Guy Burgess, who had booked passage for them on a cross-Channel steamer. The men disembarked in France and had not been seen since.

• On Monday, May 28, an unidentified man told security authorities that he believed that Maclean and Burgess had gone to Moscow to "serve their idealistic purposes." Melinda Maclean also reported her husband missing to the Foreign Office.

• No one could explain the reason that Burgess, who was not suspected of anything other than being a dissolute, had gone with Maclean.[3]

The State Department scrambled to find the real story behind this implausible sequence of events. They got no help from the British embassy, which seemed to be genuinely in the dark; the FBI, which had only a few hours' head start but had infinitely greater investigative capacities; or the CIA, the first in America to realize what had happened.

The CIA apparently knew no later than Monday, May 28. Early that afternoon, Alfred Corning Clark, the head of the CIA's New York station, where he was "liaison to corporate America," rushed into the offices of *New York Times* managing editor E. L. James with an urgent request. The CIA wanted the *Times* to put Samuel Pope Brewer, their correspondent in Spain, on immediate leave of absence to work for the CIA.

"James was too good a newspaperman not to smell a rat," Harrison Salisbury wrote later about the unusual request. "Although he didn't know what kind of rat it was," James turned Clark down flat. Afterward, he wondered about the urgency. And why Brewer?

When the news broke ten days later that Maclean and Burgess had vanished, James correctly concluded that Clark's visit must have been connected to their disappearance. But he still did not know how. That was because Kim Philby's name was completely unknown at the time, and it would be years before his name was publicly linked to the case. The pieces did not finally fall into place until Philby himself bolted for Russia; Brewer had known Philby when they both were covering the Spanish Civil War (Brewer was then with the *Chicago Tribune*).[4]

The CIA must have received its first tip from the French, upon whom British authorities were forced to rely once they had realized that Maclean and Burgess were on the Continent. The French, for their part, were notoriously indifferent about keeping secrets, especially those that did not compromise them. (When the story finally broke, it came from sources not in England, but in France.)[5]

It should come as no surprise that the CIA immediately suspected Philby of complicity. They did not know about the search for "Homer," nor anything about Maclean, but they knew something about Burgess, thanks to Bill Harvey, the man whose wife he had insulted so egregiously. Philby had deluded himself into believing that the profuse apology he had phoned to Harvey the morning after the dinner party had been accepted. Something beyond personal animosity was nagging at Harvey, however. He wondered what would explain the improbable link between the highly touted Philby, and a despicable lowlife like Burgess? Even before he had heard that Burgess had fled with Maclean, he began digging into Philby's background.[6]

"Harvey was smart, with a nose for a spy," Peter Wright, a British counterintelligence officer wrote in his best-selling *Spycatcher*.

"While others paused for doubt, Harvey pursued Philby with implacable vengeance."[7]

* * *

In England, among those who knew something had gone terribly wrong, an eerie calm prevailed between May 28—when the diplomats disappearance had been discovered—and June 7, when their escape became public. On May 30, MI5 came to Tatsfield to question Melinda, whose baby was due in two weeks. She told them that Donald had brought a man named Roger Stiles home on Friday night. Later, he and Donald had driven off for a "business appointment" from which they never returned. "Stiles" was subsequently identified as Guy Burgess.[8] Also on May 30 Alan Maclean was summarily recalled to London; his diplomatic career was over. Meanwhile, Harriet and Mrs. Dunbar rushed to England so that they could be at Melinda's side.[9]

For all the debilitating leaks suffered by the Foreign Office during the preceding few years—not a few of which can be attributed to Maclean—the realization that he was a spy and that he had taken flight to elude his accusers was a remarkably well-kept secret. Things appeared normal inside the Foreign Office. Even Robert Cecil and his American Department colleagues were unaware "that anything was amiss." Before Donald left, there had been a minor flap about whether the British should refer to the disputed island territories off Argentina as "the Falklands" or "the Malvinas." In an attempt to resolve this pressing issue, Sir Francis Evans, back from New York and not yet appointed ambassador to Israel, sent a memo to the American Department on May 29: "Mr. Maclean, may I have your views please?"[10]

When Cecil finally was made aware of the situation, he realized that senior officials were gripped by a paralysis of disbelief. Permanent Under Secretary of the Foreign Office William Strang and his top advisers had nine days to prepare for the shocked reaction Parliament and the public were certain to have once the story broke. But they did nothing:

The Diplomatic Service with its links to the throne had always gone on the assumption that its loyalty was irrefragable; that its status and

tradition set it apart from, and above, the rest of the Civil Service . . .
At one blow this whole framework of mutual confidence and trust had
been shattered; it had been built up over more than a century and it
could not be reconstructed.[11]

Until the last moment the Foreign Office clung desperately and
irrationally to the hope that Burgess and Maclean could be captured
and returned, and the whole ugly episode suppressed. That possibility vanished when Larry Solon, the American-born Paris correspondent for the London *Daily Express,* received an anonymous tip on
the night of June 6 that the French police were searching for two
missing British diplomats whose last names were Burgess and Maclean. Unable to obtain verification for the story from the Foreign
Office, Solon's editors decided to print the story but omit the names.
Almost immediately the Foreign Office "collapsed and ceased to
function. The Office banged and barred the door, pulled down the
blinds and tried to block the keyhole."[12]

June 6 had been a routine day in Washington; President Truman
had presided that morning over the ninety-third meeting of the
National Security Council, which agreed to consider at its June 18
meeting a proposal to amend the McMahon Act so that atomic
information could be exchanged with the British. The initiative was
certain to be passed, primarily because Secretary of Defense George
C. Marshall and CIA Director Bedell Smith, both of whom had
formed deep wartime ties with the British, were solidly behind it.[13]

That afternoon Linwood Williams, a salesman at Mayflower Motors, called Esther Whitfield to tell her that "an individual who
happened to see Burgess's car sitting on the Mayflower car lot
without a license plate inquired of him if it were for sale." This must
have been a relief for Esther. She had taken on legal responsibility
for the car, and it had proved to be nothing but a headache. It
somehow had rolled down the incline of Philby's driveway on May 7
and crashed into her car and Philby's as well. She was responsible
for obtaining insurance estimates for all three cars, and Burgess's
had to be towed to two different garages. Burgess would want at
least $750 for his car, Esther told Williams, adding that she "expected
momentarily to hear from him."[14]

That evening Ambassador Franks and his staff entertained Washington's political, diplomatic, and social elite at the British embassy's annual garden party in honor of the King's birthday. Little did they realize that only blocks away at FBI headquarters, developments were occurring that would forever alter the world of British diplomacy.

The FBI, apparently within an hour or two after Solon had called his paper in London, had just been alerted to Maclean's flight. This is an immensely controversial point. For decades a number of British Foreign Office and security officials fostered the notion that the FBI was a full partner in the "Homer" investigation. It has even been claimed that Hoover not only knew Maclean was to be questioned, but pressured the British to delay doing so. Lamphere's assertions that prior to June 6 the Bureau did not even know Maclean's name, let alone that he was a suspect who had escaped on May 25, have evoked gasps of disbelief in London.[15]

Documents obtained under the Freedom of Information Act, however, prove that Lamphere was correct. Hoover did not order a "name check," the first step in an FBI investigation, until the afternoon of June 6. When the urgent teletype went out from Bureau headquarters to the FBI's New York and Washington field offices, Hoover and his associates thought Maclean had lived in New York, were unsure how long he had remained in the United States, and did not know how to spell his name:

> NY search name Donald McLean and Mac Lean thru fortythree to fortyfive telephone directories in effort to identify NY address. Conduct immediate and discreet investigation verify address if located and develop data re wife's background. WFO [Washington field office] check I&Rs [Intelligence and Research in the State Department] and State Records re McLean and wife.[16]

The next morning, Thursday, June 7, the front page of London's *Daily Express* shouted the news that "Yard Hunts Two Britons."

"It was the biggest news blockbuster since the blitz on London," Solon recalled without excessive immodesty years later. Cecil confirms that "the news bursts forth in the *Daily Express* with a crescendo of horns, trumpets, tubas and trombones . . . the towers of Whitehall [seemed] to totter."[17] As the presses were rolling in the early morning hours, Philip Jordan, Prime Minister Attlee's press secretary and a long-time friend of Donald Maclean who knew that his disappearance would become public the next day, awoke from his sleep, cried out, and fell back, dead of a heart attack at age forty-eight.[18]

The phone rang at "a horribly early hour" at Philby's house the morning of June 7. It was Geoffrey Patterson, MI5's man at the British embassy, calling to tell Philby that a lengthy "Most Immediate" cable had just come in from London. Patterson's secretary was on leave. Could Philby ask Esther to come down and help out? According to Philby, when he arrived at the embassy several hours later, both Patterson and Esther were looking pale and distraught. Then, says Philby, the following exchange took place:

"Kim, the bird has flown," Patterson said in an urgent half-whisper.

"What bird? Not Maclean?" Philby responded.

"Yes," Patterson answered. "But there's worse than that . . . *Guy Burgess* has gone with him." At that, Philby says, in what may be one of the few truthful statements in his book, his shock was no longer feigned.[19]

Dean Acheson was not in a good mood as he drove to work that morning. He dreaded yet another appearance (his sixth) before a special Joint Senate Committee investigating America's sorrowful Far Eastern policy. Republicans were trying to prove that the loss of China and MacArthur's dismissal were part of a conspiracy that the Democrats had entered into with Stalin at Yalta. Suddenly, he heard on the radio the news that Donald Maclean had disappeared. Although he would later tell the Senate committee that he did not know either Maclean or Burgess, as soon as he arrived at his office, Acheson exclaimed to Jack Hickerson, "My God, that sonofabitch [Maclean] knew everything."[20]

While Acheson was making his way to Foggy Bottom, the New York field office sent Hoover the first rudimentary facts about Maclean:

Rebutel [re bureau teletype] June six. Donald Duart Mac Lean and wife Melinda Marling Mac Lean, nee Melinda Marling, arrive US May six fortyfour on Queen Elizabeth. Both interviewed under Foreign Travel Control.

Sometime that same morning Philby and Patterson undertook the embarrassing assignment of explaining to the FBI what had happened. First they saw Mickey Ladd who took the news with "remarkable calm." Ladd did not reproach them, Philby maintains, because he was compromised by a somewhat quirky friendship he had maintained with Burgess.[21]

Then he and Patterson performed their mea culpas for Lamphere. Philby was sure that he had fooled another gullible American with his feigned distress and confusion: "[Lamphere] ventured a few theories in his solid, earnest way, which suggested that he was still far from the truth," unless he were a consummate actor, Philby wrote later. Lamphere was not a consummate actor. But neither was Philby the expert dissembler that he fancied himself. Lamphere remembers the meeting vividly:

> Patterson and Philby came in. I'm not saying much. They're not saying much. I know one thing for sure: I've been lied to for a long time by MI5.
>
> I'm doing a lot of thinking; they're doing a lot of thinking. I'm thinking, "Maclean has fled. Burgess, who had been in Philby's house, has fled with him. Surely Philby tipped-off Maclean."[22]

Others had reached the same conclusion. The first time Mackenzie came face to face with Philby after Maclean's flight, "I looked at him, and he looked at me and we both knew." Philby later conceded as much: "I thought I caught a shrewd glint in his eyes." And at the CIA, Bill Harvey was compiling his case to show that Philby was a long-term Soviet agent.[23]

No one—neither the British embassy, the CIA, nor the FBI—bothered to apprise the State Department about this or any other aspect of the case. The early afternoon edition of the June 7 *Washington Star* had a front-page wire service story about the latest developments. But Acheson, anxious for inside information, sent a "Secret/NIACT" [Night Action, Awaken the Ambassador if necessary] cable to Douglas in London at 6:00 P.M. Washington time (11:00 P.M. London time):

> DEPT obviously anxious receive Embassy's reaction McClean [*sic*] Burgess case plus any evaluation available from FONOFF [Foreign Office] other than its statements to press.

Is reported MI-5 investigation extra precaution or does FONOFF have good reason believe men have defected?

Brit Emb apparently uninformed except for press reports.

Acheson[24]

By June 7, therefore, the pattern for the cover-up was established. The British were withholding information from the Americans. The CIA was withholding information from the FBI, which was withholding information from the State Department. The AEC would then join the fray and withhold information from all the others and Congress as well. Each organization in Washington and London was determined to protect itself.

Whitehall was furiously pumping out falsehoods and disinformation at a rate that would have been the envy of the purveyors of truth at Tass and *Pravda*. Maclean and Burgess were characterized as incorrigible degenerates who suffered from "repeated drunkenness, recurrent nervous breakdowns, sexual deviation and other human frailties." They may not have defected at all, went one story, but simply gone off to Europe on a drinking spree.[25]

This soothed *The Washington Post*. The two diplomats, it assured its readers in a Saturday morning, June 9, lead editorial, "may not have absconded to Russia after all, [but] merely went off on a prolonged toot." The editorial bemoaned "the jitteriness of our times" and admonished news organizations for needlessly frightening people. This presumably applied to its own paper, whose headline the previous day had proclaimed "British Diplomats Disappear; Flight to Russia Feared."[26]

"Whatever the reasons for their disappearance," the not so easily assuaged *New York Times* editorialized on Monday, "there is no longer any escape from the conclusion that the incident is ugly, sordid and sinister." They may be dead, murdered, or "behind the Iron Curtain and that is the worst thought of all" (though Burgess and Maclean could have been expected to dissent on that point).[27]

On Tuesday, June 12, the State Department pleaded with the British embassy "to contact Christopher Warner [a senior FO official] in an effort to establish an "agreed [Anglo-American] line." When there was no response from London, Acheson three days later

sent another "NIACT" cable to Douglas requesting "your intervention to secure soonest necessary INFO on agreed treatment" so that
the Department's line would "be in agreement with British on
attitude to take in case it develops McLean [sic] and Burgess have
defected." But, as Cecil reports, a coordinated cover-up "found no
favor in London."[28]

Meanwhile, a reporter from *The Washington Times Herald,* probably tipped off by someone at Mayflower Motors, appeared at the
garage. She was exploring a rumor that Burgess had lived beyond
his means and wanted to see the Lincoln. She failed to examine the
car, however, thereby missing a scoop, as the FBI discovered the
next day.[29] Inside, they found graphs and charts on the strength of
American armed forces, and defense expenditures for the United
States from 1943 to 1950, and maps of various defense installations.
FBI records do not reflect what, if any, classifications they bore.
They also found in the glove compartment 5 by 7 inch photos of a
small boy and girl whose ages were estimated to be six. Finally, they
found a tattered copy of *The Complete Stories of Jane Austen,* Burgess's
favorite author, whose sales he must have boosted considerably
because he was forever leaving her books behind in cars, apartments,
and offices.[30]

The day of reckoning for MI5 was at hand. Its chief, Sir Percy
Sillitoe, and Arthur Martin, Lamphere's counterpart, had to fly to
the United States to explain the "Homer" fiasco to Hoover. Determined to slip out of the country unnoticed, they made reservations
on a British Overseas Airways stratocruiser to New York. Later, in
an effort to deceive the press, the reservations were canceled. But
minutes before the flight departed, a black saloon car drove directly
to the plane with Sillitoe in the back seat and Martin driving,
"disguised" as his chauffeur.

The charade fooled no one, and their pictures were in all of the
London papers the next day. But the inability of Britain's counterintelligence chief to get himself inconspicuously out of the country
should clarify one point. It did not require Soviet moles burrowed
away inside Britain's security agency to explain how two bumbling
and unstable amateurs like Maclean and Burgess could skip the
country right under MI5's nose.

Sillitoe did manage to avoid one embarrassment. Before he and

Martin arrived in Washington, Philby had been recalled. Wanted by SIS for questioning, he left Washington on Sunday, June 10, the day before the MI5 chief arrived.[31] Hoover was not thrilled at the prospect of meeting someone he considered a loser. He agreed to see Sir Percy, but admonished his staff, "I am having no newsreel photographs of me" with Sillitoe.[32]

"Most of what I have to tell you relates to Philby," Martin told Lamphere. "We now have the gravest suspicions of him," he added, as he turned over dossiers on Philby, Burgess, and Maclean. Among the items that caught Lamphere's eye were the clues that Krivitsky had provided to the British in 1940. He thought they were sufficient that "if British Intelligence services had been more on their toes," Philby and Maclean could have been rolled up then. He was also staggered when he realized for the first time the level at which Maclean had operated in Washington.[33] Martin produced a shorter memorandum stating the case against Philby. In addition to Krivitsky's evidence, there was his marriage to Litzi, the Volkov affair, and his connection to Burgess.[34]

Two days later, Harvey slapped down a memorandum on CIA Director "Beetle" Smith's desk outlining almost the same case. He was not merely suspicious of Philby; he believed that "Kim Philby was a Soviet agent, the very counterintelligence officer that Volkov had tried to tell the British about."[35]

The memorandum was sent with a tough cover letter (drafted by Harvey) from Smith to SIS chief Menzies. It snapped every rung in the SIS ladder Philby had been climbing for the past decade. Menzies called Philby in and told him that Smith's letter precluded any possibility of Philby's returning to Washington. After that, says Philby, he was not surprised when he was summoned to the head office a second time and told that he would have to resign.[36]

CHAPTER TWENTY-ONE

Those who become obsessed with a puzzle are
not very likely to solve it.

Cyril Connolly[1]

THE MYSTERY OF THE
MISSING DIPLOMATS

Maclean and Burgess vanished without a trace, leaving behind a
throng of questions which, even after scores of books, hundreds of articles, and decades of speculation, remain unanswered—
Was Maclean tipped off? Why did Burgess go with him? Did the
Soviets arrange their escape?

Of the many who have written about this story, none has been
disposed to concede that the answers may never be known. Almost
every account concludes with an effort to pull together all the strands
and tie them into a single bow. This task is made ever more difficult
because new twists and turns in the story cause old strands to unravel
or new ones to sprout. The result of trying to seamlessly fuse them
into the story line is a plot that more closely resembles a series of
knots than a neat bow.

On the morning of September 11, 1953, Melinda, who had moved
to Geneva after publicly complaining about the harassment that she
and her sons had had to suffer, disappeared. At the time there was
no certainty that Donald was even alive, and Mrs. Dunbar suspected
nothing when Melinda left that morning, saying she and the children
were going to spend a weekend with an old friend. It was only when
Mrs. Dunbar was later cleaning out the Geneva apartment that she

found evidence that Melinda had been plotting her flight for months. It was another two years before Melinda finally wrote from Moscow.[2]

One year later, a London paper published Soviet defector Vladimir Petrov's claims that Burgess and Maclean were long-term Soviet agents whose escape was masterminded in Moscow. The former Soviet intelligence operator seemed to blend the obvious (that they were spies), and perhaps a lucky guess (that they had been recruited at Cambridge), with some information that was absolutely incorrect (contending, for instance, that both Maclean and Burgess had been under investigation, when it was only true of Maclean).[3]

Although he admitted that his information was all secondhand, Petrov's story was the spark that ignited long-smoldering resentment by politicians, the press, and the public toward the British government's infuriating obtuseness. Whitehall tried to douse the inflamed passions with a terse four thousand-word "White Paper" dated September 23, 1955. It admitted that in 1951 Maclean was suspected of being a Soviet agent, and that *"he was alerted and fled the country together with Burgess."*[4] Although admitting that Maclean had been a spy and that he had been tipped off was a Copernican revolution for the government, everyone else had reached that conclusion long before.

"If, after four years, this tissue of palpable half-truths and contradictions is the best that the Government can produce," snorted Labour MP Richard Crossman, "the impression of 'covering up' is more strongly substantiated than ever." Dame Rebecca West denounced it "an insult to any reasonable man's intelligence," and later wrote that the White Paper "was bound to be inept, but [it] was so to an unnecessary degree."[5]

The real issue was the identity of the Third Man.[6]

In Washington Hoover was orchestrating a whisper campaign to put Philby's name into play, and in so doing set in motion a series of events that ended up clearing him. Just two days after the White Paper was issued, Walter Winchell, Hoover's favorite journalistic outlet, used his popular Sunday night radio show to exhort:

Attention Sherman Adams [President Eisenhower's chief of staff] . . .
Burgess and Maclean, the top British intelligence agents, fled to Russia

following a tip that they were watched by Scotland Yard for being Russian spies. The person who tipped them off is another top British intelligence agent . . . the FBI refused to give this man any information for over three years but other American intelligence departments opened up their very top secret files for him.[7]

It was a masterful accomplishment for Hoover. In one stroke, he had enshrined with monumental inaccuracy the FBI's vigilance, maligned the CIA, and sent out the word that the FBI director was open for business. He did not have long to wait.

At midafternoon the following Thursday, a reporter with the International News Service called Hoover. He had already been told by a British source that Kim Philby was the Third Man (Philby's name, it was later claimed in England, "had been hawked about for months"). Could the FBI confirm that?[8]

"[You're] apparently on the trail of some very hot information," Hoover encouraged him. His notes continue:

I told him Philby was a heavy drinker, and because of his close association with Burgess, *was suspected of having tipped off Burgess to the investigation being conducted; that if Philby had not actually done so, he was at least in the position of having access to this and other highly confidential information* . . . There was no mention of Philby's name [in the White Paper] apparently because of lack of direct proof against Philby and the fact that Philby was in contact with lawyers and threatening heavy libel suits if any paper prints his name in connection with this matter.[9]

At the time, the name Harold Adrian "Kim" Philby was completely unknown to the British public, as was the fact that he had ever worked for British intelligence, or that he had been forced out of the SIS because of the Burgess-Maclean scandal. Further, Britain's strict libel laws prohibited the possibility in England of publicly linking Philby's name to the case without risking a ruinous suit.

Just as with the Hiss-Chambers case almost exactly eight years before, it was a cat and mouse game over libel that gave this case its next bizarre twist. All statements made in the House of Commons are beyond the reach of libel. On October 25, therefore, nearly a month after Hoover had confirmed the suspicion of Philby, Lieutenant Colonel Marcus Lipton, a Labor MP, demanded to know whether Prime Minister Anthony Eden had "made up his mind to cover up at all costs the dubious Third Man activities of Mr. Harold Philby . . ."[10]

Lipton's emphatic inquiry compelled the government, or so it claimed, either to let his charge of treason stand, or to deny it. On November 7, Foreign Secretary Harold Macmillan "was at his most urbanely authoritative" as he rejected his own government's three-week-old position that Maclean "had been alerted," by proclaiming that it had no reason "to identify [Philby] with the so-called 'third man,' *if, indeed, there was one.*"[11]

Exonerated, a euphoric Philby held a packed press conference three days later at his mother's apartment. Relaxed, charming, and confident (even the stutter was gone) he was the personification of public rectitude. He had been prevented from defending himself before, he explained, because of his fidelity to the Official Secrets Act and his fear of saying anything that might embarrass the British security services, whose well-being he put ahead of his own. He defied Lipton to repeat his charges outside of the House of Commons. Unlike Chambers, Lipton immediately backed down, and issued a public apology.[12]

His SIS associates shared Philby's glee. "Good old Kim" had never done anything wrong, they had angrily argued from the start. If it looked to outsiders, those not trained in the Great Game (such as MI5 and the FBI), that he had, it was only because he played the game with such daring. His reward was to become a victim of McCarthyism, a fall guy for the loathsome Hoover, left without a job worthy of his abilities. Senior officials at the SIS arranged with the *Observer* and *The Economist* to hire Philby as their Middle East correspondent. He left for Beirut, it is assumed, also back on the SIS payroll.[13]

In February 1956 the Soviet government finally issued its equivalent of a White Paper delivered by its trophies, Burgess and Maclean. In their first public appearance the two handed a statement to four journalists gathered at a Moscow hotel room (two British, two Soviets). According to this version Burgess and Maclean were idealists, not spies, who had come to Russia to promote mutual understanding. Because his political views were out of step with the warmongering policies of London and Washington, Maclean knew he was under surveillance. This is the reason that their spur of the moment departure had to be organized by Burgess.[14]

Even the combined efforts of the British and Soviet governments, however, could not induce a persistent group in MI5, the CIA, and the FBI to exonerate Philby. Finally, late in 1962, Nicholas Elliott, one of Philby's greatest admirers, flew out to Beirut and confronted "good old Kim" with the obvious—he had been lying. By then Philby, who knew that the noose was tightening, was well on his way to becoming a broken-down alcoholic. After making a partial confession to Elliott, he vanished from Beirut.[15]

His disappearance forced the government to weather a cloudburst of rage for its seemingly inexhaustible supply of ineptitude and deception. Soon the rancor dissipated, however, and Philby receded into the background, still largely unknown.[16]

It was not until late 1967, when an exhaustive investigation was published by *The Times* (London), that the British public finally learned that Philby had once been the head of Soviet counterintelligence, linkman to the CIA and the FBI, and well on his way to the SIS's upper reaches. Philby emerged from this account as a romatic revolutionary, an idealist who followed his convictions all the way to Moscow. Soon his name was inseparable from such sobriquets as "Masterspy" or "The Spy of the Century." Even Allen Dulles called him "the greatest spy the Russians ever had," and other CIA men similarly joined in to inflate his reputation—the subtext: Yes, we were fooled, but we were fooled by the best.

The Times's success in penetrating the government's wall of secrecy, even in the face of official intimidation, made its effort a monument to investigative journalism. Paradoxically, however, it deepened the mystery, because its portrayal made Burgess's decision to go with Maclean not just unnecessary and quirky, but downright incomprehensible. Why, if Philby were so important, would the Soviets have doomed him by taking Burgess out with Maclean? They surely knew that this would turn the spotlight of suspicion on Philby.[17]

Moscow was as irritated as London by such speculation. To silence it, they published another official version under Philby's byline. It was the sort of project in which Philby delighted (and for which he reportedly received $50,000 for the British rights).[18]

All the nonsense by Burgess and Maclean about not being spies was repudiated. Philby also insisted that Maclean's flight to Moscow, far from being an impulse organized by Burgess, was the result of a plan crafted by him and the Soviets. The story, according to Philby, is that it was axiomatic in Moscow that because Maclean was an "old comrade" he must be rescued. At the last minute Philby and the Soviets decided to use Burgess in a very limited role. Since it would look suspicious if Burgess returned to London just before his friend Maclean disappeared, he got himself booked for speeding three times to trigger his involuntary return. Once back in London Burgess was to meet with a Soviet contact, then see Maclean at the Foreign Office and shove a piece of paper across his desk telling him he was under surveillance and setting a time and place for a later meeting with his Soviet control. That was it. Any further involvement ran too high a risk of linking Burgess to Maclean's escape, thus endangering Philby.[19] To help divert suspicion from himself in the investigation that would follow Maclean's disappearance, Philby made a positive contribution to solving the "Homer" case by reminding London of Krivitsky's description of Soviet agents working in the Foreign Office. This backfired, however, because the revelation was of such blinding brilliance that London began closing in on Maclean much faster than they otherwise would have. When Philby learned they were getting close, he had to tell Burgess to make haste. Burgess had left his Lincoln in the embassy parking lot. Philby used this as a pretext to send him a thinly veiled warning: act at once or it will be too late, your car will be sent to the scrap heap. The totally unexpected happened when Burgess, contrary to all instructions, went with Maclean.[20]

This account is a complete fabrication. Of course, it was not written to serve truth but, as *The New York Times* pointed out, to "discredit Western intelligence organizations and to improve the image of the Soviet Union's secret service." To this a third purpose can be added—that of cementing the Philby legend.[21] It has worked with remarkable success, proving again Bok's axiom that the person who reveals a secret gains considerable control over how others see it.[22]

Philby has offered his book as an insider's guide for those trying to pick their way through the mysterious labyrinth of the Burgess-

Maclean case. Although his map is filled with bogus trails, false directions, and mislabeled signposts, it has taken on a life of its own even among skeptics. For instance, his assertion that the FBI was heavily engaged in the search for "Homer" was taken as gospel for two decades.

Why would Philby fabricate such a story? Because it made him appear crucial to the Soviet effort to rescue Maclean, while making the Americans appear inept. "The FBI was still sending us reams about the embassy charladies," he haughtily complained. "The enquiry into our menial personnel was spinning itself out endlessly." But the FBI, as Lamphere later corrected, was not sending the British reams of anything because the British had completely frozen the Americans out of the "Homer" investigation.[23]

Equally enduring has been Philby's gratuitous claim that he re-surrected the Krivitsky material. That is, even though Krivitsky's efforts to identify Soviet agents inside the Foreign Office had been in the news frequently between 1948 and 1951 (because of his ties to Whittaker Chambers and the Hiss case), not a single British official involved in the search for "Homer" had had the wit—except for Philby—to suggest rechecking Krivitsky's description of Soviet agents operating inside the Foreign Office.[24]

Nothing contributed more to the legend of "Philby, Masterspy," however, than his claim that he and the Soviets had engineered Maclean's escape by manipulating a variety of Anglo-American officials. "The governor," Philby gloated (referring to Battle's com-plaing after Burgess was "booked" three times for speeding) "re-acted just as we had hoped," as did the State Department, the ambassador, and the Foreign Office.[25]

Burgess was not booked for anything, however. Turck had gotten the only ticket issued that day, and if Burgess had had fifty dollars, Turck would never have been left alone to panic and turn on him. It was from Turck's affidavit that Lyon, Binford, and Battle learned that Burgess had been stopped (but not booked) twice before he got to Petersburg. And it was only after Binford sent him Turck's affidavit that Battle had become so enraged, which triggered the complaint to the State Department.[26] Burgess did not know about the affidavit and so could hardly have anticipated the reaction that it would precipitate. Upon returning to Washington, he had had every reason to believe that the unpleasant incident in Petersburg was behind him.[27]

It was not the scheming Philby and his elite Soviet commrades who had engineered Burgess's recall. It was an uneducated, homosexual drifter.[28]

The British and Soviet governments have been working almost as partners on this story. For the first seventeen years, Whitehall shouldered the burden of the cover-up, trading national honor and public integrity to protect something it called its "secrets." But during the last twenty years, the Soviets have taken the lead (through their agents Philby and Blunt) in creating new layers of deceptions and diversions. The British have certainly gotten the short end of this bargain, because Soviet versions merely reinforce the image that the British government was populated by officials whose virtues included treason, duplicity, ineptitude, incompetence, and moral depravity. The prewar reputation of British intelligence for global eminence, went from "invincible and impregnable, [to] incompetent and incontinent."[29]

★   ★   ★

Perhaps the complete story could only be reconstructed at some kind of roundtable discussion among British, Soviet, and American officials as there has been on the Cuban missile crisis. The U.S. government has at least opened up many of its files. In 1990, it is a better bet that the KGB will open its files before the British (whose "secrets" cupboard might well be embarrassingly empty).

Meanwhile, it is useful to review the basic questions and consider at least one new answer.

1. *Why did the Soviets, who had never rescued a non-Russian-born citizen before, want to save Maclean?*

Because he was an "old comrade"? Yet, Klaus Fuchs had been a pretty good "old comrade" too, and they did not save him. Because he could be useful in Moscow? Nuclear physicists like Fuchs and Alan Nunn May would have been far better investments than a broken-down drunk of a diplomat, and Moscow did not save them from the dungeon. Because *Maclean* wanted out? Surely the Rosenbergs would have preferred the Soviet Union, too, but all they got was the electric chair. To keep Maclean from cracking and giving Philby away? But the moment Burgess went, Philby was dead in the water anyway.

Others have argued that the reason the Soviets did not save Nunn May and Fuchs is that this would have cast suspicion on Philby. But knowledge of Nunn May was so widely held for so long in three countries that it would hardly have implicated Philby if he had finally bolted for Russia. Almost the same was true of Fuchs, who cast suspicion upon himself. Besides, if Volkov's demise did not raise doubts about Philby, it would seem that he was untouchable.

The specter is always held up that Maclean could not have withstood the skillful and hard-nosed Skarden who gained legendary fame for "cracking" Fuchs. But that is a vastly inflated reputation. For over two months, Fuchs voluntarily suggested that he was a security risk. Finally, Skarden merely accused Fuchs of what he himself had been hinting at: he was a Soviet agent. Skarden did not crack Fuchs, Fuchs cracked Fuchs.

2. *Even if the Soviets had intended to rescue Maclean, why would they have informed Philby of their plans?*

With London refusing to share its investigation with Washington and nothing coming back the other way, there is very little that Philby had to offer the Soviets. Indeed, the fact that MI5 did not notify Patterson until June 6, only hours before the news broke publicly that Maclean had fled, reflects how irrelevant the Washington liaison function was to those pursuing Maclean.

3. *Why did the Soviets need to involve Philby, Burgess, and Blunt in the rescue effort?*

Party veterans like Beria (later Stalin's chief of the KGB) had mastered underground life during the czarist period. They had shuttled agents in and out of countries, including Britain, for decades undetected. This, along with their ruthlessness, was what the vaunted reputation of Soviet intelligence was based upon. It is absurd to suggest that to extricate Maclean they suddenly needed the help of one junior officer and two amateurs with a total of two years of field experience, two of whom during the most critical period were a useless three thousand miles away.[30]

Yet, according to most accounts, on the night of Friday, May 25, Burgess picked up Maclean at his Tatsfield home and they raced to Southampton, where they barely caught the last ferry leaving England.[31]

Called upon to explain what had happened, especially the reason that Burgess accompanied Maclean, Philby claims to have fooled the FBI with the explanation that the Soviets had taken Burgess because he had no future in England, was generally at the end of his tether, and, if left behind, might endanger other agents. Once in Moscow, he told another story. It was no longer the Soviets who bore the responsibility for Burgess's having gone to Russia—and destroying Philby's career—it was Guy himself, acting in defiance of the Soviet plan.[32]

"The whole thing was a mess, an intelligence nightmare, and it was all due to that bloody man Burgess," Philby told Knightley in 1988. "The KGB never forgave him. They kept us apart in Moscow to avoid recriminations over what had happened."[33]

4. *What if the Soviets were* not *involved in Maclean's flight from England?*

When Burgess returned to Britain on May 7, he was met by Anthony Blunt who, if he did not know before, quickly learned that Maclean—and thus the whole Cambridge network—was in mortal danger. Sir Anthony, Surveyor of the King's Pictures, director of the prestigious Courtauld Institute, internationally renowned art critic, lecturer, and author, had more to lose than any of the others.

How could he be sure that Moscow would not allow Maclean to go the same way as Alan Nunn May, approximately twenty Canadian public servants and elected officials (all identified by Gouzenko), Klaus Fuchs, Harry Gold, the Rosenbergs, and countless other Soviet agents? Perhaps Blunt conspired with Burgess in a rogue operation to get Maclean out of the country. Donald, cowering at the prospect of jail, was eager to leave—not initially for Russia, but perhaps for Switzerland to have time to sort things out and wait for Melinda to join him before deciding what to do next.[34]

One reason for believing this possibility is that, as far as is known, Burgess and Maclean rendezvoused at Tatsfield. They did so secure in the knowledge that MI5 did not tail Maclean once he had boarded his train for home.[35] Leaving aside *how* they may have known this, the more important point is that if Tatsfield was a safe rendezvous for Burgess, it also would have been safe for the Soviets. If Moscow had wanted to get Maclean out of the country, they could have sent an experienced Soviet operator to pick him up and take him to some secluded coastal spot to board a Russian trawler. They would not have had to depend on Burgess and the cumbersome and risky Channel ferry. If Maclean were caught fleeing with a Soviet agent, at least Philby would not have been automatically compromised.[36] Instead, Maclean's escape had all the characteristics of an improvised operation with no clear destiny, and bereft of the resources and skill normally associated with Soviet intelligence.

From everything that is known about Burgess, it is almost certain that when he left England on May 25, 1951, he never thought that he was leaving England forever. Whether he was forced to go to Russia or was tricked into going by being told that in a few weeks he would be allowed to return to England, is unknown. But Guy Burgess never would have chosen to live in Russia, where homosexuality was a capital offense and gay clubs were nonexistent.[37]

His principal pastime in Moscow, until he finally died there of alcoholism, was seeking out Western visitors. Like a junkie in need of a fix, he craved gossip about his friends and the literary and political heavies in London. Once he went backstage at the Bolshoi to see the actor Michael Redgrave. They had known each other at Cambridge. During a walk around Moscow, Burgess repeated dejectedly several times: "They had only wanted me to deliver Donald Maclean . . . they had only wanted me to deliver him."[38]

He never accepted that he was doomed to the drab life of the Soviet Union. He never had any real job, never learned the language, and never became a citizen. He may not have been in Lubiyanka prison, but Guy Burgess was a prisoner nonetheless. If, when Philby arrived twelve years later, the Soviets found it necessary to keep him from Burgess (then only months from death), it may have had less to do with avoiding recriminations with each other than with their mutual discovery that the Soviets had betrayed them both.

Whether Maclean's flight was masterminded from Moscow, or was a Blunt-Burgess rogue operation, there is one unassailable truth—Guy Burgess ended up in Russia only because the Soviets wanted him there. This is the one empirically verifiable fact in the entire mystery of his disappearance from England.

If the Soviets were worried that if he were left behind in London Burgess posed a possible threat to Philby, they did not have to take him to Moscow. This only assured that Philby, their most valuable penetration operation, was ruined. They could have simply killed Burgess. Guy was the one person who could have been fished out of the Thames, or found robbed and knifed in an alley behind one of his homosexual haunts, and everyone would have agreed that he had met his logical end. There would not have been a soul in all of England—including his mother—who would have suspected another more sinister plot.

Even if Burgess had proceeded with Maclean in defiance of Soviet instructions (the story Soviet intelligence apparently fed Philby), they could have arranged for him to be fished out of the Adriatic Sea or found in a Venetian hotel, complete with a suicide note of the same vintage as the convincing ones found with Krivitsky. This may not have entirely shielded Philby, but it certainly would have contained the damage.

Philby claims the Soviets never forgave Burgess. But surely if he were half as clever as is claimed, Philby knew the moment he heard the news that Burgess had gone with Maclean that it was the Soviets, not Guy, who left him out to dry. Moscow did not gamble with Philby's future. They did not even sacrifice it. They threw it away.

Why? Who can say? How can one acknowledge Stalin's twisted mind and demand logical answers? He was rapidly losing his grip, the Kremlin was slipping into another one of its power struggles, and Beria was consolidating his vast power (even Stalin feared him). Minor purges were reverberating throughout Russia. Perhaps in this land where high crimes and misdemeanors pass for politics someone had a score to settle with Comrade Kim.

Whatever the reason for the Soviet betrayal of Philby—ineptitude or vengeance—he was reinstated following Stalin's death in March 1953 and Beria's execution a few months later. It was another decade before he finally fled to Moscow and began his life's work: reinventing his past.

With the help of eager mythmakers in both the East and the West, Philby was able to portray himself as a vital cog in a Soviet apparatus that was governed by fiendishly clever and ruthless minds. Yet what Philby unwittingly revealed, to use the description employed by Conor Cruise O'Brien in his review of another defector's expose, "is something more alarming" about Soviet intelligence. It is "a cumbersome, ill-informed, mutually suspicious, apprehensive and dimly improvising elite."[39]

Philby didn't seem to notice. For he took far greater pride in boasting that the embrace between Stalin and his British hirelings never loosened.

> It is no good clearing Hollis if you accept that
> there was a high-level penetration without
> providing another candidate.
>
> Peter Wright on the historical imperative
> for a mole.

EPILOGUE

In late August 1963, Guy Burgess, age fifty-two, was the first of Stalin's Englishmen to die. He had lived a life of misery in Russia. Within weeks of his arrival, a gang of toughs knocked out half of his teeth. The government stripped him of all privileges, though they did eventually let him take a male companion. One of the last to see him was Willard Straight, Michael's older brother and then vice-chairman of Rolls-Royce. As always, Guy was still wearing his Old Eton tie. "He loves the old country," Straight reported.[1]

The Macleans were among the small group of mourners, along with Guy's brother Nigel. Although he and Guy had long before had a falling out and no longer saw or spoke to each other, Maclean, his eyes welling up with tears, gave a very moving tribute. According to *The New York Times,* he looked truly grieved. No Soviet or Communist Party officials attended; neither did Kim Philby, who had been in Russia for eight months. Perhaps Soviet officials still feared "recriminations."[2]

Philby's private life was even messier at the end of his career than it had been at the beginning, if that is possible. Aileen had been left in London with the children when he went to Beirut. Within a year, she died a tormented death at age forty-seven, convinced that her husband was a Soviet spy.

In Beirut, Samuel Pope Brewer, then *New York Times* Middle East correspondent, took Philby under his wing, introduced him to colleagues, invited him to parties, and often asked Kim to join him and his wife, Eleanor, for meals. This is the same Brewer whom the CIA had tried to recruit to investigate Philby just after the flight of Maclean and Burgess (an effort that neither Brewer nor Philby ever seemed to know about).

Philby and Eleanor soon were having an affair; after her Mexican divorce, they were married. She followed him to the Soviet Union, where their constant companions were Melinda and Donald Maclean. It was apparent that the Maclean marriage had completely broken down, and soon Kim and Melinda were having an affair. After Eleanor left Russia, Melinda left Donald and moved in with Philby.

Donald was deeply humiliated by this. Moscow's expatriate community is small and its members are desperately dependent upon one another to make life bearable. To that small and hapless group, Melinda's defection from Maclean's bed to Philby's was the most sensational event next to President Kennedy's assassination. It would be inaccurate to believe that Donald had found any measure of happiness before this. The same loathing that had made so much of Cambridge disagreeable to him still dominated his attitude.

Yet he had found a measure of tranquillity in Russia that had eluded him in the West. At last the great con game was over. For the first time since he was twenty-one, his survival did not depend on his ability to lie and deceive. Relieved of the pressure of being constantly on guard, he tried to establish himself as a serious statesman. He learned Russian, worked in a foreign policy "think tank," and grew close to the refusniks and intellectuals who were battling the Dark Ages of Brezhnev.

He was never able, however, to shake the curse that had forever shackled his name to Guy Burgess. It was almost always Burgess-Maclean, too, rarely the other way around—a pair of dissolute, slightly daffy diplomats, made notorious as homosexual traitors. It would have been difficult to disentangle his persona from Burgess's, and Maclean, who refused to speak to Western journalists, never tried. No one else did, either.

Thus, he was unable to ever establish his pretension of being an international statesman whose life's journey had been directed by deeply held convictions. This image received a further setback in 1970 after he published a boring, shallow, polemic on British foreign policy.

For a while he exchanged letters with his friend Philip Toynbee. They revived some of the old drinking jokes. But after he ardently defended the ruthless way in which the Red Army crushed the 1956 Hungarian revolution, Toynbee, appalled, said "it was a letter I found impossible to answer." They never corresponded again.[3]

Fergus, Donald Jr., and young Melinda were raised as Russians. Fluent in the language, they all married Russians and had children. Melinda returned to the United States alone in 1976. Soon Maclean's children began to desert him as well. Daughter Melinda, then in her mid-twenties and a divorced mother herself, left shortly for America. The boys, with their wives and children, were next. All are alive and living in the West.

For Donald, the departure of each was like cutting off another limb. He had formed deep attachments to his grandchildren. Once all had left him, he must have realized that he remained behind not because he was a hostage to his conscience, but because he was just another inmate. He had never been completely cured of drink, and he now had little else to comfort him.

Donald Maclean died in March 1983 at the age of sixty-nine. His brother Alan was with him at the end and stoically remarked, "He died content." Unlike Burgess, he was given a hero's funeral. *Izvestia* called him "a man of high moral principle"; high-ranking Soviet and Party officials were present. Philby did not attend. Later Maclean's ashes were quietly flown to Britain where they were interred in English soil, near a fading stone memorial acknowledging his father's service to his country.

Melinda Maclean, who lives in the New York City area, now seventy-four, refuses to talk to any writer or journalist. Her sister Harriet lives in New York City. Their mother, the amazing Mrs. Dunbar, lived into her nineties. Alan Maclean had a successful career with the Macmillan publishing company and is now retired.

In 1963 Michael Straight went to the FBI and confessed his sins. In 1969, President Richard M. Nixon, fully aware of Straight's past, appointed him deputy chairman of the National Endowments for the Arts.[4] Among those Straight informed on was Anthony Blunt. Sir Anthony, too, confessed, but was granted immunity and allowed to live his privileged life as a millionaire member of the Establishment. MI5 questioned him numerous times both before and after his confession. His greatest consistency was in his lying, which he performed effortlessly and without remorse. In 1979 he was finally exposed publicly as a spy and was only then stripped of his knighthood (conferred in 1956) and his Royal appointment. His "White Paper" came in the form of an interview with a group of journalists during which he pumped out half-truths, distortions, and lies with all of the old gusto.[5]

Two weeks after Donald's death, Blunt collapsed and died at age seventy-five in his elegant sixth floor apartment near Marble Arch. Life had been extremely good to him. The last four years had created some slight discomfort, but nothing of the magnitude of the despair that Burgess experienced for twelve years and Donald for thirty-two, nor Philby's thirty-seven years—half his life—of useless inactivity.

★ ★ ★

Bill Harvey was a Cold War general in the front ranks of the East-West subterranean warfare. His end came when he was sucked into the vortex of the Kennedy administration's obsession with Fidel Castro. Eventually, he crossed swords with Robert Kennedy and was forced into retirement. He died an alcoholic in Indianapolis. His wife Libby returned to her native Kentucky where she eventually committed suicide.

James Angleton thrived in the ever-expanding CIA, but he had turned bitter and distrustful, not to mention paranoiac, having realized how completely he had been taken in by Philby. To the end of his life, Angleton imagined that he and Kim were still locked in a duel, with Philby masterminding moves from Moscow.[6]

Convinced that a Soviet mole had burrowed his way into the CIA, Angleton tore the Agency apart to find it, creating more havoc and impairing its operations more effectively than any mole possibly could have. This led some insiders to conclude there was, indeed, a Soviet mole loose in the Agency—in the person of Angleton.

During the CIA's "Wild West" days, when the gloves were off and anything was permissible, Angleton directed operations to spy on American citizens and open their mail. In 1974 this finally blew up in his and the CIA's faces, and he was forced to resign. Some felt that his departure was a victory for the Kremlin; others believed that he was a burnt-out case who took the Agency down with him.

Philby was the last to depart. He died on May 11, 1988 in Moscow, two years to the day after Jim Angleton died in Washington.

Angleton was not the only one who succumbed to mole fever. In England a group of agents became convinced that MI5's long series of failures could only be explained by the presence of a Soviet mole at the organization's top. An ideal candidate was found in Sir Roger Hollis, the MI5 director-general from 1956 to 1965. Hollis was ideal because he had been unpopular among his colleagues and of mediocre talent. Most of all, however, by the time the accusations were flying, he not only had ceased to be director of MI5, he had ceased to live.

The conspiracy-minded agents took their story to Chapman Pincher, the science reporter for *The Daily Express* at the time when it broke the story about the disappearance of Burgess and Maclean. He became an instant disciple. (Pincher would claim that he made his case on the "facts." As his primary source, Peter Wright confirms, however, it was really more a matter of faith, "as another man might have faith in God.")[7]

"The existence of such a source," Pincher intoned in one of the two books he wrote indicting Hollis, "would explain virtually everything which appeared to be mysterious about the defection of Maclean, including the fact that Burgess accompanied him."[8]

For true believers the discovery of the Soviet mole produced the same kind of almost mystical experience that communism induced among the Thirties generation:

The whole universe falls into a pattern like the stray pieces of a jigsaw puzzle assembled by magic at one stroke. There is now an answer to every question, doubts and conflicts are a matter of the tortured past—a past already remote, when one had lived in dismal ignorance in the tasteless, colorless world of those who *don't know*. Nothing henceforth can disturb the convert's inner peace and serenity—except the occasional fear of losing faith again.[9]

Each lingering question about the Burgess-Maclean-Philby case was effortlessly solved once Hollis was accepted as the mole. Pincher's 850-page bill of particulars includes Hollis's "habit of walking home after staying late at the office." His route, it was explained, took him past places where he could have left material in Soviet drop boxes. Equally incriminating was his fondness for wearing his old school tie as did the spy Burgess. And perhaps the most damning evidence of all, Hollis liked golf the way the spy Philby liked cricket.[10]

As he builds up to his grand finale, Pincher—in one page—riddles Hollis's corpse with a burst of fire that includes five *would haves* ("he would have read . . . He would also have been more inclined . . ."); four *could haves* ("the leak could have come . . . a regular Soviet agent could have alerted . . ."); three *ifs* ("If an MI5 officer . . . If someone in MI5 . . .") and one invocation of something called *the existing conspiratorial rules*.[11]

Pincher claims to have extensive sources within British, American, Australian, and Canadian intelligence, and in some chapters forty percent or more of his footnotes have the simple entry of "Confidential information to the author." He explains that this was necessary to protect his sources from the crushing retribution of the Official Secrets Acts, although he does not remind his readers that the spy Kim Philby, too, hid behind the Official Secrets Act in 1955, as did the spy Anthony Blunt in 1979.

Hollis may have been the best spy the Soviets ever had, the spy of the century, the perfect spy. But none of this is evident from what has been written about him. The British historian John Keegan believes that the evidence amassed by Pincher is not convincing one way or the other, because all of it is entirely circumstantial. "On internal evidence alone, therefore, Pincher's case can be made to fall quite as easily as it can be made to stand up."[12] Cecil is even more blunt. "There [is] no scintilla of evidence" that his accusers have produced against Hollis he concludes.[13]

As is true of Marxists, mole-hunters claimed that their cause sprang from historical necessity. As Wright explained:

It is no good clearing Hollis if you accept that there was high-level penetration without providing another candidate. I think the circumstantial evidence that has been set out for the high-level penetration of MI5 is irrefutable. And Hollis is the best candidate. And if it wasn't Hollis, who else was it?

In 1987 when Wright published his own book, the British government did him the inestimable favor of trying to suppress *Spycatcher*, thus assuring its success as a worldwide best seller. The book is subdued compared with Pincher's, and Wright does not make even a fraction of the claims that Pincher had attributed to his "confidential sources."[14]

Perhaps we can hope that Moscow and London will yet permit the Soviet and British sides of the Philby–Burgess–Maclean story to be told.

SOURCES AND NOTES

For books the author, title, year and place of publication appear in the first citation. Thereafter, only the author's last name and relevant page numbers are given, except in cases where additional information is needed to distinguish between authors sharing the same surname, or where one author has more than one work cited.

Abbreviations:

FBI: The files on the Philby-Burgess-Maclean case, consisting of over three thousand documents, are available in the Federal Bureau of Investigation Reading Room, Washington, D. C., File No. 100–374183. This has been shortened to "FBI: Philby Files." All possible details are provided, but the documents are heavily excised and in some places the dates, the sender and recipient, and the page number have all been deleted.

For years, the FBI issued updated "Summary Reports" for Cabinet-level officers or ranking members of the American intelligence community. The first was issued on June 19, 1951; they continued to be compiled well into the 1960s. The one used most frequently for this book is dated November 5, 1955.

Additional FBI files have been obtained under the Freedom of Information Act (FOIA) and are designated as, for instance, "FBI: Roosevelt File." These also include information on Alger Hiss from Hoover's O & C Files (Official and Confidential Files) which were intended to be destroyed without being integrated into the Bureau's main file system. Many were not, however, and over the years have been released under FOIA. My use of "FBI: Hiss File" is unique to these and other documents released since 1984, which are not to be confused with the Bureau's voluminous Hiss Files, which I did not peruse (though there may be an overlap between items which I have obtained and documents which are in the original Hiss collection).

DOS: Hundreds of State Department documents were released pursuant to my FOIA requests. Though these documents were released piecemeal on the basis of a series of specific requests, I cite them as, e.g., "DOS: Krivitsky File." This is my designation, not the State Department's.

DOE: Documents released under FOIA from the Department of Energy primarily cover the Atomic Energy Commission.

NA: National Archives of the United States, Washington, D. C. Nearly all citations are from documents available in the Diplomatic Section.

FO: These are the Foreign Office files available in the Public Record Office, Kew, England. Material found in files other than those originating with the Foreign Office has the prefix, "PRO:"

RDGD: In 1975, Carrollton Press of Arlington, Virginia published the first volume of Recently Declassified Government Documents consisting of U. S. Government documents which had been released through a variety of means including FOIA and automatic declassification procedures. The first volume was called a Retrospective Collection because it included documents that were released prior to 1975 (cited as RDGD/1975 RC). In 1981 Carrollton Press became part of Research Publications of Woodbridge, Connecticut.

FRUS: Foreign Relations of the United States series, including year, volume number and page. Published by the United States Government Printing Office, Washington, D. C.

PREM: The Prime Minister's Operational File (PREM 3) and the Prime Minister's Confidential File (PREM 4) contain both the Churchill-Roosevelt correspondence as well as unsent drafts, and internal correspondence between Churchill, his ministers and staff. Because of Professor Warren Kimball's definitive work on the Churchill-Roosevelt correspondence, a collection of the PREM files are available at Rutgers University in New Brunswick, N. J.

SPECIAL COLLECTIONS: Robert T. Crowley, a career CIA official, has collected a large number of documents through FOIA. He has generously allowed me use of these papers, particularly those concerning the Krivitsky case.

Mrs. Ruth Levine allowed me to examine her late husband Isaac Don Levine's correspondence and other papers.

Louis Waldman's papers are in the Manuscript and Archives section of the New York Public Library.

INTRODUCTION

1. Dr. Edna R. Fluegel, "The Burgess-Maclean Case," *American Mercury:* Part I, February 1957, pp. 7–13; Part II, March 1957, pp. 127–134; Part III, April 1957, pp. 68–77; NA\Senate Judiciary Files, Memorandum from Edna Fluegel to Bob Morris, May 21, 1956; for FBI "review," see FBI Philby Files, W. A. Branigan to A. H. Belmont, January 28 and March 6, 1957.

2. Michael Straight, *After Long Silence* (New York, 1983). One of the first and still one of the best books on this story was by three British journalists, Bruce Page, David Leitch, and Phillip Knightley, *Philby: The Spy Who Betrayed A Generation* ,London, 1968), hereafter, Page. The book received generally high marks from the FBI, but in reviewing it W. A. Branigan noted, "The weakest portion of the book deals with Philby's stay in the U. S. from 1949 to 1951 and from this it can be

assumed that their sources in the U. S. were not as cooperative as their British sources." This shortcoming extended in even greater terms to the period Maclean and Burgess spent in the United States; see FBI Philby Files: Branigan to W. C. Sullivan, June 28, 1968.

3. Richard M. Helms, interview with author, March 26, 1985.

4. Matthews reported by Wright in FO371/51719, March 14, 1946.

5. Geoffrey Hoare, "Questions they're still dodging," *News Chronicle* (London), September 24, 1955, emphasis added.

PROLOGUE

1. Ruth Levine, interviews with author, February 21 and August 28, 1989.

2. The previous owner of 38 East 64th Street had been John Bouvier III, father of Jacqueline Bouvier Kennedy.

3. Whittaker Chambers, *Witness* (New York, 1952), p. 196.

4. *The Saturday Evening Post* published Krivitsky's articles in five installments between April 5, 1939 and June 15, 1940. These articles became the basis for his book Walter Krivitsky, *In Stalin's Secret Service* (New York, 1939).

5. On the twenty-fifth anniversary of Krivitsky's death, Flora Lewis wrote a 15,000 word article in the *Washington Post* entitled "Who Killed Krivitsky?,"; see the *Washington Post,* February 13, 1966; "I joined," in Krivitsky, *In Stalin's Secret Service,* p. 4.

6. For Krivitsky's defection, see *The Times* (London) and *New York Times,* December 7, 1937; for Trotsky quote, see Lewis, "Who Killed Krivitsky?"

7. Lewis, "Who Killed Krivitsky?"

8. For accounts of the Krivitsky-Chambers meeting, see Chambers, *Witness,* pp. 459–463; Isaac Don Levine, *Eyewitness to History* (New York, 1973), pp. 190–191; Lewis, "Who Killed Krivitsky?"; and Allen Weinstein, *Perjury* (New York, 1978), p. 327.

CHAPTER ONE (pp. 1–31)

1. Milovan Djilas, *Conversations with Stalin* (New York, 1962), p. 187.

2. Lewis, "Who Killed Krivitsky?"

3. In June 1940 the Immigration Service was transferred from the Department of Labor to the Department of Justice, see Francis Perkins, *The Roosevelt I Knew* (New York, 1946), p. 361.

4. Krivitsky's situation was truly complicated. He was traveling under a combination of French and American documents, including a "Titre d'Identité et de Voyage" issued in Paris on October 5, 1938, and an American visitor's permit issued by the American embassy in Paris; see Waldman Papers, Folders Two and Four.

5. Krivitsky's arrival is documented in the Crowley Files, "Intelligence Memo,

War Department, G-2, Military Intelligence," December 19, 1938 from Busbee (NFN-No First Name given), to Assistant Chief, Governor's Island; undated Memorandum by F. K. Ross, G-2. Bullitt's role was further confirmed by Director of the Immigration Service James L. Houghteling to I. D. Levine, which Levine relates to Dorothy Thompson in a letter dated June 6, 1939 in the Levine Papers.

6. *New York Times,* June 16, 1937.

7. For purges, see Leonard Shapiro, *The Communist Party of the Soviet Union* (New York, 1971), pp. 421–424; for eyewitness account of the trials, see Charles E. Bohlen, *Witness to History* (New York, 1973), pp. 47–54; "secret agreements," in Isaac Deutscher, *Stalin* (London, 1968), pp. 368–369; Hugh Thomas, *The Spanish Civil War* (New York, 1961), p. 342.

8. *New York Times,* July 30, 1937; "lying," in Louis Fischer, *Men and Politics* (New York, 1966), p. 435; "death," in *New York Times,* ibid.

9. *New York Times,* June 24, 1937.

10. Shapiro, pp. 424–425.

11. George F. Kennan, *Memoirs 1925–1950* (Boston, 1967), pp. 67–70; *New York Times,* November 13, 1939.

12. For Tukhachevsky, see Deutscher, pp. 375–376; Shapiro, pp. 423–434; Maxim Litvinov, *Notes For A Journal* (New York, 1955), p. 280.

13. George W. Baer, ed., *A Question of Trust: The Memoirs of Loy Henderson* (Stanford, Calif., 1986), pp. 93–95; Martin Weil, *A Pretty Good Club* (New York, 1978), pp. 490–495.

14. Lewis, "Who Killed Krivitsky?"

15. Louis Waldman, *Labor Lawyer* (New York, 1944), p. 347.

16. Lewis, "Who Killed Krivitsky?"

17. A second Soviet census lowered the number to ten million. Robert Conquest puts it at seven million, while others have estimated five million. See Alex Nove in *The New Republic,* November 3, 1986.

18. For State Department thinking at the time, see Bohlen, pp. 52–55.

19. David N. Kandelacki, a fellow Georgian and Stalin's childhood friend, pursued the Nazis with such single-mindedness as to be embarrassing. In a meeting with Dr. Hjalmer Schact, acting Minister of Economics and president of the Reichsbank, Kandelacki suddenly "stammered out something about an Eastern Pact." Schact icily replied that any such conversation should be initiated by Russia's ambassador with the German foreign minister. But not even Litvinov knew of the overtures, or that Kandelacki was reporting directly to Stalin by special courier; see *Documents on German Foreign Policy,* v. 4, p. 453, Schact memorandum dated July 15, 1935; v. 5, document 312, dated May 6, 1936; Shapiro, p. 490; Thomas, *The Spanish Civil War,* p. 342. Stalin informed Litvinov of his special channel in February 1937, just as a whole series of new approaches were initiated; see Litvinov, *Notes,* p. 284.

20. DOS: Krivitsky File, Memorandum of Conversation, drafted by Edward Page, January 17, 1939; Levine, *Eyewitness to History,* p. 189.

21. DOS: Krivitsky File, Memorandum of Conversation, drafted by Loy Henderson, March 15, 1939.

22. I. D. Levine, *Eyewitness,* p. 189; Ruth Levine interviews.

23. Christopher Andrew, *His Majesty's Secret Service* (New York, 1985), p. 423.

24. The State Department was willing to fan the flames. On November 18, 1939 Messersmith sent Hoover a curt note expressing the view that the Department saw no advantage in having the FBI interview Krivitsky; see DOS: Krivitsky File, Messersmith to Hoover.

25. See "The FBI as Our Counterspy," in *Hoover's FBI* by William W. Turner (New York, 1971), pp. 264–279.

26. On May 1, Immigration Services denied Krivitsky's request for an extension of his stay. Weeks of wrangling followed, culminating in Immigration Services June 28 demand that Krivitsky's insurance company either submit proof that he had left the country or forfeit their bond. Finally, with the intervention of Henderson and others at the State Department as well as Waldman's heroic efforts, Immigration agreed that if the French would extend their documents for a specified period, the United States would extend Krivitsky's visitor's permit until December 31, 1939; see Waldman Papers, Folder 2.

27. DOS: Krivitsky File, Memorandum to the Files, July 11, 1939, drafted by Ruth Shipley; Warren to Messersmith, May 19, 1939.

28. Beatrice Berle and Travis B. Jacobs, eds., *Navigating the Rapids, 1918–1971: From the Papers of Adolf Berle,* (New York, 1973), p. 229.

29. Appearance before Uhl in *New York Times,* July 7, 1939; visa extension in NA\861.20200/6-1047.

30. Ruth Levine interviews; Lewis, "Who Killed Krivitsky?"

31. For "open letter," see *The Nation,* August 26, 1939.

32. *New York Times,* August 22, 1939.

33. Chambers, *Witness,* p. 463.

34. For Edwin C. Fischel's definitive account of Stimson's action, see *FILS, Foreign Intelligence Literary Scene,* October 1985, v. 4, No. 5, pp. 4–6; for Stimson's account, see Henry L. Stimson and McGeorge Bundy, *On Active Service* (New York, 1948), p. 188; also George Lardner, Jr., The *Washington Post,* May 18, 1986.

35. For often contradictory accounts of this meeting, see Chambers, *Witness,* pp. 463–466; Levin, *Eyewitness,* pp. 192–195; Berle and Jacobs, pp. 249–250; Weinstein, pp. 328–330.

36. William L. Shirer, *The Rise and Fall of the Third Reich* (New York, 1962), pp. 813–814n.

37. Lewis, "Who Killed Krivitsky?"

38. For accounts of this meeting, see ibid.; Levine, *Eyewitness,* p. 196; Levine's testimony before the Senate Internal Security Subcommittee Hearings, June 6 & 7, 1956, USGO, Part 28; also *Plain Talk,* a magazine which Levine edited between October 1946 and May 1950, see September 1948, v. 2, No. 12. Later a select number of articles were published by the same name in book form; see *Plain Talk* (New York, 1975), p. 207; D. Cameron Watt, "Francis Herbert King: A Soviet Source in the Foreign Office," *Intelligence and National Security,* April 1988, pp. 62–82.

39. Henderson May 20, 1979 letter to Peter Masley, in Levine Papers; for Foreign Office action, see David Dilks, ed. *The Diaries of Sir Alexander Cadogan, 1938–1945* (New York, 1972), pp. 207–208, 227–228, 235; John Costello and Andrew give September 4 as the date of Lothian's telegram to Cadogan; see Costello, *The Mask of Treachery* (New York, 1988), p. 345; Andrew, *His Majesty's Secret Service,* p. 432. Levine's later recollection that it occurred after the September 17 Soviet invasion of Poland is probably in error; see *Plain Talk,* September 1948, v. 2, no. 12.

40. Levine, *Eyewitness,* p. 196.

41. NA\761.62/09–2239.

42. *New York Times,* October 12, 1939.

43. For details of Krivitsky's British mission including the stipulation that he could not leave from American soil; see FBI: Krivitsky Files, "Memorandum to the Director," April 10, 1944; Lewis, "Who Killed Krivitsky?" The Immigration Service was characteristically unconcerned about Krivitsky's whereabouts. "It's not our business where he goes," they wrote Waldman, "as long as he leaves."; see Waldman Files, Folder Two, November 25 from Director Houghteling to Waldman.

44. Levine on security, *Plain Talk,* p. 146; Havemeyer, *New York Times,* October 10, 1939; for immigration problems, see *New York Times,* July 7 and October 19, 1939.

45. Krivitsky's December 26 departure date is confirmed in correspondence from Waldman to the insurance company that carried a bond on him; see Waldman Papers, Folder 2, Waldman to SAI, January 4, 1940. Berle reported the Krivitsky-Henderson call to the FBI on December 27; see FBI: Krivitsky File, p. 3 "Memorandum to the Director", undated, probably between February 12 and 20, 1941. During his February 1941 visit to her farm, Krivitsky told Marguerite Dobert that he went to England via submarine; Dobert interview with the author, March 18, 1989. In his initial preparations, Waldman had booked Krivitsky First Class passage on the Cunard line using an alias, but it could be that once Krivitsky was in Canada, the British made other arrangements; see Waldman Papers, Folder Five, Waldman's undated, handwritten notes. For other details see Waldman, p. 352. For a report of Krivitsky's mysterious absence from New York City, see *New York Times,* December 30, 1939.

46. Krivitsky's date of arrival is in Gordon Brook-Shepherd, *The Storm Petrels* (London, 1977), p. 172; for Foreign Office account of Tyler Kent, see FO371/51681; for the political impact of the Kent affair on U. S. politics, see Richard Whalen, *The Founding Father* (New York, 1964), pp. 309–320; Malcolm Muggeridge, *Chronicles of Wasted Time: The Infernal Grove* (New York, 1974), p. 108.

47. James J. Angleton, one-time CIA counterintelligence chief, told me that Kent was working for the Soviets and was fingered by Krivitsky; James J. Angleton interview with author, February 23, 1984. Krivitsky told Levine that a member of Ambassador William Bullitt's staff in Moscow spied for the Soviets; see *Plain Talk,* September, 1948, v. 2. No. 12 and October, 1948, v. 3, No. 1. Ambassador Kennedy assumed that Kent was working for both the Germans and the Soviets (corroborating Krivitsky's assertion that the two services were working hand in

hand). Still, most writers believed Kent was a German agent until Nigel West, an MP and writer on British intelligence, asserted that MI5 had reclassified Kent a Soviet mole; see *The Times* (London), December 10, 1983. This claim was echoed by Anthony Masters, *The Man Who Was M* (London, 1984), pp. 82–87. Others such as American intelligence expert Robert Crowley believe that Kent was—as he claimed—on a mission to destroy Roosevelt politically and was not under the control of any foreign power. For an excellent historiography of the Tyler Kent case, see Hayden B. Peake in *FILS* (Foreign Intelligence Literary Scene), March–April 1986, v. 5, No. 2, and May–June 1986, v. 5, No. 3; see also, Warren F. Kimball & Bruce Bartlett, "Roosevelt and Prewar Commitments to Churchill: The Tyler Kent Affair," *Diplomatic History,* November 1965, pp. 291–311; Richard J. Whalen, *The Founding Father* (New York, 1964), pp. 310–320.

48. "Disaster," in Kimball and Bartlett, op. cit., p. 294; "destroyed," in Whalen, op. cit., p. 309.

49. For details of Krivitsky in the U. K., see, Costello, pp. 348–349 and Brook-Sheppard, p. 182; for an error-filled account, see Nigel West, *MI5* (New York, 1982), pp. 72–73.

50. Lord Gladwyn, letter to author, February 18, 1986. He also asserted that his interview with Krivitsky appears in *The Memoirs of Lord Gladwyn* (London, 1972), which is not so. It might be that he did include it originally, but that it may have been subsequently excised by the Foreign Office.

51. For Levine's description of the Foreign Office spy based on information given to him by Krivitsky, see Levine testimony, Senate Internal Security Subcommittee, June 6, 1956, USGPO, Part 28; *Plain Talk,* September, 1948, v. 2., No. 12 and October, 1948, v. 3, No. 1. His description matches Philby's; see Kim Philby, *My Silent War* (New York, 1983), p. 175; Robert Cecil, *A Divided Life* (London, 1988), p. 64.

52. According to Alan Maclean, his older brother was recruited while at Cambridge and went into the Foreign Office only because he was subsequently instructed to do so by the Soviets. Before then, Donald had ruled out any possibility of government service. Alan Maclean, interview with author, January 16, 1985, London.

53. For Maclean's family background, see Geoffrey Hoare, *The Missing Macleans* (New York, 1955), p. 57; for King George letter, see *The Times* (London), June 6, 1932; for FO interview of Maclean, see Andrew Boyle, *The Fourth Man* (New York, 1979), p. 114.

54. Berlin's mission was not, as many authors have asserted, the result of any scheme by Burgess. Sir Isaiah's assignment was conceived wholly separate from any of Burgess's machinations. Letter to author from Sir Isaiah Berlin, September 29, 1989. See also Harold Nicolson, *The War Years 1939–1945* (New York, 1967) v. 2, pp. 98, 124.

55. Ibid.

56. Ibid.

57. Ibid.; Cripps was appointed June 2 and arrived in Moscow June 12; for Burgess's visa dated July 8, 1940, see NA\701.4111, Burgess, Guy 7–840.

58. Straight, *After Long Silence,* pp. 110, 122–123, 129–130.

59. Ibid. "willing," p. 130, "escape" etc., p. 135; Corcoran, p. 136; Burgess arrival, p. 142.

60. Ibid., pp. 142–143.

61. Ibid., p. 156; Straight phone interview, March 19, 1991.

62. John D. Hickerson, interview with author, February 5, 1986.

63. Straight told me about the Roosevelt letter, which he does not mention in his book, on March 12, 1988. Both the National Archives and Hyde Park have a record of a letter regarding Straight being sent from FDR to the State Department, but neither has an actual copy; see NA\111.24/131 1/2, July 29 FDR to the Department of State. Straight's appointment appears in The Registry, Department of State, GPO, October 1940. Straight's account of the events of this period are sometimes inaccurate. For instance, Cripp's Indian mission was still two years away. In 1940, he was in Washington as an apologist for the Soviet invasions of Finland and Poland, and to justify the Nazi-Soviet Pact. Straight claims that he personally was counseling Stalin to abandon the pact, via messages to Moscow; see Straight, pp. 141–144. Straight's account of Kennedy's role in the 1940 campaign and the circumstances under which he resigned are inaccurate, see Straight, pp. 315–316.

64. Krivitsky reentered the United States on October 31, 1940; see Waldman Papers, Folder Four. In 1989, two Soviet historians with access to KGB files confirmed what Westerners had long suspected—Trotsky's assassination was directed by Soviet intelligence on Stalin's orders; see *Washington Post, New York Times,* September 10, 1988; and *Washington Post,* January 5, 1989. Trotsky made the comment to J. B. Matthews who worked for the Dies Committee; see *Washington Star,* February 11, 1941.

65. Ruth Levine interviews.

66. Paul Wohl, "Walter E. Krivitsky," *Commonweal,* February 28, 1941, pp. 462–468. Krivitsky's wife told Waldman that Wohl was a Soviet agent who worked for Krivitsky in Switzerland and France; see Waldman Papers, Folder 2, undated notes of conversation. The two had a bitter falling out in the United States over money.

67. Weinstein, p. 67.

68. Chambers, pp. 483–486.

69. Lewis, "Who Killed Krivitsky?"

70. According to information received by Waldman, Dobert became a Soviet sympathizer after he quit the Nazis, including for an indefinite period after he arrived in America. But according to those same sources, he had since abandoned communism; see Waldman Papers, Folder 3, "Memorandum and Calendar of Events on the Death of General Krivitsky," p. 9, undated, hereafter Waldman Memo.

71. The account of Krivitsky's visit to the farm is based on author's interview with Marguerite Dobert, March 18, 1989. The suggestion that Krivitsky was driven to the farm is in *The Washington Star,* February 11, 1941.

72. *New York Times,* February 12, 1941.

73. Waldman arrived in Washington at eleven o'clock on the night of Monday,

February 10. After viewing Krivitsky's body at the morgue, he met with police, and then made a statement to the waiting press calling for an FBI investigation. The following morning after Hoover refused to take his call, he met with Inspector Rosen who said that "the FBI would not investigate regardless of whether Krivitsky's death was murder or suicide."; see Waldman Memo, pp. 5–6.

74. On February 10, 1941, the FBI's C. H. Carson advised E. A. Tamm that the Bureau "wants a very discreet check into the matter of Krivitsky's death," particularly to know of any Soviet involvement, "although we must conceal our interest"; see FBI: Krivitsky File, Carlson to Tamm. But a "Memorandum For The Director," dated February 12, 1941, confirms Hoover's edict that the Bureau stay out of the case. In March Hoover informed the New York FBI office that "the Bureau is not interested in determining whether Krivitsky was murdered or whether he committed suicide"; Hoover had the original of Shipley's memo and Berle saw to it that he got the others as well; see FBI: Krivitsky File, "Memorandum for the Attorney General from John Edgar Hoover," February 11, 1941; DOS: Krivitsky File, "Memorandum of Ruth Shipley" July 11, 1939. She wrote on it "Original to FBI."

After Levine's June 6, 1956 appearance before a Senate subcommittee, op. cit., the FBI—who never questioned Levine about either Krivitsky or Chambers—analyzed his testimony. It concluded that remarks by Levine should have been brought to Hoover's attention. A. F. Belmont wrote, "I consider the error mine." Hoover responded: "It is shameful. I don't get the complete picture particularly in a matter of such delicacy. I now flatly refuse to allow FBI to become involved in any way in this matter." Because everything else has been excised from the copy of that analysis released under FOIA, it is not possible to know what Hoover was referring to; see FBI: Krivitsky File, "Memorandum for Mr. Belmont, ADDENDUM", 6/15/56.

75. Although after nearly fifty years it has become an article of faith that the door was "locked from the inside," Waldman, after using the maid's passkey, attests that it was impossible when using the passkey to know whether or not the lock had been engaged from inside. That is, whether the door was locked or unlocked, the degree of resistance and the sound was the same. When Thelma Jackson entered the room that morning, Waldman concluded, she "was in no position to say whether the door on the inside was open or locked." see Waldman Memo, p. 8.

76. Krivitsky's death generated nationwide headlines. Between February 11–14 *The Washington Star* and *The Chicago Daily News* provided excellent coverage. The various stages of the police investigation were chronicled by both papers in great detail. Waldman, who interviewed the police extensively about their investigation, confirms all the points raised by the press; see Waldman Memo.

77. *Washington Post*, February 13, 1941; Whether or not she grasped that she was providing what police would use as the clinching evidence for a suicide verdict, Mrs. Dobert herself told Mrs. Krivitsky that she was not convinced. In one of several heartrending notes that she sent the widow, Mrs. Dobert wrote, "Circumstances point to suicide. Walter's behavior absolutely not. To me it is completely puzzling."; see Waldman Papers, Folder Two, M. Dobert to Tanya, February 13 and 14, 1941.

78. Until now copies of the original notes have never been seen. For all the different versions and Waldman's efforts to get corrected copies released, as well as his futile efforts to obtain the originals, see Waldman Papers, Folders 2, 3, & 7.

79. Lewis, "Who Killed Krivitsky?"

80. A decade later Mrs. Krivitsky was still trying to obtain the original suicide note. True to form, Hoover refused to be of any help and referred her to the Metropolitan Police. In 1989 the D. C. police assured me that all records in the case had been destroyed decades ago; see FBI: Krivitsky Files, "Memorandum to the Director," April 12, 1951.

81. Mrs. Krivitsky and Mrs. Dobert eventually came to believe that Krivitsky committed suicide to save his family.

82. M. Dobert and Ruth Levine interviews. Antonia Porfirjera was born February 19, 1902 in St. Petersburg.

83. The FBI pegs Straight's official resignation date as February 28, 1941. Other records indicate that it was not until May; it was announced in the May 5, 1941 issue of *The New Republic*. But in his book, Straight links his decision to leave the Department to the appointment of John Winant as ambassador to the Court of St. James; see Straight, p. 157. Winant was unanimously confirmed by the Senate on February 10, the day that Krivitsky's body was found. The two stories shared front page billing on February 11.

84. Report No. 15 found in the Senate Judiciary Files, National Archives, dated April 8, 1954, "RE: The Murder of General Walter Krivitsky in Washington, D. C." For Chambers on Parilla, see *Witness*, p. 252; The FBI did receive a report that George Mink, an American citizen and head of the Communist Party's seaman's organization, was involved in stalking and killing Krivitsky; see FBI: Krivitsky File, Sackett to Hoover, February 20, 1941. For Mink also see Chambers, *Witness*, pp. 302–303n; William R. Corson and Robert T. Crowley, *The New KGB* (New York, 1986), pp. 295, 466–467.

85. Straight, p. 140. From 1969 to 1977 Straight was the deputy chairman of the National Endowment for the Arts. His June 18, 1963 confession to the FBI about his work for the Soviets was sent to the White House where it read and initialed on August 9, 1969 by President Nixon's chief of staff, H. R. Haldeman; see FBI: Straight File.

86. Krivitsky, p. 255; Lewis, "Who Killed Krivitsky?"

87. *The New Republic,* February 22, 1941.

CHAPTER TWO (pp. 33–40)

1. Carl Jung, *Modern Man in Search of Soul,* quoted in Sissela Bok, *Secrets: On the Ethics of Concealment and Revelation* (New York, 1982), p. 8. The Swedish-born Bok has taught ethics at the Harvard Medical School and is now a professor of philosophy at Brandeis University.

2. The term was coined by a Royal Canadian Commission whose report is

extensively used throughout this chapter. *Report of the Royal Commission Appointed to Investigate the Facts Relating to the Circumstances Surrounding the Communication by Public Officials and Other Persons in Positions of Trust of Secret and Confidential Information to Agents of a Foreign Power* (Ottawa, June 27, 1946). Hereafter, noted as RCC. See especially, "Motivation of Agents," pp. 57–58.

3. RCC, p. 83.

4. Kim Philby, *My Silent War* (New York, 1983) p. 14.

5. RCC, p. 77, speaks to the Canadian situation. The British analysis of that report noted this passage with alarm and was unable to point to a contrary example in England; see, FO371/54705. British security authorities would claim Flora Solomon's 1963 statement that Philby tried to recruit her in 1936 was a crucial piece of evidence against him; see Flora Solomon, *A Woman's Way* (New York, 1984), pp. 225–226; Peter Wright, *Spycatcher* (New York, 1987), pp. 172–173, pp. 246–249; Based on his interviews with Philby, Phillip Knightley also believes "no one would be able to say that they had been approached by the Russian intelligence service, only that they had been *obliquely* sounded out by a friend." (emphasis added); see Knightley, *Philby: The Life and Views of the K. G. B. Masterspy* (London, 1988), p. 45. Hereafter *Masterspy*. There is no known example where a failed recruitment was reported to American authorities prior to 1946.

6. David Dallin, *Soviet Espionage* (New Haven, Conn., 1955), pp. 443–445; Chambers, *Witness,* pp. 37–42; Elizabeth Bentley *Out of Bondage* (New York, 1951), p. 210.

7. RCC, p. 44.

8. For the system of files see RCC, pp. 44–45 and Hede Massing in *This Deception* (New York, 1951), p. 165.

9. Both T. E. B. Howarth, *Cambridge Between Two Wars* (London, 1978), p. 158, and Straight, p. 60 have the same numbers for communists and socialists. Straight provides the numbers for cells in 1935.

10. Bok, *Secrets,* p. 6.

11. Hugh Trevor-Roper, "Acts of the Apostle," *The New York Review of Books,* March 31, 1983.

12. RCC, p. 72.

13. Leon Trotsky, *My Life,* quoted in Bok, *Secrets,* p. 49.

14. *Washington Post,* July 12, 1987.

15. *New York Times Sunday Magazine,* "American Traitors: A Study in Motives," May 22, 1948.

16. Weinstein, p. 341; RCC, p. 75; Trevor-Roper, op. cit.

17. Irving Howe and Lewis Coser, *The American Communist Party* (New York, 1962), quoted in *The New Republic,* July 1, 1985.

18. Dallin, *Soviet Espionage,* p. 443; *New York Times Sunday Magazine,* "American Traitors: A Study in Motives," May 22, 1948.

19. Robert Cecil, *A Divided Life,* pp. 77, 128.

20. Dallin, *Soviet Espionage,* p. vii.

21. Alexander Orlov, *Handbook of Intelligence and Guerilla Warfare* (Ann Arbor, Mich., 1963), pp. 9–11.

22. Richard Helms interview with author, March 26, 1985; also for Maclean's standing with Moscow, see Philby, p. 173. John Keegan, British historian, believes Maclean, not Philby caused greater damage; see John Keegan, "Greatest Spy Tag Unwarranted," *Daily Telegraph,* May 12, 1988.

23. Christopher Andrew, and Jeremy Noakes, *Intelligence and International Relations, 1900–1945,* (Exeter, 1987), pp. 16–17; for more on Churchill, see Andrew, *Her Majesty's Secret Service,* pp. 448–449.

24. Robert Conquest, *The New Republic,* September 15 and 22, 1986.

CHAPTER THREE (pp. 41–57)

1. Dmitri Mirsky, *The Intelligentsia of Great Britain,* translated by Alec Brown (New York, 1935), p. 22.

2. Patrick Seale and Maureen McConville, *Philby: The Long Road to Moscow* (New York, 1973), p. 13.

3. Mirsky, p. 113; Keynes quoted in Straight, p. 93.

4. The great surge in CUSS's membership occurred the year after Philby graduated, Straight, pp. 60–62; Howarth, p. 158.

5. Hewlett Johnson, *The Soviet Power* (New York, 1941), p. 96.

6. Eleanor Philby, *Kim Philby: The Spy I Married* (New York, 1968), pp. 93–94.

7. The friend was Tom Milne; see Seale, p. 50; Page, p. 75; Harold Evans, *Good Times, Bad Times* (New York, 1984), p. 52; Trevor-Roper, "The Philby Affair," *Esquire,* April 1968, p. 6; and Knightley, *Masterspy,* p. 34. For Philby's lack of impact at school, see Seale, pp. 12–13; for Le Carré, see Page, p. 30.

8. John Lehmann, *In My Own Time* (Boston, 1969), p. 141; Muriel Gardner, *Code Name Mary* (New Haven, Conn., 1983), p. 43ff; Page, pp. 78–86; for Krivitsky in Vienna at the same time, see Krivitsky, p. xii.

9. Seale, p. 64.

10. "Directed," in E. H. Cookridge, *The Third Man* (New York, 1968), p. 24; Philby, p. 14; Chapman Pincher seems to believe he was recruited in Vienna; see *Too Secret Too Long* p. 159; Barrie Penrose and Simon Freeman believe he was recruited while at Cambridge; see Penrose and Freeman, *Conspiracy of Silence* (New York, 1987), p. 170; for children, see Page, p. 86.

11. Boyle, *The Fourth Man,* p. 442.

12. Knightley, *Masterspy,* p. 45.

13. Page, p. 47.

14. Page on Vienna, pp. 81–86. The book by Page, *et al.* was based on a series of articles published in the *Sunday Times of London* starting on October 1, 1967; Philby, pp. 8–9; see also Penrose and Freeman, p. 170.

15. Knightley, *Masterspy,* pp. 39, 42.

16. Gardner, *Code Name Mary,* p. 43ff, Lehmann, pp. 137–146.

17. Seale, p. 64.

18. Page, p. 85.

19. "Game," in Seale, pp. 60, 65; for the Vienna experience, see Pincher, *Too Secret Too Long*, p. 159; Boyle, *The Fourth Man*, pp. 125–126; T. S. Eliot quoted in Boyle, p. 126.

20. Litzi originally in Page, p. 86. She said this in 1967 when Philby was in Moscow and she was a filmmaker in East Germany. By then, Philby's absurd claim notwithstanding, there was no reason to perpetuate phony stories about events that had taken place twenty-three years earlier. For Philby's 1988 response, see Knightley, *Masterspy*, p. 44.

21. Le Carré in Page, p. 29. Philby never provided a reason for becoming a spy. Instead, he told Knightley that he became a communist after concluding "that the rich had had it too damn good for damned long and that the poor had had it too damned bad." This led *The New York Times* to conclude that *Masterspy* "offers the reader no real insights into the shadowy workings of Mr. Philby's psyche, no persuasive new theory as to the reasons for his betrayal."; see Knightley, *Masterspy*, p. 33; *New York Times*, March 21, 1989.

22. Edward R. F. Sheehan, "The Rise and Fall of a Soviet Agent," *The Saturday Evening Post*, February 15, 1964; Nigel West, "Infamy of the Third Man," quoted by Hayden B. Peake, "The Philby Mystique," FILS (Foreign Intelligence Literary Scene) v. 7, No. 3, pp. 4–5; *The Guardian*, May 13, 1988.

23. Le Carré in Page, p. 33.

24. Eleanor Philby, p. 77; Knightley, *Masterspy*, p. 229; Boyle, *The Fourth Man*, p. 123.

25. Eleanor Philby, pp. 94–95.

26. Bok, *Secrets*, p. 25.

27. Martin Gilbert, *Winston Churchill: The Wilderness Years* (London, 1981), p. 221.

28. Philby, p. 9; Shapiro, *Communist Party*, pp. 486–487.

29. Ibid.; see also Robert Conquest, *Stalin and the Kirov Murder* (New York, 1989), pp. 30–31.

30. Philby, p. 9.

31. Muggeridge, "Refractions on the Character of Kim Philby," *Esquire*, September, 1967, p. 168; Muggeridge on Goebbels, quoted in Boyle, *The Fourth Man*, pp. 139–140; Le Carré, Page, p. 30.

32. Page, p. 54; also for St. John Philby, see Robert Lacey, *The Kingdom* (New York, 1984), pp. 128–133.

33. Philby claimed the 1931 election soured him; see Philby, p. 12.

34. RCC, p. 82. Also see George Watson, "Were the Intellectuals Duped?" *Encounter*, December 1973, pp. 21–31.

35. Philby, p. 9; also for Nazi associations to cover communists tracks, see Knightley, *Masterspy*, pp. 51–52; Pincher, *Too Secret Too Long*, pp. 160–161; Andrew, *Her Majesty's Secret Service*, p. 407; Penrose and Freeman, pp. 171–172.

36. Between 1934 and 1936, CUSS's ranks swelled from two hundred to six hundred; by 1938 its membership roles numbered one thousand, nearly 20 per cent of the entire undergraduate body; see Straight, pp. 60–62; Howarth, 158.

37. Bok, *Secrets,* p. 25.

38. Page, p. 114.

39. Ibid., p. 117.

40. Page, op. cit., Seale, op. cit., and Knightley, *Masterspy,* either do not mention or fail to examine Philby's curious indifference to the Nazi-Soviet Pact.

41. According to Knightley, *Masterspy,* pp. 71–72, in Brussels Philby flippantly ordered German beer as the Nazis were rolling through Belgium and suggested a round of golf in a German-occupied French town. Fitzroy Maclean tells how Philby ostentaciously wore his Franco medal, see *Take Nine Spies* (New York, 1978), p. 244. Columnist John O'Connell recalled Philby's contemptuous attitude toward the British Expeditionary Force as it was being forced into retreat; see *New York Daily News,* October 23, 1955. Philby, p. 22.

42. In the summer of 1940, Harry St. John Philby urged Saudi Arabia's King Ibn Saud to throw in his lot with the Nazis as the probable and, to him, the preferred winner. An enraged Foreign Office ordered Philby arrested at the first British port he reached, which turned out to be Karachi. He was released but rearrested once back in England, and thrown into prison as a Nazi sympathizer; see Page, pp. 59–60; and Records of the Office of Strategic Services, Memorandum from Joseph Charles to Dr. William Langer, June 16, 1944, courtesy of John Taylor, Military Division of the National Archives, Washington, D. C.

43. For Lockhart's appointment as the Director-General of the Political Warfare Executive, see Kenneth Young, ed., *The Diaries of Sir Robert Bruce Lockhart 1939–1965* (London, 1980), v. 2, p. 68.

44. For Philby's marital problems, see FBI: Philby Files, June 19, 1951 Summary Report, Section VII; also, Solomon pp. 209–211.

45. Trevor-Roper, "The Philby Affair," *Esquire,* op. cit., p. 6; Andrew King, a career MI6 intelligence officer, also claims that he advised his superiors that he had been a communist at Cambridge; see Penrose and Freeman, p. 443.

46. Trevor-Roper, ibid., pp. 3, 6; see also Page, pp. 171, 162–171.

47. "Revelations," in Dilks, *Cadogan Diaries,* pp. 520–521; "implying," in Martin Gilbert, *Road to Victory* (Boston, 1986), p. 385.

48. For Stalin's reaction to Sikorski's charges, see Ministry of Foreign Affairs of the U.S.S.R, *Stalin's Correspondence with Churchill and Attlee 1941–1945* (New York, 1965), pp. 120–130.

49. For Sir Owen O'Malley's vivid and moving report on the massacre, see Warren Kimball, *Churchill & Roosevelt: The Complete Correspondence* (Princeton, 1984), v. 2, pp. 389–402. In 1987 Gorbachev pledged to fill the "blank spots" of Soviet history. When a joint Polish-Soviet commission to consider the evidence on Katyn moved slowly, the Polish government declared "everything indicates" the Poles were killed by the Soviet Secret police. Finally in April 1990, Gorbachev admitted this was true. He apologized and gave to Poland KGB documents detailing the executions. *Washington Post; New York Times,* March 8–9, 1989 and April 14, 1990.

50. Ivan Maisky, *Memoirs of a Soviet Ambassador* (London, 1965), pp. 365–371.

51. For the best, indeed almost the only, account of Sikorski's death and the subsequent Court of Inquiry, see David Irving's *Accident: The Death of General Sikorski* (London, 1967).

52. The CIA's long-held suspicions about Sikorski's "accident" were resurrected in 1968 by Le Carré's suggestion that Philby could possibly be implicated in Sikorski's death; see Page, p. 33; undated CIA Publication, *Intelligence in Recent Public Literature,* pp. 95–99, released under FOIA, November 14, 1980.

53. Maisky, p. 365, says "there arrived from Moscow a telegram requesting me to fly urgently to the USSR" to show Stalin's disapproval of the Allied decision not to open a second front. Stalin's anger and disappointment over this decision was immense. But the decision had been made in late May and communicated to him on June 4, a month before Maisky's "urgent" recall. By then Stalin had vented his disappointment in messages to Churchill and Roosevelt, denouncing the decision but accepting it as final. It would have been futile and moot to have recalled Maisky in July. As it turned out, Maisky never returned to his London post. For Stalin's reaction to the Second Front decision and his aspersions on Sikorski's loyalty, as well as the value assigned to Sikorski by Churchill, see *Stalin's Correspondence with Churchill and Attlee, 1941–45,* op. cit, pp. 127–141.

CHAPTER FOUR (pp. 59–70)

1. Hoare, pp. 201–202.

2. Cyril Connolly, "A Personal Study of The Missing Diplomats," *U. S. News and World Report,* September 23, 1953, pp. 58–64. Also published in *The Sunday Times of London,* September 21 and 28, 1952, and in book form as *The Missing Diplomats* (London, 1952).

3. For background on Sir Donald, see Hoare, pp. 55–60; Donald Maclean's obituary, *New York Times,* March 12, 1983; Trevor Wilson, *The Downfall of the Liberal Party 1914–1935* (Cornell, N. Y. 1966), pp. 191, 218, 244, 291.

4. In addition to Klugman and Maclean, other Gresham communists included Roger and Brian Simon, and Bernard Floud; see Cecil, *A Divided Life,* p. 17.

5. Cecil, *A Divided Life,* pp. 20–21.

6. For Maclean's unsuccessful experience with a younger student in the back seat of a car; see Cecil, *A Divided Life,* p. 20; "adolescent," in Rebecca West, *The New Meaning of Treason* (New York, 1964), p. 221; Connolly, "A Personal Study of the Missing Diplomats," op. cit. p. 59; also Hoare, p. 207.

7. Cecil, *A Divided Life,* p. 27.

8. Maclean wrote this when he reviewed R. D. Charques's *Contemporary Literature and Social Revolution* for *The Cambridge Left* (Winter 1933–1934), quoted in Seale, p. 45.

9. Neal Wood, *Communism and the British Intellectuals* (London, 1959), pp. 97–98.

10. Maclean expressed these views in a February 1934 letter to *Granta,* a magazine published in Cambridge, England. Quoted in Howarth, pp. 214–215.

11. Wood, *Intellectuals,* p. 111.

12. The passage was from a letter V. I. Lenin wrote to Comrade Pokrovsky, which Lenin quoted in his *A Brief History of Russia.* After Maclean fled to Moscow, Hoare was permitted to go through his library and discovered the underlined passage; see Hoare, p. 185, emphasis added.

13. Before publishing a biography on Maclean, Robert Cecil wrote two penetrating pieces which combined his personal knowledge of Maclean, Philby, and Burgess with his experience as a diplomat and in intelligence matters; all are recommended reading. "Elegant young man," in *A Divided Life,* p. 30; also, see "Legends Spies Tell," *Encounter,* April, 1978, No. 50, pp. 9–17 ("mask," p. 9); also, Cecil's "The Cambridge Comintern" appears as a chapter in *The Missing Dimension* (London, 1984), pp. 169–198, Christopher Andrew and David Dilks, eds.

14. John Connell, *The 'Office'* (New York, 1958), p. 336.

15. Whittaker Chambers tried to explain to his Soviet handler, Boris Bykov, that his network of agents were committed communists who did not want, would not accept, and would be outraged by gifts of money. Bykov was incapable of understanding the point. "All right, so they are Communists," he finally blurted out. They would still have to accept money because "who pays is boss, and who takes money must also give something."; Chambers, *Witness,* pp. 414–415; also on this point, see Bentley, *Bondage,* p. 210; Dallin, *Soviet Espionage,* p. 22.

16. Knightley, *Masterspy,* pp. 262–263.

17. Penrose and Freeman did not include Klugman in a group of known Soviet agents, but instead put him in the category of "unknown."; see *Sunday Times of London,* July 23, 1989; it is certain Klugman did help recruit others for Soviet intelligence; Wright, p. 249.

18. Cecil, *A Divided Life,* pp. 29–33.

19. Alan Maclean, interview with author, January 16, 1985; Cecil, *A Divided Life,* pp. 35–37.

20. "Weathercock," in Cecil, *A Divided Life,* pp. 36–37. The way the FBI later got the story, "During his university days Maclean admitted to his mother that he had some Communist leanings. But he subsequently told her he had changed his mind,"; see FBI Summary Report; "irresolute," in Connell, p. 329.

21. Quoted in Boyle, *The Fourth Man,* p. 114; Fitzroy Maclean tells of a similar episode in *Take Nine Spies,* pp. 237–238; the exam results were published in *The Times* (London), September 25, 1935; Soviet defector Vladimir Petrov later told the Australian court of inquiry that Soviet recruiters routinely sent to Moscow the list of those who passed such examinations; see DOS: Petrov File, American Embassy in Canberra to the Secretary of State, August 30, 1955.

22. Cecil, *A Divided Life,* pp. 39–41; "revolution," in Eleanor Philby, p. 82.

23. Cecil, *A Divided Life,* p. 64; Brook-Shephard, *Storm Petrels,* p. 185.

24. "White hope," in Connolly, "A Personal Study of the Missing Diplomats," *U. S. News and World Report,* p. 59, op. cit.; Alan Maclean interview. Vladimir

Petrov, also stated that Maclean was recruited "while still in college." Ambassador Sir Roger Makins in Washington confirmed to the State Department that the British government accepted Petrov's statement as true; see DOS: Petrov File, Herbert Hoover, Jr. to Secretary of State, July 19, 1955.

25. Winston Churchill, *Blood, Sweat and Tears* (New York, 1941), p. 427.

26. "Paris," in Cecil, "The Cambridge Comintern," *The Missing Dimension,* p. 175; also Cecil, "Legends Spies Tell," *Encounter,* op. cit., pp. 10–11.

27. FRUS, 1944, The Second Quebec Conference, "The Joint Chiefs of Staff to the Secretary of State," Top Secret, pp. 252–253. The need to establish global bases was in accord with Roosevelt's thinking; see Kimball, *Churchill and Roosevelt,* v. 3, p. 237.

28. FRUS, 1944, The Second Quebec Conference, "Memorandum by the Deputy Director (Matthews) . . . ," p. 253. Valentine Lawford, who served with Maclean as a Third Secretary in Paris, confirms that both he and Maclean knew Matthews well; from interview with author, March 21, 1986. One plausible way that Maclean might have obtained the document was by virtue of his membership on the Combined Civil Affairs Committee chaired by John J. McCloy, later High Commissioner to Germany and the first president of the World Bank. Maclean "Had access to all, or nearly all, documents circulated," according to Matthews, who was also on the committee. The committee was an adjunct of the British-American Combined Chiefs of Staff and dealt with war-related political and economic problems; see DOS: Maclean File, Matthews to W. M. Chase, Department security, November 17, 1955.

29. For how the Stalin-enforced isolation affected Foreign Office policy, see FO371/47852; for American policy, see Bohlen, pp. 36, 45.

30. Details of the Casual Sources report and the London-Moscow-Washington exchanges can be found in FO371/47852.

31. Bohlen, p. 45.

32. Maclean's promotion in NA\701.4111/4–1745.

CHAPTER FIVE (pp. 71–85)

1. For descriptions of Maclean in Washington see the *Washington Star,* June 7, 1951; *New York Times,* March 12, 1983, and Cecil, *A Divided Life,* pp. 73–74; "picture" from John D. Hickerson, interview with author, October 3, 1984.

2. John Balfour, *Not Too Correct An Aureole* (London, 1983), pp. 113–114.

3. Letter, Hoare, p. 192; for Halifax appointment see *New York Times,* August 20, 1939; Jebb, p. 125; Dilks, *Cadogan Diaries,* pp. 277, 280.

4. "Team," in Earl of Birkenhead, *Halifax* (London, 1965), p. 480; also Cecil, *A Divided Life,* p. 70.

5. Cecil, *A Divided Life,* p. 74.

6. "Terroristic acts," in *Washington Post,* June 15, 1945. Churchill To Truman,

June 7, 1945, NA/Leahy Files, Folder 98. For the story of the Polish leaders see Z. F. Stypulkowski, *Invitation to Moscow* (London, 1951).

7. For the Hopkins-Stalin talks see Robert Sherwood, *Roosevelt and Hopkins* (New York, 1948), pp. 887–916; W. Averell Harriman and Elie Abel, *Special Envoy* (New York, 1975), pp. 459–471; FRUS, 1945, v. 5, pp. 317–339; Churchill, *Triumph and Tragedy* (New York, 1962), pp. 496–497.

8. Rebecca West, *The New Meaning of Treason,* pp. 221–222.

9. For the British War Cabinet Security Committee's *Reports of the Cipher Committee,* which spells out the procedures by which classified documents were received and transmitted, see FO850/46A & FO850/185 (which mentions Maclean), FO115/4262 and 4295.

10. For the final discussion on the Polish prisoners, see Sherwood, pp. 909–910; Harriman, pp. 469–470; Bohlen, pp. 219, 223; see also Kennan, *Memoirs,* p. 212; Murphy thought Hopkins was optimistic when he stopped in Berlin on his way back to Washington, see Robert Murphy, *Diplomat Among Warriors* (New York, 1964), p. 260; Herbert Feis has a more upbeat interpretation of the Hopkins-Stalin talks, see Herbert Feis, *Between War and Peace: The Potsdam Conference* (Princeton, 1960), pp. 97–116.

11. For Maclean's attitude about the postwar period see Donald Maclean, *British Foreign Policy* (New York, 1970), pp. 40, 54–55.

12. Churchill to Truman No. 73, June 4, 1945, Harry S. Truman Library, Independence, Mo.; *Washington Post,* June 12, 1945.

13. William Hillman, *Mr. President* (New York, 1952), entry for June 13, 1945, p. 122.

14. *Washington Post,* June 14–15, 1945.

15. Ibid., June 14, 1945.

16. "Chronic liar," H. G. Nichols, ed. *Washington Despatches 1941–1945* (Chicago, 1981), pp. 241–242; The information on the investigation that follows, unless otherwise noted, is taken from the FBI report dated July 31, 1945 and transmitted from J. Edgar Hoover to the White House on August 17 entitled *"Leaks to Press Regarding the Hopkins-Stalin Conversations in Moscow."* It can be found in the 1975 Retrospective Collection of Recently Declassified Government Documents, 251A.

17. Sherwood, p. 910.

18. Maclean was, however, adept at dealing with the media and a skilled leaker as well. When Malcolm Muggeridge was in Washington as a British correspondent, he frequently attended press briefings conducted by Maclean. "There is no doubt that Maclean knew his stuff," Muggeridge later recalled, though he did find him "a dull, humourless and rather pompous young man who tried a bit too hard to appear agreeable and relaxed . . . He was far too much of a cold fish beneath the polished surface charm." Quoted in Boyle, *The Fourth Man,* pp. 302–303. During the Anglo-American negotiations over bases (Chapter Eight), Maclean advised the FO "we leaked this to [*New York Times* correspondent] Reston" on instructions from London. Maclean explained that while the preferred place for the leak had been through an outlet in Teheran, "We took the view that the likelihood of such a press

leak in Teheran securing wide publicity was remote. Unfortunately Reston wrote his account as tho the State Department had leaked it," which caused State a number of problems. FO115/4246. Several weeks later, when England had come out on the short end of a Reston story leaked by State, Maclean cabled London, "There is nothing new about this except the fact that Reston continues to succeed in keeping the public well posted on what was supposed to be a series of secret talks and negotiations!", see FO371/59772.

19. David Karr, then twenty-six, once a Fuller Brush salesman, would go on to become a Hollywood producer and secret White House liaison to the Kremlin during the Carter administration, before dying mysteriously in Paris in 1977. Though Pearson ridiculed charges that he had been a communist, Karr admitted to the FBI he had been "on the staff of the *Daily Worker* for four years," see FBI: David Karr File, Nichols to Tolson, January 25, 1943; Nichols to Tolson, December 30, 1950. For Hoover's reaction, see his handwritten note on April 26, 1943, Memo Nichols to Tolson. As Senator McCarthy zeroed in on him, Karr confessed to Nichols that "he had been foolish; that in his ambitions to become a newspaperman he had done things that were uncalled for . . . he had given aid and comfort to Communists and Communist front groups years ago; that he had a tremendous obligation to the country to rectify this; that he would do anything, go any place, make any sacrifice to discharge his obligation to his country."; see Nichols to Tolson, January 5, 1951. According to FBI records, in a 1955 passport application Karr submitted a 50-page affidavit freely admitting his communist past and activities, now claiming it was because of his anit-Nazi sympathies and to combat anti-Semitism; see Belmont to Boardman, November 4, 1955. In 1945, Karr's wife Madeline worked for *Free World,* the Michael Straight-funded magazine which was edited by his brother-in-law Louis Dolivet, a suspected Comintern agent.

20. Sherwood, p. 135.

21. Clark in Thomas M. Franck and Edward Weisband, *Secrecy and Foreign Policy,* eds. (New York, 1974), pp. 203–204, 210.

22. For reference to and copies of the Hopkins-Churchill exchanges see NA\860c.00/6–445; Sherwood, p. 910; Churchill, v. 6. *Triumph and Tragedy,* op. cit., pp. 497–498; NA\740.00119 [Potsdam] 6–645.

23. From the earliest days of the Roosevelt-Churchill correspondence, the Foreign Office and the British embassy in Washington insisted that they receive copies of Churchill's messages to high-ranking American officials. After some initial reluctance, Churchill agreed. By the time he became Prime Minister, the system was almost automatic. Eventually it was Churchill himself who became most emphatic about the Washington embassy's being kept informed about all details of the Anglo-American relationship. This became a source of irritation for the State Department and especially the JCS, according to George Elsay who worked in the White House Map Room. Roosevelt would frequently share his early thinking on matters with Churchill, but withhold it from his own advisers. The JCS or the State Department would learn of the President's attitude only after Churchill shared it with the embassy, which would then press American officials for more details; from Elsay,

interview with author, June 12, 1984. For the routing of Churchill's communications both as first lord of the admiralty and prime minister see Sir Llewellyn Woodward, *British Foreign Policy in the Second World War* (London, 1970), pp. 334–335n; Joseph Lash, *Roosevelt and Churchill 1939–1941* (New York, 1976), pp. 61–62.

24. During the war Peter Dwyer had worked with Sir William Stephenson's British Security Coordination in New York. He was then assigned to the embassy as MI5/MI6 liaison with the FBI and later the CIA. He was replaced in the autumn of 1949 by Philby. NA\701.4111/Dwyer, Peter; Robert Lamphere and Tom Shachtman, *The FBI-KGB War* (New York, 1986), pp. 126–131.

25. On June 6, the FBI made a series of highly publicized arrests in New York, including two State Department officials, all of whom were charged with passing state secrets to a foreign power. Involved were thousands of documents passed over several years to *Amerasia Magazine,* a small, left-leaning New York publication. But the FBI had bungled the case badly, getting most of their evidence from illegal wiretaps and break-ins. Critics wondered how such a large espionage operation could have lasted so long without becoming enmeshed in FBI nets; see Harvey Klehr and Ronald Radosh, *Amerasia,* (New York, 1988).

26. Interview with John Taylor, head of the Military Division of the National Archives who arranged for me to be provided with copies of Numbers 72 and 73 directly from the Truman Presidential Library in Independence, Missouri.

27. Lamphere devotes a chapter to the breakthrough on the Soviet code in *The FBI-KGB War,* pp. 78–98. He remembers the Soviets changing their code at the end of May. But the cutoff may not have been that abrupt, and there were no other exchanges between Churchill and Truman during that period that would have had the importance of Numbers 72 and 73. See also David C. Martin, *Wilderness of Mirrors* (New York, 1980), pp. 38–39.

28. FBI: Philby Files, Undated report to Hoover from the New York Field Office, NY 65–15546, pp. 4–5; FBI June 19, 1951 Summary Report.

29. Interview with Harriet Marling Sheers, April 19, 1985; Hoare, pp. 71–73.

30. Interview with C.W.H. Dunbar, June 7 and 8, 1951 in FBI June 19, 1951 Summary Report.

31. Sheers interview.

32. Dunbar, FBI interview, op. cit. The Dunbars were divorced in April, 1945.

33. Hoare, p. 74.

34. *Life,* October 16, 1944, pp. 27–33.

35. The embassy's housing problems and Wright's purchase are in FO115/4260; Maclean's living arrangements are detailed in a number of FBI documents, the first an "Urgent" teletype to Hoover from the Washington field office dated June 12, 1951; "Rich Friend" in Hoare, p. 72; also Sheers interview.

36. FBI, June 19, 1951 Summary Report reports the exact date of the lease was January 19; Hoare, pp. 71–74; Cecil, *A Divided Life,* pp. 83–84 and *The Missing Dimension,* p. 187.

37. Cecil, *A Divided Life,* p. 89.

38. Hoare, pp. 81, 196, 201.

CHAPTER SIX (pp. 87–96)

1. Pincher, *Too Secret Too Long,* p. 205.

2. Information provided to the author by Joseph Alsop in letters and interviews between October 1984 and August 1985.

3. RDGD, 1975 R C, 70A.

4. Hickerson, interview with author, October 3, 1984.

5. "Vision," in Eleanor Philby, p. 115.

6. Hoare, p. 201.

7. Maclean, *British Foreign Policy,* p. 54.

8. Hoare, pp. 193–194, emphasis added.

9. Pincher, *Too Secret Too Long,* p. 205.

10. Cecil, "The Cambridge Comintern," *The Missing Dimension,* p. 183.

11. Page, *et. al.* were the first to reveal the Volkov episode. They did not identify Reed by name, though Knightley did some years later. See, Page, pp. 196–200 and Knightley, *Masterspy,* pp. 135–139. Both quote Reed's conclusion about Philby, Page, p. 199 and Knightley, p. 138. Chapman Pincher claims to have received a letter from John Reed, though he spells his name Read; see Pincher, *Too Secret Too Long,* pp. 204–206.

12. For a detailed account of the Volkov affair see Robert Cecil, "The Cambridge Comintern," *The Missing Dimension,* pp. 182–185; for Peterson see Dilks, *Cadogan Diaries,* pp. 286–87.

13. Igor Gouzenko, *This Was My Choice* (London, 1948), pp. 262–268.

14. Gouzenko, p. 270; "official," in Pincher, *Too Secret Too Long,* p. 206.

15. J. W. Pickersgill and D. F. Forster, eds. *The Mackenzie King Record* (Toronto, 1970), v. 3, 1945–1946, pp. 6–10.

16. Ibid., pp. 11–15.

17. FBI: Gouzenko Files 100–342972–26; note from Hoover, September 12, 1945; Nunn May in Ladd to Tamm, September 11, 1945; also Ladd to Hoover, September 12, 1945; Hoover to Tamm, Ladd, Tolson, September 13, 1945.

18. This also explains the reason that at Potsdam, when Truman told Stalin that the United States had developed a bomb "of unusual destructive force," the Russian dictator greeted the news with indifference. Truman, *Year of Decisions* (New York, 1955), v. 1, p. 416.

19. NA\FW 861.20242/9–1845.

20. Pickersgill and Forster, *King Record,* pp. 40–42; FBI: Hiss Files, Memo to Tolson, Tamm, Ladd, Carson from Hoover, October 11, 1945 details the Acheson-Hoover meeting.

21. Paul Gore-Booth, *With Great Truth and Respect* (London, 1974), pp. 144, 374–75.

CHAPTER SEVEN (pp. 97–109)

1. For John Connell on how Maclean would "sabotage what he was there ostensibly to promote," see, *The 'Office',* p. 331.

2. Testimony of Yuri Rastvorov before the Senate Judiciary Subcommittee, April 12, 1956, Part 14, US GPO.

3. Philby, p. 173; Cecil, "The Cambridge Comintern," *The Missing Dimension,* p. 185.

4. For Nazi-Soviet intrigue on the Straits, see Anthony Read and David Fisher, *The Deadly Embrace* (New York, 1988), pp. 517, 521, 539; Shirer, *The Rise and Fall of the Third Reich,* pp. 1060–62. For Soviet postwar efforts, see FRUS, 1944, Yalta Papers, 897–906; Edward Stettinius, *Roosevelt and the Russians: The Yalta Conference* (New York, 1949), 267–269; Harry Howard, *Turkey, the Straits & U. S. Policy,* (Baltimore, Md., 1974), pp. 210–215; Hugh Thomas, *Armed Truce* (New York, 1987), pp. 389–394.

5. Not every Senator was sold. Senators Arthur Vandenberg and Tom Connolly, the Republican Party's most respected foreign policy experts, thought, as Vandenberg put it, Byrnes would have been wonderful "for any other job,"; see Norman A. Graebner, *An Uncertain Tradition: American Secretaries of State in the Twentieth Century* (New York, 1961), p. 206.

6. For Byrnes's attitudes about negotiating with the Soviets, see Walter Mills, ed., *The Forrestal Diaries* (New York, 1951), pp. 262–263; For Byrnes's fatal negotiations with Molotov at the December 1945 Moscow conference, see Kennan, *Memoirs,* pp. 286–289.

7. For Soviet demands, see Joseph Jones, *The Fifteen Weeks* (New York, 1955), pp. 60–61; also, Graham Ross, ed., *The Foreign Office and the Kremlin* (Cambridge, 1984), pp. 238–240.

8. Howard, p. 222.

9. FRUS, 1945, v. 8, pp. 1248, 1257; Howard, p. 233.

10. FRUS, 1945, v. 8, pp. 1252.

11. For McDermott, see FO371/48698; "perhaps," in FO371/48775.

12. "Nyet!" in Murphy, pp. 278–279; "Stalin wants," in Howard, p. 225; see also Bohlen, p. 235; James F. Byrnes, *Speaking Frankly* (New York, 1947), p. 77; Truman, *Memoirs,* v. 1, pp. 377–378; William D. Leahy, *I Was There* (New York, 1950), p. 409.

13. NA\767.68119/10-1345

14. Wilson cable, in 761.67/10–2045; contents shared with British, FO371/48775; "die," in Howard, pp. 220, 233, and Mills, *The Forrestal Diaries,* p. 97.

15. NA\767.68119/10-2045.

16. Bevin in Howard, p. 228; "I think," in FO371/48698. The Turkish Foreign Office later adopted the phrase about "severing the British Empire jugular at Suez"; see FRUS, 1947, v. 5, p. 2.

17. FO371/48698.

18. Harriman, FRUS, 1945, v. 8, p. 1258; "Hand in hand," in FO371/48775; Henderson to Wright, FRUS, 1945, v. 8, p. 1258, note 75; For Henderson's December 1945 assessment of the Near East, see FRUS, 1946, v. 7, pp. 1–6.

19. For Maclean-Wright review of American proposal and call to Henderson, see NA\867N.01/10-2445 and FRUS, 1945, v. 8, pp. 1258–1259; For dispatch of American proposal from the British Embassy, see FO371/48698.

20. *New York Times,* October 30 and October 31, 1945.

21. Department of State, Verbatim Reports, Press Conferences, v. 16, (1945) No. 55, pp. 1–6, US GPO.

22. For Halifax report to London of Byrnes's call, see FO371/48699. In a subsequent cable about Byrnes's characterization of the proposal the U. S. had sent Turkey, Halifax emphasized that the secretary said it had been sent "without (repeat without) consultation with the British."

23. FRUS, 1945, v. 8, pp. 1266–1267.

24. Eleanor Philby, p. 84.

25. For routing of American proposal and Peterson's account of meeting, see FO371/48699; For ground rules Henderson had imposed in earlier instance, see FO371/48775 and FRUS, 1945, v. 8, pp. 1262–1263.

26. Byrnes's first cable was routinely drafted, cleared and then dispatched to Wilson at 3 p.m. Washington time. His second cable, countermanding the first, was dispatched at 7 p.m.; see NA\767.68119/10–3045; see also FRUS, 1945, v. 8, pp. 1263–1268.

27. NA\761.67/11–145.

28. "Would rather," in Adam B. Ulam, *The Rivals: America and Russia Since World War II* (New York, 1978), p. 258; for Victor Rothwell's conclusion that Soviet embassies between 1946 and 1953 were "morbid tombs" whose terrified occupants could perform few of the normal duties of diplomats, see his *Britain and the Cold War 1941–1947* (London, 1982), p. 233.

29. For Wilson meeting with Vinogradov, see NA\767.68119/11–345.

30. Wilson letters in NA\767.68119/11–545. For other mix-ups that followed transmittal of the American paper to the British, see FRUS, 1945, v. 8, pp. 1265–66.

31. For Bevin's assurances to the British embassy that he was investigating the leak, see FO371/48699 and NA\767.68119/11–745; for Henderson's report of Maclean's assurances to Byrnes, Acheson, et. al., see NA\767.68119/11–745.

32. "I do not propose," in FO371/48699 and FRUS, 1945, v. 8, p. 1269, note 87; for the reaction of Turkish Foreign Minister Erkin, who thought "the effect of the American proposals would be to turn the Black Sea into a Soviet naval base," see Howard, p. 237, and FO371/48699, Peterson to FO, November 5.

33. FO371/48699.

34. Howard, p. 238.

35. FO371/48699.

36. Kennan, *Memoirs,* p. 286; for British aspersions on Byrnes, see "personality reports" in FO371/44620; "lie," in FO371/48699.

37. FRUS, 1947, v. 5, pp. 350–351.

38. FO371/48775, minute dated November 4, 1945.

39. NA\867.20/9–2947; FRUS, 1947, v. 5, p. 352, note 1.

40. Hillman, *Mr. President,* pp. 22–23; Truman, *Memoirs,* v. 1., pp. 551–552; Thomas, *Armed Truce,* p. 393.

41. Loy Henderson, phone interview with author, July 14, 1985.

CHAPTER EIGHT (pp. 111–125)

1. FRUS, 1946, v. 5, 35–36.

2. *Washington Post,* December 5, 1989.

3. For the Bermuda Conference, see *The New York Times,* February 16 and 17, 1946; see also NA\841.796/2–746; and FRUS, 1946, v. 1, 1472–74 for disputes.

4. Wright was on leave from February 18 to March 6. He departed Washington permanently on March 31; see FO115/4229 and NA\701.411/Wright, Michael; There has been much confusion and debate about when Maclean was Head of Chancery. Both Hoare and the FBI erroneously concluded that he held that position from the spring of 1945 on; see FBI: Philby Files, undated memorandum to Boardman, p. 3; Hoare, p. 199. Cecil is more accurate in saying that Maclean was acting Head once Wright left Washington; see "Legends Spies Tell," *Encounter,* April 1978. But as has been shown, he was acting Head from at least mid-February, and during the summer of 1945, he shared many of the duties if not the title, according to Gore-Booth, op. cit., pp. 144, 374–375.

5. During the height of Maclean's work with Gore-Booth and the running of the chancery, he was vitally involved in security matters including renovations of the cipher room on the chancery's second floor. The Soviets have a long history of bugging foreign embassies, including the British embassy in Moscow in the 1940s and the American embassy in Moscow in the 1980s. If they did not exploit Maclean's supervision of the renovation work on the cipher room in 1946, it was an uncharacteristic restraint; see FO850/185.

William Codrington was made an unpaid adviser on security in 1940 after Krivitsky's warnings. He sent a friend, Ralph Thomas to Washington to take charge of embassy security. During 1945–1946 Thomas, who had no experience and was largely ignored, reported to Maclean (including, for instance, in arranging security for a 1946 United Nations visit by Bevin). His reports to Codrington betrayed his insecurity: "in the course of this work I have made some very real friends."; see FO850/46A; Cecil, *A Divided Life,* p. 64; "The Cambridge Comintern," in *The Missing Dimension,* pp. 181–182.

6. "For the Ambassador," in FRUS, 1946, v. 2, pp. 27–28. The subject was an impending meeting of the Council of Foreign Ministers; for Halifax rescinding order, see FO115/4229.

7. For Churchill and Roosevelt on bases, see Robert Dallek, *Franklin D. Roosevelt and American Foreign Policy, 1932–1945* (New York, 1979), pp. 243–247; Lash, *Roosevelt and Churchill,* pp. 206–212; Kimball, *Churchill & Roosevelt,* v. 1, pp. 57–59; The British possessions were Bermuda, the Bahamas, Jamaica, Antigua, Newfoundland, Trinidad, British Guiana, and St. Lucia.

8. Mahon in *Washington Evening Star,* April 9, 1945; Leahy in *New York Times,* August 11, 1945; see also Nichols, ed., *Washington Despatches,* p. 616; NA\811.24590/ 4-545; Chicago *Tribune,* April 9, 1945 quoted in Christopher Thorne, *Allies of a Kind* (New York, 1978), p. 664.

9. According to Leahy, Roosevelt was anxious to secure "a series of strategic

bases all over the world," but they were to be controlled by the United Nations; see Leahy p. 314. But that was not de Gaulle's understanding; see Kimball, *Roosevelt & Churchill,* v. 3, p. 237.

10. "As long," in Thomas, *Armed Truce,* p. 601, note 23.

11. Mills, *Forrestal Diaries,* p. 141; "stepping stones," in J. N. Henderson, *The Private Office* (London, 1984), p. 48.

12. FO371/44671, January 17, 1946.

13. "Find out," in FO115/4238; "Washington," in FO371/44671, October 2, 1945 by Orme Sargent.

14. Attitudes on Hickerson in FO115/4238.

15. Henderson, p. 59.

16. "It would," in FO115/4238. Byrnes had expressed the same sentiment but more gently in late September, and primarily for Tarawa; see FO371/44671.

17. "List," in FO115/4238; for strategy behind the negotiations, see Thorne, pp. 663–664; as Commander in Chief of the Atlantic forces Dennison played a dramatic role during the 1962 Cuban Missile Crisis.

18. Hickerson interview.

19. For Maclean's reports, see FO115/4238 and FO371/51682.

20. "Treating us," in FO371/51682.

21. FO115/4238, emphasis added.

22. Baruch in Richard N. Gardner, *Sterling-Dollar Diplomacy* (New York, 1969), pp. 189–190.

23. Nichols, ed., *Washington Despatches,* p. 616.

24. For an analysis of the loan, see *New York Times,* September 9, 1945.

25. "The Americans," in FO371/44671; for British reaction, see Gardner, *Sterling-Dollar Diplomacy,* pp. 227–28.

26. Gardner, p. 224.

27. Ibid., p. 237–238.

28. For Halifax report on exchange with Vandenberg, see FO371/44671.

29. R.F. Harrod, *The Life and Times of John Maynard Keynes* (New York, 1951), pp. 597–598; "conditions," in Robert J. Donovan, *Conflict and Crisis,* (New York, 1977), p. 186.

30. "Loan," in *New York Times,* February 11 and 15, 1946.

31. "Embarrassing," and "great assistance," in FO115/4238; "solely," in FRUS, 1946, v. 5, p. 39; "bows," in FRUS, 1946, v. 5, p. 45.

32. For Evat proposal, see FRUS, 1946, v. 5, pp. 36–37, 40–43.

33. Ibid., pp. 35–36.

34. Ibid., p. 38.

35. For Maclean's report on May 2 Hickerson meeting, see FO115/4238.

36. Maclean-Hickerson in FRUS, 1946, v. 5, pp. 37–38. It is worth noting, given the British government's later diminution of the American Department when Maclean headed it, that Mason—constantly at Bevin's side during these important Anglo-American negotiations—was then head of the American Department.

37. Harriman in FRUS, 1946, v. 5, pp. 43–44.

38. *New York Times,* May 10, 1946; *Manchester Guardian,* May 10, 1946; *London Times,* May 13, 1946.

39. NA\841.014/5–1446.

40. *Daily Express, Daily Telegraph,* May 14, and *Manchester Guardian,* May 15, 1946.

41. FRUS, 1946, v. 5, pp. 45–46.

42. Ibid.

43. Ibid., pp. 44–45.

44. Director of the Central Intelligence Group Hoyt S. Vandenberg to Leahy, August 27, 1946, RDGD, 1975 RC, 245B. The report covers activities much earlier because Zhukov had been demoted and had disappeared from Moscow by July; see *New York Times,* March 9, 1946; Deutscher, pp. 546–547.

45. Montgomery Hyde, *The Atom Bomb Spies* (New York, 1980), pp. 70–75.

46. Gardner, *Sterling Diplomacy,* p. 342.

47. Hickerson interview, October 3, 1984.

CHAPTER NINE (pp. 127–143)

1. Hiss interview with David Wigg, *The Times* (London), June 23, 1973 at the time of the Watergate scandal.

2. Weinstein, pp. 350–351.

3. FBI: Hiss Files, Statement of Alger Hiss, February 14, 1942. Though the names have been excised, documents obtained from the State Department show that the FBI attached to Hiss's statement the names of twelve informants; see DOS: Hiss Files, Shaw to Hoover, March 26, 1942. Shaw later testified as a character witness for Hiss; see Weinstein, p. 203, for another opinion, see Bohlen, p. 94.

4. Hiss interview with author, April 10, 1985.

5. According to Hoover, "Bentley furnished voluminous information to this Bureau," see FBI: Philby Files, Summary Report.

6. King told Acheson and Truman that Gouzenko had described a spy who was very close to Stettinius at San Francisco. The Prime Minister wrote in his diary on February 6, 1946, "I was surprised when I saw the particular person [Gouzenko] mentioned filling the position he did."; see Pickersgill and Forster, *King Record,* v. 3, p. 140, emphasis added; see also James Barros, "Alger Hiss and Harry Dexter White: The Canadian Connection," *Orbis,* v. 21, No. 3, 1977, pp. 593–605; FBI: Hiss Files, Nichols to Tolson, June 21, 1956.

7. For Hoover-Acheson meeting, see FBI: Hiss Files, Memorandum for Mr. Tolson, *et. al.,* October 11, 1945.

8. The first official FBI report naming Hiss as a Russian operative was dated November 27, 1945. It was sent to the White House and later to the State Department. The surveillance was initially on Hiss's home, and later expanded to include his State Department office from August to October 1946, see Weinstein,

pp. 357, 364. FBI documents detail the Maclean-Hiss contacts from October onward, FBI: Philby Files 1955 Summary report, p. 36, XVII. "Maclean and Hiss."

9. For December 13 meeting, see NA\501.BC/12–1345; "Dear Hiss," in NA\501.BC/12–1545. This is the only instance found in either American or British archives where Maclean addressed an American colleague with such presumed familiarity. On the 22nd Hiss sent Maclean a memo and Maclean phoned Hiss to ask questions about it; see NA\501.BC12–15–2545.

10. Greece in NA\501.BC/9–1346 and FRUS, 1946, v. 7, pp. 216–218; Africa trusteeships in FRUS, 1946, v. 1, pp. 631–632, another instance when Maclean signed "for the Ambassador." When Hiss's desk calendar for September 1946 was made an exhibit in one of his trials in 1956, its notation "McLean [sic] Brit. Emb." caused a stir. Mid-level FBI agents were unable or unwilling to provide any explanation in response to press inquiries, even though at least at the senior levels of the Bureau the contacts between Hiss and Maclean were well known; see FBI: Philby Files, Nichols to Tolson, February 28, 1956 and New York to Director, March 21, 1956. Years later Alan Weinstein also tried to find a connection between Hiss and Maclean, but did not and concluded that the matter ended with the meeting on the 14th; see Weinstein, pp. 363–364.

11. For Byrnes's initial reaction to the Hiss allegations, see FBI: Hiss Files, November 30, 1945 Memorandum, Hoover to Tolson, et al., which details the November 27 Byrnes-Hoover meeting. That Hoover was a master of intrigue, plotting and manipulation is demonstrated in a series of meetings and conversations between March 19–21, 1946 with Byrnes, Attorney General Tom Clark, and various members of Congress. Hoover designated the memoranda detailing these meetings be placed in his Official and Confidential Files (O&C Files). Though these files were "to be destroyed after action is taken and not sent [to official FBI] files," many were not, and in recent years have been released under FOIA. The exchanges between Hiss-Byrnes-Hoover-and Clark which follow are all taken from the March 19–21 memoranda.

12. Immediately after Hiss left his office, Byrnes called Hoover to report on their meeting. As soon as he hung up with Byrnes, Hoover purposefully aroused Clark's ire over Byrnes's session with Hiss. See Hoover O&C Files, Memorandum to Tolson, et al., March 21, 1946; Hiss met with Ladd on March 25, see FBI: Hiss Files, Ladd memorandum, March 25, 1946.

13. "No further," in Weinstein, p. 358; "terminated," in DOS: Hiss File, undated memorandum, "Security Information."

14. For Winchell broadcast, see DOS: Hiss Files, Klaus to Panuch, October 1, 1946.

15. Several sources provided James Barros with details about how Acheson conspired to circumvent Hiss at the time the State Department was formulating its response to Britain's sudden withdrawal from Turkey and Greece. The British, however, did not inform the Department of their decision to pull out until February 11, 1947. Hiss resigned from the State Department in December 1946; see Barros, "Alger Hiss and Harry Dexter White," Orbis, op. cit., pp. 602–603.

16. Chambers in Weinstein, p. 366.

17. "Strength," in Pickersgill, ed., *King Record* v. 3, pp. 17, 41; Djilas, *Conversations With Stalin,* pp. 114–115; "calculation," in C. L. Sulzberger, *A Long Row of Candles* (Toronto, 1969), p. 479.

18. Text of the Gromyko Resolution in FRUS, 1946, v. 1, pp. 892–893; text and news accounts, *New York Times,* August 30 and August 31, 1946.

19. For troop estimates, see *New York Times,* May 3 and November 11, 1945 and April 17 and June 3, 1946; for British estimates of Soviet strength, see FO371/56848; U.S. estimates in NA\861.20/2–2546. For Stalin order to demobilize, see September 18, 1946 report of Soviet Military Intentions, Papers of Harry S. Truman, President's Secretary's Files, RDGD, 1975 RC. The true number of Russian war dead was unknown until 1959 when Western demographers, using Soviet census data, concluded that Russia had suffered twenty million war dead; see Deutscher, pp. 535–536 and *Wall Street Journal,* August 11, and November 19, 1945.

20. "Talking tough," in *New York Times,* March 16, 1946.

21. For US troop demobilization, see *New York Times,* May 17, November 20, 1945, and August 31, 1946; also, *Time,* October 14, 1946.

22. "Detailed," in *New York Times,* August 31, 1946.

23. For troop strength information available to Maclean, see FO371/46410, FO371/47917, and FO115/4257. For Maclean and JSM, see Cecil, *A Divided Life,* pp. 74–75.

24. "Latest Developments," in FO115/4257 and FO371/47917; estimates of American naval manpower, FO371/46410.

25. NA\501.BC/9–1346.

26. FRUS, 1946, v. 1, p. 967.

27. RDGD, 1975 RC, 75A.

28. FRUS, 1946, v. 1, p. 962.

29. For "Public Opinion Report to the Secretary," (a periodic report), see NA\501.BB/10–1846.

30. For memorandum of Hiss-Maclean phone conversation, see NA\501.BB/10–246 and FRUS, 1946, v. 1, 960–961. The FBI discovered that they had records of Hiss-Maclean phone conversations on June 7, 1951: "According to [deleted, but assumed to be technical surveillance], on October 19, 1946, Alger Hiss twice conferred with Donald Maclean concerning one of the topics on the UNGA agenda dealing with troops of the UN in non-enemy territories. Later in the day Hiss was again in contact with Maclean also concerning a proposed resolution," see FBI: Ladd to Hoover, June 7, 1951; Summary Report.

31. Hiss-Maclean October 19 and 21 phone conversations, FRUS, 1946, v. 1, pp. 960–961; Maclean to Byrnes and Byrnes to Hiss, NA\501.BB/10–2146.

32. Bevin first spelled out his objections to Byrnes in Paris: "Your suggestion would lead to very grave difficulties for the British Command and I must tell you frankly that we are opposed to it. There are fundamental reasons for this which I will explain to you confidentially this afternoon." In the meantime, Byrnes was assured, the British "would vote against any U.N. resolution requiring disclosure of their troops abroad." see NA\501.BB/9–246 and FRUS, 1946, v. 1, pp. 896–897.

33. For strain on Royal Navy, see NA\501.BB/11–645.

34. NA\501.BB/10–2346 and FRUS, 1946, v. 1., pp. 962–963.

35. FRUS, 1946, v. 1, pp. 966–968. Bevin departed England Saturday, October 26 and arrived New York, Saturday, November 2.

36. FRUS, 1946, v. 1, p. 969, emphasis added.

37. *New York Times,* October 30, 1946.

38. FRUS, 1946, v. 1, pp. 978–979.

39. *New York Times,* Thursday, October 31.

40. For Austin's speech revisions, see NA\501.BB/10–2946 and 10–3046; also FRUS, 1946, v. 1, pp. 972–979. Disarmament debate can be followed in *The New York Times,* November 20–22, and 25–28, 1946.

41. Hiss had hopes of becoming the State Department's man on atomic energy; see Weinstein, pp. 357, 363.

42. Cecil, *A Divided Life,* pp. 75–76.

43. Weinstein, pp. 363–364. The FBI's own strange handling of the Hiss-Maclean allegations can be seen in FBI: Philby Files, Nichols to Tolson February 28, 1956 and New York to Hoover, March 21, 1956.

44. I spoke with Hiss by phone on September 17, 1984, and interviewed him at his New York apartment on April 10, 1985. I reviewed with him all the exhibits, including his handwritten notes of meetings with Maclean. He recalled the pressing United Nations issues at the time. "But I just do not recall any meetings with Maclean." For another view of Hiss's constant bewilderment, see Straight, p. 231. For Burgess's opinion, Boyle, *The Fourth Man,* p. 320.

45. Cecil, *A Divided Life,* p. 76; Philip Toynbee, "Maclean and I," *Observer,* October 15, 1967.

CHAPTER TEN (pp. 145–161)

1. *The Journals of David E. Lilienthal: The Atomic Energy Years* (New York, 1964), v. 2, pp. 11, 26.

2. FBI: Philby Files, LaPlante to Waters, June 7, 1951.

3. FBI: Philby Files, Nichols to Tolson, June 8, 1951, with handwritten notation at bottom by Hoover.

4. June 8, 1951 Pike to McMahon. Released by the Department of Energy on August 27, 1987 in response to the author's FOIA request.

5. The Trust was negotiated in London in March 1944 and the Declaration of Trust between Britain, America was signed in mid-June 1944. The CDT was codenamed the "Insecticide Committee," and its campaign to control the world's sources of high-grade uranium was codenamed "the Murray Hill Project," Leslie Groves, *Now It Can Be Told* (New York, 1983), pp. 170–74.

6. Between June 9 and June 13, 1951 the FBI interviewed AEC staffers Roy B. Snapp, Chief of the Office of Special Projects; Attorney A. A. Wells, John K.

Gustafson, Manager for Raw Materials, and former AEC General Manager Carroll Wilson, see FBI: Philby Files, June 9, 1951 interviews, pp. 2–4.

7. The British Scientific Mission notified the AEC on August 23, 1948 that the pass was no longer needed. AEC records show that Maclean did not surrender the pass until August 27, his last day in Washington; see FBI: Philby Files, La Plante to Waters, June 15, 1951 and Belmont to Boardman, October 26, 1955. See also Lewis L. Strauss, *Men and Decisions* (New York, 1963), pp. 266–267. In 1954 Strauss led the highly controversial campaign to strip Robert Oppenheimer of his security clearance. In 1959 Strauss was nominated by Eisenhower to be Secretary of Commerce. But the Senate, concluding he was "guilty of an outright misrepresentation" and lacking in integrity, rejected the nomination. The Senate did not reject another Cabinet nominee until John Tower 30 years later; see Philip M. Stern, *The Oppenheimer Case* (New York, 1969), pp. 441–446.

8. FBI: Philby Files, Ladd to the Director, June 26, 1951; on July 3, Strauss called Ladd to tell him that he had found among his papers a copy of the memorandum authorizing a pass for Maclean; see AEC Review, Roach to Belmont, November 7, 1955.

9. FBI: Philby Files, Belmont to Ladd, August 2, 1951, emphasis added.

10. FBI: Philby Files. In a memo from Ladd to Hoover dated June 7, the heading is:

UNKNOWN SUBJECT WAS:
[Deleted]
Espionage—R.

But no effort was made to excise the heading of the June 28, 1951 memo from Hoover to the CIA, which I obtained under the FOIA.

11. DOS: Maclean Files, Eastland to Dulles, October 11, 1955, emphasis added.

12. For September 21, Butler to Makins, see PRO/AB16–2; Dr. Wilfrid Mann, a British physicist who arrived at the Canadian atomic energy project at Chalk River, Canada, on July 27, 1946, was suggested by David E. H. Pierson. But Makins opposed him because he was "too inexperienced to fill the bill," see PRO/AB16–2. Later Andrew Boyle, operating at least in part under false leads planted by former CIA counterintelligence chief James Angleton as part of a vendetta he had with Mann, implicated Mann as a Soviet spy sent to help Maclean. This thesis was convincingly rejected by Alan Weinstein in *The Washington Post*, January 25, 1980. Later Mann wrote *Was There A Fifth Man?* (Oxford, 1982).

13. Rickett to D. E. H. Pierson, January 17, 1947, PRO/AB16–2.

14. Vincent Jones, *Manhattan* (Washington, 1985), pp. 227–228.

15. *A Report to the President by Special Committee of National Security Council on Atomic Energy Policy with respect to the United Kingdom and Canada,* March 2, 1949, in RDGD, 1975 RC, pp. 19–23. Hereafter *NSC/AE.*

16. None were more suspicious of the British, and more opposed to sharing information with them, than Groves. Yet, even he conceded that Churchill was the

most enthusiastic and effective friend that the Manhattan Project ever had. He could sense even from London when the project was stymied because of Washington inertia, and he would intercede with Roosevelt to give the project a new impetus; see Groves, p. 408.

17. NSC/AE, p. 32.

18. "You are," in FO115/4223; for July 4 CPC meeting, see FRUS, 1945, v. 2, p. 12. Marshall's official order to the army was not issued until July 25. Maclean notes that "this clause [in the Quebec agreement] was strictly complied with before the American atomic attack on Hiroshima."; see Maclean, p. 53; for a fascinating postscript see Acheson, *Present at the Creation* (New York, 1969), pp. 715–716.

19. "Cable No. 1," in FRUS, 1946, v. 2, p. 37, emphasis added; for public reaction, see *New York Times,* November 17 and 18, 1945. According to one observer at the Mayflower, the prevailing attitude of the conference was "The Atomic Bomb is just too dreadful, too awful, too-too-too—Everybody must do something about it quick. What are you doing? What Am I doing?—We must all do more."; see Alice Kimbell Smith, *A Peril and A Hope* (Chicago, 1965), pp. 227–228; also Donald A. Strickland, *Scientists in Politics: The Atomic Scientist Movement, 1945–46* (Lafayette, Ind., 1968), pp. 2–9, 58–59.

Maclean and Balfour did most of the planning for Attlee's participation in the November 15 Conference. As one State Department meeting broke up, Donald and an American official walked towards the elevator still deep in discussion over the agenda, unaware "a posse of journalists were closing in on us with notebooks at the ready." But, says Balfour, "they shut-up like frightened clams when I pointed out that they were encircled by the press," Balfour, pp. 114–115.

20. FBI: Philby Files, Hoover handwritten note, Ladd to Strickland, December 5, 1945; Barros, "Alger Hiss and Harry Dexter White," *Orbis,* op. cit., p. 597.

21. It was while waiting for the ceremonies to be completed that Vandenberg made his suggestions to Halifax about "sweeteners" for the British loan, FO371/44671.

22. *New York Times,* March 20, 1946.

23. Teller later recanted, conceding that science provides no special insight to public affairs, and that scientists, like movie stars, ought to restrain themselves less they be taken too seriously, Richard Rhodes, *The Making of The Atomic Bomb* (New York, 1986), p. 770.

24. A pioneering work in this deception was William Reuben, *The Atom Spy Hoax* (New York, 1955). A more contemporary version can be found in Gregg Herken, *The Winning Weapon* (New York, 1982), pp. 97–113.

25. Churchill seems to have been the recipient of perpetually bad advice from his science adviser Lord Cherwell, who was cheering the break-up of the Anglo-American atomic partnership so that the Americans would no longer hamper the British effort. "If it becomes necessary," he told Churchill, "we could put up a better plant than the one in the USA . . . Incidentally, there are various dodges, which the Americans think we do not know, by which the power of this explosive can probably be multiplied four or five times." See PREM/3/139/2, "The Tube Alloys Positions," from Cherwell to the PM.

26. "No reason," in *New York Times,* October 9, 1945, and Donovan, *Conflict and Crisis,* p. 132; "open exchange," in *New York Times,* November 16, 1945.

27. Francis Williams, *Twilight of Empire: Memoirs of Prime Minister Attlee* (New York, 1962), p. 99; Howe quoted in *New York Times,* February 17, 1946.

28. Pickersgill, *King Record,* p. 75; Churchill in PREM 3/139/2.

29. Groves, p. 170.

30. Vincent Jones, *Manhattan,* p. 8.

31. Ibid., pp. 64–65; Groves, pp. 33–35, is considerably kinder to Sengier.

32. V. Jones, *Manhattan,* p. 295.

33. Acheson, pp. 140–141.

34. FRUS, 1947, v. 1, pp. 789–792.

35. Baruch in *Washington Post,* February 4, 1947; for Acheson's view of Baruch's reputation, see Acheson, p. 154.

36. Richard E. Hewlett and Oscar E. Anderson, Jr., *The New World, 1939/1946: A History of the Atomic Energy Commission* (University Park, Pa., 1962), v. 1, p. 541.

37. FRUS, 1947, v. 1, pp. 792–793.

38. Van Hodrick comments reported in NA\855.6359/2–1047.

39. DOS: Atomic Energy Files, February 19, 1947 cable from the American embassy in Brussels.

40. *New York Times,* March 12–17, 1947.

41. Spaak in FRUS, 1947, v. 1, pp. 793–794, 812, 822–824; Makins to Rickett, PRO/AB16–2, July 17, 1947.

CHAPTER ELEVEN (pp. 163–185)

1. FRUS, 1947, v. 1, p. 807; interview by author with former CDT staff member who requested anonymity, March 19, 1985.

2. Maclean, p. 273.

3. Meeting, FRUS, 1947, v. 1, pp. 785–789; for Acheson on FDR, see Acheson, p. 3, for Quebec, p. 164; also Walter Isaacson and Evan Thomas, *The Wise Men* (New York, 1986), pp. 134–135.

4. FRUS, 1947, v. 1, pp. 794–795.

5. Ibid., pp. 798–799.

6. Margaret Gowing, *Independence and Deterrance: Britain and Atomic Energy, 1945–1952* (New York, 1974) v. 1, *Policy Execution,* pp. 103–104, 243.

7. Curiously, British historian Anthony Glees concludes that while Maclean and the Belgian Communists "could have made matters very difficult for M. Paul Spaak" they did not do so. Glees believes that the Communists never learned about the secret preemptive buying agreement because Maclean, "evidently stayed silent." Glees's offers this as proof that Maclean "could have done worse damage than he did." See Anthony Glees, *The Secrets of the Service* (London, 1987), p. 354.

8. FRUS, 1947, v. 1., p. 802.

9. Ibid., pp. 802–803.

10. Ibid., p. 817, emphasis added.

11. FO115/4335, Inverchapel to Attlee, March 10, 1947.

12. Dates for Maclean's London visit, March 28 to April 6 are in PRO/AB16 and FBI Summary Report based on files from the Immigration and Naturalization Service.

13. Herken, pp. 196–197.

14. For meeting, see FRUS, 1947, v. 1, pp. 804–806; Lilienthal, *Journals,* v. 2, p. 172; Richard G. Hewlett and Francis Duncan, *Atomic Shield 1947/1952: A History of the United States Atomic Energy Commission* (University Park, Pa., 1969), pp. 47–48.

15. For illumination of this attitude, see "Statement of Effect of Atomic Weapons on National Security and Military Organization," issued by the Joint Chiefs of Staff, January 1946, *Washington Post,* July 22, 1985.

16. "Shock," in Hewlett and Duncan, *Atomic Shield,* p. 47.

17. PRO/AB16–388, June 21, 1947, Longair to Cockcroft.

18. PRO/AB16–408, July 11, 1947.

19. PRO/AB16–2, A. King to Munro, March 18, 1947; the U. S. had a 60-inch cyclotron in 1939; see Hewlett and Duncan, *Atomic Shield,* p. 229.

20. For JCAE meeting, see Lilienthal, *Journals,* v. 2, pp. 175–176; Hewlett and Duncan, *Atomic Shield,* pp. 274–275; for Maclean-Gullion, see FO115/4311.

21. "Live wire," in PRO/AB16–388, Munro to Rickett, March 20, 1947; "commission," in PRO/AB16–388, March 18, 1947.

22. May 10 meeting with Wilson in PRO/AB16–388; "impossible to comply," in FRUS, 1947, v. 1, p. 793.

23. "Cheering news," in Gowing, v. 1, pp. 242–243.

24. May 12 meeting with Wilson in PRO/AB16–388.

25. "Pleased," in Lilienthal, *Journals,* v. 2, p. 177.

26. For Acheson meeting with JCAE, see FRUS, 1947, v. 1, pp. 806–811. Acheson had been chosen as the bearer of bad news because he had no role in negotiating the original agreements and because he was scheduled to leave government in two months anyway, see Acheson, pp. 167–168; the British embassy in Washington reported the meeting to London via cable on May 14, presumably by Maclean. Curiously, the report to London characterized Acheson's appearance as "successful," with no hostile reaction by the Committee: "We have taken this hurdle without mishap."; see AB16–285, May 14; for Vandenberg's reaction, see Arthur Vandenberg Jr., ed. *The Private Papers of Senator Vandenberg* (Boston, 1952), p. 361; For Hickenlooper's reaction, see FRUS, 1947, v. 1, pp. 833–834.

27. For Baruch's estimate of when the Soviets would have an atomic weapon see *New York Times,* February 4–5, 1947; for Groves, see FRUS, 1946, v. 1, p. 1198; Peter Wyden, *Day One: Before Hiroshima and After* (New York, 1984), p. 157 and Herken, p. 112; for Central Intelligence Group estimate, see October 31, 1946, RDGD, 1975 RC; for CIA December 15, 1947 estimate, see FRUS, 1947, v. 1, pp. 903–905.

28. For Gullion, see FRUS, 1947, v. 1, pp. 832–833; Danish physicist Niels Bohr also proved prophetic, see FRUS, 1948, v. 1, p. 508; Brooks Atkinson, the Broadway

critic turned war correspondent, had perhaps the keenest anticipation of Soviet abilities; see the *New York Times,* November 25, 1945.

29. Arnold Kramish, *Atomic Energy in the Soviet Union* (Stanford, Calif., 1959), pp. 120, 170–171.

30. FRUS, 1947, v. 1, p. 829.

31. The Soviet Union's uranium sources were nearly all low-grade and on the fringes of its borders, areas that were thinly populated and offered no transportation. Beginning in January 1943, Soviet intelligence tried every method possible to obtain uranium from the United States. See Dallin, *Soviet Espionage,* pp. 457–458; "microgram," in Wyden, p. 90.

32. Hyde, *The Atom Bomb Spies,* pp. 29–30.

33. Dallin, *Soviet Espionage,* p. 458.

34. Kramish, pp. 26–27, 119–120; and Hewlett and Anderson, *The New World,* p. 548.

35. FRUS, 1945, v. 2, pp. 84–89; reported to UK in PRO/AB16–285. Groves also conceded that the Soviets might have large deposits of low-grade uranium, and in time the "discovery of new deposits is not improbable," but "they could not be developed in the next decade" unless "no consideration is given to cost."

36. "Maclean attended," in FBI: Philby Files, June 13 teletype to Hoover from New York.

37. Acheson before JCAE, FRUS, 1947, v. 1, p. 806; Richard Hewlett in phone interview with author, May 14, 1985.

38. CDT engineer on Maclean, interview with anonymous source, March 19, 1985.

39. Byrnes in Herken, p. 57.

40. Kirk and Spaak in FRUS, 1947, v. 1, pp. 836–837.

41. Press reports in NA\855A.6359/8–647.

42. FBI: Philby Files, Memorandum to CIA Director from Hoover, October 3, 1955. There was no "O" building around the Reflection Pool, though there was an "O" building in a different part of town. All in all, this further undermines the credibility of Hoover's allegations.

43. Toynbee, *Observer,* "Maclean and I," op. cit.; Hoare, pp. 196–201.

44. Edmund A. Gullion, interview with author, October 16, 1984; translations from European clips can be found in FO/711.4011/2–1248.

45. For Fuchs, see Carroll Wilson to F. N. Woodward at the British Commonwealth Science Office in Washington, August 19, 1947 in FO115/4313.

46. DOE Files: August 6, 1947, T. O. Jones from D. Dean. In all, MI5 cleared Fuchs eight times.

47. Both Robert C. Williams and Norman Moss detail Fuchs espionage activities during this period; see Williams, *Klaus Fuchs, Atom Spy* (Cambridge, Mass., 1987) and Moss, *Klaus Fuchs* (New York, 1987).

48. Lilienthal, *Journals,* v. 2, p. 255; "rare forums," in Gowing, v. 1, p. 112.

49. Molotov in FRUS, 1947, v. 1, p. 861.

50. DOE Files: The AEC's report on security was part of its annual Report to the Congress submitted to the JCAE on July 22, 1947.

51. DOE Files: Attendees and procedures in memo dated November 12, 1947, Harold A. Fidler to Bryan LaPlante; results of conference in LaPlante to Wilson February 4, 1950.

52. Gowing, *Independent and Deterrence: Britain and Atomic Energy, 1945–1952*, (New York, 1974), v. 2, Policy Execution, p. 144.

53. In its July 22, 1948 annual Report to The Congress, the AEC referred to the conference but gave no indication that atomic weapons had been discussed. However, Wilson acknowledged that they had been discussed in his June 9, 1951 FBI interview, op. cit.; although the FBI and Gowing later expressed uncertainty over whether Fuchs actually attended the conference, his November 11 arrival on a British flight and subsequent itinerary can be found in NA\841.01b11/12–1747.

54. FRUS, 1947, v. 1, pp. 869, 881. Maclean's copy of the report can be found in FO115/4313.

55. Moss, *Klaus Fuchs,* p. 110.

56. Hickenlooper to Marshall, August 21, 1947, FRUS, 1947, v. 1, pp. 833–834.

57. FRUS, 1947, v. 1, p. 867.

58. Ibid., p. 873.

59. Lilienthal, *Journals,* v. 2, p. 266.

60. FRUS, 1947, v. 1, pp. 878–879.

61. For Lovett, see ibid.; Acheson, p. 178.

62. Donovan, *Conflict and Crisis,* p. 290; Harry Bayard Price, *The Marshall Plan and Its Meaning* (New York, 1955), pp. 60–61.

63. FRUS, 1947, v. 1, p. 839.

64. For Lovett to Douglas, December 4, see *ibid.,* pp. 879–881; For December 6 Lovett to Marshall (who was in London), see *ibid.,* pp. 885–886. In November Carroll Wilson did confide in Cockroft that "Congressional leaders are asking some embarrassing questions about the supply of uranium in the context of the Marshall Plan." But there is no indication Cockroft connected this to England's stockpile; see PRO/AB16–388; Gowing, v. 1, pp. 248, 277–279.

65. FRUS, 1947, v. 1, p. 906.

66. Gowing, v. 1, p. 243.

67. For December 10 CPC meeting, see FRUS, 1947, v. 1, pp. 889–894; for *Modus Vivendi,* see also Gowing, v. 1, pp. 251–254 and Hewlett and Duncan, *Atomic Shield,* pp. 281–283.

68. Gullion interview with author; There is some indication the term originated with the British; see Gowing, v. 1, p. 119.

69. Lilienthal, *Journals,* v. 2, p. 282; FRUS, 1948, v. 1, p. 678; Hewlett, v. 2, p. 283, Gowing, v. 1, p. 251.

CHAPTER TWELVE (pp. 187–211)

1. FBI Summary Report, "Interviews with Maclean's Neighbors," names deleted, p. 131.

2. Eleanor Philby, p. 158.

3. Hoare, pp. 201, 207.

4. Cecil, "Legends Spies Tell," *Encounter,* op. cit., p. 10; White House ball in Hoare, pp. 48–49.

5. For other domestic problems, such as the hiring and firing of maids, see Cecil, "Legends Spies Tell," *Encounter,* p. 14; FBI Summary Report, p. 130, and an undated teletype from the New York FBI bureau; Hoare, p. 74.

6. "Protect her," in Hoare, p. 75, "not easy," p. 48.

7. *Ibid.,* p. 193.

8. Penrose and Freeman, pp. 333–334; "row," in letter to the author from Sir Isaiah Berlin, September 29, 1989.

9. Hoare, p. 193; Melinda eventually was very open about Donald's homosexual pursuits; see Hoare, p. 97; Howard S. Terrell, who was married to Catherine Marling, Melinda's youngest sister, told the FBI that according to the "family grapevine . . . Maclean is homosexual."; see FBI Summary Report, "Interviews Concerning Maclean."

10. Hoare, p. 204.

11. *New York Times,* January 23, 1948.

12. For Maclean on Greece, see FRUS, 1947, v. 5, pp. 350–352, September 29, 1947.

13. Acheson, p. 219.

14. Kennan, *Memoirs,* p. 279; and *Russian and the West* (Boston, 1960), p. 386.

15. *New York Times,* January 22 and 23, 1948.

16. Soviet inventions, similar to those Hitler published in 1940, can be found in *Documents and Materials Relating to the Eve of the Second World War* (New York, 1948); *New York Times,* April 27, 1948. The story of the captured German archives is a fascinating one. All three powers were looking for the Windsor File, detailing the Nazi flirtations of the Duke of Windsor both when he was on the throne and after he abdicated. At one point Maclean was dispatched to the State Department to demand that the Americans destroy their copy of the file; an infuriated Acheson refused; see NA\862.414/8–2045.

17. "The news," and "witness," in Donovan, *Conflict and Crisis,* p. 360; for Masaryk's death see, Claire Sterling, *The Masaryk Case* (New York, 1969); Sulzberger, *A Long Row of Candles,* pp. 26–27.

18. Czech U. N. Representative Dr. Jan Papanek quoted in the *1949 Collier's Year Book,* pp. 225–226.

19. Isaacson and Thomas, *Wise Men,* p. 447; J. N. Henderson, *Private Office,* p. 59, would later write that "without Hickerson's unclenching faith in the [NATO] Pact it would never have happened."

20. FO115/4359. Embassy cables throughout the next several months made it clear that they regarded Hickerson and his staff as the engine pulling the Western Alliance train. According to Hickerson, Inverchapel had trouble seeing Marshall with the frequency that No. 10 Downing demanded. When Inverchapel discovered Hickerson was from Marshall, Texas, he would often deliver messages to the

American staffer and then assure London, "Marshall connection made," or some other contrivance, Hickerson interview, October 3, 1984.

21. "Will Russia," in Donovan, *Conflict and Crisis*, p. 359; "prepare," and speech in Daniel Yergin, *Shattered Peace* (Boston, 1977), pp. 351–354.

22. Ronald Steel, *Walter Lippmann and the American Century* (Boston, 1980), pp. 450–451. Finland, after being accused by *Izvestia* of skullduggery for trying to join the World Bank, was summoned to Moscow to negotiate "a friendship treaty." A jittery Norwegian government then asked Washington and London "what help they might expect to receive if attacked;" see, FRUS, 1948, v. 3, pp. 46–48; FO115/4348; Donovan, *Crisis and Conflict*, p. 363.

23. "Fearing," in FO115/4348; for the role Guy Burgess played in these same events, see Tom Driberg, *Guy Burgess: A Portrait With Background* (London, 1956), p. 80.

24. For Maclean-drafted note, see FO115/4348, March 14, 1948.

25. For atomic weapons, see FRUS, 1948, v. 1, pp. 700–701; also Mills, *Forrestal Diaries*, pp. 406–407. Though rumors and speculation on this had appeared in the British press, the government did not make its official announcement until May 12, 1948 in answer to a question in the House of Commons; see *Parliamentary Debates*, vol. 450, cols. 2128–29.

26. DOS: Maclean Files, letter from security officer Carl E. Westrum to Jack Minor, September 24, 1951.

27. FRUS, 1948, v. 3, pp. 69–70.

28. "Deception measure," in ibid., and FO371/68067, March 22, 1948; Jebb crowed, in FO115/4348, March 26, Jebb to Roberts at the FO; also see Jebb, p. 216.

29. "Work," in *Time*, March 29, 1948; "I led," in FO371/68067, March 22, 1948; "chief advisor," in Jebb, pp. 215–216. Inverchapel was well past his prime when he came to Washington, and bored by his work and surroundings; he therefore relied heavily on Maclean whom he thought was "a sweetie." See Cecil, *A Divided Life*, p. 79; Balfour, p. 105.

30. NA\840.00/3–2348; and FRUS, 1948, v. 3, p. 64.

31. The observation about "predatory animals," was transmitted in a report to London on March 26, between the third and the fourth session of the talks. See FO115/4348.

32. March 25, FO115/4348.

33. The talks were formally known as the "United States-United Kingdom-Canadian Security Conversations." For summations of each session and the results, see FRUS, 1948, v. 3, pp. 63–75.

34. "The problem," in FO115/4348; Bevin response in FRUS, 1948, v. 3, p. 69.

35. Ibid.

36. For Denmark's anxiety, see FRUS, 1948, v. 3, pp. 67–68.

37. Cecil, *A Divided Life*, pp. 86–87, C. Wieber and B. Zeeman, International Affairs, (London) v. 59, No. 3, 1983, p. 363.

38. Ibid.

39. "Truman," in FO115/4348; for Truman's domestic opposition, see William

E. Leuchtenburg, *In the Shadow of FDR,* (Ithaca, N.Y., 1983), pp. 25–33; Steel, p. 452.

40. When withdrawal was proposed as an option to Truman on June 28 he said flatly, there is "no discussion on that point, we are going to stay period." See Mills, *Forrestal Diaries,* p. 454.

41. "Would most," in Herken, p. 254.

42. "Weak," in Steel, p. 459; Murphy, p. 316.

43. Strobe Talbott, ed., *Kruschev Remembers* (Boston, 1970), pp. 361–372.

44. Paul Johnson, *Modern Times* (New York, 1983), p. 440; Murphy, pp. 314–317.

45. Yergin, pp. 349, 380.

46. Marshall in Mills, *Forrestal Diaries,* p. 373.

47. Troop strength in ibid., pp. 374–376.

48. War plan in Herken, p. 248.

49. Mills, *Forrestal Diaries,* p. 374; Pentagon study in Marshall to Forrestal, FRUS, 1948, v. 1, pp. 541–542.

50. David Alan Rosenberg, "U. S. nuclear stockpile, 1945 to 1950," *The Bulletin of the Atomic Scientists,* May 1982, pp. 25–30.

51. Yergin, p. 382.

52. Cecil, *A Divided Life,* p. 83.

53. Ibid.; for Clay, see Yergin, p. 384.

54. Herken, p. 197; Truman in John M. Blum, *The Price of Vision* (Boston, 1973), p. 530; "no document," in Rosenberg, "U.S. nuclear stockpile," op. cit., p. 25; Senator McMahon quoted in *New York Times Sunday Magazine,* July 10, 1949.

55. As late as 1956 the State Department wanted to omit any reference to Maclean's knowledge of America's uranium requirements in a letter to Senator Eastland. It was finally included because "we must assume" Eastland had seen the McMahon letter; see DOE Files: January 16 draft and February 21, 1956 letter to Eastland, emphasis added.

56. DOS: Maclean Files: Jack K. McFall to McMahon, August 13, 1951. Also FRUS, 1951, v. 1, pp. 752–755; DOS: Maclean Files: Memorandum to Gerald Smith, December 2, 1955, emphasis added. Smith, a career disarmament specialist who would hold a number of important positions from the Truman to the Nixon administrations, inexplicably did not pass this information to his superiors. Instead, he told them that "nothing of significance was found" as a result of the review. Thus, the June and August 1951 letters to McMahon stood as "definitive." See Smith to Chase, December 9, 1955.

57. Rosenberg, op. cit., 26; estimates in *New York Times Sunday Magazine,* July 10, 1949.

58. It would have taken at least six weeks—two weeks to assemble thirty bombs and four weeks to load them—to get even America's stunted arsenal airborne; see Rosenberg, op. cit., p. 26; One reason that Truman did not want the planes to carry bombs—aside from the problems already mentioned—was that he wanted to keep control of its use. "[I'm not going] to have some dashing lieutenant colonel decide

when would be the proper time to drop one," he told Forrestal; see Mills, *Forrestal Diaries,* p. 458. He also insisted "this is no time to be juggling an atom bomb around," Lilienthal, *Journals,* p. 391; See also Steel, p. 453, and Mills, *Forrestal Diaries,* pp. 451–460.

59. According to Lilienthal, the size of the atomic arsenal did not increase between 1945–1948; see Herken, pp. 239, 258–260. Khrushchev acknowledges that Stalin rarely shared information with the Politburo. Stalin first "carefully selected, limited and weighed" anything they received. "He felt no urge to exchange opinions with others," and he certainly would not have felt compelled to share secret intelligence either. As much as the Europeans and the Americans, he manipulated crises for his own domestic needs. After all, the Soviet government had to convince the masses that their deprivations and hardships were the result of Russia's encirclement by warmongering capitalists. It would ill-behoove Stalin to suggest that the threat was not real; Talbott, ed., *Khrushchev Remembers,* pp. 133, 174.

60. For Berlin access, see Murphy, pp. 260–264, 317.

61. Mills, *Forrestal Diaries,* p. 457.

62. *Time,* February 23, 1948.

63. *Time,* May 31, 1948.

64. On February 24, 1956, an article by Maclean appeared in the *Daily Herald* (London) in which he correctly pointed out "It was the British Government which initiated the whole idea of NATO. I have reason to remember this since, when a First Secretary at the British Embassy in Washington, I was myself attached to the British party which, with the assistance of Canadian representatives, argued the case for the "Treaty." Yet, in *British Foreign Policy,* p. 55, he refers to these talks as if all his knowledge was acquired only after he was in Moscow and read the memoirs of Anglo-American statesmen.

65. For security arrangements, see FRUS, 1948, v. 3, pp. 151–152.

66. At the time the United States started intercepting Soviets transmissions, the Soviet Union was an ally of Germany. By the autumn of 1946 the FBI was getting intercepts from thirteen countries; see James Bamford, *Puzzle Palace* (New York, 1983), pp. 314–315. See also David C. Martin, *Wilderness of Mirrors* (New York, 1980), pp. 35–41.

67. Lamphere, pp. 78–86.

68. But Maclean still had three good years of espionage work in front of him, and the security meetings proved to be an excellent source. Lovett ordered a detailed report for the representatives on Europe's military plans in case of war and "their actual and potential sources of military supplies," Henderson, p. 23.

69. Harriet Marling Sheers interview, op. cit.

70. See Djilas, *Conversations with Stalin,* pp. 127–128 for Molotov's and Stalin's scheming.

71. For CIA activity in Italian elections, see Thomas Powers, *The Man Who Kept the Secrets* (New York, 1979), pp. 30–31.

CHAPTER THIRTEEN (pp. 213–223)

1. FBI: Rushmore Files. On March 18, 1946, the FBI was told by a confidential informant that Rushmore had a source—who turned out to be Whittaker Cham-

bers—who was prepared to take the stand and testify that Hiss was a communist. Rushmore hinted at this in his own column and passed it on to others; he would subsequently "name names" and work for Joe McCarthy prior to a dramatic suicide.

2. Richard M. Nixon, *Six Crises* (New York, 1962), p. 2; Weinstein, pp. 4–8.

3. *Time,* December 13, 1948.

4. Weinstein, pp. 8–15.

5. Ibid., p. 37.

6. Hiss made the "same single source" claim in a letter to John Foster Dulles, Eisenhower's future secretary of state and chairman of the Carnegie's board of trustees, Weinstein, p. 17; for Bullitt connection, Weinstein, p. 331.

7. On September 25, 1948, Hiss finally filed a slander suit in the amount of $50,000 against Chambers. When Chambers mocked the action, Hiss added another $25,000 to the amount; see Weinstein, p. 161.

8. For Hiss's August 25 appearance and press reaction, see Weinstein, pp. 44–51.

9. Maclean's farewell, in Cecil, *A Divided Life,* p. 84; Gullion interview.

10. Gullion interview.

11. Straight, p. 229.

12. *New York Times,* March 19, 1948. After Truman fired Wallace, Straight hired him at *The New Republic,* where he was not just an editor, but a deity. He was featured in all the promotional advertisement. His speeches were advertised on the cover and printed in full. Books about him were heavily promoted. During his brief tenure the magazine lost over $500,000, which was felt even by someone of Straight's considerable wealth. See *Time,* February 23, 1948.

13. Straight, p. 209.

14. Ibid., pp. 254–256. Wallace was the candidate of the Progressive Party, which was created and completely controlled, as Straight admits, by the American Communist Party. The hapless campaign became so discredited that by the time the election rolled around even *The New Republic,* though it once printed a cover demanding TRUMAN SHOULD QUIT, endorsed the president.

15. Ibid., pp. 256–258, Straight does not mention Dolivet's involvement in the Wallace campaign, but does talk about other aspects of their relationship. For State Department on Dolivet, see NA\032 Wallace, Henry A./4–347 to 4–1747; NA\711.61/5–148.

16. Straight, p. 229.

17. Straight statement to the FBI June 18, 1963. Based on research connected with this book, Straight admitted in a November 12, 1985 interview that his long-held impression must have been incorrect.

18. Belinda Compton Straight, phone interview with author, April 15, 1985; Welderhall, letter to author July 9, 1986. Dr. Welderhall died in 1990. Straight and his wife divorced in 1969.

19. Straight, p. 231.

20. Burgess in Gorowny Rees, *A Chapter of Accidents* (New York, 1972), p. 165; Philby, p. 155.

21. Valentine Lawford, interview with author, March 21, 1986; also see Lawford in Cecil, *A Divided Life,* p. 89; FBI: Philby Files, interview with Lawford on June 15, 1951.

22. FBI Summary Report, "Interviews Connected With Maclean." Albert Parker, a federal government worker rented the house at 3326 P Street. He had met Maclean twice, and thought him pleasant. But his impression was jarred when his daughter Charlotte found the letter. It had been discarded by the time the FBI interviewed Parker nearly three years later. *New York Times,* September 1, 1945; *Plain Talk,* September, 1948, v. 2, No. 12.

CHAPTER FOURTEEN (pp. 225–241)

1. Philip Toynbee, "Maclean and I," *Observer,* October 15, 1967.

2. For reports of threats against Western ambassadors, see FO141/1254, November 26, 1948.

3. Maclean to Wright in FO141/1377, October 30, 1949.

4. "Caffery," in FO141/1377, Campbell to FO, October 22, 1949; Sir James Murray, interviews with author, February 6 and March 19, 1986.

5. "No need," in FO141/1333, September 25, 1949; Farouk cable in FO141/1345, June 14, 1949.

6. The January date was included in the British White Paper of September 1955. The date was confirmed in the FBI's November 1955 Summary Report.

7. Hoare, pp. 75–77; For another dinner party see Malcolm Muggeridge, *Like It Was* (London, 1982), p. 299.

8. Hoare, pp. 79, 96; for changes in Melinda, see also Cecil, *A Divided Life,* p. 95.

9. For Nile expedition, see Cecil, pp. 97–98; Hoare, pp. 82–84; Page, p. 237.

10. Maclean's complaints had reached the ears of several officials at the American embassy in Cairo, see FBI Summary Report, p. 134.

11. FO141/1315, April 28, 1949.

12. For Maclean interview with Gallad and the minutes from his colleagues including the *Economist* quote, see FO141/1339.

13. DOS Maclean File: "Memorandum to the Ambassador," July 28, 1951 and letter to C. Lewis Jones from Gordon H. Mattison, August 9, 1951.

14. FRUS, 1949, v. 6, pp. 198–203; FO141/1345, March 14 and June 14, 1949.

15. *New York Times,* September 24, 1949; Robert J. Donovan, *Tumultous Years* (New York, 1982), p. 101; Vandenberg, p. 518.

16. *New York Times,* November 11 and 25, 1945, and September 24, 1949.

17. For estimates on when Russia would get the bomb, see FRUS, 1947, v. 1, pp. 832–833; Kramish, p. 123; FRUS, 1948, v. 1, p. 508; *New York Times,* September 24, 1949.

18. For Tizard, see Kramish, p. 221. This charge was echoed by Senator McMahon, who had originally dismissed Gouzenko's story as an invention by

Groves and the American military. "Now we appreciate more than ever that Russia started her espionage of the atomic project while she was still fighting as an ally" in 1943, he told his Senate colleagues; see *New York Times,* September 28, 1949.

19. *New York Times,* September 26, 1949.

20. Lamphere, pp. 132–135; Hyde, *The Atom Bomb Spies,* p. 119; Gowing, v. 2, p. 145. In her official history, Gowing says London was first contacted in August; Hyde puts the date for Perrin at September 5; Lamphere says it was not until mid-September. R. C. Williams, however, found an FBI request to the AEC on Fuchs, dated September 13, that is, after Lamphere's first visit to compare reports; see Williams, *Klaus Fuchs,* p. 119.

21. Gowing, v. 2, p. 145.

22. Lilienthal, *Journals,* pp. 634–635; see also George Arneson, *The Foreign Service Journal,* June 1969.

23. Damage estimates for Fuchs can be found in Gowing, v. 2, pp. 138, 150; Hewlett and Duncan, v. 2, pp. 415–416; *New York Times,* May 5, 1950 and January 29, 1988; *Washington Post,* January 29, 1988.

24. PRO/AB16–858.

25. Hewlett and Duncan, v. 2, pp. 312–313.

26. Donovan, *Tumultous Years,* p. 134; *New York Times,* January 23, 1950.

27. FBI Summary Report, p. 133; for Caffery, see Sulzberger, *A Long Row of Candles,* p. 806.

28. Phillip W. Ireland was assigned to the American embassy in Cairo during Maclean's tenure. He thought Faiza and her retinue were more "fun loving" than immoral, FBI: Philby Files, "Interviews in Connection with Maclean"; Murray interviews.

29. DOS: Maclean Files, July 28, 1951 Memorandum, op. cit.; Hoare, p. 82; Both Hoare and Cecil tend to discount the likelihood that Maclean was a participant in the orgies or became outrageously indiscreet. Nor did the FBI give much weight to a report from an American that Maclean was "one of a ring of 12 people who were regarded as homosexuals and possibly dope addicts." The source may have discredited himself by assuring the FBI that Maclean frequently dressed as a woman and may have escaped "to Buenos Aires disguised [all 6'4" of him] as a woman."; see FBI: Philby Files, Nichols to Tolson, June 30, 1951.

30. Hoare, p. 78; Cecil, *The Missing Dimension,* p. 189; Harriet Sheers interview.

31. FBI Summary Report, p. 133; Hoare, p. 80. The Duke's visit to Egypt was reported in *London Times,* January 29, 1950. He was married to Elizabeth who became the Queen of England in June 1953. He later became Prince Philip.

32. Cecil, *A Divided Life,* pp. 99–100.

33. Ibid., p. 106.

34. Murray interviews; FBI Summary Report, p. 133.

35. Cecil, *A Divided Life,* pp. 100–106, quotes extensively from Toynbee's unpublished diary, and unless otherwise noted quotes attributed to Toynbee are from those passages; Hoare, p. 81; DOS Maclean Files: July 28, 1951 memo, op. cit.

36. DOS Maclean File: August 9, 1951 letter, op. cit.

37. Toynbee, *Observer,* "Maclean and I," op. cit.

38. Ibid., they first entered an apartment shared by Sheila Engert, an instructor at the American University in Cairo, and Jacqueline Brannerman, a secretary at the U. S. embassy. Miss Brannerman was home alone and asleep. Toynbee and Maclean then went to the adjoining apartment of Eunice Taylor, secretary to Caffery and Mrs. Ellen Speers, whose husband worked for the Arabian-American Oil Company. Sheila Engert interview in FBI Summary Report, "Interviews in Connection with Maclean." Miss Taylor might later have gotten somewhat paranoid about Maclean. She was serving at the American embassy in Moscow in 1951 when he defected.

39. DOS Maclean File: Interview with Ambassador Jefferson Caffery, February 16, 1956. Caffery also pointed out that when the Cairo press printed the story they reported most of the facts, including the names, incorrectly. Other accounts of Maclean's last days in Cairo can be found in Hoare, pp. 84–86 and Page, pp. 240–241.

40. Hickerson and Lawford interviews with author.

41. Hoare, pp. 86–87.

42. Cecil, *A Divided Life,* p. 107.

CHAPTER FIFTEEN (pp. 243–255)

1. Memorandum prepared by the Central Intelligence Agency, on "Strengths and Weaknesses of the Hoxha Regime in Albania," dated September 12, 1945 contained in RDGD/ 1975 RC.

2. *Caronia* in *New York Times,* October 8, 1949.

3. Philby, p. 155.

4. The agreement, known as the UKUSA agreement, was renewed in 1947; see Costello, p. 521; Bamford, pp. 314–315.

5. Lamphere, pp. 129–130.

6. Ibid., p. 129.

7. Robert Lamphere, interview with author, December 10, 1985; Philby, p. 169.

8. Lamphere interview and Lamphere, p. 130.

9. Lamphere interview.

10. Ibid. For some reason, in his book Philby felt compelled to sometimes refer to Ladd as "Johnny Boyd"; see Philby, pp. 168–169.

11. Lamphere interview.

12. Ibid. A number of British authors, notably Chapman Pincher in *Too Secret Too Long,* Peter Wright in *The Spycatcher,* and John Costello in *Mask of Treachery,* blame British inaction on MI5 chief Roger Hollis who they contend was a Soviet mole.

13. Knightley, *Masterspy,* pp. 77–78; "Pipe-smoking" in Wright, p. 185.

14. James J. Angleton, interview with author, February 23, 1984.

15. McCarger, writing under the non de plume of Christopher Felix, reviewed several books on Philby; see *New York Times Book Review,* Sunday June 2, 1968.

16. Nicholas Bethell, *Betrayed* (New York, 1984), p. 33.

17. CIA September 12, 1949 memorandum, *op. cit.*

18. Leonard Mosley, *Dulles* (New York, 1978), pp. 494–495.

19. Bethell, p. 90.

20. Philby, p. 155.

21. Bok, p. 84.

22. Costello, p. 518; FBI Summary Report, pp. 24–25; The letter to CIA Director Bedell Smith from Hoover, November 20, 1951 states that Philby met with Litzi in Paris in August 1939 on his way back from Spain.

23. Williams, pp. 117, 129.

24. "Newspapers," in Williams, p. 167; also see Ronald Radosh and Joyce Milton, *The Rosenberg File* (New York, 1983), pp. 38–41.

25. Lamphere, pp. 147–152.

26. Philby, p. 170. The FBI were flabbergasted by this KGB-authorized admission, because communists and fellow travelers always maintained that the Rosenbergs were complete innocents, victims of Hoover's witchhunts, a theory finally obliterated by Radosh and Milton. The finishing touch came when former premier Nikita Khrushchev recalled how Stalin spoke of the Rosenbergs "with warmth," as he described their service to the Soviet Union as spies; see *Time,* October 1, 1990, p. 75.

27. Hoare, pp. 89–90.

28. Hoare, p. 91; Cecil *A Divided Life,* pp. 109–110.

29. Connolly, *U.S. News and World Report,* September 25, 1953, p. 60; Hoare, p. 94.

30. Cecil, *A Divided Life,* pp. 78–79.

31. Cecil, *A Divided Life,* pp. 112–113.

32. Page, p. 250.

33. Hoare, p. 97. "Mother gave Hoare Melinda's letters . . . he probably gave her too much to drink," Harriett said later about the intimate letters which appeared in *The Missing Macleans.* "I was outraged, I wanted to sue."; from Harriet Sheers interview.

34. Hoare, pp. 94–95. Information from Gordon H. Mattison, a career Foreign Service Officer who retired in 1968 after an extensive career mostly in the Middle East. He was on the same ship as Mrs. Dunbar.

35. DOS Maclean File: Cable dated July 16, 1951 from Acheson to the American embassy in Cairo based on a report the Department received from its Madrid embassy.

36. Alan Maclean interview.

CHAPTER SIXTEEN (pp. 257–262)

1. Harry S. Truman, *Years of Trial and Hope* (New York, 1956), v. 2, p. 343.

2. For anticipation of trouble spots, see Kennan, *Memoirs,* pp. 484–485; David

Rees, *Korea: The Limited War* (New York, 1964), pp. 18–31; "The best damn army," Hickerson interview, October 3, 1984.

3. For policy statements on Korea and Acheson travel, see R. Rovere and A. Schlesinger, Jr., *The MacArthur Controversy* (New York, 1965), pp. 100–102; MacArthur also told the British Ambassador in Tokyo that "Korea is doomed to be a Soviet satellite," FO371/84094, September 26, 1947.

4. For call to Truman, see Acheson, p. 402 and Truman, v. 2, p. 332.

5. Jebb mistakenly refers to his arrival as Wednesday, June 27. Immigration and Naturalization records confirm that he and Alan Maclean arrived on Wednesday the 28th. See Jebb, p. 229.

6. Even if the Soviets had been present to veto the U.S. resolution, the Allies under Article 51 could have taken it to the Western dominated General Assembly where it would have passed. See D. Rees, *Korea,* p. 34.

7. Interview by author with Marshall biographer Forrest C. Pogue, November 18, 1987; for background on MacArthur during this period, see William Manchester, *American Caesar* (Boston, 1978), pp. 457–472.

8. These reports were part of a series the CIA was providing the White House in the aftermath of the invasion and can be found in RDGD/1975 RC.

9. Truman, v. 2, p. 343.

10. Deutscher, pp. 608–609.

11. Philby, p. 171.

CHAPTER SEVENTEEN (pp. 263–279)

1. Maclean interview with author.

2. Connolly, *U.S. News & World Report,* September 25, 1953, op. cit., p. 59.

3. Muggeridge, *The Infernal Grove,* p. 107.

4. Straight, p. 94.

5. *New York Times,* October 24, 1984. Bates played Burgess in the television production "An Englishman Abroad."

6. Blunt, *The Times* (London), November 21, 1979; for Burgess's inclusion at a Frankfurter dinner party, see Isaiah Berlin, *Personal Impressions* (New York, 1982), p. 81; G. Rees, *A Chapter of Accidents,* p. 110; Felix Frankfurter, *Felix Frankfurter Reminisces* (New York, 1960), p. 259.

7. "Heroes," in Penrose and Freeman, p. 196; Cecil, *A Divided Life,* p. 131.

8. Edward R. F. Sheehan, "The Rise and Fall of a Soviet Agent," *Saturday Evening Post,* February 15, 1964, p. 34; Hugh Trevor-Roper, "Acts of the Apostles," *The New York Review of Books,* March 31, 1983, p. 4.

9. Connolly, *U.S. News & World Report,* September 25, 1953, op. cit.

10. FBI: Philby Files, June 15, 1951 interview with Isherwood in report to Hoover dated July 18, 1951.

11. Lord Greenhill, *The Times* (London), September 7, 1977.

Sources and Notes

12. Susan Mary Alsop, *To Marietta From Paris* (New York, 1975), p. 131. She later married columnist Joseph Alsop.

13. McNeil later told Sulzberger that Burgess had been strongly anti-American because he had been jilted by an American lover. McNeil also said that he assumed that Burgess had been killed by Maclean somewhere in Europe. Many attributed McNeil's early death in 1955 to the strain and shock of Burgess's defection. See Sulzberger, *A Long Row of Candles,* pp. 412, 654.

14. For Burgess at Brussels, see Page, p. 203; Penrose and Freeman, p. 317.

15. These and other stories accompany nearly every description of Burgess, and can be found, for instance, in Penrose and Freeman, p. 317 and Page, pp. 203–205.

16. Burgess was a private secretary for the Minister of State from December 31, 1946 to August 1947. His official starting date with the Far Eastern Department was November 1, 1948; see FBI Summary Report. In 1981 a young British graduate student found documents in the Public Record Office that shattered Whitehall's forty-year insistence that Burgess never had access to classified information. The student found Burgess's comments and signature on a batch of documents, including intelligence reports that detailed Western estimates of the level of Soviet military aid flowing to China; see *The Times* (London), February 2, 1981.

17. Harold Nicholson, *The Last Years: 1945–1962* (New York, 1968), v. 3, p. 184.

18. "Pathological," in Penrose and Freeman, p. 326. For more on Burgess's "hatred of Americans," see John S. Mather, ed., *The Great Spy Scandal* (London, 1955), p. 34.

19. Knightley, *Masterspy,* p. 100. Later Philby argued that because his and Burgess's careers as spies were so intertwined, if Burgess were found out, he would be done in anyway. By having Burgess live in his house he, Philby, could try to make Burgess behave. The best that can be said about this bit of strategy is that it was a spectacular misjudgment and a total failure; see Philby, pp. 171–172.

20. Greenhill, *The Times* (London), September 7, 1977.

21. David M. Oshinsky, *A Conspiracy So Immense* (New York, 1983), pp. 179–182.

22. Costello, p. 540; Penrose and Freeman, p. 328.

23. Seale, p. 208.

24. "Constantly," in James Angleton memorandum dated June 18, 1951 and released by the CIA under FOIA; also Page, p. 243.

25. Angleton interview.

26. In separate interviews with the author, both Angleton and Sir Robert Mackenzie confirmed this cover story. Ludicrous as it was, some in the FBI took the bait. A June 21, 1951 report by the Washington field office to Hoover referred to Esther as Burgess's "girl friend." Hoover knew otherwise. In his June 19 report his first item on Burgess was that "he is a known homosexual."

27. "Objections," in Greenhill, September 7, 1977, op. cit. Mackenzie interview.

28. Francis J. Thompson, *Destination Washington* (London, 1960), p. 207; "goats," in Philby, pp. 171–172.

29. The embassy set-up was described by Mann in interviews with the author from 1984 to 1986, and in his *Was There A Fifth Man?*, pp. 78–79; see also Thompson, pp. 207–209.

30. Greenhill, September 7, 1977, op. cit.

31. The cable reported ominously that "moving of troop trains north along Pin-Han Railway over the last two months has been continuing," and that "railway stations north of Shanhaikuan have had all name placards etc. removed and now only display numbers."; see FO115/4483.

32. FRUS, 1950, v. 7, p. 563.

33. FBI: Philby Files, undated report from the FBI Washington field office, pp. 77. All quotes attributed to State Department officials are contained in this report. The names have been deleted by the FBI.

34. FBI Summary Report, pp. 77, 87–89; Greenhill, September 7, 1977, *op. cit.*

35. Henry Latrobe Roosevelt was one of the FDR's first appointments. He served as assistant secretary of the Navy from March 17, 1933 until February 27, 1936, and died in office.

36. Unless otherwise noted, all information concerning the Roosevelts originates with FBI interviews and correspondence to them from Burgess. As will be seen, the Roosevelts were among Burgess's victims, and not a breath of suspicion was ever directed at them. Their files were released to the author under the FOIA.

37. Joseph Alsop, interviews and letters to the author from 1984 to 1986.

38. Grace Lockwood, letter to author, January 12, 1986.

39. Robert Grant, interview with author, June 27, 1985; FBI Summary report, "Interview with Grant," June 19, 1951, pp. 30–32.

40. Lawford and Horst, interview with author, March 21, 1986 in Oyster Bay; FBI: Philby Files, interview with Lawford, June 15, 1951.

41. Lord Gladwyn, letter to author, February 18, 1986.

42. FBI: Philby Files, extensively documented Burgess's travels. During one thirty-two day stretch in November and December he spent sixteen nights at the Sutton, including thirteen nights during November. He spent additional time in New York during this period, but stayed with friends or at other hotels. This was at a time when a delegation from the People's Republic of China was expected at the United Nations, though they did not finally arrive until after Burgess left New York. The FBI also picked up reports that Burgess was trying to get to Canada in November. It is worth nothing that E. Herbert Norman, a high-ranking Canadian diplomat had then been recalled to Ottawa for interrogation about his communist past. In 1963, Straight told the FBI that Norman had been a member of his communist cell at Cambridge. Years later, as the stories about him persisted, Norman, then Canadian ambassador to Egypt, committed suicide by jumping off a building in Cairo; see Straight, p. 229; FBI: Straight File, June 18, 1963 interview.

43. Sulzberger, *A Long Row of Candles*, p. 481.

44. Donovan, *Tumultous Years*, pp. 291–294.

45. FBI: Philby Files, interviews with State Department employees, op. cit.

46. Martin Gilbert confirms the visit and the exchange, see Gilbert, *The Wilderness Years,* p. 235. According to Trevor-Roper, after he returned to London, Burgess sent Churchill "a long lecture on the correct foreign policy to be adopted by Britain."; see Trevor-Roper, *New York Review of Books,* March 31, 1983. Burgess claimed that when he gave him the book, Churchill told him that if he ever returned to power and Guy wanted to join his regime, he need only present the book to his gatekeepers. Aileen Philby told Angleton she did not believe that Burgess had such a book; see Angleton memo. op. cit.

47. Eden had traveled from Washington to Canada to accept an honorary degree from McGill University. Burgess retold the book episode in a tape recording he made in New York just before he sailed back to England. He also penciled-in Eden's comment in his prized book. See Stephen Spender, *Journals 1939–1983* (New York, 1986), p. 214. Photostats of Eden's handwritten note have appeared in several London newspapers and in Driberg's book on Burgess.

CHAPTER EIGHTEEN (pp. 281–304)

1. Sir Frederick Hoyer-Millar to FO, in FO115/4486.

2. FBI: Philby Files, Hoover to the Attorney General, October 6, 1955. This was presumably based on Philby's "interrogation" during 1951 and 1952.

3. According to their mutual friend Goronwy Rees, Donald "was the apple of Burgess's eye." see G. Rees, p. 129; Burgess's visits to Alan Maclean's apartment in letter to author from Alan Maclean, April 28, 1986; "shared," in letter to author from Lord Gladwyn (Jebb), February 18, 1986.

4. "Kim was," from Alan Maclean interview with author, January 16, 1985; Harriet, who visited Melinda nine times in Russia, also found Philby charming and fascinating "except when he got drunk, then he became a bore."; from Harriet Marling Sheers interview, April 9, 1985.

5. Cecil, *A Divided Life,* pp. 112–113.

6. G. Rees, p. 191.

7. When he first reported this exchange, Cyril Connolly did not identify the person whom Maclean challenged to turn him in; see Connolly, *U.S. News and World Report,* September 25, 1953 *op. cit.* Some years later Page *et al.* provided a slightly modified version of the exchange, and identified Culme-Seymour whom they interviewed; see Page, p. 253.

8. Cecil, *A Divided Life,* p. 114; Philby, p. 172.

9. Cecil, *A Divided Life,* p. 111–112.

10. "Donald had," in Hoare, p. 96.

11. "He," in ibid.; Cecil, *A Divided Life,* p. 116.

12. "Principally," in Hansard, November 7, 1955, 1495. In his definitive book *The Foreign Office,* Lord Strang, who was Permanent Under Secretary at the Foreign Office when Maclean was appointed the head of the American Department,

described the duties of the American Department thus: "Advise the Secretary of State as to the policy to be followed in regard to the political, economic and other relations between this country" and other countries including the U.S. "Study and analyze the reports from H. M. Representatives . . . issue instructions on behalf of the Secretary of State . . . maintain relations with representatives" of other countries including the U.S. Quoted in Connell, *The 'Office'*, p. 327.

13. When it issued its White Paper in September 1955 and during the ensuing parliamentary debate, the British government insisted critical papers were denied Maclean once he was a suspect. In fact, they speculate, it was precisely this denial of top secret documents that may have tipped off Maclean to the fact that he was under investigation. But the earliest date anyone has offered for when Maclean appeared on the "short list" of suspects is March, 1951, well after he could have inflicted the greatest damage in terms of the Korean War. See *Report Concerning The Disappearance of Two Former Foreign Office Officials* (hereafter The White Paper), September 23, 1955 (HMSO), pp. 10–11.

Roger Makins and Robert Cecil both agree that Maclean was denied sensitive documents. But since Makins was also on this list, he too would have been denied the same access he claims he, as Maclean's superintending under secretary, denied Maclean. And Cecil reports that right up to the time Maclean took flight, "none of us in the American Department was aware that anything was amiss." Yet if the flow of top secret documents had suddenly ceased, he and everyone else in the Department, including Maclean, would have noticed something was very much amiss. For Makins, see Anthony Glees, *The Secrets of the Service*, p. 363; for Cecil, see *A Divided Life*, pp. 135, 139, 140.

Penrose and Freeman believe Makins was not on the list of suspects because he wasn't in Washington at the relevant times. Robert Mackenzie, however, has confirmed to me Philby's contention that Makins was one of five on the list. Further, Makins arrived at the Washington embassy on January 6, 1945. The FBI had intercepts of Soviet transmissions from New York to Moscow containing information passed by "Homer" at least as late as May 1945. So Makins overlapped sufficiently long during the period "Homer" was operating from the embassy so as not to be automatically eliminated on that grounds. For list see Philby, p. 176; confirmed by Mackenzie during interview with author, January 17, 1985, London; for Makins dates in Washington, see NA\701.4111/Makins, Roger; for dates of intercepts, see Lamphere, pp. 84–85.

It doesn't take very long in the Public Record Office to appreciate how thoroughly government weeders have depleted official files of the evidence which would contradict the government's claims about information available to Maclean. For instance, of the sixteen files in the Far Eastern Department, FO371/84094/258–278, covering a several week period in 1950, seven can be found which were copied to the American Department. All, it should come as no surprise, have low or no classification and contain copies of routine press clippings. What is even more striking is what is missing.

Most of the messages from the Washington embassy to the Foreign Office have been purged from the available files of the Far Eastern Department. These would have contained some of the most secret and sensitive information on Korea and have been purged presumably because they would show that either the embassy or the department copied the contents to the American Department. Most of the surviving American Department's Files covering the period of Maclean's tenure, conveniently, deal exclusively with Latin America.

14. According to Penrose and Freeman, Maclean was a chief suspect by March; Cecil believes the final evidence identifying him was known in early April, but he was on a "short list" much earlier. See Penrose and Freeman, p. 344; Cecil, *A Divided Life,* p. 117.

15. FO371/92757.

16. Cecil, *A Divided Life,* "access" in p. 118, "cabinet" in p. 123.

17. "We can," in D. Rees, *Korea,* p. 315; for Kennan's assertion that "we needed no international mandate to make this action proper", see *Memoirs,* p. 490. Of the approximately 800,000 ground troops under the Eighth Army at the war's end, 44,000 were from Allied countries; see D. Rees, *Korea,* p. 33.

18. For Bradley-Tedder see, for instance, FO371/84102, November 2, 1950, and FO115/4486, July 17 & July 26, 1950; Hoyer-Millar in FO115/4486, July 27, 1950, emphasis added.

19. FO115/4487, embassy to FO, August 18, 1950.

20. MacArthur also assured Air Vice-Marshal C. A. Bouchier that he held the British Chiefs of Staff in a much higher regard than the FO; see FO371/84904.

21. See for instance Franks's cables on Korea in FO371/84093, July 14, 1945. On his first day Maclean received a report from Washington that the U.S. had no confirmation of Communist Chinese fighting in Korea; see FO371/84110, November 1, 1950.

22. Manchester, *American Caesar,* pp. 597–598.

23. Hutchison's colleague K. M. Panikkar, India's ambassador to the People's Republic of China, thought Hutchison was an "excellent man, but did not claim to be much of a politician." Formerly Commercial Minister in Nanking, his assessments in the PRC were often contradictory and unreliable and were hotly disputed within the Foreign Office right up to the time of his recall and retirement early in 1951; see K. M. Panikkar, *In Two Chinas* (London, 1955), p. 94; a Mr. Buzzard particularly challenged Hutchison's reporting; see FO371/84109, Files 1023–28.

24. Panikkar, p. 108.

25. Kennan, *Memoirs,* p. 491; "We hope," in Truman, v. 2, p. 359.

26. Chou warned Panikkar on October 3, as U.S. troops were moving north, that "if American armed forces crossed the 38th parallel, China would send troops into North Korea to participate in its defense." However, the British, as Hubert Graves at the embassy advised the State Department, "do not take too seriously Panikkar's fears, believing him volatile and an unreliable reporter." Truman considered the warning "Communist propaganda," observing that the Indian ambassador had "played the game of the Chinese Communists fairly regularly."; for October 3 warning, see FO371/84109; Truman, v. 2, pp. 361–362; Graves in FRUS, 1950, v. 7, pp. 793–794.

27. Jebb in FO371/84098, September 29, 1950; for conditions in China at the time, see Max Hastings, *The Korean War* (New York, 1987), pp. 132–133.

28. "Were not prepared," in FO371/84109, September 27, 1950; "their internal," in FO371/84109, September 28, 1950.

29. Acheson, p. 466.

30. "Sniveling dependency," in Maclean, *British Foreign Policy,* p. 43. Other things remained the same. The divisive leaks that occurred whenever Maclean was around continued at a rapid clip once he returned to active duty. As the Foreign Office was vetoing one MacArthur initiative after another, a UPI story datelined London claimed that British diplomats regarded plans coming out of Washington as "dangerous." The State Department was livid and immediately accused London of planting the story. Bevin denied it and vowed "to trace the source of this report, which is of course without foundation." As usual, nothing more was done; see FO371/84112, November 8, 1950.

31. Kennan, *Memoirs,* p. 497.

32. Franks in FO115/4487.

33. "Indefensible," quoted in Manchester, *American Caesar,* p. 603; Douglas MacArthur, *Reminiscences* (New York, 1964), p. 365; order broadened in FO371/84112, Franks to FO, November 7, 1950 and MacArthur, p. 365.

34. For Bevin on Soviet air force, see FO371/84124, December 7, 1950, Minister of Defense to British embassy Tokyo; on hot pursuit, FO371/84137, FO to embassy, December 11, 1950; for Washington's case for hot pursuit, see FRUS, 1950, v. 7, pp. 1144–45; for Bevin's response, see *ibid.,* p. 1172; also Courtney Whitney, *MacArthur: His Rendezvous With History* (New York, 1956), pp. 406–407; Truman, v. 2, pp. 375–376; Acheson, p. 464.

35. For CIA estimates, see Hastings, p. 131; for bombing of bridges, see FO371/84102, embassy to FO, November 8, 1950, and RDGD/1975 RC, 73B.

36. "Understand," in FRUS, 1950, v. 7, pp. 1173–74; "no ultimatum," in FO371/84112, Bevin to Jebb, November 9, 1950.

37. "Bolt," in Hastings, p. 138; Gascoigne in FO371/84103.

38. "Warning," in FO115/4486, July 26, 1950; for Bevin's opposition to new offensive, see FRUS, 1950, v. 7, p. 1172–73, November 17, 1950; and FO371/84103 November 13, 1950; for a more candid expression of Bevin's frustration, see FO371/84103, Bevin to Franks, November 22, 1950.

39. For Acheson's November 22, 1950 response, see FO371/84103.

40. Wilfrid Mann interview with author, April 16, 1984.

41. Rovere and Schlesinger, p. 144.

42. "If successful," in ibid.; for preparation and first days of offensive, see also Manchester, *American Caesar,* pp. 604–608.

43. "Men," in Michael Kernan, *The Washington Post,* December 1, 1984, interviews with Chosin survivors; Manchester, *American Caesar,* pp. 608–612.

44. Hastings, p. 130ff; *The Guardian* quoted in D. Rees, *Korea,* p. 110.

45. FO371/84110.

46. "Contradictory," in Joseph C. Goulden, *Korea: The Untold Story* (New York,

1982), pp. 275–276; *New York Times,* October 7, 1950; *Time,* November 13 and 20, 1950; "the Dean," in FO371/84112, November 4, 1950.

47. Troop estimates in FO371/84110; "threaten," in Manchester, *American Caesar,* p. 601; "a new," etc., in Rovere and Schlesinger, p. 138.

48. "They really," in D. Rees, *Korea,* p. 114; Hutchison, FO371/84112, November 4, 1950; CIA in Manchester, *American Caesar,* p. 604.

49. James M. Gavin, *Atlantic,* June 1965.

50. James Van Fleet, *U.S. News & World Report,* September 30, 1955.

51. Cecil, *A Divided Life,* p. 125.

52. "Must know," in FO371/84109, *op. cit.*

53. "Bottomless," in Rees, p. 171. Indications are that Truman never wanted to use the bomb, and that rather than considering it America's "political ace," he considered it a political liability. Franks, according to Hastings, believed "the Adminstration never seriously considered the use of nuclear weapons in Korea." However, the point is that the Chinese did not, or at least should not have known this; see Hastings, p. 181; for PRC dismissal of the atomic bomb as innocuous and a "paper tiger," see D. Rees, *Korea,* pp. 106, 141.

54. Franks to FO in FO371/84112.

55. For Suiho dam, see Hastings, p. 126 and D. Clayton James, *Triumph & Disaster* (Boston, 1985), pp. 498, 520; for bombing of the dam in June 1952, see D. Rees, *Korea,* pp. 378–379 and Hastings, p. 267.

56. Manchester, *American Caesar,* p. 598.

57. *Washington Post* and *New York Times,* December 1, 1950.

58. Franks cable in FO371/841112; "Truman's fingers," in Roger Dingman, *International Security,* Winter, 1989, p. 66; British military officers in Korea emphatically rejected using the bomb, concluding "if the atom bomb were used in Korea it would be ineffective in holding up the Chinese advance . . . inevitably bringing in the Soviet Union Air Force and might lead to World War III."; see FO371/84124, December 7, 1950.

59. For Maclean's role in briefing, see Cecil, *A Divided Life,* p. 123.

60. Maclean's copy of summit, FO371/84105. When the State Department was still trying in March 1956 to piece together what Maclean may have known about Korea, they reexamined the Attlee-Truman transcript. It was still considered so hot that after reviewing it, one senior official sent it back to the European Division because "in my office we do not normally keep material of a classification above secret, [so] I would prefer not to retain this extra copy of the Truman-Attlee conversations."; see DOS: Maclean File, R. A. Kidder to E. A. Lister April 5, 1956.

61. Acheson, p. 478.

62. For U.S. record of Truman-Attlee talks, see FRUS, 1950, v. 7, pp. 1362–1465; for U.K., see FO371/84105.

63. FRUS, 1950, v. 7, p. 1395.

64. FO371/84105.

65. For "limited war," see Donovan, *Tumultous Years,* p. 318.

66. FO371/84105.

67. Ibid.

68. Such talks had taken place among the Americans in early December, including the identification of islands. But the minutes do not reflect they were discussed in the same detail with the British; see Goulden, pp. 408–410 and FO371/84105.

69. For discussion of atomic weapons, see Acheson, pp. 481–485; Donovan, *Tumultous Years*, p. 318; FRUS, Korea, 1950, v. 7, p. 1462; FO371/84105. The Attlee-Truman understanding was not reflected in the summit's official record. It did appear in Franks's notes and in a memorandum for the record retained in Acheson's office; see Goulden, pp. 400, 668.

70. Donovan, *Tumultous Years*, p. 318.

71. JCS in Dingman, op. cit., p. 67. Dingman provides the definitive history of the debate on whether or not to use atomic weapons, which continued throughout the Korean conflict.

72. "Reassurance," in Hastings, p. 181; "rightfully," in Hewlett and Duncan, v. 2, p. 533.

73. "Not dead," in FO371/84124, December 12, 1950; the Cabinet paper was "among secret documents that I retrieved from [Maclean's] steel filing cabinet after his flight."; see Cecil, *A Divided Life*, p. 123.

74. For meetings in Moscow, see Talbott, *Khrushchev Remembers*, pp. 367–368.

75. Bohlen, pp. 294–295.

76. Talbott, *Khrushchev Remembers*, p. 367.

77. Talbott, *Khrushchev Remembers*, pp. 367–372. Khrushchev admits he didn't attend any of the key meetings affecting Korea, but his account was collaborated many years later by Li San Cho, the North Korean ambassador to Moscow at the time the meetings took place. "Kim Il Sung discussed his plans to seize the South with Stalin in advance and won the Soviet dictator's approval," Li San Cho told *The Moscow News* in 1990. Lin San Cho later became the deputy chief of staff of the North's armed forces during the war. See *New York Times*, July 6, 1990.

78. "Avowed," in FO371/84109, September 30, 1950; S. L. A. Marshall quoted in Manchester, *American Caesar*, p. 607.

79. Acheson, pp. 472–474.

80. "How Two Spies Cost U.S. a War," *U.S. News and World Report*, September 30, 1955. Burgess, of course, was the other.

81. In early May, (weeks after the FO would falsely claim Maclean was cut off from receiving top-secret documents), Washington inquired of England and Australia if they would support immediate and massive retaliation against Chinese air bases in Manchuria if air strikes were launched from there. Both said yes. Interestingly enough, no such Chinese attacks ever occurred; see FO371/92758, dated May 10, 1951.

82. FBI Summary Report, Section XXII, p. 44. The "observation" was added as an addendum.

CHAPTER NINETEEN (pp. 305–324)

1. Kermit Roosevelt, phone interview with author, November 1984.

2. Cicely Angleton, phone interview with author, October 2, 1984.

3. Thomas Powers describes how Richard Helms "was conspicuously lacking in the old money" common to so many in the CIA's early days. It implied that he needed his job for the paycheck and could not afford to be confrontational because he had no personal fortune to support him if he were to resign or be fired; see Powers, *The Man Who Kept the Secrets,* p. 55.

4. Martin, *Wilderness of Mirrors,* p. 52.

5. All remarks attributed to Lamphere in this chapter come from an interview with the author, December 10, 1985.

6. Robin Winks, *Cloak and Gown* (New York, 1987), p. 348.

7. Wilfrid and Miriam Mann, interviews with author, from April 1984 to October 1986.

8. Mackenzie, interview with author, January 17, 1985.

9. For "The Spy Who Came To Dinner," *The Washingtonian,* October 1984, I interviewed everyone who had been at the dinner party who was then still alive, except Philby who did not answer my letters (Gerry Dack's whereabouts was unknown). The Manns were particularly helpful; his own account appears in *Was There A Fifth Man?* pp. 81–86; see also Martin, pp. 47–48.

10. Mann, 59; Gowing, v. 2, p. 151.

11. Angleton memorandum, op. cit.

12. Philby, p. 171.

13. Alsop interview.

14. Angleton interview and Angleton memo, op. cit.

15. Angleton interview and Angleton memo, op. cit. He did not know in 1951 that one of the largest blots in Burgess's Foreign Office copybook came when he publicly identified the Iberian British security chief as he was dining in a Gibraltar restaurant; see Page, pp. 203–204.

16. FBI investigators questioned Citadel President General Charles P. Summerall who reported that his request for a speaker was addressed to Ambassador Franks, and the response came over Franks's signature. It is certainly possible, but highly doubtful, that this was done by subordinates and that Franks was unaware of the request or the selection of Burgess; see FBI: Philby Files, June 16, 1951 teletype from FBI Office in Savannah to Hoover.

17. Sam Mellichamp, interview with author, October 5, 1985. All quotes, remarks, and observations attributed to Mellichamp are from this interview.

18. David A. Lyon III, interview with author, October 5, 1985. All quotes, remarks and observations attributed to Lyon are from this interview.

19. Francis W. Binford, interview with author, October 5, 1985. All quotes, remarks, and observations attributed to Judge Binford are from this interview.

20. FBI: Philby Files, affidavit signed by James A. Turck and sealed by David R. Lyon for the State of Virginia on February 28, 1951.

21. FBI Summary Report. In describing Turck in this report as a homosexual, Hoover clearly rejected Turck's contention that he was not.

22. FBI Summary Report, "Interviews in Connection with Burgess."

23. FBI Summary Report, interviews with Summerall and Josephine Pinckney.

24. *Charleston News and Chronicle,* June 8, 1951 and FBI interviews with Summerall and other attendes. The next day, in an effort to make amends, Burgess called on several Citadel officials, one of whom was named James Bond.

25. Battle to Simmons, March 14, 1951; see Battle Papers, Virginia State Archives, Richmond, Virginia.

26. Smith in Ray Cline, *Secrets, Scholars, and Spies* (Washington, 1976), p. 108.

27. Information from Mr. and Mrs. Kermit Roosevelt; in his book *Countercoup* (New York, 1978), p. 109, Roosevelt suggests that because of Burgess he became suspicious of Philby before May 1951. But on other occasions, including in our conversations, he wisely backed away from that assertion. For Philby on Kermit Roosevelt, whom he dubbed "the quiet American," see Mosley, *Dulles,* p. 326.

28. Seale, p. 211.

29. FBI: Philby Files, Turck affidavit to the FBI dated June 13, 1951. Philby mentions that he had bought a "camera, tripod and accessories"; see Philby, p. 180.

30. Burgess asked Emily Roosevelt if he and his mother could be guests at Gippy Plantation. She wrote back and urged him not to come, but he showed up at her doorstep anyway, claiming that her letter must have arrived in Washington after he left. Mrs. Roosevelt had heard all about his earlier trip, and with George Wharton Pepper (whose wealthy father had been a U.S. Senator) and Fitz Eugene Newbold (head of a prominent financial clan) as house guests, she was taking no chances. She took in his mother, but asked Guy to stay in a nearby motel; see FBI: Rosevelt File, Emily Roosevelt's interview with FBI agents, June 12, 1951.

31. Battle Papers: Simmons to Battle, March 30, 1951; C. D. Steele to Simmons, April 7, 1951. Tommy Thompson maintains that Franks was in London when the material arrived from the State Department, and that it was sent to him there so he could respond to it immediately. None of the documentation on the case supports this scenario. If it were sent to London, however, it is possible it either went directly or was copied to Maclean. Thompson does complain that it took the FO "their usual long time to decide what to do"; see Thompson, pp. 212–213. For Franks's travel see *New York Times,* March 10 and March 28, 1951.

32. On April 13 Burgess telegrammed Philby: "Both [he and his mother] arriving directly after lunch Saturday fourteenth. Lincoln arriving independently." They flew back together because Burgess's Lincoln had broken down. During a twenty-four hour period in Charleston, Burgess rented one car, drove it thirty-five miles, returned it, rented a second car, and drove it 144 miles before returning it. FBI: Philby Files, June 18, 1951 teletype from Savannah to Hoover; Greenhill, op. cit.

33. Greenhill, op. cit.; Battle Papers: C. D. Steele to Simmons, April 18, 1951. Simmons did not notify Battle until April 30.

34. Straight, pp. 71, 80.

35. Ibid., pp. 230–231.

36. Ibid., pp. 249–250.

37. Philby, p. 176.

38. Ibid.; Mackenzie interview confirmed that these were the names on the list, and that Philby convinced him Gore-Booth was Hoover.

39. At a press conference on September 18, 1955 the Foreign Office admitted "definite suspicion had fallen on Maclean by April"; see *The Times* (London), September 19, 1955; Cecil, *The Times,* and Costello refine the date to April 17; see Cecil, *The Missing Dimension,* p. 191; *The Times* (London), January 2, 1982; Costello, p. 549. During the period Gore-Booth was serving with Maclean at the embassy, his pregnant wife was also in New York where she eventually gave birth to twins; see Cecil, *A Divided Life,* p. 140.

40. Philby, p. 172.

41. Alan Maclean interview; FBI Summary Report.

42. FBI: Philby Files, undated teletype from New York.

CHAPTER TWENTY (pp. 325–336)

1. Wire service items can be found in, FBI: Philby Files; DOS: Maclean Files.

2. Gullion interview; Lawford interview; information to author from Moultrie Ball (who is related to Emily Roosevelt); Farmer in Richard Deacon, *The British Connection* (London, 1979), pp. 174–175. On May 18, Anglo-American atomic cooperation was placed on the NSC agenda. However, "the disappearance of MacLean (sic) and Burgess and the crowded calendars of the members of the [NSC] combined to postpone the consideration of" the proposal; see FRUS, 1951, v. 1, pp. 786–787.

3. DOS: Maclean Files.

4. Since the Franco regime was trying to expel Brewer for a series he was doing on corruption, James wondered whether the CIA was trying to remove a thorn in Franco's side. Brewer worked for the OSS during the war. When he was hired by *The New York Times* he promised to sever all ties with American intelligence. Years later the *Times* realized that he probably never did; see Harrison Salisbury, *Without Fear or Favor* (New York, 1980), pp. 501–504. It was probably Allen Dulles, knowing that he had ties to Philby from some years back, who recommended using Brewer in May 1951. CIA Director Smith later requested that the FBI interview Brewer. Brewer provided the FBI attache in Madrid with the FBI's first information about Philby's bizarre domestic arrangements; see FBI: Philby Files, November 7, 1951 Urgent Teletype from Madrid to Hoover; November 20, 1951 memorandum Hoover to Smith.

5. Robert Mackenzie was in Paris for the Tripartite Security Working Group, composed of British, French, and American security authorities. He was lecturing the French about their sloppy security methods when he was called away to take a call from his boss Carey-Foster, who told him the news about Maclean. It came as a jolt to Mackenzie who knew all about the "Homer" investigation. But the "most humbling experience of all" he later recalled, was to have to walk back into the room to ask for French help in hunting down the British diplomats; from Mackenzie interview; see Cecil, *A Divided Life,* p. 146.

6. Philby, p. 189.

7. Wright, *Spycatcher,* p. 147.

8. Both Foreign Office and MI5 officials would claim that MI5 wanted to postpone confronting Maclean until after Melinda had gone into the hospital so they could search the house. She and her mother told Hoare that when MI5 did come to the house, they "did not trouble to examine the mass of papers [Donald] left behind." Of course, it is possible that they searched the house when Melinda was in the hospital. But with her family at Tatsfield in such numbers, it is unlikely that it was ever as abandoned as MI5 had originally evisioned; see *News Chronicle* (London), September 24, 1955; 1955 White Paper, p. 4

9. Francis Marling, Melinda's father, an oil executive from Chicago, flew to England to open his own investigation. He confronted British authorities demanding answers to his son-in-law's disappearance. After several frustrating months, he returned to Chicago bitter and angry. On the eve of the first anniversary of Donald's disappearance he died of a heart attack at age fifty-nine; see Hoare, pp. 104–105; *New York Times,* May 19, 1952.

10. "Amiss," in Cecil, *A Divided Life,* p. 140; on May 29 a telegram also arrived from an agitated British ambassador in Sweden who had apparently been addressed by the American Department as the ambassador to Norway. "Dear Head of Department (whom I do not know). I suffered under the delusion that I was his Majesty's representative at Stockholm not Oslo." Cecil responded on June 6 on behalf of Maclean "who is away." He blamed the mistake on a typist; see FO371/90436.

11. Cecil, *A Divided Life,* p. 147.

12. Connell, p. 326.

13. FRUS, 1951, v. 1, p. 787; on June 6 the NSC also received a CIA report entitled U.S. *Policy on Soviet and Satellite Defectors,* RDGD, 1978 Collection.

14. FBI Summary Report. According to Williams he talked to the prospective buyer on June 5 and called Whitfield on the morning of June 7.

15. The most avid proponent of this view has been Sir Patrick Reilly, a senior Foreign Office official who from 1949 to 1953 had special responsibilities for intelligence, and was the chairman of the Joint Intelligence Committee. He argues that regardless of what Lamphere may have known, the British directly informed Hoover of all developments with respect to Maclean; see Glees, pp. 358–363. This led Cecil to conclude that Hoover may have held out on his own lieutenants and then claimed ignorance when Maclean got away. The absence of any documentation in FBI files, Cecil suggests, is part of a U.S. government cover-up to protect friendly governments; see Cecil, *A Divided Life,* pp. 126–127. Carey-Foster similarly insists that the Americans were kept fully informed; see Penrose and Freeman, p. 344.

16. FBI: Philby Files, June 6 Urgent Teletype from Hoover to the New York and Washington field offices.

17. Larry Solon, *Headlines All My Life* (London, 1957), pp. 263–266; Cecil, *A Divided Life,* p. 145.

18. As told to Andrew Boyle by Kitty Muggeridge in Boyle, *The Fourth Man,* p. 382.

19. Philby carefully avoids telling the date Patterson received MI5's cable. He does mention that after receiving it he and Patterson, as instructed by MI5, went directly to see Lamphere. It has long been assumed, given the spin Philby put on the story, that MI5's cable was dispatched on Monday, May 28, and arrived at the embassy early on the morning of May 29. But the June 6 FBI teletype directing a name search, plus Lamphere's own recollection, means either the MI5 did not dispatch their cable to Patterson until the night of June 6, or—most unlikely—the cable was sent and received earlier but Patterson did not immediately report its contents to the FBI; see Philby, pp. 177–180; Lamphere, p. 231 and Lamphere interview. In 1988, Costello offered a scenario that has Philby and Patterson receiving the MI5 cable and informing the FBI on May 26, but this would require that Lamphere held back from his colleagues; see Costello, pp. 561–562.

20. Hickerson interview; *Washington Post,* June 8, 1951.

21. There may be an element of truth to this. Ladd would have found Burgess's vulgarity alluring, and very likely spent more time with him than he wanted Hoover to know. Lamphere confirms that Ladd would been attracted to Burgess's dark side. But he also believes that Ladd would have drawn Burgess out on his anti-Americanism and not forgotten it; see Philby, 179–180; Lamphere interview.

22. Philby, p. 180; Lamphere did not think that Philby was an active Soviet spy, only because he found him so lazy and lacking in initiative that he could not believe that Philby was working very diligently for anyone; from Lamphere interview, and Lamphere, p. 231.

23. Mackenzie interview; Philby, p. 184.

24. DOS: Maclean Files, 741.13/6–751.

25. DOS: UP story summarizing British statements, taken off wire service at 2:20 P.M., June 8, 1951.

26. *Washington Post,* June 8 and 9, 1951.

27. *New York Times,* June 11, 1951.

28. DOS: Maclean Files, 741.13/6–1551; Cecil, *A Divided Life,* p. 149.

29. FBI Summary Report, p. 90.

30. FBI: Philby Files, Summary Report, pp. 91–92. Burgess also left behind books by Austen in the car that he rented on the day of May 25, as well as in his London apartment.

31. Lamphere confirms that by the time he met with Martin on June 11, Philby had been recalled to England; see Lamphere, p. 237; Hoover claims that "a representative of [Philby's] organization [SIS] did come to this country and accompany Philby back when he was recalled,"; see FBI: Philby Files, Hoover to Tolson, et al., September 29, 1955.

32. FBI: Philby Files, Nichols to Tolson, June 11, 1950.

33. Lamphere, pp. 231–235.

34. Ibid., pp. 236–237.

35. Martin, p. 54.

36. So convinced was Philby that he had snowed Harvey with his charming contrition the morning after the dinner party that he and Burgess celebrated by

climbing into bed with a bottle of champagne. That same morning, Wilfrid Mann, who had had too many martinis at the dinner party to drive home, returned to 4100 Nebraska to retrieve his car. When he came to the house, Aileen told him to go upstairs and "say hello to the boys." Although Mann was surprised to find "the boys" together in bed, neither he nor Aileen read anything homosexual into it. Jim Angleton, however, did. "If Mann had told me that when it happened I could have destroyed Philby," Angleton told me with bitterness some years later. "It would have destroyed Philby's cover for Burgess that he was in the house as 'Esther's last chance for marriage.' "

This was the beginning of a vendetta Angleton waged against Mann that culminated in his planting the story that Mann was a Soviet agent. In *The Fourth Man,* Andrew Boyle, based on his interviews with Angleton, has Mann—whom he dubs "Basil" (Mann's middle name)—appearing, mostly at incorrect times and places, as a Soviet agent assisting Maclean; from Mann and Angleton interviews. When Philby later discoverd Harvey's role in his dismissal, his reaction was somewhere between comically absurd and insufferably asinine. Philby believed Harvey had an obligation not to discover that he was a Soviet spy, and did so only as a "retrospective exercise in spite," because of Burgess's insult to his wife; see Philby, p. 189.

CHAPTER TWENTY-ONE (pp. 337–349)

1. Connolly, *U.S. News and World Report,* September 25, 1953, p. 58.

2. For Mrs. Dunbar, see Hoare, pp. 121, 130–131; for Melinda's state of mind, see Cecil, *A Divided Life,* pp. 152–158. Rebecca West maintains Melinda's complaints were exaggerated; see, R. West, *The New Meaning of Treason,* p. 230. According to a report that reached John Foster Dulles, Melinda went from Switzerland to Austria by train, and then continued to Russia via auto. "It was a matter of touch and go," the report continued, "one of the children started to cry and complained about a pain. Mrs. Maclean became frightened and thought it might be appendicitis. She wanted to take the child to a hospital. It took the driver no end of trouble to persuade her to cross the border. She met her husband after her arrival in Russia." See DOS: Maclean File, Telegram To the Secretary of State from The Hague, November 4, 1955. The final plans may have been made when she spent six weeks that summer at the home of widower Douglas MacKillop on Majorca, the largest of the Balearic Islands off the coast of Spain. MacKillop, a stocky San Francisco native in his late thirties, had been a State Department foreign service security officer who had worked with the Marshall Plan in Paris at the same time as Jay Sheers, Harriet's husband.

Because Tomas Harris lived on Majorca, and because of the near certainty that he was involved in Donald Maclean's flight, there is good reason to believe that he helped plan her escape while she was in Majorca. MacKillop was interviewed by journalist Rene MacColl; see *Daily Express* (London), September 25, 1953.

3. Petrov defected in Australia on April 3, 1954. The Australian government

issued its report on September 14, 1955, and *The People* published it in London on September 18. He discusses Burgess and Maclean in his book *Empire of Fear* (New York, 1956), pp. 271–275. There is speculation that the Soviets had been indifferent to Maclean's pleas to allow Melinda and the children to join him in Russia. It is possible that Bruno Pontecorvo, whose standing increased greatly because of his help in developing a Soviet hydrogen bomb—successfully tested only weeks before Melinda's disappearance—intervened with Soviet authorities on Maclean's behalf. During the years that Donald and Melinda were in Paris, her aunt was a close friend of the Joliot-Curie's whom she often visited. Pontecorvo worked for the Joliot-Curie's at the same time, and he and his wife were of similar age and background to Donald and Melinda. See "Another Lady Vanishes," *World,* v. 1, No. 5, January 1, 1954, pp. 18–20; for latest historical information on the Soviet hydrogen bomb, see *New York Times,* October 8, 1990.

4. 1955 White Paper, p. 7, emphasis added.

5. Crossman in *Hansard,* November 7, 1955, p. 1535; R. West, *The New Meaning of Treason,* p. 238; for editorial that "these damaging and somewhat disgraceful admissions by the Foreign Office were not spontaneous" but forced by Petrov's disclosures, see *Washington Post,* September 21, 1955.

6. The first to be referred to as the Third Man was Bernard Warren Miller, an American medical student who had met Burgess aboard the *Queen Mary* and who was one of the last persons to see Burgess in London before he fled with Maclean; see *Daily Express* (London), June 21, 1951 and *New York Herald Tribune,* June 22, 1951.

7. FBI: Philby Files, Winchell text in undated memorandum to Boardman. There were obvious inaccuracies. Neither Burgess nor Maclean were members of British intelligence, Burgess was not under suspicion, and Philby was in Washington less than two years.

8. "Hawked about," in *Hansard,* op. cit., p. 1590.

9. FBI: Philby Files, Hoover to Tolson *et al.,* September 29, 1955, emphasis added.

10. Lipton inferred his tip had come from the CIA. Also see Knightley, *Masterspy,* pp. 192–197; Page, pp. 295–299.

11. "Third man," in *Hansard,* op. cit., p. 1501. Morrison continued to insist there had been a tip off; see *Hansard,* op. cit., p. 1521; Page, pp. 299–300.

12. Edwin Newman, who later became a nationally known correspondent for NBC, was at the press conference in Dora Philby's South Kensington apartment. "What I remember most vividly about that news conference," he recalled some thirty years later, "was that all the British reporters refused to ask him questions about Burgess and Maclean." Newman's questions about Philby's relationship to the two men were met with glares by his British colleagues. Such questions, it was made clear to the American, smacked of contemptible McCarthyism. "It was simply unacceptable to ask him if he was the Third Man," Newman explained. He stated that he did not believe Philby at the time and was not at all surprised when he defected to Moscow. Edwin Newman, telephone interview with author, October 10, 1986.

13. Knightley, *Masterspy*, p. 198.

14. *Facts on File,* February 8–14, 1956, pp. 49–50; see also, Driberg, pp. 91–105. This is essentially the same story Blunt, the unidentified friend, gave immediately after their flight; see *Daily Express* (London), June 7, 1951.

15. For Elliott-Philby, see Wright, pp. 184, 194. This precipitated another crisis in Anglo-American intelligence relations because Angleton, concerned about the myopia of the SIS old boy network, claims to have extracted a commitment from London that they would never interrogate Philby without first notifying him, and that such an interrogation would never take place on foreign soil. In an effort at damage control, Elliott flew from Beirut to Washington to share Philby's "confession" with Angleton; from Angleton interview. FBI agents in Beirut managed to get into the Philby's apartment where they examined both Kim's and Eleanor's typewriter ribbons to see if they could pick up any clues to Philby's disappearance. It proved fruitless, see FBI: Philby Files, W. D. Griffin to Conrad, July 10, 1963.

16. The government's official explanation by Edward Heath, Lord Privy Seal to the House, can be found in *The Washington Star,* July 1, 1963.

17. Page, *et al.,* believe that the Soviets never planned to take Burgess with Maclean. In trying to find "the explanation that fit the facts," they assume that the Soviets were determined to save Maclean, that it was essential for them to involve Burgess in the escape plan, but that because Burgess was an amateur he made mistakes. Once in France, he realized that he might have left a trail behind, and so decided to go on to Moscow. The Soviets, knowing that he was in too deep to go back, took him, thus dooming Philby; see Page, pp. 262–269.

18. FBI: Philby Files, Cutto to De Loach, *et al.,* April 26, 1968.

19. He went over all this, says Philby, in a Washington restaurant that he does not name. But the description he gives could only be the Peking Restaurant on Connecticut Avenue, a favorite hang-out, Angleton confirmed, for members of the British and American intelligence community. Philby chose it because each booth was (and still is) equipped with a speaker, and the music would make it impossible for anyone to eavesdrop on their conversation; see Philby, p. 176.

20. Philby, pp. 174–177.

21. *New York Times,* March 18, 1968; after lengthy interviews with Philby twenty years later in Moscow, Knightley came to much the same conclusion: "Philby's account in his book can now been (sic) seen for what it really is—an attempt to cover up a Russian intelligence mess in which his own blunders played no small part . . ."; see Knightley, *Masterspy,* p. 179.

22. Bok, p. 84.

23. Philby, p. 173; Lamphere, pp. 231–232. As Pincher points out, "writers, including myself, have made an assumption . . . [that] London was at pains to keep the U.S. authorities fully and immediately informed," *Too Secret, Too Long,* p. 173. Carey-Foster continued to insist that the FO kept the FBI fully informed; see Penrose and Freeman, p. 344. Cecil maintains that the FBI was kept informed until April when London feared that if the FBI were told about Maclean, they would tell the State Department, which shows surprising FO naivete about FBI-State relations; see Cecil, *A Divided Life,* pp. 135–136.

24. For Krivitsky in the news, see for instance, *New York Times,* September 1, 1948, January 6, 1949, September 16, 1949 and August 1, 1951; For acceptance of Philby's claims, see Philby, p. 175, Page, 269, Seale, p. 212; Pincher, *Too Secret Too Long,* p. 437; Penrose and Freeman, p. 340; Cecil, *A Divided Life,* p. 131; Costello, p. 547. Wright, the one person who could confirm that Philby had done so, does not.

25. Philby, pp. 173–178; Seale, pp. 212–213; Penrose, pp. 339–340. Cecil dissents, see Cecil, *A Divided Life,* pp. 129–131; Knightley has a mixed acceptance; see Knightley, *Masterspy,* pp. 173–179.

26. The only reason that Burgess did not have cash was that he had to pay for emergency repairs in Richmond; see FBI: Philby Files, Turck interview.

27. Neither Lyon nor Turck told Burgess about the affidavit. Battle's complaint may have been the detonating event in Burgess's recall. But there is every reason to believe that to Burgess, Franks emphasized as much if not more his repeated embassy security violations, his bad judgment, and his poor performance. See White Paper, p. 35, and Greenhill, op. cit. Battle may have planted the seed for the subsequent distortions by Burgess and Philby. In a June 8, 1951, UP story, the Governor was the first to suggest that Burgess's recall was the result of his complaint to the State Department. Burgess's assertion that he talked about it with Sumner Welles is fabrication—just Burgess's way of engaging in more name-dropping; see Driberg, p. 85.

28. Costello, p. 547, is correct in saying that Burgess was deliberately speeding, hoping to get stopped. But this derives from Burgess's peculiar fascination with diplomatic immunity. He viewed it as a privilege of the elite that was wasted unless it was used. Journalist Blair Bolles for instance, describes how Burgess would pass up legal parking places until he found an illegal one. When he left Petersburg, Burgess had no tickets. Yet, he did not get stopped again—at least there is no record—for the remainder of this trip or on a subsequent one to South Carolina taken before he was finally called in by Franks; see FBI: Philby Files, Bolles interview, July 14, 1951. Philby's inventions are too numerous to itemize, but among some of the others: He claims that Menzies personally contacted Hoover about his appointment. But FBI files contain no evidence of any such cable from Menzies; see Philby, p. 154; FBI: Philby Files, Memorandum Brannigan to W. C. Sullivan, undated, p. 3. Nor is there any record that Philby met with Hoover after the flight of Burgess and Maclean as he claims; see Boardman, p. 6; Philby, p. 185; Lamphere maintains he did not, Lamphere interview.

Because Philby needlessly falsified the pretext he used to warn Burgess—who left his car not in the embassy parking lot but at Philby's home—it must be assumed that his claim that he sent such a warning is also invented; see Philby, p. 177; FBI: Philby Files, Summary Report, "Investigation In Connection With Burgess Automobile," pp. 87–92; see also, Costello, p. 557. Philby's account also conflicts with his later claim to Knightley that the Soviets had set the date for May 25. If this were so, telling Burgess to hurry up would have been pointless, unless Philby means to suggest that Burgess had the authority to override Moscow. Blunt, a pathological liar if ever there was one, could not resist embellishing the story; see Penrose and Freeman, p. 358; Knightley, *Masterspy*, p. 178; for Blunt's veracity, see Wright, pp. 219, 253, 263; Costello, pp. 47–48; Penrose and Freeman, p. 340.

29. "Invincible," in David Cannadine, *New York Review of Books*, March 27, 1986.

30. After Philby first claimed that Burgess was at the center of the escape plan, Page, *et al.*, wrote "One can only say that if the Soviet secret service was relying on Burgess for operational plans . . . it was a less formidable operation than we have been lead to believe."; see Page, p. 269. Some writers have tried to read into Burgess's leisurely return via ship a confirmation that Philby knew something about when Maclean was to be confronted. It meant nothing of the sort. So short was the time between Burgess's recall and the time he sailed, that the embassy was later forced to apologize to the State Department for not immediately returning Burgess's diplomatic tags. "Sir Oliver Franks very much regrets that as Mr. Burgess' departure took place at unusually short notice the normal procedure for collecting diplomatic identification . . . was not followed . . ." NA\601. 4111/9–551. The embassy booked Burgess on the *Queen Mary* as part of a small British delegation returning to England. Burgess and Philby had absolutely no say in the matter; see FBI Summary Report; Penrose and Freeman, p. 340; Pincher, *Too Secret, Too Long*, p. 184.

31. The pickup at Tatsfield is based on statements first made by Melinda and later by Burgess, and can be challenged for this reason alone.

Pincher alleges that MI5 has "officially" branded Melinda a liar who was converted by Donald to communism. No reliable sources are, of course, given, and Wright does not make such a claim in his book. But those who knew her, such as Hoare and Cecil, do not believe that she had any communist views, or very strong political views of any stripe. They saw her later flight to Russia as the act of someone overwhelmed at the prospect of either remarrying or raising three children without a father, making her guilty of bad judgment rather than treachery; see Pincher, *Too Secret, Too Long*, pp. 193–194.

32. Philby, pp. 184–185.

33. Knightley, *Masterspy*, p. 179. After his interviews with Philby, Knightley suggests an account that implies that KGB operators were a group of highly independent entrepreneurs. He suggests, for instance, that Burgess's Soviet control in London authorized him to go to Russia, unaware that this would be a disaster for Philby because he did not know that the two had been living together in Washington. But it seems inconceivable under the rigid centralization of Stalin and Beria, where the predictable reward for individual initiative was a bullet in the brain, that any Soviet intelligence operator would have authorized Burgess to go to Moscow without obtaining the highest clearance. This goes as well for any Soviet intelligence officials on the Continent who subsequently handled them (this also assumes, of course, that the Soviets were involved in executing the escape of Burgess and Maclean); see Knightley, *Masterspy*, pp. 176–179.

34. Philby almost suggested that some such arrangement should have been considered; see Knightley, *Masterspy*, p. 178. The initial cover story devised by

Burgess and Blunt and faithfully repeated by Jack Hewitt, Burgess's boyfriend, was to set up an alibi for Maclean and Burgess to have gone to Paris; see *Daily Express* (London), June 22, 1951.

35. Burgess's allegation that Maclean knew he was not being followed outside London helped feed various conspiracy theories; see for instance, Pincher, *Too Secret, Too Long*, p. 194. Burgess drove one hundred thirty miles using the Austin he rented at 2:00 P.M. It is about eighty miles from London to Southampton, though Tatsfield is to the east of the most direct route; see *Daily Express* (London), June 11, 1951.

36. Obviously if the Soviets knew that Tatsfield were a safe haven, they could have been in touch with Maclean directly even before May 25, obviating any need for Burgess and Maclean to push scrawled notes across Donald's desk, as Burgess and Philby claim.

37. Isherwood put it best: "I have the strongest personal reasons for not wanting to go to Russia and I should think Guy Burgess would have exactly the same sort of reasons. We both happen to have exactly the same sort of tastes, and they don't meet with the approval of the Soviets. In fact, I'm told they liquidate chaps with our views—rather beastly don't you think?" Quoted in *Time,* June 25, 1951.

38. Michael Redgrave, *In My Mind's Eye* (New York, 1983), pp. 192–194. "Write me, it's bloody lonely here," Burgess beseeched Redgrave. It was during this 1958 tour of the Shakespeare Memorial Company that Burgess met Coral Browne. Their sessions and correspondence became the basis for the dramatization *"An Englishman Abroad."*

No one escaped Burgess's attentions, including Randolph Churchill, see *Evening Standard,* Feb. 23, 1959.

39. Conor Cruise O'Brien, *New York Review of Books,* April 11, 1985. He was reviewing Arkady N. Shevchenko's *Breaking with Moscow*.

EPILOGUE (pp. 351–357)

1. Cookridge, pp. 261–262.

2. *New York Times,* September 5, 1963.

3. Toynbee, "Maclean and I," *Observer,* October 15, 1967.

4. On August 9, 1969 the FBI sent a copy of Straight's June 18, 1963 FBI confession to H. R. Haldeman, President Nixon's White House chief of staff; see FBI: Straight File, Memorandum to the Director from WFO [Washington Field Office].

5. Blunt did his friend Tomas Harris a grave injustice by insisting that he was not a Soviet agent. During his MI5 interrogation, Blunt would repeatedly deny that someone he knew was a Soviet agent. Then, after being confronted with evidence, Blunt would admit he had lied and that yes, so-and-so was indeed an agent; see Wright, pp. 219, 253, 263 and Penrose and Freeman, p. 430. Blunt's ludicrous pretensions notwithstanding, Moscow hardly provided him with a complete list of

all their agents. Blunt could only identify with certainty the handful he recruited. He was in no position to know the hundreds of others recruited by the Soviets. So his denial about Harris is at best meaningless. Harris was involved in the flight of Maclean and Burgess and may have helped plot Melinda's flight as well. See Deacon, *The British Connection*, pp. 174–182.

6. During a marathon interview session with the author, Angleton brought out a full-page advertisement then running in newspapers across the country. It offered a $100,000 reward for information about a series of assassinations including those of the Kennedy brothers and Martin Luther King. The advertisement's clear implication was that Angleton could somehow be tied to each one. Angleton smiled with satisfaction. "That's Kim, I know that's Kim. He's behind all this." Wright had a similar experience; see *Spycatcher*, pp. 308–309.

7. "Facts," in Pincher, *Their Trade is Treachery* (London, 1981), p.x; "faith," in Wright, p. 381.

8. "Existence," in Pincher, *Too Secret Too Long*, p. 184.

9. Richard Crossman, ed., *The God that Failed* (New York, 1950), p. 23.

10. "Tie," and "golf," in Pincher, *Too Secret Too Long*, p. 36; "habit," in Pincher, *Their Trade Is Treachery*, p. 36. Pincher's case collapses on the first page of his over 800-page indictment of Hollis. Pincher claims that a 1974 report by Lord Trend concluded that MI5 had probably been infiltrated and that Hollis was the most likely candidate. Prime Minister Thatcher, however, denied this characterization of the Trend Report was true and Wright, Pincher's chief source, conceded it was not. Lord Trend, Wright has confirmed, "concluded that Hollis was not an agent of the Russian Intelligence Service."; see *Their Trade Is Treachery*, pp. 1–2; Wright, p. 381; Andrew, *Her Majesty's Secret Service*, p. 504; Penrose and Freeman, p. 488.

11. Pincher, *Too Secret Too Long*, p. 190. These unstated "rules" are apparently subject to change. On the day that *Philby*, by Page, *et al.* was published, Pincher denounced it because the "assumptions on which the book is built are not credible and are in conflict with the way Soviet espionage works." Specifically, he rejected as contrary to the rules of conspiracy the assertion that Philby and Maclean knew each other was a spy and that Philby told Burgess about Maclean. Yet, in his own books Pincher later subscribed to these same notions; see *Daily Express* (London), February 19, 1968; *Too Secret Too Long*, p. 183.

12. *New York Review of Books*, March 14, 1985.

13. Cecil, *A Divided Life*, p. 137; also, Penrose and Freeman, pp. 428–451.

14. In reviewing Wright's book, John Gross found "much of it is convincing, some of it is disturbing. But he also undermines credibility by the ease with which he indulges speculations and suspicions—most obviously in the case of the belief that gives his book its central thrust, his conviction that the late Roger Hollis, director of M.I.5 from 1956 to 1965, was a Soviet agent."; see "Books of The Times," *New York Times*, July 21, 1987.

SELECT BIBLIOGRAPHY

Acheson, Dean. *Present at the Creation.* New York: W. W. Norton, 1969.

Akhmedov, Ismail. *In and Out of Stalin's GRU.* Frederick, MD.: University Press of America, 1984.

Alliluyeva, Svetlana. *Twenty Letters to a Friend.* New York: Harper & Row, 1967.

Alsop, Joseph. *FDR—A Centenary Remembrance.* New York: Washington Square Press, 1982.

Alsop, Susan Mary. *To Marietta From Paris 1945–1960.* Garden City, New York: Doubleday & Co., 1975.

Ambrose, Stephen E. *Eisenhower, Soldier, General of the Army, President-Elect—1890–1952,* v. 1. New York: Simon & Schuster, 1983.

Anderson, Jack. *Confessions of a Muckraker.* New York: Random House, 1979.

Andrew, Christopher. *Her Majesty's Secret Service: The Making of the British Intelligence Community.* New York: Viking, 1985.

———, and Dilks, David, eds. *The Missing Dimension: Governments and Intelligence Communities in the Twentieth Century.* London: Macmillan, 1984.

———, and Noakes, Jeremy. *Intelligence and International Relations, 1900–1945.* Exeter, Eng.: University or Exeter, 1987.

Balfour, Sir John. *Not Too Correct an Aureole.* London: Michael Russell, 1983.

Bamford, James. *The Puzzle Palace: A Report on America's Most Secret Agency.* New York: Penguin Books, 1983.

Barron, John. *KGB Today: The Hidden Hand.* New York: Reader's Digest Press, 1983.

Bendiner, Robert. *The Riddle of the State Department.* New York: Farrar & Rinehart, 1942.

Bentley, Elizabeth. *Out of Bondage.* New York: Devin-Adair, 1951.

Berle, Beatrice Bishop, and Jacobs, Travis Beal, eds. *Navigating the Rapids 1918–1971: From the Papers of Adolf A. Berle.* New York: Harcourt, 1973.

Berlin, Isaiah. *Personal Impressions.* New York: Penguin Books, 1982.

Bernikow, Louise. *Abel.* New York: Ballantine Books, 1980.

Beschloss, Michael R. *Kennedy and Roosevelt: The Uneasy Alliance*. New York: W. W. Norton, 1980.

Bethell, Lord Nicholas. *The Great Betrayal: The Untold Story of Kim Philby's Biggest Coup*. New York: Time Books, 1984.

Birkenhead, Second Earl of. *Halifax: The Life of Lord Halifax*. Boston: Houghton-Mifflin, 1966.

Blackett, P. M. S. *Fear, War and the Bomb: Military and Political Consequences of Atomic Energy*. New York: McGraw-Hill, 1949.

Blum, John Morton, ed. *The Price of Vision: The Diary of Henry A. Wallace, 1942–1946*. Boston: Houghton Mifflin, 1973.

Bohlen, Charles E. *Witness to History*. New York: W. W. Norton, 1973.

Bok, Sissela, *Secrets: On the Ethics of Concealment and Revelation*. New York: Pantheon Books, 1982.

Boyle, Andrew. *The Fourth Man*. New York: Dial Press, 1979.

Bradley, Omar, and Clay, Blair. *A Soldier's Story*. New York: Henry Holt & Co., 1951.

Bright-Holmes, John, ed. *Like It Was: The Diaries of Malcolm Muggeridge*. New York: William Morrow, 1982.

Brook-Shepherd, Gordon. *The Storm Petrels*. London: Collins, 1977.

Bullitt, William C. *For the President Personal and Secret*. Boston: Houghton Mifflin, 1972.

Bundy, McGeorge. *Danger and Survival*. New York: Vintage Books, 1990.

Burke, Michael. *Outrageous Good Fortune*. Boston: Little, Brown & Co., 1984.

Byrnes, James F. *Speaking Frankly*. New York: Harper, 1947.

Casey, Lord. *Personal Experience 1939–1946*. New York: David McKay & Co., 1962.

Cave Brown, Anthony, and MacDonald, Charles B. *On A Field of Red*. New York: G. P. Putnam's Sons, 1981.

———. *The Last Hero: Wild Bill Donovan*. New York: Vintage Books, 1984.

Cecil, Robert. *A Divided Life*. London: The Bodley Head, 1988.

Chamberlain, W. H. *The Russian Revolution, 1917–1921*. London and New York: Ayer & Co., 1935.

Chambers, Whittaker. *Witness*. New York: Random House, 1952.

Churchill, Winston S. *Blood, Sweat, and Tears*. New York: G. P. Putnam's Sons, 1941.

———. *The Second World War*, vols 1–6 New York: Bantam Books, 1961–1962.

Cline, Ray S. *Secrets, Spies and Scholars*. Washington: Acropolis Books, 1976.

Colby, William, and Forbath, Peter. *Honorable Men: My Life in the CIA*. New York: Simon & Schuster, 1978.

Colville, John. *The Fringes of Power: 10 Downing Street Diaries 1939–1955*. New York: W. W. Norton, 1985.

Connell, John. *The 'Office': The Story of the British Foreign Office 1919–1951*. New York: St. Martin's Press, 1958.

Connolly, Cyril. *The Missing Diplomats*. London: Queen Anne Press, 1952.

Conquest, Robert. *The Great Terror: Stalin's Purges of the Thirties*. New York: The Macmillan Co., 1968.

———. *Stalin and the Kirov Murder*. New York: Oxford University Press, 1989.

Constantinides, George C. *Intelligence and Espionage: An Analytical Bibliography*. Boulder, Co: Westview Press, 1983.

Cook, Fred, J. *The FBI Nobody Knows*. New York: Macmillan, 1964.

Cookridge, E. H. *The Third Man*. New York: G. P. Putman's Sons, 1968.

Copeland, Miles. *The Game of Nations*. New York: Simon & Schuster, 1969.

Corson, William R. and Crowley, Robert T. *The New KGB*. New York: Morrow, 1986.

Costello, John. *Mask of Treachery*. New York: William Morrow & Co., 1988.

Crossman, Richard H. S., ed. *The God that Failed*. New York: Harper & Row, 1950.

Dallek, Robert. *Franklin D. Roosevelt and American Foreign Policy, 1932–1945*. New York: Oxford University Press, 1979.

Dallin, David J. *Soviet Espionage*. New Haven, Conn.: Yale University Press, 1955.

Deacan, Richard. *The British Connection*. London: Hamish Hamilton, 1979.

Dilks, David, ed. *The Diaries of Sir Alexander Cadogan 1938–1945*. New York: G. P. Putnam's Sons, 1972.

DeJonge, Alex. *Stalin And the Shaping of the Soviet Union*. New York: William Morrow, 1986.

Derbian, Peter, and Gibney, Frank. *The Secret World*. New York: Ballantine Books, 1982.

de Toledana, Ralph. *Lament for a Generation*. New York: Farrar, Straus & Giroux, 1960.

Deutscher, Isaac. *Stalin*. London: Pelican Books, 1968,

Djilas, Milovan. *Conversations With Stalin*. New York: Harcourt, Brace, 1962.

Donovan, Robert J. *Conflict and Crisis: The Presidency of Harry S. Truman, 1945–1948*. New York: W. W. Norton, 1977.

———. *Tumultous Years: The Presidency of Harry S. Truman, 1949–1953*. New York: W. W. Norton, 1982.

Driberg, Tom. *Guy Burgess: A Portrait with Background*. London: Weidenfeld & Nicolson, 1956.

Dulles, Allen. *The Craft of Intelligence*. Westport, Ct: Greenwood Press, 1977.

————. *The Secret Surrender*. New York: Harper & Row, 1966.

Eden, Anthony. *Full Circle*. Boston: Houghton Mifflin, 1960.

————. *Facing the Dictators*. Boston: Houghton Mifflin, 1962.

Eisenhower, Dwight D. *Crusade in Europe*. Garden City, N.Y.: Doubleday, 1948.

————. *The White House Years: Waging Peace, 1956–61*. Garden City, N.Y.: Doubleday & Co., 1965.

Epstein, Edward Jay. *Legend: The Secret World of Harvey Oswald*. New York: McGraw-Hill, 1978.

Evans, Harold. *Good Times, Bad Times*. New York: Atheneum, 1984.

Eveland, Wilbur Crane. *Ropes of Sand: America's Failures in the Middle East*. New York: W. W. Norton, 1980.

Farago, Ladislas. *The Game of the Foxes*. New York: Bantam Books, 1971.

Feis, Herbert. *Between War and Peace: The Potsdam Conference*. Princeton: Princeton University Press, 1960.

Finletter, Thomas K. *Power and Policy*. New York: Harcourt, Brace & Co., 1954.

Fischer, Louis. *Men and Politics: Europe Between the Two World Wars*. New York: Harper & Row, 1966.

Foote, Alexander. *Handbook for Spies*. Garden City, N.Y.: Doubleday & Co., 1949.

Franck, Thomas M., and Weiband, Edward, eds. *Secrecy and Foreign Policy*. New York: Oxford University Press, 1974.

Frankfurther, Felix. *Felix Frankfurther Reminisces*. New York: Reynal & Co., 1960.

Gaddis, John Lewis. *The United States and the Origins of the Cold War, 1941–1947*. New York: Columbia University Press, 1972.

Gardner, Muriel. *Code Name Mary*. New Haven, Conn.: Yale University Press, 1983.

Gardner, Richard N. *Sterling-Dollar Diplomacy*. New York: McGraw Hill, 1969.

Gehlen, Reinhard. *The Service*. New York: Popular Library, 1972.

Gilbert, Martin. *Winston Churchill: The Wilderness Years*. London: Macmillan, 1981.

————. *Winston S. Churchill: Road to Victory 1941–1945*. Boston: Houghton Mifflin, 1986.

Gladwyn, Lord. *The Memoirs of Lord Gladwyn*. London: Weidenfeld & Nicolson, 1972.

Glees, Anthony. *The Secrets of the Service: British Intelligence and Communist Subversion 1939–1951*. London: Jonathan Cape, 1987.

Gore-Booth, Paul. *With Great Truth & Respect*. London: Constable, 1974.

Goulden, Joseph C. *Korea: The Untold Story of the War*. New York: McGraw-Hill, 1983.

Gouzenko, Igor. *This Was My Choice*. London: Eyre & Spottiswoode, 1948.

Gowing, Margaret. *Britain and Atomic Energy, 1939–45*. London: Macmillan & Co. Ltd., 1964.

————. *Independence and Deterrence: Britain and Atomic Energy, 1945–1952*. 2 vols. New York: St. Martin's Press, 1974. Vol 1: Policy Making; Vol 2: Policy Execution.

Graebner, Norman A., ed. *An Uncertain Tradition: American Secretaries of State in the Twentieth Century*. New York: McGraw-Hill, 1961.

Graves, Robert, and Hodge, Alan. *The Long Week-End: A Social History of Great Britain 1918–1939*. New York: W. W. Norton, 1963.

Grew, Joseph C. *Turbulent Era: A Diplomatic Record of Forty Years*. 2 vols. Boston: Houghton Mifflin, 1952.

Groves, Leslie. *Now It Can Be Told: The Story of the Manhattan Project*. New York: Da Capo Press, 1983.

Halberstam, David. *The Best and the Brightest*. Greenwich, Ct: Fawcett Crest, 1972.

Halifax, The Earl of. *Fullness of Days*. London: Collins, 1957.

Harriman, W. Averell, and Abel, Elie. *Special Envoy to Churchill and Stalin 1941–1946*. New York: Random House, 1975.

Harrod, Roy. *The Life and Times of John Maynard Keynes*. New York: Macmillan, 1951.

Hastings, Max. *The Korean War*. New York: Simon & Schuster, 1987.

Hayter, Sir William. *The Kremlin and the Embassy*. New York: Macmillan & Co., 1966.

Henderson, J. N. *The Private Office*. London: Weidenfeld & Nicolson, 1984.

Henderson, Loy. *A Question of Trust: The Memoirs of Loy H. Henderson*. Stanford: Calif.: Hoover Institution Press, 1986.

Herken, Gregg. *The Winning Weapon: The Atomic Bomb in the Cold War: 1945–50*. New York: Alfred A. Knopf, 1982.

Hewlett, Richard G., and Anderson, Jr., Oscar E. *The New World, 1939/1946*. Vol. 1: A History of the United States Atomic Energy Commission. University Park, Pa.: Pennsylvania State University Press, 1962.

Hewlett, Richard G. and Duncan, Francis. *Atomic Shield, 1947/1952*. Vol. 2: A History of the United States Atomic Energy Commission. University Park, Pa.: Pennsylvania State University Press, 1969.

Hillman, William. *Mr. President*. New York: Farrar, Straus & Young, 1952.

Hinsley, F. H., Thomas, E. E., Ransom, C. F. G. and Knight, R. C. *British Intelligence in the Second World War: Its Influence on Strategy and Operations*. 3 vols. London: Her Majesty's Stationary Office, 1979, 1981, 1984.

Hoare, Geoffrey. *The Missing Macleans*. New York: Viking Press, 1955.

Howard, Harry N. *Turkey*. Baltimore, Md.: Johns Hopkins University Press, 1974.

Howarth, T. E. B. *Cambridge Between Two Wars*. London: William Collins, 1978.

Hullen, Bertram. *Inside the Department of State*. New York: Harper & Row, 1939.

Hull, Cordell. *The Memoirs of Cordell Hull*. 2 vols. New York: Macmillan Co., 1948.

Hyde, H. Montgomery. *The Atom Bomb Spies*. New York: Ballantine, 1980.

Irving, David. *Accident*. London: Collins, 1967.

Ismay, General Lord. *The Memoirs of General Lord Ismay*. New York: Viking Press, 1960.

Isaacson, Walter, and Thomas, Evan. *The Wise Men: Six Friends and the World They Made*. New York: Simon & Schuster, 1988.

James. D. Clayton. *The Years of MacArthur: Triumph & Disaster 1945–1964*. Boston: Houghton Mifflin, 1985.

Johnson, Hewlett. *The Soviet Power*. New York: International Publishers, 1941.

Johnson, Paul. *Modern Times: The World from the Twenties to the Eighties*. New York: Harper & Row, 1985.

Jones, Joseph Marion. *The Fifteen Weeks: An Inside Account of the Genesis of the Marshall Plan*. New York: Harcourt Brace Jovanovich, 1955.

Jones, Vincent C. *Manhattan: The Army and the Atomic Bomb*. Washington, D. C.: Center of Military History, U. S. Army, 1985.

Kahn, David. *The Codebreakers*. New York: New American Library, 1973.

Kaznacheev, Alexandr. *Inside a Soviet Embassy*. Philadelphia: J. B. Lippincott Co., 1962.

Kennan, George F. *Memoirs 1925–1950*. Boston: Little, Brown & Co., 1967.

———. *Russia and the West Under Lenin and Stalin*. Boston: Little, Brown & Co., 1961.

Kimball, Warren F., ed. *Churchill & Roosevelt: The Complete Correspondence*. 3 vols. Princeton: Princeton University Press, 1984. Vol. 1: Alliance Emerging, October 1933—November, 1942; Vol. 2: Alliance Forged, November 1942—February 1944; Vol. 3: Alliance Declining, February 1944—April 1945.

Kirkpatrick, Lyman. *The Real CIA*. New York: Macmillan, 1968,

Klehr, Harvey. *The Heyday of American Communism: The Depression Decade*. New York: Basic Books, 1984.

———, and Radosh, Ronald. *Amerasia*. New York: W. W. Norton, 1983.

Knightley, Phillip. *Philby: The Life and Views of the K. G. B. Masterspy*. London: Andre Deutsch, 1988.

Kramish, Arnold. *Atomic Energy in the Soviet Union*. Stanford: Stanford University Press, 1959.

Kravchenko, Victor. *I Chose Freedom*. New York: Charles Scribner's Sons, 1946

Krivitsky, Walter G. *In Stalin's Secret Service*. New York: Harper & Row, 1939.

Kuniholm, Bruce R. *The Origins of the Cold War in the Near East.* Princeton: Princeton University Press, 1980.

Lacey, Robert. *The Kingdom: Arabia and the House of Saud.* New York: Harcourt Brace Jovanivich, 1982.

Lamphere, Robert J., and Shachtman, Tom. *The FBI-KGB War: A Special Agent's Story.* New York: Random House, 1986.

Langer, William. *In and Out of the Ivory Tower.* New York: Random House, 1977.

Lawford, Valentine. *Bound for Diplomacy.* London: John Murray, 1963.

Larabee, Eric. *Commander in Chief.* New York: Harper & Row, 1987.

Leahy, William D. *I Was There.* New York: Whittlesey House, McGraw-Hill, 1950.

Lash, Joseph P. *Roosevelt and Churchill 1939–1941: The Partnership That Saved the West.* New York: W. W. Norton, 1976.

Lehmann, John. *In My Own Time: Memoirs of a Literary Life.* Boston: Little, Brown & Co., 1969.

Leuchtenburg, William E. *In the Shadow of FDR: From Harry Truman to Ronald Reagan.* Ithaca, N.Y.: Cornell University Press, 1983.

Levine, Isaac Don. *Eyewitness to History.* New York: Hawthorne Books, 1973.

———, ed. *Plain Talk.* New York: Arlington House, 1975.

Lewis, Flora, *Red Pawn.* New York: Doubleday & Co., 1965.

———. "Who Killed Krivitsky?" *Washington Post,* February 13, 1966.

Lillienthal, David E. *The Journals of David E. Lilienthal.* Vol. 2: *The Atomic Energy Years.* New York: Harper & Row, 1964.

Litvinov, Maxim. *Notes for A Journal.* London: Andre Deutsch, 1955.

MacArthur, Douglas. *Reminiscences.* New York: McGraw-Hill, 1964.

Maclean, Donald D. *British Foreign Policy: The Years Since Suez 1956–1958.* New York: Stein and Day, 1970.

Maclean, Fitzroy. *Take Nine Spies.* New York: 1978.

MacNeice, Louis. *The Strings are False.* London: Faber and Faber, 1982.

Maisky, Ivan. *Memoirs of a Soviet Ambassador.* London: Hutchinson, 1968.

Manchester, William. *The Glory and the Dream: A Narrative History of America 1932–1972.* New York: Bantam Books, 1979.

———. *American Caesar.* Boston: Little, Brown & Co., 1978.

Mann, Wilfrid Basil. *Was There a Fifth Man?* Oxford: Pergamon, 1982.

Martin, David C. *Wilderness of Mirrors.* New York: Harper & Row, 1980.

Massing, Hede. *This Deception.* New York: Duell, Sloan & Pearce, 1951.

Masterman, J. C. *The Double Cross System in the War of 1939–1945.* New Haven, Conn: Yale University Press, 1972.

Masters, Anthony. *The Man Who Was M: The Life of Maxwell Knight*. London: Blackwell, 1984.

Mather, John, ed. *The Great Spy Scandal*. London: Daily Express Books, 1955.

McJimsey, George. *Harry Hopkins: Ally of the Poor and Defender of Democracy*. Cambridge, Mass.: Harvard University Press, 1987.

Miller, Joan. *One Woman's War: Personal Exploits in MI5's Most Secret Station*. Dublin: Brandon, 1986.

Mills, Walter, ed. *The Forrestal Diaries*. New York: Viking, 1951.

Ministry of Foreign Affairs of the U.S.S.R. *Correspondence Between the Chairman of the Council of Ministers of the U.S.S.R. and the Presidents of the U.S.A. and the Prime Ministers of Great Britain During the Great Patriotic War of 1941–1945; Stalin's Correspondence with Churchill and Attlee 1941–1945*. New York: Capricorn Books, 1965.

Mirsky, Dmitri. *The Intelligentsia of Great Britain*. New York: Covici Friede, 1935.

Mosley, Leonard. *Dulles: A Biography of Eleanor, Allen and John Foster Dulles and Their Family Network*. New York: Dial Press, 1978.

Moss, Norman. *Klaus Fuchs*. New York: St. Martin's Press, 1987.

Muggeridge, Malcolm. *Chronicles of Wasted Time: The Infernal Grove*. New York: William Morrow & Co., 1974.

Murphy, Robert. *Diplomat Among Warriors*. Garden City, N.Y.: Doubleday & Co., 1964.

Nichols, H. G. *Washington Despatches 1941–1945: Weekly Political Reports From the British Embassy*. Chicago: The University of Chicago Press, 1981.

Nicolson, Harold. *Diaries and Letters 1930–1962*. Nigel Nicolson, ed. 3 vols. New York: Antheneum, 1966, 1967, 1968. vol. 1: 1930–1939; vol. 2: 1939–1945; vol. 3: 1945–1962.

Nixon, Richard M. *Six Crises*. New York: Pocket Books, 1962.

Orlov, Alexander. *Handbook of Intelligence and Guerrilla Warfare*. Ann Arbor, Mich.: University of Michigan Press, 1963.

Oshinsky, David M. *A Conspiracy So Immense: The World of Joe McCarthy*. New York: Macmillan & Co., 1983.

Page, Bruce, Leitch, David and Knightley, Phillip. *Philby: The Spy Who Betrayed a Generation*. London: Penguin Books, 1969.

Panikkar, K. M. *In Two Chinas*. London: Allen & Unwin, 1955.

Pearson, Drew. *Diaries 1945–1959*. New York: Holt, Rinehart & Winston, 1974.

Peierls, Rudolf, *Bird of Passage: Recollections of a Physicist*. Princeton: Princeton University Press, 1985.

Penkovsky, Oleg. *The Penkovsky Papers*. Garden City, N.Y.: Doubleday & Co., 1965.

Penrose, Barrie, and Freeman, Simon. *Conspiracy of Silence: The Secret Life of Anthony Blunt*. New York: Farrar Straus Giroux, 1987.

Perkins, Francis. *The Roosevelt I Knew*. New York: Viking Press, 1946.

Petrov, Vladimir and Evdokia. *Empire of Fear*. New York: Frederick A. Praeger, 1956.

Philby, Eleanor. *Kim Philby: The Spy I Married*. New York: Ballantine Books, 1968,

Philby, Kim. *My Silent War*. New York: Ballantine Books, 1983.

Pickersgill, J. W. and Forster, D. F., eds. *The Mackenzie King Record*. vol. 3, 1945–1946. Toronto: University of Toronto Press, 1970.

Pilat, Oliver. *The Atom Spies*. New York: G. P. Putnam's Sons, 1952.

Pincher, Chapman. *Their Trade is Treachery*. London: Sidgwick & Jackson, 1981.

———. *Too Secret Too Long*. New York: St. Martin's Press, 1984.

Pogue, Forrest C. *George C. Marshall: Statesman 1945–1959*. New York: Viking Penguin, 1987.

Poretsky, Elizabeth K. *Our Own People: A Memoir of Ignace Reiss and his Friends*. Ann Arbor, Mich.: University of Michigan Press, 1969.

Powers, Richard G. *Secrecy and Power: The Life of J. Edgar Hoover*. New York: The Free Press, 1987.

Powers, Thomas. *The Man Who Kept the Secrets: Richard Helms and the CIA*. New York: Alfred A. Knopf, 1979.

Price, Henry B. *The Marshall Plan and Its Meaning*. Ithaca, N.Y.: Cornell University Press, 1955.

Radosh, Ronald, and Milton, Joyce. *The Rosenberg File: A Search For The Truth*. New York: Vintage Books, 1984.

Ranelagh, John. *The Agency: The Rise and Decline of the CIA*. New York: Simon & Schuster, 1986.

Read, Anthony, and Fisher, David. *The Deadly Embrace: Hitler, Stalin, and the Nazi-Soviet Pact 1939–1941*. New York: W. W. Norton, 1988.

Redgrave, Michael. *In My Mind's I: An Actor's Autobiography*. New York: Viking, 1983.

Rees, David. *Korea: The Limited War*. New York: St. Martin's Press, 1964.

Rees, Goronwy. *A Chapter of Accidents*. New York: The Library Press, 1972.

Report of the Royal Commission Appointed to Investigate the Facts Relating to and the Circumstances Surrounding the Communication by Public Officials and other Persons in Positions of Trust of Secret and Confidential Information to Agents of a Foreign Power. Ottawa: H.M. Controller of Stationary, 1946.

Report of the Royal Commission on Espionage. Sydney: Government Printer for New South Wales, 1955.

Reuben, William A. *The Atom Spy Hoax*. New York: Action Books, 1955.

Rhodes, Richard. *The Making of the Atomic Bomb*. New York: Simon & Schuster, 1986.

Roosevelt, Kermit. *Countercoup: The Struggle for the Control of Iran*. New York: McGraw-Hill, 1979.

Ross, Graham, ed. *The Foreign Office and the Kremlin*. Cambridge: Cambridge University Press, 1984.

Rothwell, Victor. *Britain and the Cold War 1941–1947*. London: Jonathan Cape, 1982.

Rovere, Richard H. and Schlesinger, Jr., Arthur J. *The MacArthur Controversy*. New York: Farrar, Strauss & Giroux, 1965.

Salisbury, Harrison. *Without Fear or Favor*. New York: Times Books, 1980.

Seale, Patrick, and McConville, Maureen. *Philby: The Long Road To Moscow*. New York: Simon & Schuster, 1973.

Serge, Victor. *Memoirs of a Revolutionary 1901–1941*. London: Oxford University Press, 1963.

Shapiro, Leonard. *The Communist Party of the Soviet Union*. New York: Vantage Books, 1971.

Sherwin, Martin J. *A World Destroyed: The Atomic Bomb and the Grand Alliance*. New York: Alfred A. Knopf, 1975.

Sherwood, Robert E. *Roosevelt and Hopkins: An Intimate History*. New York: Harper & Brothers, 1948.

Shevchenko, Arkady N. *Breaking with Moscow*. New York: Knopf, 1985.

Shirer, William. *Berlin Diary: The Journal of a Foreign Correspondent 1934–1941*. New York: Popular Diary, 1961.

———. *The Rise and Fall of the Third Reich*. New York: Crest Books, 1962.

Sinclair, Andrew. *The Red and the Blue: Cambridge, Treason and Intelligence*. Boston: Little, Brown & Co., 1986.

Smith, Alice Kimball. *A Peril and a Hope: The Scientists' Movement in America: 1945–47*. Chicago: University of Chicago Press, 1965.

Smith, Bradley. F. *The Shadow Warriors: OSS and the Origins of the CIA*. New York: Basic Books, 1983.

Smith, Joseph B. *Portrait of a Cold Warrior*. New York: Ballatine Books, 1976.

Smith, Richard Harris. *OSS: The Secret History of America's First Central Intelligence Agency*. Berkeley, Calif.: University of California Press, 1972.

Smith, Walter Bedell. *My Three Years in Moscow*. Philadelphia: J. P. Lippincott, 1950.

Solomon, Flora, and Litvinoff, Barry. *A Woman's Way*. New York: Simon & Schuster, 1984.

Solon, Larry. *Headlines All of My Life*. London, Hutchinson, 1957.

Spender, Stephen. *Journals 1939–1983*. New York: Random House, 1986.

Steel, Ronald. *Walter Lippmann and the American Century*. Boston: Little, Brown & Co., 1980.

Sterling, Claire. *The Masaryk Case*. New York: Harper & Row, 1969.

Stern, Philip M. *The Oppenheimer Case: Security on Trial*. New York: Harper & Row, 1969.

Stettinius, Edward R. Jr. *Roosevelt and the Russians: The Yalta Conference*. Garden City, N.Y.: 1949.

Stimson, Henry L., and McGeorge, Bundy. *On Active Service in Peace and War*. New York: Harper & Brothers, 1948.

Strauss, Lewis L. *Men and Decisions*. Garden City, N.Y.: Doubleday & Co., 1963.

Straight, Michael. *After Long Silence*. New York: W. W. Norton, 1983.

Strickland, Donald A. *Scientists in Politics: The Atomic Scientist Movement, 1945–1946*. Lafayette, Ind.: Indiana University Press, 1968.

Stypulkowski, Z. F. *Invitation to Moscow*. London: Thames and Hudson, 1951.

Sulzberger, C. L. *A Long Row of Candles: Memoirs and Diaries, 1934–54*. Toronto: Macmillan Company, 1969.

Talbott, Strobe, ed. and trans. *Khrushchev Remembers*. Boston: Little, Brown & Co., 1970.

Thomas, Hugh. *The Spanish Civil War*. New York: Harper & Row, 1961.

————. *Armed Truce: The Beginnings of the Cold War 1945–1946*. New York: Atheneum, 1987.

Thompson, Francis J. *Destination Washington*. London: Hale, 1960.

Thorne, Christopher. *Allies of a Kind*. New York: Oxford University Press, 1978.

Tompkins, Peter. *The Murder of Admiral Darlan*. London: Weidenfeld & Nicolson, 1965.

Troy, Thomas F. *Donovan and the CIA: A History of the Establishment of the Central Intelligence Agency*. Frederick, Md.: University Press of America, 1981.

Truman, Harry S. *Memoirs*. Vol. 1. *Year of Decisions*, Vol. 2. *Years of Trial and Hope*. New York: Doubleday, 1955–1956.

Truman, Margaret. *Harry S. Truman*. New York: William Morrow, 1973.

Turner, William W. *Hoover's FBI: The Men and the Myth*. New York: Dell, 1971.

Ulam, Adam B. *The Rivals: American & Russia since World War II*. New York: Penguin Books, 1978.

Vandenberg, Arthur H. *The Private Papers of Senator Vandenberg*. Boston: Houghton Mifflin, 1952.

Waldman, Louis. *Labor Lawyer*. New York: E. P. Dutton, 1944.

Weil, Martin. *A Pretty Good Club: The Founding Fathers of the U.S. Foreign Service.* New York: W. W. Norton, 1978.

Weinstein, Allen. *Perjury: The Hiss-Chambers Case.* New York: Alfred A. Knopf, 1978.

West, Nigel. *MI5: British Security Service Operations 1909–1945.* New York: Stein and Day, 1982.

———. *The Circus: MI5 Operations 1945–1972.* New York: Stein and Day, 1984.

———. *GCHQ: The Secret Wireless War 1900–1986.* London: Weidenfeld & Nicolson, 1986.

West, Rebecca. *The New Meaning of Treason.* New York: Viking Press, 1964.

Whalen, Richard J. *The Founding Father: The Story of Joseph P. Kennedy.* New York: New American Library, 1964.

Wheeler-Bennett, Sir John. *Action This Day: Working with Churchill.* New York: St. Martin's Press, 1969.

Whitney, Courtney. *MacArthur: His Rendezvous With History.* New York: Alfred A. Knopf, 1956.

Williams, Francis. *Twilight of Empire: Memoirs of Prime Minister Clement Attlee.* New York: A. S. Barnes and Co., 1962.

Williams, Robert Chadwell. *Klaus Fuchs: Atom Spy.* Cambridge, Mass.: Harvard University Press, 1987.

Wilson, Trevor. *The Downfall of the Liberal Party 1914–1935.* Ithaca, N.Y.: Cornell University Press, 1966.

Winks, Robin W. *Cloak & Gown: Scholars in the Secret War 1939–1961.* New York: William Morrow, 1987.

Wise, David, and Ross, Thomas B. *The Espionage Establishment.* New York: Random House, 1967.

———. *The Invisible Government.* New York: Vintage Books, 1974.

Wood, Neal. *Communism and the British Intellectuals.* London: Gollancz, 1959.

Woodward, Sir Llewellyn. *British Foreign Policy in the Second World War.* 2 vols. London: H. M. Stationary Office, 1962.

Wright, Peter, with Greengrass, Paul. *Spycatcher: The Candid Autobiography of a Senior Intelligence Officer.* New York: Viking Press, 1987.

Wyden, Peter. *Day One: Before Hiroshima and After.* New York: Simon & Schuster, 1984.

Yardley, Herbert O. *The American Black Chamber.* New York: Ballantine Books, 1981.

Yergin, Daniel. *Shattered Peace: The Origins of the Cold War and the National Security State.* Boston: Houghton Mifflin, 1977.

Young, Kenneth, ed. *The Diaries of Sir Robert Bruce Lockhart, 1939–1965,* vol. 2. London: Macmillan & Co., 1980.

Zhukov, G. K. *The Memoirs of Marshall Zhukov.* New York: Delacorte Press, 1971.

INDEX

About the Author

Verne W. Newton is the award-winning writer/producer of *Harry Hopkins: At FDR's Side*, a PBS feature documentary which aired nationwide in October 1989. Newton's work has also appeared in *The New York Times*, *The Boston Globe*, *The International Herald Tribune*, *The Nation*, *The Washington Monthly*, and *The Wall Street Journal*.

From 1977 to 1980 Newton worked in the State Department as a senior official with the Agency for International Development. Among his many duties he was liaison to the White House and a member of several presidential delegations, including those led by U.N. Ambassador Andrew Young to the South Pacific and Africa.

Prior to moving to Washington he worked for a private New York investment firm.

Born in Long Beach, California, he was raised in Iowa and later received a B.A. degree in pre-law, philosophy, and history from American University in Washington, D.C. He also attended Syracuse University on scholarship as a Ph.D. candidate in European Intellectual History.

In addition to his book and film projects, he writes scripts for *The Creative Factory*, a Florida-based production, and has traveled extensively in Europe, Africa, and Asia, frequently as a consultant to the National Democratic Institute for International Affairs.